COGNITIVE AND LINGUISTIC ANALYSES OF TEST PERFORMANCE

edited by
Roy O. Freedle
Educational Testing Service
Princeton, New Jersey

Richard P. Duran
University of California
Santa Barbara, CA

Volume XXII in the Series
ADVANCES IN DISCOURSE PROCESSES
Roy O. Freedle, Editor

ABLEX PUBLISHING CORPORATION
Norwood, New Jersey

Library of Congress Cataloging-in-Publication Data

Cognitive and linguistic analyses of test performance.

(Advances in discourse processes ; v. 22)
Bibliography: p.
Includes index.
1. Examinations—Evaluation.   2. Examinations—
Interpretation.   3. Linguistic analysis (Linguistics)
4. Cognition in children.   I. Freedle, Roy O.
II. Durán, Richard P.   III. Series.
LB3060.8.C65   1986   371.2'6   86-10888
ISBN 0-89391-295-6
ISBN 0-89391-366-9 (pbk.)

Ablex Publishing Corporation
355 Chestnut Street
Norwood, New Jersey 07648

Contents

Preface to the Series

Roy O. Freedle
Series Editor

This series of volumes provides a forum for the cross-fertilization of ideas from a diverse number of disciplines, all of which share a common interest in discourse— be it prose comprehension and recall, dialogue analysis, text grammar construction, computer simulation of natural language, cross-cultural comparisons of communicative competence, or other related topics. The problems posed by multisentence contexts and the methods required to investigate them, while not always unique to discourse, are still sufficiently distinct as to benefit from the organized mode of scientific interaction made possible by this series.

Scholars working in the discourse area from the perspective of sociolinguistics, psycholinguistics, ethnomethodology and the sociology of language, educational psychology (e.g., teacher–student interaction), the philosophy of language, computational linguistics, and related subareas are invited to submit manuscripts of monograph or book length to the series editor. Edited collections of original papers resulting from conferences will also be considered.

Preface

Interpretation of test performance most traditionally involves examination of statistical and psychometric evidence that tests are reliable and valid indicators of constructs. A second concern is that tests are verifiably useful predictors of performance in criterion settings. By contrast, cognitive science and discourse analysis research give us new tools and approaches by which to begin a more intensive analysis of the constructs and corresponding skills which tests measure. The latter are the approaches characterized by the contributors to this volume.

The contributors considered together link linguistic and cognitive descriptions of items with analyses of problem-solving behavior on verbal test items. They provide us with valuable, fresh approaches to understanding what tests really measure given their objectives and how we might improve the design of tests to meet their intended purposes.

The focus on tests as a domain of interest has implications for cognitive and linguistic theory. It provides us with a useful and important educational context within which researchers can realize and evaluate the extension of theory into real situations of everyday practical worth. We are all aware that tests often serve as key practical decision-making devices that society uses to guide the selection of candidates for schools and employment, hence study of test behavior in light of cognitive science research can help establish the scientific strengths and limitations of test use.

The contributors to the present volume do not concern themselves intrinsically with psychometric theory. The integration of these approached with psychometric theory represents an exciting area for further exploration which, unfortunately, falls outside the scope of the volume. However, as we summarize below the approach that each chapter has taken we shall point out some of the more obvious implications that each chapter has for issues such as diagnostic test development; indeed, one of the practical consequences of the studies and ideas reported in this volume are suggestions for guiding the construction of new tests of diagnostic information for individual test takers. Such information can provide test users with qualitatively richer information regarding the skills and skills development of examinees than is now possible with existing norm referenced and criterion referenced aptitude and achievement tests. We will consider this possibility in greater detail below.

While the nine chapters in this volume reflect approaches combining linguistic and cognitive analyses, we have arranged them by presenting three chapters reflecting a primary cognitive orientation first. The chapter by Curtis provides us with a useful overview of the recent history of how cognitive science has begun to examine the processes, strategies, and underlying lexical knowledge that influence success on verbal test items. Curtis contrasts two main approaches—the cognitive correlates versus the cognitive components approach. The cognitive correlates approach seems to account for individual differences in verbal test scores only in a very general way, basing its conclusions on gross relationships between measures of aptitude and measures of performance based on the information processing requirements of cognitive tasks. Most of Curtis' review is concerned with providing evidence for the second approach which stresses the identification of explicit skills and processes used in problem solving and individual differences in enacting these skills and processes in the solution of vocabulary and analogy test items. Individuals of high and low verbal ability seem to use different strategies which interact with their available knowledge for word meanings, especially for hard items. Low verbal ability subjects in Curtis' research were prone to utilize immediately available definitional knowledge of words and more obvious relationships pairing words as the source of information for their problem. High ability subjects were more prone to examine, reflect upon, and modify their inital understandings of words and the relationships construed among words. This result relates to the next chapter by Freedle & Fellbaum.

Duran, Canale, Penfield, Stansfield and Lisken-Gasparro in the first chapter conduct a systematic linguistic and test performance description of the Test of English as a Foreign Language (TOEFL). They base their description on a range of criteria, calling into consideration the distribution of structural characteristics of the language occurring on the TOEFL and also the relationship of the examinee to the language and item tasks occurring on the TOEFL. They conclude that examinee's performance on the TOEFL demands a wide range of linguistic and communicative competencies and that the strength of the test in this regard lies in its lengthier item types intended to assess comprehension of oral and written discourse. Longer items present examinees with a greater variety of grammatical structures, sociolinguistic demands and discourse forms which must be properly recognized and operated upon in order to solve test items correctly. The chapter suggests that use of abbreviated item types with little information about a context of communication severely limits the value of items in assessing the linguistic competencies of examinees. The concluding section of the chapter outlines steps which might be taken to improve the communicative characteristics of language proficiency tests.

Freedle & Fellbaum found that the degree to which a "lexical repetition" strategy was used varies according to ability level of *groups* of individuals. Low ability groups use this strategy much more than do high ability individuals. Had individuals (rather than ability groups) been studied, they might have provided a closer match to some of the results reported in Curtis' review. Freedle & Fellbaum were concerned not only with finding evidence for strategies that differentiate high from low ability groups in responding to paraphrase-like items (taken from the TOEFL) but also in studying what special linguistic properties might influence item difficulty. They show how their results can be used to help item writers write items more efficiently at the very hard and very easy ends of the difficulty spectrum—a practical result since such items are empirically very difficult to discover. Basically, their study disclosed two strategies followed by examinees which were closely related to item difficulty: a lexical inference matching strategy between item stem and option, and a lexical repetition matching strategy. These results suggest that when items are difficult and presumably hard to understand for non-Native speakers of English, some examinees fall back on strategies matching individual words in answer options with words occuring in item stems. Given this strategy, diagnostic tests might be designed to "neutralize" this effect by making all options to have the same lexical overlap with the stem. This should encourage the test taker to focus more on relevant processing of phrases and clauses.

The two final chapters by Chittenden & Scott also have a strong cognitive orientation but deal with young children as test takers. Chittenden's chapter reveals that children can differ in reading strategies used at the very early levels of reading instruction. By the end of the primary grades, two groups of students showed the same reading level proficiency (based on teacher ratings and California Achievement Test scores in reading) even though initially they had been chosen because they differed in the kinds of strategies they used in learning to read aloud. One group of children used the following strategy: they anticipated meanings as they moved through a text. They were more willing to guess at a word and keep going even if they made mistakes. The other group of children had a different style: they adopted a very 'focused' approach to reading stressing comprehension of the most immediate vocabulary and constituents they encountered. Interestingly, when these latter children ran into a difficulty, they tended to stop reading rather than push ahead. Chittenden provides evidence that the second group was initially better adapted to perform under the constraints of some of the reading comprehension items presented. Yet while these early tests favored one group over the other, they basically ended up at similar ability levels by the end of the primary years. Chittenden's paper suggests to us that perhaps there is a natural way to extend some of Curtis' conclusions into a developmental framework.

The chapter by Haney & Scott presents some interesting empirical evidence for how children differ in their response to reading comprehension test items. Ambiguity in interpreting and understanding reading comprehension items is an old issue as their literature review suggests, but they have tackled this old issue by interviewing children to discover empirically how children interpret a variety of items, and in so doing, they attempt to discover the variety of sources that can contribute to an item's ambiguity. Ambiguity is a troublesome issue, as one might expect because the degree to which an item can be legitimately interpreted in any one of several competing ways must necessarily lessen the contribution of that item to a test's content validity and also, ultimately, an items desirable psychometric characteristics. The authors present evidence that ambiguity contributes to two results of psychological importance—it reveals that children can have a particular skill but fail to exhibit it because an item is not structured clearly enough, and also that the converse can happen. That is, children can get an item correct but in fact not possess the necessary skill for understanding the item clearly. They can get it right for the wrong reasons. Interestingly, though, the authors conclude that while their interview technique shows many reading items they examined to be ambiguous, the situation, while undesirable, may not be as disastrous as some critics of testing have suggested. Thus, while elimination of ambiguity it items is important in the test development process, one still can use total test scores on a test with undetected imperfections to obtain useful information about the relative proficiency of children with respect to some skilled domain (or, too, one can still use a combined test score across many such items and still have a useful predictive measure relating reading to other behavioral measures). This view is consistent with assumptions underlying most psychometric models of test performance and predictive validity. However, postulation of error or guessing components in psychometric models of test scores cannot improve the quality of test items, and, further, the psychometric efficiency and reliability of test items is reduced as guessing and error components contribute more to item performance. A goal of test development should be to reduce and eliminate content characteritits of items which contribute to randomlike performance on the part of examinees. As the practice of test construction catches up with cognitive and linguistic theory, one of the most useful application of cognitive and linguistic analyses of test performance can be to help improve the proper interpretation of test performance and overall effectiveness of tests.

The middle group of four chapters focus primarily upon linguistic analyses of test performance and on cognitive interpretations of discourse found in test items. The opening chapter in this section is by Paul Kay, known widely for his early work on color perception with Berlin and for his research in sociolinguistics. In his paper Kay introduces for us the notion on an "ideal reader." The notion of an "ideal reader" helps focus attention on how comprehension of a test item is built up sequentially from the linguistic cues presented in test items. As Kay points out, this development of meaning can lead to a convergence upon the intended meaning of the item or else to systematic departures from the intended meaning reflecting specific linguistic and cognitive strategies. The notion of the ideal reader is a useful analytic tool for guiding analysis of factors contributing to accurate versus inappropriate comprehension of verbal test items. It seems likely that the idea of an "ideal reader" as described by Kay will provide future researchers with a useful guide to empirical work in both test development and research on the construct validity of verbal tests.

The next chapter by Langer, a colleague of Kay, in fact, makes use of this idea of an "ideal reader" to help interpret children's interpretation of several reading passages. She develops a notation system that allows tracking how the interpretation of a test changes as new material is added to the interpretation.

Fellbaum's chapter illustrates how the development of a detailed linguistic scoring system can help us understand which features of items help to contribute to item difficulty. The type of item she is concerned with is Sentence Completion; this item type typically involves locating which word or words best fill in deletions in a test sentence. She finds several contributors to item difficulty. Both her paper and that by Freedle & Fellbaum (this volume) suggest that one must distinguish between relationships that exist between an item stem and its response options, as they influence item difficulty, and relationships that contribute to item difficulty based on features of the item stem in isolation. As additional work is done in this area we will thus be able to state the individual language comprehension strategies and linguistic characteristics of items that influence item difficulty from at least two sources: the item stem source and a separate source due to the relationship between the response options and the stem.

The chapter by Freeman evaluates the use of particular readability formula as the basis for constructing items reflecting different levels of reading difficulty in light of the linguistic features of items. One can legitimately question whether a simple readability formula would be sufficient to generate items with known content validity and other psychometric characteristics for a realm as complex as reading. Yet, the fact appears to be that the item writers of the passages which Freeman criticizes only used the formula as a starting point—that is, they later edited test items to improve their content characteristics and language. Nevertheless Freeman's paper is a useful reminder that in matters of language testing, one must not assume that use of a rigid small-scale formula is adequate to guide construction of items in ways that systematically sample complex language structures as found in a wide range of reading passages. In a similar vain, the "small-scale" regression formula presented in the Freedle & Fellbaum chapter is intended as only a first step in uncovering linguistic structures and processes that contribute to difficulty among the paraphrase-like items studied by them.

In scanning the chapters one sees that the Kay and Langer chapters, along with the Haney & Scott and Chittenden papers together suggest approaches to understanding test behavior, which with further refinement and interpretation in terms of cognitive theory of performance might ultimately contribute to developmental approaches to assessment of skills such as early reading skills. The chapter by Curtis suggests the need for explicit cognitive models of verbal test performance that generate scientifically verifiable or dismissable predictions about the verbal problem solving of individuals given their cognitive characteristics.

Also one sees that the chapters as a whole indicate that the data from non-English examinees (as analyzed by Freedle & Fellbaum, and Duran et. al.) and analyses of test items from a second language learning point of view need not constitute an impediment towards eventual development of detailed cognitive and linguistic analysis of test performance. It remains to be seen, though, whether one can as readily extend the cognitive-linguistic analysis of individual test items to a point where developmental trends in acquiring competence in a second-language is possible.

We mentioned at the beginning of these introductory comments that there are several practical implications of these chapters. We suggest that the new interest in constructing diagnostic tests will greatly benefit from refinement and extensions of the particular techniques developed in this volume and from other approaches that draw even more richly on current theories.

Diagnostic tests are meant, if narrowly conceived, to provide critical information concerning limited development of skills or knowledge that an individual test taker has which leads him or her to choose *particular* types of wrong options. Under this narrow conception one attempts to develop test items where the response options clearly point to one limited skill area versus another. So if a student consistently chooses one type of erroneous response (among many such items) one might use a pattern of erroneous choices to make recommendations (say, to a teacher) identifying areas of knowledge or skill that need strengthening or development. Several of the chapters in the present volume imply that this narrow focus cannot be approached simplistically. Two points merit attention. First the chapters suggest that a *prior* step in developing diagnostic tests is some clear knowledge of what strategies people use to guide response selection when they are not sure of the correct response. Such general strategies (such as "choose the option that has the greatest lexical overlap with the item stem") can be so powerful and persuasive as to swamp any diagnostic information that may have been built into the structure of the response options.

A second point, arguing against simplistic approaches to diagnostic assessment is the importance of postulating skill development models as a basis for diagnostic tests. The chapters by Curtis, Kay, and Langer, address this question to some extent. Inappropriate or erroneous performance on test items may vary qualitatively according to examinee's mastery of the content or skill domain tested. Ideally diagnostic tests might indicate not only what an examinee can and cannot do, but also what skill areas and content knowledge areas are most amenable to immediate versus long term training. In order for such approaches to be feasible it will b necessary to formulate models of skills development appropriate to training interventions. In this way assessment and training might ultimately be interlocked and empirically validated.

The editors
Princeton, N.J.
and Santa Barbara, Calif.

CHAPTER 1

TOEFL From a Communicative Viewpoint on Language Proficiency: A Working Paper*

Richard P. Duran
University of California, Santa Barbara
Michael Canale
Ontario Institute for Studies in Education
Joyce Penfield
Rutgers University
Charles W. Stansfield
Judith E. Liskin-Gasparro
Educational Testing Service

PREFACE

This report examines the content characteristics of the Test of English as a Foreign Language (TOEFL) from a communicative perspective based on current research in the area of applied linguistics and language proficiency assessment. The method of analysis used in the study represents one among a number of possible approaches. Communicative competence is a relatively recent perspective on language use. This approach emphasizes the effects of situational context on the use and meaning of language forms. Such an approach would have been considered inappropriate two decades ago, when the emphasis of linguistic analyses was on discrete units, generally considered apart from context. Only in time will it be possible to assess the utility of a situational perspective on language-to-language assessment practice.

The approach adopted is not intended to address psychometric issues that arise in evaluating the construct and criterion related validity of the TOEFL test; these important issues deserve attention in the context of a report with that specific purpose. The goal of this work is to describe the content characteristics of TOEFL items and sections in terms of a framework for communicative competence and in terms of related factors that can affect performance on language

* The opinions and views expressed in this report do not necessarily reflect the positions or policies of Educational Testing Service or the Test of English as a Foreign Language Program. This chapter originally appeared as TOEFL Research Report 17. Reprinted with permission.

1

proficiency tests. As noted in the introduction to the report, the framework used to describe TOEFL is exploratory in nature and the detailed findings reported should be viewed as such. A great deal of reflection and judgment is necessary in any content validity study and, thus, in applying the framework to describing TOEFL. As a result, different investigators might vary in the detailed findings that would emerge from their interpretation and application of the framework to the description of TOEFL.

It is important to note also that the report rarely takes into account the actual process by which the TOEFL test is developed and produced. The absence of the viewpoint of test development professionals has allowed the investigators to render an independent description of TOEFL. While such independence has its virtue in terms of the intellectual process of conducting the work described, there are also shortcomings that arise from this procedure. Professionals responsible for the development and production of TOEFL tests along with the actual TOEFL test specifications represent important resources for a fuller understanding of the content characteristics of TOEFL. This should be kept in mind when reading the report.

R.P.D.
C.W.S.

FOREWORD

The research described in this report required the collaboration of a number of investigators. The research team involved specialists in several overlapping content areas: foreign language teaching and proficiency assessment, applied linguistics and sociolinguistics, and psycholinguistics. Michael Canale of OISE and the University of Toronto authored Section II of the report, concerning advances in language proficiency assessment research and a theoretical framework for evaluating the characteristics of TOEFL. He also authored portions of Section V concerning possible improvements in proficiency assessment instruments and contributed a preliminary checklist of communicative skills, based on Munby (1978) and Canale and Swain's (1980) previous research. Joyce Penfield of Rutgers University, assisted by Richard Duran, authored Sections III and IV of the report with contributions by Charles Stansfield and Judith Liskin-Gasparro. These discuss the use of an expanded skills checklist to describe TOEFL, and the results of applying the checklist to describe a TOEFL instrument. Scoring of the sample TOEFL test was done by Penfield and Richard Duran. Charles Stansfield and Judith Liskin-Gasparro of Educational Testing Service (ETS) authored the portions of Section IV discussing use of the ILR scale to describe the proficiency levels of TOEFL test sections and items. Richard Duran of ETS directed the project and authored the remaining portions of the report. All of the collaborators and their assistants contributed to the final editing of the report, which was coordinated by Richard Duran and Charles Stansfield.

Thanks are extended to the TOEFL Research Committee, the TOEFL Committee of Examiners, and the TOEFL Program for feedback on earlier versions of this report; the authors have made discretionary revisions of the report based on this feedback. Thanks are also extended to E. Leta Davis, Michaele Mikovsky, and Peggy Thorpe for their coding and transcription of data concerning the TOEFL test analyzed. Davis also assisted in coordinating aspects of the final report development. Special thanks go to Jessie Cryer, Thelma Benton, Faith Thompson, and Marian Helms for their typing and manuscript preparation. Finally, thanks are extended to Nancy Parr for editing and proofreading the report manuscript.

I. INTRODUCTION

1. Background to the Report

Advances in foreign language teaching and language assessment research over the past decade have suggested that language proficiency testing theory and practice might benefit from an examination of issues related to communicative competence. This report summarizes findings of a project that investigated the relevance of some of these issues to the Test of English as a Foreign Language based on a theoretical model of communicative competence and the validity of language tests. The orientation toward communication and language use adopted in this report is representative of but one approach that is current in the field of foreign language teaching and testing. It is important to note at the outset that the TOEFL test is intended to evaluate only certain aspects of the English proficiency of persons whose native language is not English. A communicative description of TOEFL should be expected to be sensitive to what the test currently measures as well as to aspects of proficiency that it does not measure. The examination of the TOEFL test based on the communicative approach to language assessment advocated in this report is exploratory. It is based on some widely cited and discussed perspectives on the communicative properties of tests, but the approach taken should not be considered to provide the definitive account of the communicative properties of the TOEFL. Before overviewing the approach of the present project, it will be helpful to discuss the purpose and nature of TOEFL. Special attention will be given to describing the content and format of TOEFL test items since these are of central concern in the present study.

The TOEFL test is intended to evaluate certain aspects of the English language proficiency of persons whose native language is not English. The test is used widely by colleges and universities in the United States and Canada in reviewing the admissions qualifications of incoming foreign students whose native language is not English. In addition, it is used by other organizations and by some agencies of the U.S. government in assessing the English language qualifications of nonnative persons.

Use of the current three-section TOEFL began in 1976; up to that time TOEFL was administered as a five-section test. The total TOEFL score, computed from scores earned on each of three sections, range from 227 to 677. Further information on the use of TOEFL scores is provided in the *Test and Score Manual* (Educational Testing Service, 1983); attention is focused here on the nature of the three TOEFL sections and the characteristics of their item types.

2.   TOEFL Sections and Item Formats
The three sections of TOEFL are Section 1, Listening Comprehension; Section 2, Structure and Written Expression; and Section 3, Reading Comprehension and Vocabulary. The following descriptions of the sections call attention to the formats of items and to the skills tested by items. Some of the skills are directly relevant to components of communicative competence identified later in this report.

Listening Comprehension Section. This section is intended to measure the examinee's ability to understand English as it is spoken in the United States. The three item types in the 50-item section are statements (20 items), dialogues (15 items), and minitalks/extended conversations (15 items).

Statement items present examinees with short recorded statements by individual speakers. After hearing a statement, examinees select one of four response options (given in the test book) that is synonymous with the original statement. All of the response options for an item are either full sentences or elliptical responses. Statement items are designed to test examinees' ability to comprehend a spoken sentence based on its syntactic structure, word meaning and word usage, phonological and suprasegmental characteristics, and inferences that follow from the meaning of a sentence. Incorrect response options reflect inappropriate recognition of words, sentence structures, and speech act types that might result if the sound characteristics of words and sentence elements are not properly recognized. Incorrect responses also might arise even if examinees do comprehend written answer options—this, indeed, is a possibility for all sections and item types found on the TOEFL.

Dialogue items present examinees with a recorded conversation between two speakers. In most instances, each participant in the conversation speaks once. Following the exchange a third recorded speaker asks the examinees a question about what was said and the examinees select one of four response options given in the test book. The oral comprehension demands of dialogue items are similar to those of statement items, but they also require that examinees understand the interrelationship between turns in a conversational segment. The questions posed by the third speaker are intended to require comprehension of all conversational turns, rather than one turn alone. Questions probe examinees' recognition of the syntax of the speakers' utterances, the content of what is said, and the speech acts and interrelationships among speech acts represented by the speakers' utterances. Some questions probe examinees' knowledge of word meanings, idioms, and paralinguistic cues in the context of conversation. Finally, some questions test examinees' ability to draw inferences about the characteristics of the speakers or the situations represented by the conversations.

A minitalk/extended conversation item stem consists of a recording of an extended utterance by one speaker or a recording of a conversation involving several turns between two speakers; an additional speaker then asks a series of questions. Examinees respond to each question by selecting one of four response options, printed in their test books, that are in the form of phrases or full sentences. These questions stress examinees' understanding of the situation depicted by a talk or conversation, the roles of the speakers, the intentions of the speakers, the topics of discussion, and the content of what was said. According to the TOEFL test specifications, minitalk/extended conversation items involve situations and topics representative of language use in academic settings or in the everyday life of college students.

Structure and Written Expression Section. This section consists of 15 structure and 25 written expression items, all of which are printed in the test books. Each structure item consists of a sentence with an omitted word. Examinees are required to select one of four response options consisting of a word or phrase that will complete the sentence. Only one response option is grammatically correct given the structure and content of the stimulus sentence. Items are designed to systematically probe examinees' control of syntactic features appropriate to various clause and phrase types, negative constructions, comparative forms, word ordering within sentences, and statements of parallel relationships at the phrase and clause level.

Written expression items consist of sentences, each with four underlined words corresponding to response options. Examinees are required to select the one response option corresponding to a word that is grammatically inappropriate in the context of a sentence. Grammatical points tested by these items involve agreement in the syntactic and semantic characteristics of function and content words, appropriate usage of function words, appropriate word ordering, appropriate diction and idiomatic usage, appropriate and complete clause or phrase structure, and maintenance of parallel forms. Errors in sentences reflect inappropriate omission or inappropriate inclusion of sentence elements related to the foregoing grammatical features.

Reading Comprehension and Vocabulary Section. This section is designed to measure examinees' ability to understand various kinds of reading material and the meaning and use of words. The section includes 30 vocabulary items followed by 30 reading comprehension items; all are printed in the test book. Each vocabulary item consists of a single sentence (usually, but not always, of a complex form) with one word underlined. From the four response options, examinees are to select the one that is synonymous in meaning to the underlined word. The occurrence of grammatical category and the difficulty of vocabulary is controlled for in both the item and the response options. According to the

TOEFL test specifications, sentences are representative of materials that students might encounter in books, magazines, articles, newspapers, and other printed matter.

Each reading comprehension item consists of a stimulus passage followed by a series of items pertaining to the main idea of the passage, supporting ideas or facts related to the passage, inferences based on passage information, the attitude or tone of the passage, or the application of passage information to other information. Examinees answer each question by selecting one of four answer options, which are sometimes phrases and sometimes full sentences. Some item stems are in the form of incomplete statements that must be completed with one of four response options that are phrases or clauses. Regardless of format, there is only one correct response for each reading comprehension item.

Passages used in the reading comprehension section are 100 to 350 words long and are followed by 3 to 8 questions. The specifications for the design of passages and items controls for the vocabulary characteristics, rhetorical organization of passages, and content characteristics of passages. According to the test specifications, the passages used in the reading comprehension section are representative of materials that students might encounter in school work or in situations related to college life.

A sample TOEFL test is presented in Appendix A. This test, identified as Form 3FATF5, was administered on May 14, 1983, and is the test that is described in detail in this report.

3.   Overview of Project Activities and the Report
The central goal of the project was to describe the TOEFL test in light of an approach based on recent theory and research on language proficiency assessment. The outcome of this description included some suggestions for further research on the content and construct validity of TOEFL, as well as for item and test development research. The underlying motivation was an awareness of a significant shift in language teaching pedagogy and language assessment theory that has stressed extended knowledge of how to use language in the everyday world. Accordingly, the first set of activities was to draw on the expertise of a language assessment researcher attuned to leading developments in the field who could summarize current developments in the art and science of language testing and provide a useful framework from which to view significant issues that needed treatment in describing the range of language proficiency skills assessed and not assessed by the test. The summary of important trends in the field and an overview of a framework for describing TOEFL and other proficiency tests are given in Section II.

The second major set of activities was to create procedures for utilizing the framework that was developed and then proceed to study a sample TOEFL instrument in light of the framework. We viewed the effort to operationalize and apply the framework as exploratory. To the best of our knowledge, no similar attempt has been made to describe TOEFL or any other language proficiency instrument in this manner. We realize we have much to learn and that our modest efforts were only a beginning toward a more adequate description of the content validity of language proficiency tests in general. Development of the procedures for describing the TOEFL test based on the framework is described in Section III. The resulting description of the sample TOEFL is in Section IV.

A final objective of our work was to suggest ways in which language proficiency tests might be improved with regard to both usefulness and validity given the findings of our review of TOEFL. While our concern lay most with TOEFL and how its strengths and limitations might be evaluated, we were also concerned with presenting a position on improvements that would be of value to the field of language testing as a whole. Further, it seemed important to suggest concrete steps that might be undertaken to devise new instruments for assessing extended language proficiency. Section IV of the report is devoted to these matters, and also summarizes the findings of our research on TOEFL.

II.   INVESTIGATING THE LANGUAGE SKILLS REQUIRED BY TOEFL

1.   Recent Research in Language Testing
In recent state-of-the-art reports, Spolsky (1979 and elsewhere) has distinguished three major approaches to language testing. In brief, the traditional approach has viewed language testing as an art best practiced by the language teacher, and has focused largely on what should be tested rather than on how testing should be done. The psychometric–structuralist approach views language testing as a science best practiced by measurement scientists (psychometricians) working with language scientists (linguists); the focus is on both how to test and what to test. Finally, the integrative–sociolinguistic approach is in many ways a synthesis of the other two. In this approach, language testing is viewed as both an art and a science, requiring the collective expertise of language teachers, linguists, psychometricians, sociologists, and anthropologists; the focus is on what is involved in authentic language use (sociolinguistic perspectives) and on how to measure this use through language tests (integrative techniques).

A concern expressed frequently by proponents of this third approach is that many major language tests, under the influence of the psychometric–structuralist approach, may be more objective, reliable, and administratively efficient than they are valid, acceptable, and relevant to the needs of examinees and teachers (e.g., Oller & Spolsky, 1979). This concern is also expressed about psychological and educational testing in general. For example, Messick (1981) has argued that the two most important components in psychological and educational testing are construct validity (roughly, how well we can demonstrate what we are or should be testing) and the potential social consequences of test results. Moreover, Shoemaker 1980) has assembled the sobering viewpoints of such testing experts as Buros, Throndike, and Lumsden on the extent to which achievement testing has progressed during this century; the view of Buros (1977), reported below, is typical.

> Except for the tremendous advances in electronic scoring, analysis, and reporting of test results, we don't have a great deal to show for fifty years of work. Essentially, achievement tests are being constructed today in the same way they were fifty years ago—the major changes being the use of more sophisticated statistical procedures for doing what we did then—mistakes and all. . . . In fact, some of today's tests may even be poorer, because of the restrictions imposed by machine scoring. (p. 10)

Reflecting these concerns, much recent research in language testing has addressed two issues: the construct validity of language tests and the relevance of language tests to the needs of students and teachers. We turn to some examples of this research on construct validity; the particular studies mentioned are not the only noteworthy research, but are intended to serve as convenient examples.

2.   Construct Validity Concerns

Two main lines of research on construct validity are summarized here: one dealing with theoretical frameworks of language proficiency, the other with the nature of performance on language tests.

Theoretical Frameworks for Language Proficiency. Inspired by the work of such researchers as Vygotsky (1962), Chomsky (1965), Gumperz (1971), Halliday (1973), Hymes (1974), Bruner (1975), and others, much research on language proficiency has attempted to explain three widespread and nontrivial findings in recent work on language proficiency testing (see Canale 1983a, 1983b, and 1984; and Cummins, 1983 and 1984 for references).

(a) Certain individuals (often members of language minority groups) have been misclassified as having language disorders and "linguistic deficits," that is as lacking, in a biological/maturational sense, *basic language proficiency.*

(b) Certain individuals who have studied a second language in a formal classroom setting, and who perform well on academically oriented second language tests, do not perform as well on tests requiring use of the second language for *authentic communication* outside such classroom settings.

(c) Certain individuals who perform well on tests requiring authentic communication in the second language do not perform as well on academically oriented second language tests requiring *autonomous language use*—such as in organizing one's ideas or solving a verbal math problem.

To address such findings adequately and to respond to other shortcomings of previous frameworks for language proficiency, it has been suggested that a theoretical framework with the following three general features is needed: first, basic, communicative, and autonomous language proficiencies should be distinguished; second, the types of knowledge and skills (competence areas) involved in each dimension of language proficiency should be identified; and third, the linguistic and other cognitive demands of a given language task should be considered separately (cf., Canale, 1983a, for a discussion). Following is a brief outline of both the minimal range of language related competence that could be considered and the manner in which it might contribute to the three dimensions of language proficiency.

As a preliminary range of language competence areas, one might consider those discussed by Canale and Swain (1980). Although proposed originally for describing only communicative language use, these competence areas may represent core components of overall language proficiency and hence may be useful for understanding other uses of language as well. Since these areas are discussed in detail (with references to other work) by Canale and Swain (1980) and Canale (1983b), and in the next part of this report, what follows is only an outline of their essential features.

1. *Grammatical Competence:* mastery of the language code (e.g., vocabulary and rules of word formation, sentence formation, literal meaning, pronunciation, and spelling).

2. *Sociolinguistic competence:* mastery of appropriate use (production and comprehension) of language in different sociolinguistic contexts, with emphasis on appropriateness of (a) meanings (e.g., topics, attitudes, functions) and (b) forms (e.g., register, formulaic expressions).

3. *Discourse competence:* mastery of how to combine meanings and forms to achieve unified text in different genres—such as a casual conversation, an argumentative essay, or a business letter—by using both (a) cohesion devices to relate forms (e.g., use of pronouns, transition expressions, parallel structures) and (b) coherence principles to organize meanings (e.g., concerning the development, consistency, balance, and completeness of ideas).

4. *Strategic competence:* mastery of verbal and nonverbal strategies both (a) to compensate for breakdowns in communication due to insufficient competence or to performance limitations (e.g., use of paraphrase, dictionaries) and (b) to enhance the rhetorical effect of language (e.g., use of slow and soft speech, use of literary devices).

With this range of competencies in mind, consider the three dimensions of language proficiency proposed below.

Basic language proficiency. This dimension, while not critical to the substance of this reoort, is mentioned here for the sake of completeness. It is concerned with the biological universals required for normal language development and use. Of concern, then, are not only universals of grammar that underlie grammatical competence but also sociolinguistic universals, discourse universals, universal strategies, and perceptual/processing universals. It is assumed that such universals interact with general cognitive development to set the biological upper and lower limits on possible uses, messages, and forms of language. A normal individual's actual communicative and autonomous proficiencies are thus presumably within these limits and are influenced mainly by socialization and, to perhaps a relatively lesser extent, by individual differences in personality, intelligence, aptitudes, learning style, motivation, and personal experiences.

Communicative language proficiency. The focus here is on social, interpersonal (or other-directed) uses of language through spoken or written channels, similar to what Vygotsky (1962) and others have referred to as *social speech.* It is assumed that communication is primarily a form of social interaction, in which emphasis is normally less on grammatical forms and literal meaning than on participants and what they are trying to do through language—i.e., on the social meaning of utterances. Such social meaning is qualified by contextual variables, such as roles of participants, setting, goals, and norms of interaction; authentic communication thus requires continuous evaluation, interpretation, and negotiation of various levels of information. Such contextual variables may serve to simplify communication (by providing clues to meaning) or complicate it (e.g., by imposing language-specific appropriate conditions). Although communicative language use normally involves grammatical, sociolinguistic, discourse, and strategic competencies (as identified above), the focus and greatest demand may be on sociolinguistic and strategic knowledge and skills, less so on discourse ones (e.g., cohesion devices and genre structures), and least so on grammatical competence. As such, the degree of exposure to and use of sociolinguistic rules, communication strategies, and interactional discourse features—that is, degree of socialization and acculturation with respect to a given language community—may be especially important in determining the range of communicative contexts and functions that an individual can and is willing to handle through that language.

Autonomous language proficiency. This dimension involves less directly social and more intrapersonal, representational (or self-directed) uses of language, such as problem solving, organizing one's thoughts, verbal play, poetry, and personal writing. It is similar to what Vygotsky (1962) and others have referred to as *inner speech.* Focus is less on social meaning than on personal and literal meanings; hence, contextual variables do not seem to qualify (simplify or complicate) information as much as do the language code, logical relationships among propositions, and idiosyncratic personal interpretations of these. Though immediate sociolinguistic context may be rich, it is not necessarily in focus in autonomous language uses (for example, in counting one's change at the local grocery store). The main language competencies involved would seem to be grammatical (especially vocabulary and rules for deriving literal meaning) and discourse (especially coherence principles), with less demand on communicative strategies and the least on sociolinguistic competence. Again, however, degree of socialization—e.g., degree of exposure to and acceptance of various autonomous tasks in a given language—may be viewed as a valuable index of the range of such tasks that can be performed by an individual through that same language without undue affective, linguistic, and general cognitive difficulties.

To summarize, the relationships among these three dimensions of language proficiency seem to be as follows. Basic language proficiency is comprised of those language-related biological universals that are required for communicative and autonomous language development and use. Communicative and autonomous proficiencies seem to differ in that sociolinguistic and strategic competencies may receive more emphasis in the former whereas grammatical and discourse competencies may be more in focus in the latter. In this view, it follows that one cannot adequately develop or test communicative proficiency through autonomous tasks or vice versa.

The nature of performance on language tests. Just as lack of understanding of what we are trying to measure limits the construct validity of language tests, so does our lack of understanding of how different test methods (or formats) influence performance on such tests. Careful studies have been carried out to investigate just how examinees' attitudes, perceptions, and training with respect both to formal testing and to a particular test method (e.g., multiple-choice) can affect a test score (e.g., Deyhle, 1983; Scott & Madsen, 1983); compelling arguments have been made for paying close attention to the quality of performance elicited by various test methods (e.g., Jones, 1983). The research reviewed here is that of Bachman and Palmer (forthcoming). They examine eight factors influencing language performance that may, in addition to an examinee's language proficiency, be reflected in a language test score. The important point they stress is that the type of performance elicited through certain test methods may be qualitatively different from that involved in authentic language use; to the extent that test performance does differ importantly and unpredictably from authentic performance, it may in some instances prove difficult to use a test score to draw firm conclusions about an examinee's true ability to use language.

Before outlining the eight factors cited by Bachman and Palmer, it is important to note that the range of authentic language to which learners of English as a foreign language have been exposed to is likely to be limited. Therefore, in some sense, it is not appropriate to expect that an English proficiency test such as TOEFL, used for college and university admission of foreign students, would be able to cover the widest range of authentic language use that might be judged to occur in the life of college students in the United States.

The eight factors identified by Bachman and Palmer are outlined below; then an illustration is provided to indicate how these factors can be useful in test analysis and development.

Psychophysiological skills. This factor reflects the extent to which sensory skills are called for in receptive language tasks (auditory or visual) and to which neuromuscular skills are required in production tasks (articulatory or digital).

Representation of knowledge. Here the focus is on the extent to which the knowledge required in a language task is consciously or subconsciously stored, on the one hand, and stored as a prefabricated pattern or as a rule, on the other hand.

Language use situations. Such situations may differ along two dimensions: first, the extent to which the situation is reflexive (focused on language itself) or transitive (focused on doing something with language); and second, the extent to which the situation is reciprocal (providing immediate feedback and interaction) or nonreciprocal (providing no immediate feedback nor interaction).

Context and message. Four features are distinguished here: the amount of context that must be attended to (i.e., the ratio of familiar to new information); the distribution of the message (compact or diffuse over time and space); type of message (abstract or concrete information); and control of message (whether or not the information must be consciously dealt with).

Artificial restrictions. Language performance may be limited in contrived ways at several levels: organization of discourse (e.g., changing topic from one test item to another); message (e.g., no illocutionary force); forms (e.g., contrived use of synonymy in a text to satisfy readability formula); participants (e.g., the social and personal roles assumed); and channels (e.g., a minilecture without any visual aids).

Monitoring factors. Based on Krashen's (1982) notion of the language use strategy of consciously editing or monitoring one's language production, this set of factors includes the time available to perform a task and the extent to which the task encourages attention to form and to the use of explicit, conscious language knowledge.

Affective factors. Four elements are signaled here: preference for field dependence (overall image) or independence (isolated bits of image); inhibition (e.g., in role play or oral interaction); tolerance for ambiguity (e.g., detailed versus general task description); and motivation (e.g., to sound or act like a native of the target language).

Strategic factors. This set of factors deals with the extent to which one is able to resolve various language use problems (e.g., use of paraphrase, gestures, basic sentence patterns, requests for repetition) or to enhance one's performance (e.g., use of literary devices in writing or of rhetorical devices in speaking).

Like the research on theoretical frameworks for language proficiency summarized in the first part of this section, research on the factors outlined in relation to performance on language tests bears on the issue of construct validity in language testing. Together these two sets of studies may provide a coherent basis for carrying out research both on what current language tests may actually be measuring and on how to improve language testing. The following discussion illustrates these possible applications in the context of TOEFL.

3.   A Framework for Analyzing TOEFL
The framework developed by the project staff for overviewing the TOEFL test attempted to operationalize the concerns raised in Section I on the construct

validity of language tests and their relevance to learners in North American postsecondary educational institutions. This framework has four components that were developed independently from the actual TOEFL test specifications. Consistent with the original research proposal for the work described, a modification of Munby's (1978) classification of skills was used for describing skills required by TOEFL. However, the framework also addressed other issues related to language performance on TOEFL. The framework can be summarized as follows.

1. *A domain description of competence areas.* The purpose of this description is to identify in sufficient but manageable detail the main knowledge and skills provided by TOEFL in the areas of grammatical, sociolinguistic, discourse, and strategic competencies. It has been developed independently of any consideration of TOEFL; rather, it reflects the domain descriptions presented by Munby (1978) and Canale (1983a, based on Canale & Swain, 1980). In the present context, this outline was adjusted and developed to reflect important features in the teaching of English as a foreign language.

2. *Language performance features.* Based on the work of Bachman and Palmer (forthcoming), this component attempts to identify the main features of language performance elicited by TOEFL items. The purpose of this component is to allow preliminary characterization of TOEFL item formats in terms of the extent to which each performance feature is or is not present across various item types and sections of the test.

3. *Relevance for academic and social language uses.* The purpose of this component is to allow independent judges to characterize, in a scalar manner, the content of TOEFL items, i.e., the relevance of topics, communicative functions, discourse genres, and sociocultural contexts to academic language use, on the one hand, and to social language use, on the other.

4. *Minimum mastery level.* The ultimate purpose here is to allow independent judges to characterize the difficulty of TOEFL sections and items with reference to criterion performance descriptions. A first step in investigating what level of proficiency is sufficient to perform accurately on TOEFL entails a description of TOEFL items in terms of an appropriate performance scale.

The next part of this report describes the implementation of this framework in describing the TOEFL test in detail. Before proceeding, it is useful to note that the four areas designated by the framework are important for the evaluation of any proficiency test, not just TOEFL. The generality of the approach is important; it emphasizes the extended validity of a proficiency test. All four areas cited are important to examinees taking a proficiency test and to proficiency test consumers; all four have significant bearings on the legitimacy of test score interpretation and the use of this information for valid purposes. This viewpoint contrasts with other approaches to proficiency testing, which have so often ignored the larger range of multiple links that must be established and evaluated between performance on an instrument and performance in the real world.

A second matter that deserves attention is the exploratory character of applying the framework. The areas designated in the framework are of clear significance, but the process of implementing their interpretation in describing a proficiency test is an experiment. This fact should motivate the reader to question how refinement and implementation of the framework might be improved in future contexts. What follows is an honest, and occasionally critical, portrayal of the successes and difficulties encountered in applying this framework to describing the TOEFL test.

III. PROCEDURES FOR DESCRIBING THE TOEFL

1. Overview
The TOEFL instrument found in Appendix A was described in terms of the four framework components discussed in the previous sections: (1) a domain description of competence areas based on a communicative skills checklist; (2) an analysis of the language performance features of TOEFL sections and item types; (3) an evaluation of the relevance of TOEFL section and item contents to language use in criterion settings; and (4) a preliminary description of the minimum mastery levels represented by TOEFL test sections and item types. The design of procedures to operationalize each of the four framework components is discussed in this portion of the report.

2. Procedures for Conducting the Competence Domain Description of a Sample TOEFL Test
One of the major goals of this study was to conduct a detailed examination of the various communicative skills needed to fulfill language tasks on the TOEFL test. To achieve this goal, a taxonomic list of identifiable skills entering into the communicative process was created. The domain description of competence discussed in the previous section and at length in Canale and Swain (1980) and Canale (1983b) served as the basic analytical perspective of communicative competence. From three of the four components of communicative competence presented in this perspective—grammatical, sociolinguistic, and discourse—an operationally oriented list of skills was suggested by Canale (Appendix B). Strategic competence was excluded as an area since examinees are not required to produce language as part of the TOEFL examination. The checklist in Appendix B was subjected to numerous revisions by Penfield and Duran throughout the project. This resulted in a fairly detailed list that was, in turn, modified later in the project in order to be more generic. Appendix C presents this generic skills checklist, and Appendix D summarizes data resulting from application of this checklist to the sample TOEFL test in Appendix A.

Coding an operational instrument for communicative competence that could be applied to natural communication or simulations of it was a monumental task that deserves some discussion here. At each stage in the process of designing successive versions of the skills checklist, the inadequacies of a taxonomic approach to communication became more apparent. It is clear that there is a strong interaction among elements occurring across areas of the checklist and that the taxonomic breakdown of skills did not convey much information about dependencies among skills across checklist areas. Also, in the case of oral discourse, the checklist could not capture dynamic dependencies across several conversational turns of discourse. Therefore we must qualify that the skills checklist is not intended as a conceptualization of communicative competence but rather as an operationally oriented list of discrete skills entering into communicative competence and the communicative process. As linguists from various theoretical perspectives have noted about language, communication, i.e., its integrative nature, goes beyond the sum of any identifiable discrete parts. Savignon (1983), Garvin (1978), Gumperz (1982), and others have noted that the gestalt nature of language, language usage, and communication is realized as a dynamic process, one that a taxonomy consisting of hierarchically arranged discrete, nonoverlapping categories cannot capture. In any case, despite the obvious inadequacies in a checklist approach to evaluating communicative competence, there are advantages in compiling such a list for research on proficiency testing. In this project, such a checklist is justified since it can serve as a useful analytical tool in looking at discrete skills that are tested intentionally and/or incidentally by a discrete point test such as TOEFL.

The identifiable discrete skills entering into natural communication in all of the various communicative and social contexts of language use are perhaps infinite. Consequently, those suggested in our skills checklist (Appendix D) comprise a select list of those skills that seem most salient and significant for a nonnative English speaker to learn in order to be adequately equipped to communicate in English in an American academic context. For the most part the skills selected were based on different types of meaning criteria—referential meaning, conceptual meaning, structural meaning, interactional meaning, attitudinal meaning, propositional meaning, etc. However, in conformity with the nature of English and its uniqueness compared to other languages, at some points the selectivity was based on patterns of organization or structure that may only be related indirectly to meaning. The selection of skills to be included in the checklist was based primarily on the uniqueness of English in American academic contexts. The designers of the final checklist drew heavily on their knowledge of other languages and cultures in the world, years of experience in teaching English to nonnative speakers, and sociolinguistic research. Above all, this skills checklist should only be construed as a suggested operational taxonomy of some discrete and salient skills foreign students must acquire and not as a definitive, comprehensive list of all that it takes to be communicatively competent.

3. Description of the Competence Skills Checklist

This section presents a general description of the major skills represented in the checklist (Appendix C) along with the rationale for the categorization suggested at each level in the taxonomy. The relevant portions of the checklist are cited in parentheses. Capital letters A, B, or C in parentheses indicate which of the general competencies is alluded to; digits following capital letters identify particular competencies or classes of competencies.

3.1 Grammatical Competence (Section A). This component refers to mastery of the linguistic code of English for which numerous grammars have been written, e.g., Francis (1958), *Structure of American English,* or, more recently, Leech and Svartvik (1975), *A Communicative Grammar of English,* and many others. Our skills checklist focuses on five basic dimensions of grammatical competence that are discussed in depth below: pronunciation, script or written symbols, lexicon or vocabulary, word formation or morphology, and sentence formation or syntax.

Pronunciation (Section A.1). Included in this section are skills related to the articulation of words as they combine in connected speech as well as the melodic accompaniment in prosodic patterns signaled by rate, stress, intonation, range of pitch, height of pitch, and pauses (Bolinger & Sears, 1981). Regarding the articulation of words or lexical items, a categorical distinction is drawn between those cases in which words maintain their full pronunciation form, for the most part, in connected speech (Sect. A.1.1) and those that are presented in a modified form in speech (Sect. A.1.2), reflected in such natural processes in English as vowel reduction, consonant cluster reduction, vowel deletion, palatalization, and contraction. There are pragmatic implications for making the distinction between Section A.1.1 and A.1.2 since rate of speech, degree of informality or casualness, and social context often trigger those linguistic processes mentioned in Section A.1.2.

While prosodic patterns in English are extremely complex, they have been known to play a significant role in learning how to communicate in English, given a non-English background (see Gumperz & Kaltman, 1980). There is much variation and even disagreement among researchers as to the patterns and functions of prosody in English; we have emphasized three overall meanings that prosodic phenomena participate in signaling in English: (1) neutral reference, with no extra emotional or emphatic message implied (Sect. A.1.3); (2) contrastive or emphatic meaning, where the opposite of the neutral reference is implied, marked by a variant in stress or pitch within an overall pattern (Sect. A.1.4); and (3) emotive or attitudinal meaning, marked by tempo, range of pitch, height of pitch, pauses, and other prosodic patterns (Sect. A.1.5). It is perhaps obvious at this point that the skills we have selected extend beyond an interest with denotative meaning to also include connotative meaning and the full range of meaning entailed in natural communication—even that at a more personal, emotional level. This orientation is in keeping with sociolinguistic research that describes communication as the negotiation of meaning based on inferences concerning the social and affective context of communication (Gumperz, 1982). Our treatment of prosodic patterns is not designed to describe in detail prosodic functions induced by the occurrence of particular phonological and syntactic structures in speech. Such a description of prosodic functions would be valuable as an augmentation and refinement of the current work.

Script (written symbols) (Section A.2). Skills selected within this section include graphic symbols and their combination as they are used to convey meaning in a written text. To be more comprehensive, we have selected both those symbols that are arranged into spelling patterns to form words (Sect. A.2.1) and those that signal various types of grammatical, structural, and lexical meaning with a text (Sect. A.2.2 and A.2.3). Of those graphic symbols conveyed by the letters of English, there are those that reflect the spelling patterns found in isolated words (Sect. A.2.1.1) and those that reflect modifications caused by words entering into a sentence sequence (Sect. A.2.1.2), e.g., the problematic patterns of "plan" vs. "planned" or "cry" vs. "cried."

Other graphic symbols (e.g., punctuation symbols, slashes, underlining, indentation, capitalization, italics, boldface type) serve to mark a multitude of different meanings in written English text. Teachers are most familiar with the use of these symbols, particularly punctuation marks, to mark structural meaning or structural grouping in written texts (Sect. A.2.2); they are meant to aid the reader in selecting the salient pieces of information embedded linearly in the text. There is less analytical description about other uses of the array of graphic symbols to convey different types of meaning. We have suggested the following categories of uses of some of these graphic symbols: (a) representing modifications of full word forms (Sect. A.2.3) as in the case of contractions, for example; (b) marking specific concepts (Sect. A.2.4); and (c) marking emphatic or contrastive meaning within textual units (Sect. A.2.5). We have selected these particular uses of graphic symbols as a potentially comprehensive list of various types of meaning conveyed in written texts with the help of symbols other than letters. For example, the use of quotation marks, which serve to mark a variety of different meanings ranging from direct speech to conceptual meanings such as identity (as in nicknames—Bill "Skip" Smith or titles—in "Passages. . .").

Lexicon (vocabulary) (Section A.3). Included within this skill category are the use of content words used with their neutral or literal meaning in context (Sect. A.3.1) as well as those content words used in a way that extends beyond their given literal meaning. At least two categories are distinguished among nonliteral uses of content words: (a) idiomatic expressions (Sect. A.3.2) or those instances in which words are frozen together to function as a semantic whole whose meaning cannot be determined by combining the meanings of the parts; and (b) metaphorical uses of words or expressions (Sect. A.3.3). Some very prominent types of idiomatic expressions in English that can be problematic to a learner of

English include compound nouns (Sect. A.3.2.1) and compound (two–three word) verbs (Sect. A.3.2.2) as well as numerous others that have resulted for various historical reasons (Sect. A.3.2.3). Because of the complexities involved, our analyses of idioms were not designed to examine syntactic and other structural constraints that are implicated in the appropriate use of idioms (Yorio, 1980). Category A.3.3 (metaphorical uses of words) refers to unique uses of literal words to extend their meaning and which have a clearly identifiable literal and nonliteral reference since their interpretation depends upon the association of the two references, as in: "She is the *flower* of his life." Those metaphorical uses that were no longer recognized as unique or nonconventional were categorized under idiomatic expressions, e.g., "in one ear and out the other." Content words make up only that part of the lexicon of which English speakers are most conscious and aware. Function words in English serve to bind content words together into complex patterns of meaning, often termed "grammatical meaning" by ethno-semanticists who have developed frameworks for uncovering this meaning (Mathiot, 1970). Typically, function words serve to mark specific concepts and relationships, as has been detailed by Munby (1978) and by Leech and Svartvik (1975). The most typical concepts marked by function words are included in the skills checklist (Sect. A.3.4.1–A.3.4.8). These include location and direction; definiteness and indefiniteness; quantity and amount; time, frequency of occurrence and span of time; means or instrument; possession; comparison and degree; and negation.

Morphology (word formation) (Section A.4). In addition to function words, prefixes and suffixes attached to words serve to signal grammatical meaning, as is the case with inflection (Sect. A.4.1), or to mark the class membership of the content word involved, which may or may not be the case with derivation. We have included all types of derivation, provided they occurred in a context showing the relationships shared between two words having the same stem or root (Sect. A.4.2).

Section A.4.1 includes the major conceptual meanings that inflectional suffixes in English participate in marking either completely or partially: number, as in plural nouns (Sect. A.4.1.1); possession, as in possessive nouns (Sect. A.4.1.2); person, as in third person present verbs (Sect. A.4.1.3); various simple and compound tenses (Sect. A.4.1.4); and comparison and degree, as in comparative and superlative constructions (Sect. A.4.1.5).

Sentence formation (Section A.5). Linguistic research in the past two decades has made us aware of the complexity of patterning in English at this level. It would be an impossible task to list all of these in this skills checklist; therefore, we have opted to select salient patterns that might prove problematic to a non-native speaker of English whose task is to obtain meaning from given sentences. We have begun with an assumption posed by some current theoretical linguistic views backed by psycholinguistic research (Clark and Clark, 1977; Fodor, Bever, & Garrett, 1974). According to this assumption, derivation of the meaning of sentences is based on the ability to recognize the logical subject(s), verb(s), and object(s) encoded in sentence constituents, as well as ability to recognize semantic relationships linking together the information found in sentence constituents. Given the embedding and recursive nature of English syntax, these are not easy tasks. Embedding and recursion present special problems for English language learners. For example, learners must acquire facility in detecting the syntactical and lexical markers for these phenomena and, in concert with these skills, they must develop appropriate strategies for testing alternative interpretations of the emerging left-to-right syntactic structure of sentences. Complex sentences display many clauses with numerous clausal relations, which can make the task of selecting the logical relations a confusing one for a nonnative speaker of English. Therefore, we have selected those grammatical structures that are most typical of English along with those that might seem most problematic in the recognition of the logical constituents making up sentences.

In the first group of structures are some commonly referred to by teachers as "simple sentence types" (Sect. 5.1). These are structures in which words or phrases—not clauses—participate in forming the logical relations among constituents. We have selected those well-known patterns that exhibit variation in the ordering of their logical constituents, but a variation that is systematic and suggests some sort of grammatical meaning, e.g., a question, a command, a statement. Included within these are declarative, active statements (Sect. 5.1.1); questions of any type (Sect. 5.1.2); imperatives (Sect. 5.1.3); passive constructions with or without a stated agent (Sect. 5.1.4); and THERE constructions (Sect. 5.1.5).

Section A.5.2 includes those sentences that teachers typically categorize as compound sentences. They are sentences with two main clauses and no subordinate clauses and as such have actually two sets of logical constituents bound together by some conjunction or other linking device. On the other hand, Section A.5.3 includes sentences with a main clause, from which the logical constituents are drawn, and a subordinate clause that stands outside the main clause—either preceding or following it—and adds additional semantic information to that contained within the main clause, as in: "When he's ready, he'll call" or "He'll call when he's ready," or, in reduced form: "Ready, he called."

Considered as a separate category from the type of complex sentence described in Section A.5.3 are those sentences in which clauses are subordinated within constituent members of the entire sentence—often referred to as embedding in current linguistic theory. We have chosen to include several processes or broad classes within this section that have been described in detail in recent years. Again, for the sake of minimizing excessive detail in the checklist, we will overlook some distinctions. Included in embedded structures are noun phrase (NP) complementation or nominalization (Sect. A.5.4.1), where noun phrases function as unitary constituents, and relative clause formation (Sect. 5.4.2), where subordinate clauses participate as modifiers of subjects or object constituents. In the latter case, consideration must also be given to those instances in which this particular subordinate clause is overtly signaled by relativizers, e.g., *who, which, that,* versus reduced instances in which no signal is present, as in: "The man I saw was nice."

A final sentence formation important to consider on pragmatic grounds, since some have suggested it represents a stylistic-based motivation for use, is extraposition and other forms of focus shifting (Sect. 5.5). For our purposes, we will place here all those instances in which the logical object precedes any order of the other logical constituents, as in topicalization, e.g., "That I've had enough of." or

$$\text{"That } \underset{O}{\text{I}}\text{'}\underset{S}{\text{ve had enough of}}\underset{V}{\text{."}}$$

extraposition, e.g., "What I think is that this is a difficult assignment."

$$\underset{O}{\text{"What I think}} \underset{V}{\text{is}} \underset{S}{\text{that this is a difficult assignment."}}$$

3.2   Sociolinguistic Competence (Section B).   We have relied heavily on the initial set of skills provided by Canale (Appendix A) in the development of this portion of the checklist. We have made rough attempts to expand and modify this set using various research orientations from work done on the ethnography of speaking and speech acts.

Section B.1 suggests some of those dimensions on which cultures define appropriateness when various ways of expressing the same information are available. We have selected some of the analytical factors that can be used to explain the way in which a message is presented, especially those that are socially defined. These factors include (a) status and power relationships between participants involved in communication (Sect. B.1.1); (b) topic (Sect. B.1.2); (c) setting and scene, whether formal or informal (Sect. B.1.3); (d) channel or mode of presentation, whether spoken or written (Sect. B.1.4); and (e) genre, or the general structure of presentation and format of the communication (Sect. B.1.5).

While Section B.1 includes skills that focus on the speech patterns and structuring of information from the perspective of the overall speech event or interactional event, Section B.2 includes those skills relevant at a smaller unit of analysis level, which is now termed "speech acts." It includes a selected list of possible ways in which utterances can be used within a given speech event or interaction, and the units are organized into categories of illocutionary acts or the attempt to accomplish some communicative purpose (Austin, 1962). Section B.2.1–B.2.21 lists a variety of illocutionary ways in which utterances or written pieces of language might be used communicatively. In order to capture crucial aspects of speech acts in natural communication, we have made a distinction between direct forms, in which the speech act matches the literal interpretation of the segment, and indirect forms, in which the speech act has a different meaning than the literal interpretation of the segment analyzed, e.g., where "It's hot in here," might serve as a directive to initiate the listener to open the window.

Section B.3 includes those uses of expressions that Malinowski (1944) has referred to as "phatic communication." In these instances, there is little meaning implied other than enacting a social ritual in a speech event or in marking the social role or social presence of others in a speech event. These are basically formulaic expressions with routine usage but minimal referential meaning.

Section B.4 lists some of the ways in which an indirect perspective toward a communicative event or an emotive or attitudinal orientation toward a discourse topic might be signaled either through grammatical forms or intonation. Some of the particular attitudes or emotive meaning implied that are included in Section B.4.1–6 concern sarcasm, ridicule, defeat, frustration, criticism, and doubt. Finally, Section B.5 suggests those linguistic forms or speech modes that are not typically found in broadcast or standard written English and that represent non-standard dialect forms.

3.3 Discourse Competence (Section C). This portion of the skills checklist is concerned with the way in which communicative events—be they spoken or written—are bound together to form a whole. In keeping with current work on textual analysis, we have focused on those linguistic tools that can be utilized like thread in a cloth to bind the meaning of a text together as a whole. These have been labeled cohesion devices (Sect. C.1). Since a text is also held together by an ordering of ideas or propositions—coherence—we have included some skills that relate to the organizational structuring of given texts (Sect. C.2) in both spontaneous, unplanned conversational discourse (Sect. C.2.1) and in planned, preedited discourse—whether written or spoken (Sect. C.2.2). Our observations suggest that preplanning, as opposed to spontaneity with no pre-planning, results in different structuring of the ideas in any given text, and thus would seem to have important implications for an academic use of English.

Section C.1 suggests some linguistic devices used to bind a text together according to the nature of the device itself: some are lexical (Sect. C.1.1) (e.g., pronoun reference, synonymy, word repetition, sequence markers, and so on), and some are syntactic (Sect. C.1.2) (e.g., ellipses, parallel structures, conjoined clauses). These devices have been organized in the skills checklist according to their formal nature because they can bind information in a variety of complex and different ways across different units within a text and in different manners across types of text. For example, pronoun reference can be used to bind elements of a sentence, paragraph, essay, or even book. The simplest way to handle this open variety of ways in which cohesive devices operate within the context of the skills checklist was to specify occurrence of these cohesive ties according to their immediate cohesive function at the sentence level or at the level of larger units of text. Sentence-level devices used to mark cohesion (Sect. C.1.2) were organized according to their functional nature in this process to mark conciseness (Sect. C.1.2.1); continuity (Sect. C.1.2.2); semantic relationships between clauses (Sect. C.1.2.3); and emphasis (Sect. C.1.2.4).

Coherence (Sect. C.2) represents those skills dealing with the organization of ideas within any given text beyond the boundary level of individual sentences. Most of those patterns in conversational discourse suggested by Munby (1978) have been utilized, including initiating the discourse, maintaining the discourse, and terminating the discourse (Sect. C.2.1.1–C.2.1.3). Since sociolinguistic research is still in the process of discovering the various mechanisms by which each of these skills is achieved in natural, conversational discourse, it was extremely difficult to operationalize them. There are no doubt many complex cues involved in the initiation, continuation, or termination of discourse drawn from the prosodic, kinesic, linguistic, and nonverbal systems of English that are important in American academic contexts and that .vary from other English-speaking academic contexts throughout the world. As the literature has noted (e.g., Gumperz, 1982), these cues are quite often symbols of culture that operate at an extremely unconscious level in the communication process.

Kaplan (1966) suggested many years ago that planned, written discourse also exhibited cultural patterns in its organization of ideas. We have suggested some organizational patterns that predominate written, expository texts in American academic contexts (Sect. C.4.2). Although there are many possible patterns of organization that could be utilized, as evidenced by numerous textbooks on written expository prose, we have used the framework developed and field-tested by Penfield for use with foreign students in *Essay Writing for the African World* (1979). Section C.2.2.1–C.2.2.8 suggests ways in which the predominating or salient organizational pattern of a given text might be categorized semantically, relying strongly on some typical rhetorical modes. Included are classification (Sect. C.2.2.1); illustration (Sect. C.2.2.2); definition (Sect. C.2.2.3); process or event-ordering (Sect. C.2.4); description (Sect. C.2.2.5); comparison (Sect. C.2.2.6); cause/effect (Sect. C.2.2.7); and factual development—where none of the previous categories predominate and facts are simply chained together (Sect. C.2.2.8).

3.4   Coding of TOEFL Items.   Penfield and Duran separately coded every item on the TOEFL test found in Appendix A. The initial goal was to enact fully independent coding so as to allow a comparison of agreement in coding. This did not prove entirely feasible. Duran found it necessary to study Penfield's coding of a few items in each section prior to beginning his own independent coding. This strategy was necessary since initial attempts at establishing coding guidelines working with a separate set of TOEFL items not found in Appendix A had not sufficiently resolved questions on interpretation of the checklist. Duran's agreement with Penfield's coding was nonetheless quite high, over 80 percent, though Penfield's coding revealed a higher occurrence of some phenomena, e.g., grammatical phenomena related to pronunciation. It seemed clear that Penfield's more extensive knowledge of English structure, background in phonology, and experience in teaching English as a foreign language contributed to her sensitivity as a coder. A decision was made to use Penfield's coding as the criterion coding to be discussed in this report. One exception to this involved the coding of sociolinguistic information for items drawn from Section 1 of TOEFL. It was decided to use Duran's coding in this case because it proved to be more sensitive to plausible speech acts embodied in utterances.

The coding of TOEFL items against the skills checklist involved coding up to three separate pieces of information for each item. These pieces of information included (a) the language stimulus (or stem) upon which an item was based, (b) the question (if there was one) asked of examinees for an item, and (c) the correct response option. Incorrect response options were not coded.

Appendix D presents a summary of the coding that resulted. The summary identifies when a characteristic occurred once in the language stimulus, question, or correct response to a question; the fuller data upon which the summary is based identify exactly where characteristics were found within items. Appendix D aggregates this information according to each item type within the various TOEFL sections. The disaggregated data are not presented in this report because of bulk and the difficulty most readers would have in interpreting it. (The full coded checklist is six times larger than Appendix D. While this more detailed coding is not contained in an appendix, results from it are discussed in the "Findings" section of this report.)

4.   Procedures for Analyzing Performance Features

The sample TOEFL test in Appendix A was examined in light of the eight test performance factors cited by Bachman and Palmer (forthcoming). These factors, as discussed in Section II, include:

* psychophysiological skills in test taking
* representation of knowledge
* language use situations
* context and message
* artificial restrictions
* monitoring factors
* affective factors
* strategic factors

The initial plan of research was to formulate definitions of these factors in terms of a numerical ordinal scale that could be used to rate the importance of each feature for all the TOEFL items and, in summary form, for each TOEFL section and item type. This strategy did not prove feasible to the project staff person (Duran) who was responsible for establishing the rating procedures. It was judged that such an interpretation of TOEFL in light of Bachman and Palmer's eight factors could not be carried out definitively in a first attempt, but that there would be much value in presenting a preliminary discussion about the relevance of the eight factors to TOEFL sections and item types. It seemed that such a discussion was necessary to clarify the relevant notions of performance that needed attention. The resulting analysis is presented in the section of the report detailing findings of the study.

5. Procedures for Evaluating the Relevance of TOEFL Item Content to Academic and Social Language Use Contexts

The purpose of this evaluation was to capture the extent to which TOEFL items reflect representative language that examinees might encounter in criterion settings. Presumably, these criterion settings would encompass the social and academic universe encountered by foreign students upon entering a North American university. The goal of analysis was to develop ordinal ratings of the extent to which various TOEFL items manifest social and academic content. Penfield and Duran judged that the sociolinguistic competence section of the Checklist of Competence Areas for evaluating TOEFL (Appendix C, Section B) already addressed the notion of content and that an alteration of the coding of the sample TOEFL against this portion of the checklist might accomplish the task at hand. Three ordinal rating dimensions for the category topic and authenticity were developed: academic living, academic content topic, and social naturalness. Academic living referred to the degree to which items were judged to reflect content and language use that students might encounter in everyday college life in or out of the classroom. The academic content topic dimension referred to the degree to which items might be judged as having topics that could occur as part of formal instruction at the college level. The dimension of social naturalness referred to the degree to which items in the listening comprehension section of TOEFL were judged to reflect language that foreign students might hear in everyday social interaction. The three dimensions overlap in the sense that a given TOEFL item could be judged to convey information about all three simultaneously.

Establishing an ordinal scale and criteria by which to rate TOEFL items on these three dimensions proved quite problematical. This was so because individual TOEFL items in and of themselves tend to provide a limited sample of language and a limited notion of a speech situation. Nonetheless, after an initial abortive effort was made to establish a three-point scale for each of the three dimensions, a final scale was established. On this scale, a rating of "3" indicated that an item conveyed a high and clear level of authenticity with regard to the dimension in question. A rating of "2" indicated that an item could have been an authentic sample of language, but that this judgment required a rater to imagine a language use situation or topic that was not clearly marked by the actual language of an item. A rating of "1" indicated that an item did not manifest authenticity on a dimension or that the language making up an item did not provide enough information on which to base a judgment for a given rating dimension. Based on this procedure, ratings were computed by two independent raters along each dimension for each TOEFL item. Also, average scores based on each test section and item type within section were computed. Interrater indices of agreement were also computed and examined. The raters in question were research assistants to the project.

6. Procedures for Preliminary Description of the Proficiency Level Represented by TOEFL Items

In this part of the study, Charles Stansfield and Judith Liskin-Gasparro over-viewed items on the sample TOEFL test using the Interagency Language Round-table (ILR) scale. The scale was originally developed by the Foreign Service Institute (FSI) during the 1950s as a means of measuring the language proficien-cy of government employees, especially Foreign Service officers. Subsequently, the scale was adopted by other government agencies concerned with language training, including the Civil Service Commission, the Peace Corps, and the armed forces. It is also used by the armed forces of NATO member nations. (For more information about the scale and the oral proficiency interview associated with it, see Clark [1980].)

The ILR scale used in this study to describe TOEFL items is based on the above-mentioned FSI scale. At the time of this writing, it was the most current version of the scale available. The scale was developed by the Interagency Language Roundtable, a consortium of government linguists representing the various agencies involved in language training and language testing activities. (Recently, the American Council on the Teaching of Foreign Languages (ACTFL) and Educational Testing Service have participated in meetings of the ILR by invitation.) The ILR scale is a description of proficiency in the four basic communicative skills: listening, speaking, reading, and writing.

There are eleven levels on the scale representing proficiency ranging from 0 to 5. A "plus" level is assigned to a person who fulfills most but not all of the requirements of the next highest level. The plus levels range from 0+ to 4+. There is no score higher than a level 5, which is defined as "proficiency equiv-alent to that of an *educated* native speaker." Levels on the scale are defined in paragraph-length descriptions. The November 1983 version is reprinted in full in this report as Appendix E.

The ILR descriptions for each level are based on the ability to handle various communication situations. These increase in difficulty along the scale. Two examples are the ability to understand directions on how to get from one place to another (level 1, listening), and the ability to read all materials in one's profes-sional or technical field (level 4, reading). Performance ratings on the scale reflect the ability to send or receive information in a wide variety of situations that can be associated with different levels of overall proficiency in a second language. A rating is assigned based on three criteria: the level of the text, the level of the task being asked of the examinee, and the level of the examinee's performance. Thus, the scale assumes that the ability to handle various situations effectively in a second language is hierarchical. The scale incorporates both linguistic complexity and situational competencies in its definition of communicative competence levels, and it is used by government agencies to assign a proficiency level to a communicative text. Because the scale is already being used to assign a difficulty level to a test in a test situation, it was decided to ask two persons familiar with the scale to apply it to TOEFL.

As noted earlier, in this study, Charles Stansfield and Judith Liskin-Gasparro applied the ILR scale to TOEFL. Both are familiar with the scale and certified to train other examiners in its use. They jointly evaluated items on the sample TOEFL form to gain a better understanding of the proficiency level represented by the items. They individually reviewed the form and then jointly discussed it. All items in Sections 1 and 3, and nearly all items in Section 2, were discussed and assigned ratings on the scale. Four and one-half hours of discussion were tape recorded. Subsequently, the examiners prepared the observations given in the ''Findings'' section regarding the scale and the TOEFL test.

IV.   FINDINGS

1.   Plan of Discussion

The characteristics of the sample TOEFL test in Appendix A will be discussed in terms of each of the four framework components for analyzing the validity of a language proficiency test. Findings with regard to each framework component will be discussed in the same order as used in Sections II and III of this report. At times the reader may notice that there is an overlap in the discussion of findings across framework components. This confluence is reflective of a natural overlap in issues. The various framework components were not intended to be mutually exclusive, but rather to be complementary in their scope and analyses. The task of describing the TOEFL test in light of the framework is not strictly an act of reporting objective data. Considered judgments are required that stem from the investigators' experiences and views on the structures and phenomena being described. This need to interject judgment is a characteristic of many forms of linguistic analysis and of test content validity research.

Figure 1 outlines the order of discussion of the findings and the subsection number involved. This outline is useful for understanding the logical organization of the discussion.

2.   Description of TOEFL Based on the Checklist of Communicative Skills

2.1   Summary of Findings for the TOEFL Test as a Whole.   The data under discussion here are entered on the skills checklist given in Appendix D along with instructions on how to interpret tabular entries. The terms used to describe various phenomena in this section are linked to the same terms occurring in the skills checklist. Please note that entries on the skills checklist are

Figure 1.   Outline of the Discussion of Findings

2. Description of TOEFL Based on the Checklist of Communicative Skills
    2.1   Summary of Findings for the TOEFL Test as a Whole
    2.2   Summary of Findings for Listening Comprehension, Section 1
        2.2.1   Section 1: Statements, Part A
        2.2.2   Section 1: Dialogues, Part B
        2.2.3   Section 1: Minitalks/Extended Conversation, Part C
    2.3   Summary of Findings for Structure and Written Expression, Section 2
    2.4   Summary of the Findings for Vocabulary and Reading Comprehension, Section 3
        2.4.1   Section 3: Vocabulary
        2.4.2   Section 3: Reading Comprehension
    2.5   Concluding Comment on the Checklist Findings

3. Findings Regarding Test Performance Factors Cited by Bachman and Palmer
    3.1   Overview of Issues
    3.2   Psychophysiological Skills
    3.3   Representation of Knowledge about Language and Monitoring Factors
    3.4   Language Use Situations
    3.5   Context and Message
    3.6   Artificial Restrictions
    3.7   Affective Factors
    3.8   Strategic Factors

4. Findings Regarding the Relevance of TOEFL Item Content for Academic and Social Language Use
    4.1   Rating Agreement
    4.2   Ratings of the Characteristics of Section 1 Items
    4.3   Ratings of the Characteristics of Section 2 Items
    4.4   Ratings of the Characteristics of Section 3 Items

5. ILR Scale Description of TOEFL Proficiency Level
    5.1   Section 1: Listening Comprehension
    5.2   Section 2: Structure and Written Expression
    5.3   Section 3: Reading Comprehension and Vocabulary

6. Conclusion

sensitive only to the simple *presence or absence* of skills on each item making up TOEFL test sections; these tallies are not sensitive to the *total number of occurrences* of skills *within* individual items.

The data in Appendix D reveal some broad patterns regarding the occurrence of communicative skills on various TOEFL test sections. In some instances we found a number of shared skills across all sections, but in other instances we found some patterns of skill occurrence that were unique to a given section and its item types. An important conclusion to state from the outset is that the range and complexity of skills required on various sections of the TOEFL test are directly related to the amount of language used and to the semantic and textual complexity of TOEFL items. The more language used, and the more authentic this language, the greater the number and kinds of communicative skills required of examinees. The reader should keep in mind that this conclusion should be tempered by the fact that TOEFL has an assessment purpose that is more limited in scope than assessment of the full range of communicative skills discussed here.

Some general tendencies for the entire TOEFL test to require skills found on the checklist can be noted when examining the overall frequency of occurrence of the more general classes of skills. For example, in Section 1 at the pronunciation level, recognition of use of tempo, range/height of pitch, or pauses to mark emotive or attitudinal meaning were just as frequently required of examinees as was recognition of stress and intonation to mark neutral, nonemotive reference. Each occurred in somewhat fewer than one-third of the total items in Section 1. In addition, it is equally interesting to note that examinees' need to recognize the modification of lexical items in connected speech in Section 1 occurred just about as frequently as examinees' need to recognize the modification of inherent spelling patterns of words in the remaining sections of the test.

Because the majority of the TOEFL test is presented in a written mode and all correct answer options are presented in writing, it is not surprising to find that recognition of graphic symbols plays an especially crucial role in TOEFL test performance. The table below, constructed from information found in Section A.2.2 of Appendix D, lists the percentages of items in the overall test requiring recognition of graphic symbols performing the functions or encodings listed.

To mark structural groupings:
clauses	29%
phrases	26%
Speech-based modifications:	
(e.g., contractions)	21%
To mark concepts:	
mathematical	7%
formal identity	31%

Attention now turns to data on some of the important lexical and morphological features of the language occurring in TOEFL items. The data are tabulated in Section A.3 and A.4 of Appendix D. Compounding seems to occur fairly frequently, with 58 percent of the 150 TOEFL items requiring recognition of one or more noun compounds and 31 percent requiring recognition of verb compounds. Regarding inflectional markings occurring on nouns and verbs, recognition of linguistic encoding of number seemed to be a much-required skill, as indicated by the fact that nouns marked for plurality occurred in 73 percent of the items and marking of third person singular present tense verb endings occurred in 53 percent. By far, the most typical inflectional tense markings, other than third person, were regular and irregular forms of the simple past; this occurred at least once in 46 percent of the items. Present perfect marking occurred next most frequently (28 percent of the items); past pertect and present progressive rarely occurred (7 percent and 5 percent, respectively). Qualification, case relations, and other devices to relate content words together play an important role in English language communication, and this importance was well represented by TOEFL items. Marking of specificity—definite or indefinite and often both—occurred at least once in almost every item. Other frequencies of occurrence of those functions in the 150 items across TOEFL sections in the test form analyzed are given below:

Location/direction	59%
Quantity/amount	51%
Possession	47%
Time (frequency/span	39%
Negation	37%
Comparison/degree	20%
Instrument/means	5%

Turning to Section A.5 of Appendix D, sentence formation in the TOEFL test typically exhibited the declarative, active pattern of subject–verb–object (S–V–O); this pattern occurred at least once in 88 percent of the items. Two other patterns also typically occurred: passives, at least once in 45 percent of the items; and direct, complete questions, at least once in 30 percent of the items. This points out the special importance of examinees being able to construct or at least interpret ordering of sentence elements in order to do well on TOEFL. Two types of within-sentence subordination of clauses also occurred somewhat frequently: (a) complex sentences with one or more subordinate clauses outside the main clause—at least once in 35 percent of the items; and (b) relative clauses—at least once in 34 percent of the items.

The summary tallies involving recognition skills related to sociolinguistic competence required in working TOEFL items (Section B of Appendix D) bring some important observations and raise some specific questions. For some of the sociolinguistic skills, many TOEFL items were very difficult or impossible to code with consistency across coders. For example, recognition of status/power relationships, topic, and setting/scene based on the language of items was often difficult or impossible to code unambiguously. The three skills that are cited are situational and socially derived in real-world language contexts, but TOEFL items focusing on discrete linguistic skills or neutral, written forms of communication did not typically provide enough contextual information to allow an unqualified judgment about the elicitation of these skills in understanding the language of items. Examples that especially illustrate this coding difficulty are the isolated statements making up items occurring in the vocabulary part of Section 3; by design, none of these statements is connected to another or to any other discourse context presented. Consequently, coders interpreting items based on real-world criteria for language use had to infer possible situational contexts from linguistic stimuli in isolation. And often—not surprisingly—one particular statement could be judged to entail multiple situational contexts at varying levels of generality for any one native-speaking coder. In short, the discrete-oriented, shorter TOEFL item types did not provide the coders with enough textual or situational context information to enable them to unambiguously identify the setting, or topic of discourse, and the social roles and role relationships among interlocutors depicted. This finding should be tempered by the fact that items in some TOEFL sections are designed to be content independent of each other in order to reduce the chances of item content bias. The longer, more integrative item types provided lengthier and structurally more complicated texts but, most usually, were limited in their interpersonal and social uses of language relative to authentic everyday communication. As will be seen in a subsequent section, however, the two independent judges who rated the authenticity of items found that the longer, more integrative items bore greater authenticity to actual language use.

Consistent with the findings to be presented in the section on test performance factors (Section 3), the Appendix D, Section B.1.5, data on genre indicate that, in our judgment, the isolated segments of language that make up many TOEFL test items, particularly shorter items, show a limited degree of commonality with natural communication. Overall, these data show, for example, that 13 percent of TOEFL items involved segments of conversation, while isolated statements (e.g., item language stimuli in isolation from a specified context) and limited functional statements (e.g., isolated answers to isolated questions) occurred in 71 percent and 43 percent of the items, respectively.

In authentic language use, especially that involving language at the interpersonal communication level, one typically finds a large variety of communicative purposes enacted. Most of the TOEFL test (because of its problem-solving format) emphasizes examinees' recognition of direct requests for information (39 percent of the items) and direct giving of information (97 percent of the items). A wide variety of other speech act functions typical of everyday interpersonal encounters are exhibited in Section 1, by inferring the social and cultural context indirectly signaled by the language of items. In contrast, Sections 2 and 3 (see Section B.2 of Appendix D) feature skills requiring recognition of direct giving and requesting of information.

Attention is now turned to a summary of discourse competencies required in understanding TOEFL items (see Section C of Appendix D). Although non-referential speech act functions employed in authentic language use were inferred to occur frequently only in Section 1, other discourse recognition skills typical of those required to understand textual or narrative development were prevalent across all sections of the test. Ability to recognize lexical cohesion devices was a frequent requirement on TOEFL as a whole, which is illustrated by the percentage of items demonstrating the use of cohesive devices listed:

Pronoun reference	59%
Word repetition	40%
Conjoiners	39%
Synonymy	33%

Examinees' need to recognize sentence-level devices used for cohesion and continuity also were often found; need for such skills occurred in 49 percent and 31 percent of items, respectively. The following list presents the percentages of items requiring recognition of various semantic, interclausal relationships involving conjunctive adverbs.

Contrast	28%
Result/conclusion	21%
Time	20%
Addition	18%
Condition	14%

It almost appears that occurrence of the forms of semantic conjunction listed were equally distributed intentionally.

It was expected by the designers of the skills checklist that, since the written portion of TOEFL relies on texts drawn from encyclopedic sources, textbooks, or academic journals, certain discourse structures frequently occurring in planned and edited texts would be found (e.g., classification, illustration, definition). All of these forms of text development are prevalent in student textbooks for native speakers and nonnative speakers, and they do exhibit some of the semantic rhetorical forms found elsewhere in English. Therefore, it was of some surprise to find that only two such patterns were exhibited in Sections 2 and 3 of the sample TOEFL test; these involved event sequence development and an expository text category termed "factual development." It is difficult to explain why no other forms of text development occurred, since the sample TOEFL had five reading passages in the reading comprehension portion of Section 3. It is likely that the sample TOEFL test analyzed is not representative of TOEFL tests in this regard.

The foregoing discussion was intended to give a summary overview of important communicative skills required and not required on the TOEFL test as a whole, as reflected by the skills checklist of Appendix D. The discussion was not intended to be exhaustive, but rather was guided by some important trends that emerged in the data. With this summary in mind, we now turn to a more detailed examination of the communicative skills required within each TOEFL section and item type. Discussion of each section will comment on important characteristics of the item types making up the section; the data discussed are based on a more detailed and voluminous breakdown of Appendix D data. This more detailed breakdown of data records the occurrence or lack of occurrence of every checklist characteristic for every item stimulus and correct response separately. Readers with limited interest in these details may elect to skip this next section and instead proceed to Section 3, concerned with other factors affecting performance on the TOEFL. Readers with a serious interest in the report, however, should read the next section.

2.2 Summary of Findings for Listening Comprehension, Section 1.

Section 1 consists of three parts, which differ most obviously in their length. The items in Part A, statements, consist of sentence statements that occur in isolation of any particular context in which they might naturally be found. Part B, dialogues, consists of statements by two different speakers that form an interactional unit. Part C, minitalks/extended conversation, consists of multiple sentence statements that are bound together either in a textual unit to simulate a lecture or announcement, for example, or in an interactional unit, to simulate a multiple-turn conversation between two speakers. However, the linguistic nature of Part C, even when it appears to be a conversation, makes it appear in some ways more similar to written expository prose than to informal dialogue or interactional units such as those in Part B. For example, the topic dealt with, the occurrence of complex sentence structures, and the reliance on historical and descriptive flow of information render any passages in Part C more typical of planned, edited discourse than of spontaneous, unplanned discourse so typical of conversations, dialogues, and even many lectures. Impressionistically, one has the pervading feeling, especially when listening to Part A and Part C, that edited, planned prose typical of written English contexts simulating conversation is being read from a script and spoken. This quality of speech, notable because it is crisply enunciated with no unexpected pauses and with minimal ellipsis, is no doubt intentional on the part of the developers of the TOEFL examination. Such speech helps ensure that examinees have a maximum chance to recognize the meanings of utterances; it does not require examinees to utilize speech recognition skills that deviate far from the lexical and grammatical structure of the stimulus materials. Interestingly, a similar style of speech, alluded to as "foreigner talk," has been found to occur when native speakers make a special effort to communicate with nonnative speakers (Hatch, 1983). It should be recognized, however, that authentic everyday speech, outside of situations such as those involving "foreigner talk," formal academic lectures, etc., seldom manifests the crispness of pronunciation, absence of ellipses, absence of false starts, and uniform grammatical correctness of speech found on the TOEFL test.

Because strategic competence was not included in the skills checklist framework used to analyze TOEFL, attention was not given to some important aspects of natural communication involving this kind of competence. It was not required to any noticeable extent in understanding Section 1 material. Aspects typical of spontaneous communication, such as hesitation, repair, unfinished statements, paraphrasing or rephrasing in midsentence, interjection of side comments, and many others are part of everyday natural, spontaneous communication. The checklist does not include any of these skills that are indicative of spontaneous, communicative behavior. There is no loss in this omission since, in looking at the extended conversations and minitalks, none of these particular strategies/competencies occurs. However, to a native speaker, the samples of language occurring in Section 1 may not be considered entirely representative of spontaneous speech.

In addition, in the process of applying the skills checklist to Part B, another set of skills was not included that, in this case, would have been helpful analytically. In accordance with the current popular view of communication as intimately involving negotiation of shared meaning, whereby speakers participate in shaping and directing the structuring of spoken text, more distinctions than simply how to initiate, maintain, or terminate a discourse would have been helpful. More attention should be given to knowledge of the flow of communication within speech events (Duran, 1984; Yorio, 1980). In particular, we now would recommend distinctions/recognition skills pertinent to recognizing the flow of information in a dialogue, as occurs, for example, in the sequence of the following speech acts: a direct request for information, a direct response to such a request, clarification of previous information as a response, elaboration of information, and modification of or disagreement with previous comments, suggestions, or merely emphatic comments that have little referential value but much emotional value. Other descriptors of contingent discourse behavior might also have been useful. These skills seem to play an important part in spontaneous interactional contexts whether they be brief, e.g. Part B, or extended, e.g., Part C. Although such competencies were not originally included in the skills checklist, some mention will be made of them in the discussion of Parts A, B, and C of Section 1.

Section 1 is the only TOEFL section requiring skills involving recognition of pronunciation. To some extent the pronunciation offered attempts to simulate real-life speech, as reflected by numerous uses of contractions; these occur at least once in 36 percent of the items. However, other typical modifications of isolated word-form pronunciation in connected speech—e.g., elision, vowel reduction or deletion, consonant reduction, and palatalization—occur much less frequently than they would be encountered in informal natural, English speech. The checklist data support the observation that the speech for all three parts of Section 1 is clearly enunciated. Because of the desired trait of maximal clarity of speech in a TOEFL testing context, it is lacking in assimilation patterns of spontaneous, everyday communication. When one analyzes other aspects of the linguistic content of the verbal statements in Section 1 of the test, the "careful" style, as Joos (1967) would refer to it, is presented phonetically but mixed with informal style, marked by use of idioms and colloquial vocabulary, occasional elliptical responses, contractions, and sentence formation pragmatically tailored for a particularly interactional event. For example, consider the stimulus portion of item 32 in Part B of Section 1:

A: "Didn't you tell Tom about the meeting?"
B: "Whatever I say to him goes in one ear and out the other."

In this example, there is minimal palatalization in "didn't you," minimal vowel reduction in either statement, and the contraction and idiomatic expression reflect informal style.

One final, phonetic-based comment can be made about many items presented in all parts of Section 1. Contrastive or emphatic word stress occurs at least once in about 50 percent of the stimuli for items. In Part A and B a very frequent occurrence of higher pitch patterns (level 3 or 4) occurs throughout the stimulus statements. The combination of stress and high pitch patterns on more than one segment of a statement renders an initial impression of overly dramatized speech. In the test form studied this was particularly noticeable for the female speaker (e.g., Part A, item 7), with three instances of third-level or above pitch. Perhaps an exaggerated speech style is a natural accompaniment to a careful speech style, where each word is precisely enunciated. However, the correct options for items usually involve neutral, nonemphatic, and noncontrastive referential use of language, while the actual stimulus statements they paraphrase often have attitudinal, emotive meanings that extend beyond mere referential, linguistic meaning as prompted by stress and intonation patterns.

2.2.1 Section 1: Statements, Part A. Following is a more detailed discussion of each item type making up Section 1, beginning with statement items. Idiomatic expressions in statement items are prevalent in stimuli and in correct response options; noun and verb compounds make up the most typical type. (About 50 percent of the item stimuli and 25 percent of the correct response options have one or more idiomatic expressions.) As far as function words are concerned, those used to mark either generic or specific concepts are present in more than 50 percent of the stimuli and 50 percent of the correct response options. Possession and time span concepts marked through function words are the next most frequent in occurrence (35 percent of both the stimuli and the correct response options). The most frequent inflection is the marking of simple past forms, regular and irregular; this occurs at least once in more than 50 percent of the stimuli and correct response options.

The most frequent type of sentence formation occurring is the simple sentence word ordering of declarative, active statements, prevalent in about 95 percent of the stimuli and correct response options. Other types of simple sentence word ordering, exemplified by structures appropriate for statement of questions, imperatives, passives, and existential THERE sentences, are rare, as are complex sentence patterns with subordination. Compound sentence word ordering also seems somewhat uncommon.

Because all of the stimuli and correct response options in Part A occur in unspecified social contexts, it is impossible to judge precisely which sociolinguistic recognition skills are required of examinees. There simply is not sufficient information about an interactional context to code isolated sentence statements with a high degree of certainty as to various sociolinguistic recognition skills. Even such skills as those related to topic recognition become difficult to assign on the basis of one isolated statement. Impressionistically, it appears that most statements are not marked as unquestionably pertaining to specific academic living contexts or academic classroom content topics. However, more detailed findings regarding topic are discussed in a later section of this report.

Speech act functions are difficult to code because of the lack of explicit information in statement stimuli regarding the social and interpersonal context of speech. Nonetheless, some judgments are possible when one relies on native social, and cultural knowledge of American life and, to some extent on knowledge of generalized international English usage. A little more than half of the stimuli for statement items give information simply and directly (55 percent)); the remaining stimuli may indirectly advise (e.g., the stimulus for item 6), invite (the stimulus for item 8), seek approval (the stimulus for item 7), make a suggestion (the stimulus for item 15), etc.

Linguistic devices most common at the discourse level include pronominal reference (more than 75 percent of the stimuli and correct response options) and sentence level markers of conciseness, e.g., ellipsis, clausal reduction (about 10 percent of the stimuli and correct response options).

2.2.2 Section 1: Dialogues, Part B. Idiomatic expressions are even more prevalent in Part B, occurring at least once in almost two-thirds of the stimuli for dialogue items. The majority of these idiomatic expressions are noun and verb compounds. Since these dialogues attempt to simulate informal conversation, one would expect to find such a prevalence of compounding—a process typical of colloquial, informal, or slang language usage. The occurrence of idiomatic lexical items may account in part for the difficulty of dialogue items since they reflect a colloquial, more informal use of language to which many foreign students are not exposed in formal, technical-language training.

In contrast to Part A, in Part B simple past tense inflections rarely occur. A quick glance over all the stimulus dialogues and succeeding questions suggests an extremely frequent pattern not captured in the coding of the skills checklist, but nevertheless important to recognize as a characteristic of items. First, a majority of the dialogue stimuli consists of first- and second-person interchanges—singular or plural—while all of the questions are formed in third person present singular forms, using either *"does"* or *"is"* forms. Secondly, if one searches for a critical linguistic clue or for critical semantic content for answering the question posed about a dialogue, in almost every instance the critical clue appears to exist in the second speaker's statement (Penfield judged this to occur for 86 percent of the items). Therefore, if examinees focus primarily on the second speaker's statement, they have a better chance of selecting the correct option. It is this second observation about Part B that raises the question of whether this part is in fact testing communicative skills typical of a dialogue or whether it is simply testing comprehension of a target statement in a slightly more extended context than that given in Part A. It appears possible that the language skill focus of these items may be based more on accurate recognition of the second statement as a target rather than on recognition of an integrated interactional event as a whole.

Examinees' receptive knowledge of sociolinguistic norms is difficult to code, and this seems especially evident with regard to factors related to norms of appropriateness of usage and to the social relationships of interlocutors. There is limited information about the context of communication surrounding the occurrence of dialogues. Because of this and because of the limited information about context found in the conversational turns of a dialogue, the topics treated in these items generally do not seem to clearly, directly, and unambiguously represent academic living contexts or classroom learning content topics. The stimulus dialogue for item 34 is an exception. Perhaps the most interesting and unique aspect of Part B is the use of language to accomplish communicative purposes. Most stimuli for items in Part B are not simply direct requests for or offering of information. Rather, there are several other direct and indirect communicative purposes reflected in Part B language stimuli. Indirectly expressed purposes are no doubt more difficult for non-English speakers to recognize since they involve reliance on knowledge of sociocultural norms and contexts for their accurate interpretation. Some of the indirectly expressed messages in dialogue stimuli include request for help (items 26 and 31); promise (item 26); complaint (items 25, 27, and 32); slight insult (item 32); suggestion (items 29 and 31); impatience or annoyance (items 30 and 32); advice (item 31); and denial (item 35). Perhaps the most difficult to code is the stimulus for item 35, in which both attitude and communicative purpose are expressed in a very indirect way that is also quite idiomatic and dependent on recognition of the tone of utterances.

Discourse competence recognition skills, that might be thought to be the most revealing, extend beyond the skills checklist to include concern for the turn-taking structure of dialogues, i.e., perception of the rights and obligations of interlocutors and their fulfillment of these rights and obligations. In dialogue stimuli about 20 percent of the statements made by the second speaker reflect a direct or an indirect response to the request of the first speaker; another 20 percent reflect a modification of the first speaker's comment. Other dialogues reflect elaboration of information, clarification, and suggestions offered by the second speaker in reaction to the first speaker's statement/comment.

2.2.3 Section 1: Minitalks/Extended Conversations, Part C. Part C displays a formal style of speech that closely approximates written expository prose in its vocabulary, sentence formation, and discourse structure; this formal character is called for by the TOEFL test specifications. Idiomatic forms are much less prevalent on this portion of Section 1, and this is especially noted in the reduced occurrence of noun and verb compounds. Many more competencies are required in understanding stimulus passages for Part C since the length and complexity of item stimuli are greatly increased over those in Parts A and B. The longer passages in Part C entail recognition of at least one occurrence or more of idiomatic and literal meanings of content words; literal meanings of various concepts marked by function words; and inflections for number, possession, person, and most tenses. Sentence formation recognition skills required of examinees in Part C include simple sentence word order and compound and complex sentence word order with embedded subordination, neither of which is required as much in Part A or B. The topics occurring in the stimuli passages of Part C are more identifiable as relevant to academic life or classroom content than is the case with the topics in Parts A and B. The longer passages often involve descriptive information about American geographic locations and history drawn, usually verbatim, from authentic texts. Because of their expository prose nature, most of the communicative purposes served by the connected statements comprising the stimulus passages of Part C items are simply direct communication of information. This is so even for the extended conversation in the last stimulus passage of Part C. Although this stimulus is comprised of ten conversational turns between two speakers, it consists almost entirely of information giving and requesting and involves only a limited negotiation of topic. Thus, it does not strongly resemble a spontaneous exploration between two speakers of a topic of mutual interest.

The relationship between test questions about Part C stimuli and correct response options is elliptical for about 50 percent of the questions. The occurrence of ellipses exercises examinees' skill in recognizing ellipses, though the communicative context involved is identifiable as a formal multiple-choice testing context rather than as everyday communication. Some elliptical forms in questions and correct responses consist of one word; others, one phrase. In all cases, one part of the message lies in the question and the other in the correct response option. Whether correct responses are elliptical or full sentences, each begins with a capital letter and ends with a period to mark completion. This is also true of items in both Parts B and C of Section 1.

2.3 Summary of Findings for Structure and Written Expression, Section 2.

Both item types in Section 2—structure and written expression—obviously require use of orthographic recognition skills, skills that are much more numerous and varied than those required in Section 1. For example, recognition of capitalization to mark specific concepts, such as formal identity, frequently accompanying proper names of people, places, nationalities, etc, appears at least once in almost 50 percent of the item stimuli of structure and written expression items combined. Graphic symbols to mark clausal groupings occur much more frequently in structure items (for about 33 percent of the items) than in written expression items (for about 8 percent of the items).

It is obvious that the most essential competencies or skills necessary for both parts of Section 2 are those concerned with recognition of vocabulary, word formation, and sentence formation. Correct response options seem based on conventional word orderings in English for a variety of contexts and the skills tested, including correctly recognizing an appropriate word in a sentence context; the units of a phrase required within a sentence context; the order of words or phrases required within a clause in a sentence context; the required order of words and identity of words making up an appropriate idiomatic expression within a sentence context; and the required presence or absence of inflection on words within a sentence context. The items in Section 2 require no attention to meaning developed across sentences.

In addition to the specific structural recognition skills that seem to be tested in Section 2, one can observe the prevalence of other aspects of grammatical competence that may not be tested but that exist nevertheless as part of the sentence contexts making up Section 2 items. For example, idiomatic expressions appear very often—principally compound nouns (42 percent of the time in both parts). Function words and inflections on content words are used in both parts to represent a variety of grammar-based concepts. For example, location/direction occurs at least once for 35 percent of the items in Section 2; marking of specificity occurs for almost all of the items; marking of quantity for 37 percent; marking of time for about 10 percent; possession for 37 percent; and comparison/degree for 12 percent. Inflections occur in almost all items, with plurality marked in 72 percent. Third person singular present tense and simple past tense were marked most frequently; each occurs at least once in 40 percent of the items.

With regard to sentence formation recognition skills, by far the most frequently required recognition pattern for items involves the S–V–O order of declarative, active statements; this pattern occurs for 77 percent of the items. Because of the format of Section 2 items, sentences following a grammatical question ordering of constituents never occur.

Sociolinguistic recognition skills were difficult to code for Section 2 because only isolated sentences were presented. Impressionistically, it seems that over half of the items in Section 2 deal with topics that are not linked to clearly identified academic living contexts or classroom content subject matter. However, one might judge that many topics refer to classroom content typical of secondary school or college courses in America, since so much reference is made to everyday American history or geography concepts. The findings about orthographic recognition skills required of examinees is related to examinees' knowledge of concepts that appear to occur frequently in items. Famous people, places, dates, historical events, books, or magazines that are typical of U.S. culture and background and taught in American public schools at the preuniversity and university levels appear frequently in the items in Section 2—at least once in an estimated 35 percent of the items. Noticeably, a number of references to persons, events, and entities in items utilize compound nouns that are typical of U.S. history subject matter or to American names for plants or animals.

Discourse recognition competencies required in Section 2 are minimal compared to recognition of sentence structure and vocabulary. Some recognition skills at the discourse level are required though, within the contexts of single sentences. These skills include recognition of lexical cohesion and sentence-level cohesion devices, e.g., use of pronouns, clausal reduction, parallel structuring, and transitional conjoiners binding semantic relationships between clauses.

2.4   Summary of the Findings for Vocabulary and Reading Comprehension, Section 3.   Section 3 appears more meaning oriented than Section 2. The first part of Section 3, vocabulary, tests recognition of appropriate lexical meaning as manifested by words, idioms, or phrases; the second part, reading comprehension, tests for recognition of textually manifested meaning. The two parts differ in the size or length of the item stimuli, which explains why a larger number and variety of the checklist skills were found in the reading comprehension subsection than in the vocabulary subsection.

2.4.1 *Section 3: Vocabulary.* As in all parts of Section 2, recognition of written symbols or script recognition skills are necessary in decoding the stimulus and correct response options for vocabulary items. Note that there are no question stimuli for these vocabulary items. Some of the graphic symbols that commonly occur in vocabulary items include those used to mark concepts requiring formal identify. Capitalization and/or quotes to mark names of people, cities, states, rivers, dates, and so on occurs at least once in 37 percent of the vocabulary items. The attention paid to mark formal identity in vocabulary items correlates highly with the nature of the topics dealt with in these items. About 60 percent seem to deal with topics that might be judged to be related to American history and geography. Most of the capitalization serves to mark reference to historical/geographical concepts that are part and parcel of American culture and history; this usage is intentionally built into these items. Just as we mentioned with regard to Section 2, these concepts do not appear in the correct response options, and they certainly do not themselves reference the discrete skills tested. Thus, it remains to be determined whether knowledge of these concepts helps examinees by contributing information that is useful in inferring the meaning of the targeted vocabulary items.

Other graphic symbols occurring in vocabulary items that somehow contrast in frequency of occurrence with those of the reading comprehension portion of Section 3 are those used to mark structural groupings. In vocabulary items, commas are used to set off phrases in 23 percent of the items, and to set off clauses in 10 percent of the items. In the reading comprehension portion, however, both uses of commas occur in all passages. For example, use of commas to separate clauses occurs in all reading passages used in the reading comprehension portion of Section 3. Such differences between the vocabulary and reading comprehension parts are no doubt due to the difference in length of the language stimuli presented, though the stimuli items in each section are drawn from authentic texts. In the vocabulary part only one complete sentence is presented per item, whereas in the reading comprehension part many connected sentences are presented, and questions posed for the items present yet another sentence context.

In the vocabulary part of Section 3, the stimulus portion of items frequently manifests idiomatic vocabulary, especially noun compounds, which occur in almost 50 percent of the items. Function words are fairly prevalent in the items, with location/direction most often marked (in about 50 percent of the items). Thirty-three percent of the items include marking for quantity/amount; 13 percent for time/frequency of occurrence and span; and 10 percent for comparison/degree. Certain inflections are extremely prevalent in vocabulary items. For example, marking of noun plurality occurs in 27 out of 30 items and simple past verb inflection marking in 14 out of 30. By far the most typical ordering of logical constituents in the vocabulary sentence items is that of declarative, active statements: subject–verb–object occurs in 22 out of 30 items. Passive constructions seem to occur for vocabulary items as frequently as for Section 2, and more frequently than for any other portion of the exam. Such structures can be found in almost 40 percent of the items in both the vocabulary portion of Section 3 and the structure portion of Section 2. The fact that the length of the sentence stimulus is minimal or that the sentences used are not part of clearly established textual contexts may explain why embedding occurs infrequently and why complex sentences are few in the vocabulary portion; the vocabulary part does not have any compound sentences and an average of only 10 percent of each complex sentence type. This, however, is not the case with the reading comprehension portion of Section 3, as we shall mention later. The short length of vocabulary stimuli does have an advantage: it helps ensure that examinees will not infer the meaning of the missing words solely on the basis of the meaning of words in the stimuli.

A few interrelated discourse skills are worth mentioning in relation to vocabulary items. Sentence-level cohesion devices are noticeable; clausal reduction and ellipsis is found in 27 percent of the items, and parallel structures or lists in 20 percent of the items.

In summary, we can conclude that the vocabulary portion of Section 3 tests vocabulary recognition skills as intended; other grammatical and sentence level features extending beyond vocabulary are integrated into the stimulus portions of items.

2.4.2 Section 3: Reading Comprehension. The most obvious observation about the reading comprehension subsection is that its reliance on passages as the basis for questions results in a rich sample of language for examinees to work with; stimulus passages involve almost every skill in the checklist dealing with grammatical competence and many with discourse competence. Of course, the comprehension of reading passages does not involve pronunciation recognition skills. Instead, all five passage stimuli require a large array of written symbol recognition skills. Graphic symbols used to mark formal identity occur in 63 percent of the items and options, and are more common among this item type than among any other TOEFL item type.

Noun compound lexical items, found so frequently in Section 2 and in the vocabulary portion of Section 3, occur in all reading comprehension stimulus passages, but in only five out of thirty of the corresponding question and correct answer options. The various quantifications, case relations, and semantic comparisons marked by function words occur in all five stimulus passages, with the exception of comparison and instrument or means, which occur in one stimulus passage each. Inflections of many different types occur in almost every stimulus passage, but present perfect tense markings occur in all stimulus passages, and simple past in only two out of five stimulus passages.

Particularly noticeable in reading comprehension items is the variation in sentence structure. The different complex sentence patterns identified in the skills checklist were prevalent in all five passages, with embedded structures, passives, relative clauses, and other types of subordination occurring in every passage—often repeatedly. These patterns are known to be typical of advanced expository prose, such as the prose found in college textbooks and technical writing, and, consequently, the patterns were expected. Likewise, the discourse skills required to comprehend items are quite varied and prevalent at both the lexical and sentence levels. In contrast to other item types, reading comprehension stimulus passages rely much more frequently on devices to bind interclausal semantic relationships, e.g., as realized by use of "conjunctive adverbs" serving the semantic functions of addition, contrast, result/conclusion, time, and condition. The most frequent of these functions is the use of adverbs to denote a contrast between pieces of passage information; this device occurs in four out of the five stimulus passages for reading comprehension items.

The rhetorical and semantic organization of ideas in reading comprehension passages was not always easy to code. Many of the discourse recognition skills pertaining to structuring of ideas in written text suggested in the skills checklist—e.g., classification, cause and effect, illustration, definition, description, comparison, and chronological order—were not judged to be present in any of the passages. Two passages clearly use event ordering according to the significance of events as an organizer for a passage; the other three chain information together in no apparent sequence other than as a list or as an elaboration on a particular idea initially presented. Whether the skills checklist provided an adequate system for categorizing the structuring of planned texts typical in academic reading and writing is open to debate. The alternative possibility is that the textual stimuli presented, although authentic, were not sufficiently long or sufficiently typical to tap the various patterns of organization expected in college-level reading and writing.

Two sociolinguistic competencies deserve mention. The topics dealt with in the reading comprehension passages seem fairly typical of academic classroom content. The second observation refers to the questions and correct response options. Exactly 50 percent of the questions for reading comprehension items utilize a genre that is not common in real-life communication, limited functional segments; these are isolated segments of language that are to be interpreted as "complete me" questions by examinees. In these instances, questions are incomplete statements, completed by the correct response options to form complete sentences. As mentioned previously, even though the question and correct response option form a complete statement, adequate as a full sentence, a period is *never* part of the correct response option. For example,

Question: According to the passage, most mosquito larvae develop
Correct response: (D) in bodies of still water

Interestingly, this omission of a period is required for items of this type because of ETS item editing policy to which the TOEFL program must conform. One other observation can be made about this question type: three out of fifteen total occurrences of this genre begin with the same phrase: "According to the passage . . ." In fact, in examining all thirty questions in the reading comprehension subsection, 50 percent begin with this introductory phrase. The phrase does help ensure that examinees attend carefully to the passage, but one wonders whether a greater range of synonymous phrases could be used in order to diversify the language stimuli.

In conclusion, as was mentioned previously, it seems obvious that the reading comprehension portion of Section 3 draws on a great variety of discrete English language recognition skills and, even more importantly, that it requires the integration of these skills in a manner suggestive of reading in authentic academic settings. It is also notable that the content of reading comprehension items seems to require minimal knowledge of culture and life in the United States. Questions for reading comprehension items prompt the examinee to focus often on literal meaning conveyed in passages and, in particular, to main ideas and details. There are occasional requests for implicational or interpretative meaning, and in these instances the examinee must infer the writer's viewpoint, attitude, or tone. In other questions the examinee must infer details that are not explicitly stated in reading passages; in these circumstances the examinee is urged to actively guess, speculate, or infer consequences stemming from the information in passages. This prompt is indicated by the use of words such as "probably" in questions.

2.5 Concluding Comment on the Checklist Findings. Interpretation of a single TOEFL examination in terms of the competence skills checklist, as in the present study, is exploratory, and it is not intended to comprehensively investigate the competencies required by TOEFL or to evaluate it as a generic test for the assessment of English language proficiency. In reviewing the results that have been reported, it is important to ask how similar the findings would have been if other sample TOEFL tests had been investigated. A more appropriate strategy may be to ask what checklist features are shown and not shown by a collection of TOEFL tests. A further refinement of this strategy would be to study the variability and stability in competence skills required across TOEFL examinations and thus to investigate the homogeneity in coverage of skills on the test.

3. Findings Regarding Test Performance Factors Cited by Bachman and Palmer

3.1 Overview of Issues. Consistent with the discussion of Section II of this report, concerning design of the framework to describe TOEFL, the concern here is with personal, situational, and test format factors that affect the language skills used by examinees taking the test. As mentioned in Section III under "Procedures," it will only prove feasible in the context of the present study to discuss, in a preliminary way, how the various test performance factors cited earlier might influence examinee behavior on TOEFL.

3.2 Psychophysiological Skills. Language production is not required in taking the TOEFL test, and hence, psychophysiological skills related to speaking and writing are not required (finger, hand, and arm motor skills are required in marking answer options on the test answer sheet). Section 1 of the test requires aural perception of language stimuli on all three subsections. TOEFL administration procedures, if followed appropriately, guarantee that examinees with normal hearing will have no problem clearly hearing stimuli. The fact that oral communication is not physically present as in face-to-face interaction in Parts B and C of Section 1, however, means that examinees cannot utilize visual perception to recognize proxemic and gestural cues that would enhance understanding of face-to-face interaction in real circumstances.

Because all TOEFL sections require visual processing of printed materials, acuity of vision is critical to test performance. The printed format of the test is appropriate for persons with normal vision.

3.3 Representation of Knowledge about Language and Monitoring Factors. The major issue at stake here is the kind of attention—deliberately conscious or unconscious—that examinees give to language qua language while taking the TOEFL test. If examinees consciously attend to the language of the test, calling into mind specific facts or hypotheses that they have learned as part of language instruction, they are said to be "monitoring" their language use. Such conscious examination of language has been discussed by a number of sociolinguists, and psycholinguists (e.g., by Hudson, 1980, and by McLaughlin,

Rossman, and McLeod, 1983). The notion of "monitoring" referred to here is that referred to by Krashen (1982); it can only occur consciously as a deliberate effort to evaluate language as it is produced. In this case, an individual's representation of knowledge about a language is about language as an object of formal instruction. As proficiency in a language increases, monitoring of language use typically decreases. Most persons who acquire knowledge of a second language through rich exposure to it find it unusual or unnecessary to consciously monitor their second language use. There is an exception to this pattern: some persons become highly proficient in a language and yet very actively monitor their second language use. Certain linguistic structures, such as idiomatic expressions, for example, are recognized automatically by most persons who know a language well, but persons who are learning a language through classroom instruction often have to stop and recall that they have learned an idiomatic expression as a distinctive unit, prior to understanding it or producing it.

One can only speculate, of course, on how representation of knowledge of English as just described might affect TOEFL performance. It is probable that almost all TOEFL examinees engage in much conscious evaluation of the English they encounter on the test. This is to be expected since the multiple-choice format of TOEFL test items, and the motivation to pick the correct option from among distractor options, require careful evaluation of the English in stimuli, questions, and answer options. This possibility seems more likely because distractor options for test items are so often designed to incorporate features that would lead examinees with low English proficiency to consider those incorrect options.

3.4 Language Use Situations. Based on what has been suggested in the discussion of the likely role of monitoring factors in TOEFL performance, it seems evident that taking the TOEFL test corresponds more to a "reflexive" situation than to a "transitive" situation, according to Bachman and Palmer (forthcoming). Taking TOEFL is reflexive rather than transitive because the focus of the test-taking situation and performance on test items is very much on appropriateness of language itself, rather than on communication of cohesive meaning as a primary objective. Further, TOEFL meets Bachman and Palmer's definition of a "nonreciprocal" language use situation as opposed to one that is "reciprocal." Examinees are exposed to language while they take TOEFL in only a receptive manner. Thus, there is no opportunity for back-and-forth sharing of language between examinees and others during the test.

The judgment that TOEFL displays the qualities of reflexive and nonreciprocal language use situations implies that examinees' encounter with language on the test lacks the dynamic qualities typical of much everyday face-to-face interaction. While this may be viewed as a shortcoming of the test, it should be noted that the reflexive and nonreciprocal language use emphasis of TOEFL is appropriate for assessment of some language use skills of basic importance to educational performance. There are authentic language situations (e.g., reading a William Safire column, looking up a word in a dictionary, or reading a novel by James Joyce) that also are reflexive and nonreciprocal instances of language use. The critical issue would seem to be, how wide is the range of proficiency skills that one can assess based on students' encounter with language as used on the TOEFL test?

3.5   Context and Message.   Four concerns are raised with regard to context and message. First, there is concern about the ratio of familiar to new information in language occurring in TOEFL. Familiar information is taken to be information that is conveyed in TOEFL test items, but that is already information known to examinees. In contrast, new information is information that examinees are exposed to for the first time when they take the test. This rendering of these two concepts seems overly simplistic, however. The author of this section of the report (Duran) did not uncover a clear perspective for interpreting the extent to which TOEFL items present examinees with familiar versus new information. A straightforward analysis of this question is inhibited for a number of reasons; the primary one is that no obvious criteria can be formulated to distinguish known from new information without possessing knowledge of this fact from the viewpoint of individual examinees.

A second issue concerns the distribution of meanings conveyed by language in the TOEFL test over time and/or space on the test. TOEFL items and questions are brief, and questions occur in close proximity to the language stimulus portion of items. Part C of Section 1, minidialogues/extended conversations, requires examinees to hold in memory an adequate recollection of an extended spoken message in order to answer three to five questions. It is conceivable that performance on this item type could be affected by a decay in memory for an item stimulus over time. This hypothesis may not be totally appropriate, however. Psycholinguistic research (e.g., Clark & Clark, 1977) informs us that there is an interaction between memory capacity for verbal information and facility in decoding and comprehending language. Thus, persons who perform better on Part C items may do so in large part because they have greater English proficiency and, subsequently, because they are more effective in storing the information they comprehend. This hypothesis deserves empirical attention with regard to TOEFL test performance.

A third issue concerns the abstract versus concrete semantic characteristics of language occurring in the TOEFL test. Overall, the language does not appear to be unduly abstract for college-level students. Many items are concrete, referring to commonplace social roles, entities, and situations, which are everyday. Section 1 items in particular display this quality. Other items, perhaps the majority in Sections 2 and 3, have more abstract content, referring generically to concepts, classes of objects, personal and group actions, and general situations. The abstract ideas conveyed by individual sentences or by fragments of discourse on the test are relatively easy to comprehend by educated, native speakers of English. It seems clear that in order to understand the English in TOEFL, examinees must have been exposed extensively to literate varieties of English appropriate to academic contexts and to thinking in the abstract at the college or precollege level. The content of the test is probably too abstract and academically oriented for use in assessing English proficiency for a general populace.

A fourth issue concerning context and message pertains to the intensity of thinking and problem solving activity that is induced by language in the TOEFL test. TOEFL does require examinees to engage in extensive problem solving and related cognitive activity, since the goal of examinees on individual items is to identify the one correct response option. This problem-solving activity, of course, centers on properly interpreting the language of test items. Examinees need to recognize language conventions that are appropriate to multiple-choice tests but not to other forms of communication.

In looking at the presentation of TOEFL items and instructions from a discourse framework, some interesting observations can be made. In Section 1 and Section 3 (vocabulary and reading comprehension), the examinee must play the role of audience since stimuli of various textual and contextual make-up are presented, including spoken isolated statements and texts. In some cases the request for information from the examinee about the stimulus is presented in the form of detailed instructions that precede all item stimuli (e.g., statement items, Section 1; structure and written expression items, Section 2; vocabulary items, Section 3), but in other cases the request for information about the stimulus is given after its presentation (e.g., dialogue and minitalk/extended conversation items, Section 1; reading comprehension items, Section 3). When the request for information about the stimulus follows the stimulus, it is often in a complete interrogative form (dialogue items and minitalk/extended conversation items, Section 1, and some reading comprehension items, Section 3). However, it may also frequently occur as an incomplete statement, as is typical of many reading comprehension items in Section 3. Thus, in light of the range of variation in presentation of items and item types, an answer option for a TOEFL question may complete a communicative event initiated immediately preceding it (i.e., a question and answer text may be formed). This is true of dialogue and minitalk/extended conversation items, for example. In contrast, an answer option may complete a communicative event initiated far in advance through a series of instructions about how to take a TOEFL test section.

There are numerous instances throughout the test in which some aspects of natural discourse are simulated through the question-option context typical of natural dialogues. The most obvious display of this sort of authenticity is the use of elliptical statements offered as options in over half of the dialogue and minitalk/extended conversation items of Section 1.

Finally, it is useful to offer a comment concerning the extent to which the TOEFL test draws on inferential skills or conclusions based on material not supplied directly in the stimuli. To correctly answer some TOEFL items, inferences are required that reflect extended knowledge of semantic conventions in a language and cultural norms. Some examples of inferences that examinees must make include:

a. if one is "behind," then consequently they have to "catch up"
b. if the seminar "broke up," this means everyone then "left"
c. if a gentleman has his "hands full," he will accept help from a female in carrying the load
d. reference to "front tire and seat lowering" are applicable to a "bicycle"
e. going "straight" to a place refers to time, not to spatial orientation.

3.6 Artificial Restrictions. The concern here is with restrictions in language performance that arise from the format of TOEFL test items. The focus is on the qualities of the language samples that examinees encounter on the test and whether the language in the test as a whole has authenticity in comparison to language arising in criterion settings. This question is to a large extent covered in the previous discussion on context and message, and by the discussion in Section 2 of the findings concerning the competencies required in performing on the test. The question is also briefly addressed in the next section of the findings, concerning the social and academic naturalness of language occurring in TOEFL. There is no doubt that language in TOEFL manifests artificial restrictions that result from the format of test items. It should be noted, however, that there are testing program operational restrictions in the design and use of specific test questions to assess discrete language proficiency skills. Discussion in the last section of this report will review the implications of this conclusion for the TOEFL test and for other tests of language proficiency.

3.7 Affective Factors. Affective responses of examinees to TOEFL test items is an unexplored matter. The issue, as presented by Bachman and Palmer (forthcoming) concerns the affective orientation, cognitive style, and motivation that examinees show while performing on the test. Certainly, one key matter involves the motivation of examinees to perform well, given that TOEFL scores may be a critical factor in the students' admission into a North American college. The central question is whether there are affective factors that can enhance or degrade performance on a test such as TOEFL for some individuals. At present we do not have empirical evidence on this question, and it would seem valuable to gather such information. Two practical goals for such research stand out. First, can we learn how to reduce stress, anxiety, and other affective factors by further counseling prospective test takers on good test-taking strategies? Second, are there new test item formats that can reduce the negative performance impact of affective factors? Canale (1984, in press, and in part of Section V of this report) suggests that there are ways in which both of these goals can be met. For example, design of multiple-choice proficiency tests might be altered so as to allow examinees to perceive a more naturalistic and cohesive flow of information and questions. This tactic might enhance examinees' ability to demonstrate their language competencies more fully and unobtrusively on language proficiency tests.

3.8   Strategic Factors.   Since TOEFL requires examinees to passively understand, but not produce, language, they have no opportunity to interact with others or to negotiate meaning. It is also interesting to note that Section 1 of the test does not noticeably feature strategic competence on the part of interlocutors in the stimulus portions of items. One can infer that the absence of strategic competence is due to the test development goal of making Section 1 item stimuli maximally comprehensible and brief.

4.   Findings Regarding the Relevance of TOEFL Item Content for Academic and Social Language Use

4.1   Rating Agreement.   Items from the sample TOEFL test were each rated on three dimensions of representativeness: academic living, academic content topic, and social naturalness (the last scale was used only for Section 1 items). A rating of 1, 2, or 3 was assigned each item on each scale. A 3 rating represented a judgment of clear and direct authenticity, while a 2 represented a judgment of less clear, but possible authenticity. A 1 rating indicated a judgment of ambiguous or low authenticity. Rating data were generated by two independent coders. The data that resulted for the criterion coder are summarized in Section B 1.2 of the checklist that composes Appendix D. The entries are mean rating scores for item types within given sections. Mean ratings are also provided for item types collapsed within a section.

Agreement of the independent coders was assessed by computing the number of identical ratings for items. Evaluation of the degree of agreement among raters is important, since achieving a reasonable level of agreement is necessary in order to have confidence in the findings to be discussed. Agreement was lowest for Section 2 of TOEFL and for one item type in Section 1. On Section 2, the raters agreed on only about one-half of the judgments they made about the academic life representativeness or academic content of items. This level of disagreement is due to the fact that one rater rated more items at a 1 level more often than did the other rater. Agreement levels were in the range of 66 to 70 percent on Section 1 for the academic living and academic content representativeness scales. For Section 1, there was only a 48 percent agreement in ratings with regard to the social representativeness scale. Agreement rates ranged from 77 percent to 87 percent across the academic living and academic content representativeness scales for Section 3. The low agreement rates are indicative of the difficulties encountered in providing raters with adequate criteria and training on which to base scale judgments because of the limited information about the pragmatic context alluded to by the content of items. Thus, judgments of the representativeness of language on items of each scale had an *ad hoc* character. As the ensuing discussion will show, however, some useful conclusions can be drawn from the data. In defense of these conclusions, it should be pointed out that raters' judgments tended to cluster and that they disagreed more in making ratings of 1 versus 2 than in making ratings of 2 versus 3. In the course of making ratings, judges only differed once by 2 scale points.

4.2   Ratings of the Characteristics of Section 1 Items.   As shown by the data in Section B 1.2.1 of Appendix D, the criterion judge found that Section 1 TOEFL items had relatively high social authenticity, but lower academic living and academic content authenticity. The high social authenticity ratings of Section 1 items must be interpreted cautiously, because they reflect a judgment that language clearly arose from social interaction, but not a rating of how much information there was about the nature and course of the social interaction. Despite the high social authenticity ratings, there seems to be no doubt, from a communicative viewpoint, that the social contexts depicted by TOEFL Section 1 items are limited in their rendition of everyday social contexts and communicative competencies exercised in everyday social life. With the exception of minitalk/extended conversation items, ratings of the academic living representativeness of Section 1 items averaged below 2. Minitalk/extended conversation items were judged to involve language that was more representative of situations encountered in academic life than did statements and dialogue items. Ratings of academic content representatives of topics brought out in Section 1 TOEFL items were low for statement and dialogue items, as one might expect. Minitalk/extended conversation items were found to involve topics more closely related to academic content.

4.3   Ratings of the Characteristics of Section 2 Items.   Structure and written expression items averaged a 1.5 rating in their representativeness of academic living and academic content. No 3 level judgments were made for these items on either scale. Thus, about half of the time, the criterion rater judged that items were ambiguous or not representative of academic life situations or academic content material. The extreme brevity of items in Section 2 is, no doubt, responsible for this pattern of ratings; items do not have enough linguistic context and situational reference to show clear authenticity with regard to academic living situations or academic content topics. Interestingly, and in contrast to this finding, all the materials used in Section 2 are based on sentences taken from encyclopedic sources or textbooks. The extraction of sentences from the original texts appears to result in a reduction of the academic authenticity of item stimuli when such authenticity is determined by our criteria. While Section 2 items may be useful for assessing discrete grammatical and lexical skills, they are not examples of the extended-length texts that foreign students encounter in college life and college academic study areas, outside of the confines of similar multiple-choice language proficiency tests.

4.4   Ratings of the Characteristics of Section 3 Items.   Vocabulary and reading comprehension items averaged 2 or a little under 2 in their judged relevance to academic living situations or presentation of potential academic content material. Based on the definitions of the ratings, the overall conclusion to be drawn is that the criterion rater judged, on the average, that vocabulary and reading comprehension items might be relevant to academic life or to college-level academic content materials, but that there was no clear and compelling evidence to assert overwhelmingly that they were on the average. Only two items in all of Section 3 were judged to involve language that unquestionably might come from an academic living situation or that was exemplary of college-level academic content materials. The ratings, as a whole, reflect the absence of information concerning the pragmatic meaning that could be attached to the content meaning of items.

In passing, it should be noted that the criterion coder found that some of the Section 3 items seemed more representative of high school subject matter than of college subject matter.

5.   ILR Scale Description of TOEFL Proficiency Levels
This section describes use of the ILR scale to rate the proficiency level required to answer items on various TOEFL sections.

There is some empirical evidence that the ILR scale is relevant to performance on TOEFL. In a study involving thirty-one foreign teaching assistants at American universities, Clark and Swinton (1980) found a moderate relationship between TOEFL scores and ratings on an oral proficiency interview employing a scale similar to the current ILR scale. The correlation between scores on Section 1 of TOEFL and ratings on the oral proficiency scale was .71; for Section 2 it was .57; for Section 3 it was .62; and for TOEFL total score the relationship was .71. This evidence must be interpreted with caution, however, since it may reflect the relationship between TOEFL scores and examinee performance, rather than between TOEFL scores and the situational/linguistic input material that is presented to the examinee. Nonetheless, the situational/linguistic input does serve as the context for examinee performance, and as mentioned earlier (see page 25) situational and linguistic input are organized hierarchically and therefore form a part of the descriptions of the various levels on the scale. Thus, it seems reasonable to describe the content of a second language test using the ILR scale.

Before discussing the findings, it should be noted that the ILR scale may be more suited to the analysis of integrative rather than discrete-point tests of language proficiency. This is because one criterion for a rating of level 2 and above is the availability of a corpus of language equivalent to a paragraph or more in length for any given communicative situation. Since discrete-point items are usually limited to one sentence of text or less, one encounters a diminished situational context. Thus, even though the linguistic complexity of the language in the item may be indicative of higher level skills, most discrete-point items must be classified below level 2, that is, at level 1+ or below.

5.1 Section 1: Listening Comprehension. Part A of the listening comprehension section is typical of this dilemma. This part of the test contains twenty restatement items in which the task is the literal comprehension of a single sentence that deals with concrete facts. All items in this section represent listening proficiency levels 1 or 1+, with the majority falling into the latter category. Listening proficiency level 2 involves the comprehension of multiple facts in an extended text. In Part A of this section, the message is limited to a single sentence, and the options focus on comprehension of the main idea or a single fact contained in the stimulus. Thus, most items were rated a level 1+. Only a few level 1 items were found, and these came at the beginning or the middle of this part.

The first item in Part A is illustrative of a level 1 item.

*(A) Go directly to the post office when class is over.
 (B) Let's first straighten up the classroom and then go to the post office.
 (C) That's the most direct way to the post office from our class.
 (D) The post office is straight ahead of the classroom building.

The task involves understanding simple directions one sentence long. The directions relate to "getting around," which is a "survival" (i.e., level 1) task. The stimulus is not complex; it is a simple sentence using an imperative form of the verb *to go* and everyday vocabulary. Studies in second language acquisition have found that the imperative form of English verbs is usually acquired prior to the English present tense (Burt, Dulay, & Hernandez-Chavez, 1976).

Item 3 in Part A illustrates a level 1+ item and is typical of the general level of difficulty of items in this part.

Greg thought he could do it himself.

*(A) Greg believed he could do it alone.
 (B) Greg thought he'd cut himself
 (C) Greg thought he was selfish.
 (D) Greg alone believed it could be done.

The stimulus involves an independent clause in the past tense followed by a dependent clause in the conditional tense. The dependent clause also contains a reflexive pronoun, which is the key point tested in the item. The topic is not a survival topic, but instead makes mention of a routine event that might be the

subject of a social encounter. Thus, while the syntactic and situational characteristics on the sentence are at level 2, the item must be classified at level 1+ on
the ILR scale due to insufficient context.

Some stimuli in this part contain words or idioms that also exceed level 1+ in
difficulty, such as item 19.

The encyclopedias were out of order.

The subject is a low-frequency word that could pose a problem for lower and
intermediate level learners whose native language does not use a cognate form.
The usage of *out of order,* meaning improperly arranged, can be confused with
another usage of the same idiom, meaning out of service. Indeed, one of the
distractors focuses on this type of semantic interference. Because only six words
are involved, this would also be classified at level 1+ on the ILR scale. The
classification illustrates how the ILR scale can underestimate the communicative
competence required to handle discrete-point items.

Part B of Section 1 consists of short conversations involving either a man and
a woman or two men. At the end of each conversation, a third voice asks a
question about what was said. Each speaker in the conversation has one communicative turn. Thus, the conversation involves a single exchange of messages
rather than multiple exchanges.

Since the conversation involves more than a single utterance, this item format
permits the design of items that are at level 2. Nevertheless, few of the items in
this part test level 2 listening skills as defined on the ILR scale. This is because
the conversations are normally short, followed by a single question that usually
requires comprehension of only one utterance, instead of both. (See example
items 22 and 35 on the following pages.) Since the comprehension of a single
utterance is a level 1+ task, such items are lower than level 2 in difficulty. In
fact, most of the short conversation items examined were classified at level 1+,
while some were at level 1, and a few were at level 2.

Item 21 illustrates a level 1 item.

(man)   Good morning, may I help you?
(woman)   Yes. I'd like to cash these traveler's checks first and then open a savings
          account.
(voice)   Where does this conversation probably take place?

    (A)   In a department store.
*(B)   In a bank.
    (C)   At a tourist bureau.
    (D)   At a hotel.

The item depicts a survival situation similar to one that might be encountered
by a tourist on a short sojourn in another country. The examinee need only
comprehend the general nature of the message by indicating where the situation

takes place; the item does not require the comprehension of detail. The options are phrases rather than sentences. Thus, they display the same ellipsis that is typical of normal speech. While all other Part B items on this test form contain full sentence options, the options are often slightly shorter than those found in Part A.

Although the stimulus conversation depicts a simple survival situation, the question invokes processes that are representative of normal conversation, i.e., a reliance on shared knowledge and inference. Such processes are typical of natural discourse.

As indicated above, the short duration of the stimuli often prevents items from testing level 2 skills. Although no long stimuli were found in this form, some do occur in other editions of the test. Item 22 in *Understanding TOEFL: Test Kit 1* exemplifies such items.

(man)	I can't understand why my friend isn't here yet. We agreed to meet at 10:30. It's almost 11:00. Do you think we should try to call her or go look for her?
(woman)	She probably just got tied up in traffic. Let's give her a few more minutes.
(voice)	What are these people going to do?

    (A)   Check the time for high tide.
    (B)   Go stand under the clock.
 *(C)   Wait a little longer.
    (D)   Look for the traffic light.

In this item, both utterances contain more than one sentence. The conversation meets routine social demands, and the question calls for an inference.

On the form used in this study, item 35 can also be classified at level 2.

(man)	I heard that the newspaper gave that book a terrible review.
(woman)	It depends on which newspaper you read.
(voice)	What does the woman mean?

    (A)   You should believe everything you read.
    (B)   She thinks the book is excellent.
    (C)   She wonders which newspaper he reads.
 *(D)   Reaction to the book has been varied.

The topic of this conversation is clearly above the survival level that is associated with level 1 of the scale. Also, the ability to answer the question depends on comprehension of both utterances. Finally, in order to answer the question, one must make an inference, since the correct response is not actually stated during the conversation. This ability to "understand between the lines" is associated with level 2+ on the scale. Nevertheless, the short duration of the stimulus means that the item cannot be classified beyond level 2 on the ILR scale.

In summary, most items in this part were found to fall at level 1 +. This is due to several criteria that are part of the ILR scale: i.e., the items contain short stimuli; the topic or situation is often at the survival level; the examinee is often required to understand only a single utterance.

Part C, in this form of TOEFL, consists of three listening comprehension passages. Two of them are lengthy, one is short.

The first passage is a monologue or short lecture about the high rate of deafness on the island of Martha's Vineyard, Massachusetts. (See script for the listening comprehension section, Appendix A, page 8.) The passage contains seven sentences and is just over 200 words in length; it can be classified at level 3. Although the monologue is not technical, it is a narrative that describes a sequence of situations and events and uses a deliberative style (Joos, 1967). In this sense, it is comparable to a newspaper article that discusses a topic of general interest. (Such articles are considered to be at level 3 on the ILR reading scale.) The same type of material might be heard on an educational radio program. The passage requires the examinee to follow a series of facts and then put together ideas that are interwoven with these facts regarding genetic breeding, the dominance of certain defects, etc. While the passage is definitely at level 3 in difficulty, many of the items test listening ability at level 2. They focus on facts, rather than on inferences and conclusions that can be drawn from the passage. The items could be classified at level 3 if phrased differently. An example is item 41, which is based on the last sentence in the passage.

. . . In the twentieth century the local population has mixed with people off the island, and the rate of deafness has fallen.

(voice)   According to the talk, how has the island changed in the twentieth century?

    *(A)   The patterns of marriage have changed.

    (B)   Many deaf people have regained their hearing.

    (C)   Most of the original population has left the island.

    (D)   The island has become famous for its research facilities.

The question posed by the voice calls the examinees' attention to the time frame (twentieth century) in which the action in the key occurred. Thus, no inference is required. On the other hand, an inference is signaled by the conjunction "and" in the last clause of the passage. The ability to make this inference could be tested by a similar question, such as "The rate of deafness on the island has decreased recently because." Such a question focuses on the type of listening task (inferring or concluding) that is often posed to level 3 learners of a second language. Still, this passage is the most demanding communicative task on the listening comprehension section when analyzed according to the ILR scale. It is also representative of the type of task required of a student listening to a lecture in a university classroom.

The second passage in Part C is an extended conversation between a man and a woman about California redwood trees. Each person speaks five times. Thus, the conversation contains a total of ten turns. While a considerable amount of information is divulged regarding redwood trees, the passage is not as technical as the monologue. Also, its conversational tone of a question followed by an answer tends to diminish the information load by separating it into segments. As a result, the examinee only has to listen to the information; it is not necessary to piece together a sequence of facts so they take on a larger meaning. The passage requires less cognitive processing than the monologue. The only sequence that one has to process is that trees with thick bark that live in a damp, foggy environment do not catch on fire, and therefore live a long time. Since the circumstances are contiguous in time and the conclusion is logical, the passage does not invoke the same degree of proficiency as the previous passage, which explains that repeated intermarriage produces a special set of genetic circumstances. Thus, when deafness has occurred in one generation, it may also show up several generations later because the propensity for it is carried by both parents. Because the conversation passage is easier to process than the short lecture, it would be classified at a 2+ on the ILR scale.

The items following the conversation are also straightforward. Most are restatements of the questions asked by one of the participants, and the answers are based on the responses given by the other participant. Thus, the examinee's attention is called to key facts by questions that are part of the stimulus.

The final listening passage is a short announcement of the closing of a library at the end of the day, similar to one that might be heard over a public address system. Such announcements about daily events are classified at level 2 on the ILR listening scale unless they are presented under adverse conditions, such as a high amount of static noise, etc. Radio news broadcasts, on the other hand, are usually classified at level 3 because the listener must comprehend not only the facts, but also analyses and interpretations made by the commentators. The questions deal with the factual content of the announcement and thus are designed to test level 2 listening skills.

5.2   Section 2: Structure and Written Expression.   This section of the test is composed exclusively of one-sentence discrete-point items whose function is to assess accuracy of grammar and style. In a general sense the observation is warranted that these items do not serve a communicative purpose. Thus, they are not well suited for analysis using the ILR scale. Nevertheless, some judgments can be made about the degree to which they test communicative competence using certain points raised by the scale as a criterion.

The section consists of two parts. Part A, structure, consists of fifteen incomplete sentences. In each sentence a word or phrase has been left blank. The examinee is to select from four options the one that best completes the sentence. The items focus on a wide variety of grammatical problems. Part B consists of twenty-five items in which four words or phrases in a sentence have been underlined. The examinee must identify the one underlined word or phrase that needs to be corrected or rewritten.

All of the sentences in this section are appropriate for level 2 texts or higher. One can imagine many of these sentences appearing in textbooks. Thus, lexically and structurally they are at level 3, although there is insufficient context to classify them as such. For the items to be more communicative, it would be necessary to relate them to each other or to place them in a text. A multiple-choice cloze is an example of such a context, although cloze passages usually emphasize lexical and grammatical problems equally.

Structure items seem to be slightly more communicative than written expression items. Generally, they are slightly longer and thus offer more context. In general, additional context can be used to assess more long-range constraints on an item. Many structure items function like a cloze exercise in that they utilize the constraints provided by the context of the sentence to help one select the correct completion. Written expression items focus only on the recognition of syntactic and stylistic problems.

5.3   Section 3: Reading Comprehension and Vocabulary   This section is designed to measure the examinee's ability to understand various kinds of reading materials, as well as the ability to understand the meanings and uses of words. It consists of thirty vocabulary items and 30 reading comprehension items based on reading passages. The length of the passages ranges from one hundred to three hundred and fifty words.

In the vocabulary items, the examinee is presented with a sentence that has one underlined word. The task is to select which of four options best keeps the meaning of the underlined word. From the standpoint of the ILR scale, the vocabulary items focus less on communication of meaning in context than do any other parts of the test. This is so despite the fact that examinees would need to exercise grammatical recognition skills in order to understand stimulus sentences. At least half the items can be answered without reference to their context within the sentence. Item 1 is typical of such items.

In masculine rhyme, the *end* sounds of stressed syllables are repeated.

- (A)   dominant
- (B)   vowel
- (C)   hard
- *(D)   final

While the options are all adjectives that might be associated with the noun "sounds," and therefore effective distractors for an examinee who does not know the meaning of the underlined adjective, it is not necessary to understand the context in order to answer the item correctly. This is not true of all vocabulary items, however. The following item (item 12) is context sensitive. That is, only by reading and understanding the whole sentence can one identify the correct answer. In a different context, any of the options might be considered a correct synonym for the underlined word.

The Cheyenne Indians were considered spectacular riders and fierce *warriors*.

(A)   hunters
(B)   defenders
(C)   enemies
*(D)   fighters

The vocabulary items tested in this part vary in difficulty. They would be part of the receptive lexicon of readers at level 2 to level 4. Within this range some lower-level items are *end, quarter, shy,* and *materials*. Some items that would be part of a higher level lexicon are *heyday, incessantly, ban,* and *hailed*. The nouns in this test form generally are easier than words belonging to other parts of speech, although the actual difficulty of items for each examinee would depend in part on whether the examinee's native language contained a word that shared the same derivational morpheme.

Reading Comprehension. Each form of the TOEFL test contains thirty reading comprehension items, although the number of passages may vary from form to form. The length of passages varies also, from one hundred to three hundred and fifty words. On this form, there are five passages ranging from 103 to 263 words in length. Each passage is followed by four to eight questions.

The five texts vary in difficulty from level 3 to level 4. The first passage is at level 4; the second and third are at level 3; the fourth is at level 3+; and the final passage is at level 3. All are the type of passage that might be encountered by a university student at the undergraduate level. Thus, reading comprehension appears to be the most demanding portion of the test in terms of communicative competence when judged by the ILR scale.

The first passage deals with mosquito larvae and is the most demanding. There is a heavy information load, and the passage is lacking in cohesion, characteristics that typify many authentic texts. Although the passage discusses a scientific topic, it is written for the general public rather than for scientists. One of the characteristics of a level 4 reader is the ability to "follow unpredictable turns of thought." The fact that this passage was taken from a longer text, and discusses a technical topic about which few members of the general public would have knowledge, suggests that it would invoke such skills. Another characteristic of an ILR level 4 reader is the ability to recognize all professionally relevant vocabulary known to the educated nonprofessional native. Again, the passage appears to invoke this skill.

The second passage, on oranges, is at level 3. It is a factual and historical passage written in a formal style.

The third passage, which deals with communication satellites, is also technical in nature. It employs a higher level of vocabulary, including one instance of communications industry terminology ("domsats"), which is defined in the passage. Because of its vocabulary, it might be classified as a level 3+ text, although in practice a government examiner would not consider such a short passage (103 words) to be at the 3+ level. Because the passage is not sufficiently long, it must be classified at level 3.

The fourth passage, which describes a particular type of animal behavior, contains a few technical terms along with many words that are often known by only advanced users of a second language and educated native speakers. Some of these words are *sensory, vertebrates, diurnal, predators, flock, mammals, rodents, herds, hoofed, prey, moose, dens, primate,* and *baboons.* In spite of its advanced vocabulary, the passage makes frequent use of cohesive devices, is well organized, and could be understood by a level 3+ reader. The passage is also the longest on this form (263 words).

The final passage, which discusses the problems of doing good research, is also a level 3 text. Although the vocabulary is suitable for a college audience, it does not contain low-frequency words that exemplify the highest levels on the ILR scale. While the topic discusses an academic situation, the text is a narrative and relates a frequently encountered personal experience.

The items following each passage are appropriate to level 3 texts. Quite often the questions seem to avoid testing comprehension of less frequently used terms that appear in the text, unless these are specifically defined. For instance, the passage on animal behavior is followed by questions that generally avoid the vocabulary listed above, and test comprehension of content that is also unrelated to the phrases or sentences in which this vocabulary appeared. Thus, even the more difficult reading passages do not seem particularly suited to assess highly advanced (level 4) users of English as a second language. This may not be inappropriate however, since a test designed for such bilinguals would probably confuse many native English speakers with nonnative speakers, which is a problem the current TOEFL does not have.

5.4 Conclusion. The communicative competence invoked by TOEFL items seems to be quite consistent within each item type, while deviating considerably across item types. In general, the discrete-point items were rated low on the ILR scale (from level 1 to level 2). Of these, vocabulary items generally made the least use of situational context. The monologues and extended dialogues in Section 1 and the reading passages in Section 3 were found to be the most demanding communicative tasks on the test; text difficulty ranged from level 2+ to level 4. The test items were frequently found to be of a lower level than the passages on which they were based. Even with the more difficult listening and reading passages, the more advanced communicative tasks were not assessed by the comprehension questions.

On the basis of this analysis of the test using the ILR scale, it appears that the communicative content of TOEFL, while limited in some ways, is appropriate for assessing the language proficiency of basic, intermediate, and advanced learners and of fluent users of English as a second language. However, it does not appear that the test is appropriate for identifying or discriminating among highly proficient, near-native speakers. The discourse tasks tested are not that advanced, nor are they as communicatively rich as the range of tasks on the ILR scale. This does not mean however, that examinees who attain high scores on TOEFL (i.e., 630 and above) could not perform such communicative tasks; it merely indicates that such tasks are not measured to a significant degree on the test. To be more specific, such tasks (as defined on the ILR scale) as the ability to understand fully all input on any subject within one's range of experience and to grasp all subtleties and nuances, and the ability to understand speech under unfavorable conditions, including nonstandard dialects and slang, as well as cultural references and extremely abstract prose, are not measured by the test.

Finally, it should be remembered that the ILR scale is designed to provide a global rating of communicative competence. In this analysis, it was found that discrete-point tests that focus on linguistic accuracy are not well suited for analysis by this scale. Quite often, the difficulty of such items is underestimated by the scale. While adherence to the requirement for a specific amount of context may appear to be unnecessarily strict, it must be remembered that the ILR scale is basically noncompensatory. Thus, the satisfaction of some but not all of the requirements for a particular classification is not sufficient reason for an examinee or a passage to receive that classification.

V. DISCUSSION AND DIRECTIONS FOR ITEM AND TEST DEVELOPMENT

1. Overview of This Section

This section of the report first discusses the major findings of the study. It then outlines some considerations that should be made in improving the design of language tests in general, and finally, the implications of some of these suggestions for the TOEFL test.

2. Conclusions Regarding TOEFL

The description of the TOEFL test given in this report suggests that the content of the test is directly appropriate for assessing some language skills but not others. This conclusion is based on a communicative description of the content characteristics of items only. No comprehensive research has been done investigating skills that are not assessed by the test but are important to foreign students' academic functioning. Research is needed on this question and on TOEFL's correlation with these skills. The test requires only receptive language skills on the part of examinees, and in this regard the main strength of the test lies in its assessment of examinees' ability to recognize orthographic encoding of information, grammatical appropriateness at the spoken or written sentence level, and recognition of spoken or written semantic information at the sentence or brief text level. As outlined in the TOEFL test specifications, each section and item type within a section are designed to assess examinees' recognition of a particular point or skill. The discrete skill emphasis of the instrument is enhanced by the frequent use of many items that are tailored to the skill being tested; with the exception of minitalk/extended conversation items in Section 1 and the reading comprehension items in Section 3, adjacent items never share contents that refer to the same topics.

Within the range of skills TOEFL can assess, the naturalness of language that examinees are exposed to is a direct function of the length and rhetorical complexity of the language stimuli that accompany test questions. For example, the minitalk/extended conversation items of Section 1 and the reading comprehension passages in Section 3 provide the richest integration of language phenomena, and, accordingly, these items exercise examinees' language recognition skills in the richest and most face valid manner. Both types of items are clustered into small groups of questions regarding an extended text stimuli. However, there is no evidence of a deliberate thematic connection in the topics pursued across questions in the same set.

The statements and dialogue items of Section 1 provide examinees with less language than do the two above-mentioned item types; dialogue items do require examinees to recognize the relation between a pair of utterances made by two speakers, but correct response options seem most related to the second utterance. A number of dialogue items feature speech act functions that go beyond simply giving and asking for information, and while this frequency of occurrence is not rare, occurrence of speech act forms must be inferred. The nature of the social context surrounding occurrence of dialogue items must be inferred by examinees, and there is only limited information in the linguistic and paralinguistic content of dialogues to guide this form of inference. The use of paralinguistic cues, such as stress, and modulation of intonation in speech sometimes seems to be more enunciated and hyperbolic than that encountered in casual face-to-face conversation. This finding should be weighed against the need for high acoustic quality in a tape-recorded section. Delivery of dialogue items by tape recording seems to be a constraint, in that examinees are not physically exposed to gestural and other proxemic cues that can enhance inference of meaning and intent in speakers' utterances. The speech in dialogue items is devoid of false starts, hesitations, back channel cues, and other phenomena that are associated with the exhibition and recognition of strategic competence.

The statement item stimuli are the most decontextualized examples of natural speech found on the TOEFL test. These stimuli are provided with no information about the communicative context within which they occur, and while they feature intonation, stress, and prosody that are typical of North American English speakers and have referential meaning, the specific function and purpose of utterances is not always easily inferred. While the correct, written response option for statement items is typically a paraphrase of the stimulis, on occasion examinees must infer a correct response option based on pragmatic knowledge of the real world situation the stimulus and response option are judged to refer to.

Section 2 of TOEFL, structure and written expression (along with the vocabulary portion of Section 3), utilizes the most restricted and least natural written language stimuli occurring in TOEFL. The two structure and written expression item types are designed to probe examinees' knowledge of sentence grammar and appropriate usage of words, but not range of vocabulary. The two item types consist of isolated sentence fragments or else one or two isolated sentences. No information is provided about a communicative context, and the topics of different items are always unrelated to each other. The TOEFL test specifications for Section 2 suggest that this variability is a desired goal, in order to expose examinees to a greater range of contents and topics.

A review of test method and personal factors that might affect TOEFL identified a number of ways that examinees' performance might be distorted or limited relative to situations in which authentic communication occurs. All language proficiency tests, be they direct or indirect, or discrete-point oriented versus integrative or holistic, entail some distortion of normal communicative processes from the viewpoint of examinees. The performance constraints occurring on TOEFL relative to normal communication limit the assessment of an extended range of communication skills because the test involves only language reception on the part of examinees, and because multiple-choice items present diminished situational context. However, it should be noted that TOEFL is not designed to be a test of extended communication skills. Also, such a criticism is not unique to the TOEFL test; the same criticism could be made of other proficiency tests currently in use for the same purpose of TOEFL. If the sole purpose of TOEFL is to challenge examinees with questions on specific points related to American English grammar, vocabulary, and usage, then TOEFL items perform this task. The immediate critical issue seems to be whether TOEFL might achieve its goals better with items that have greater face and content validity.

The analysis of test method and personal factors potentially affecting TOEFL performance that was presented in this report is quite preliminary. The Bachman and Palmer (forthcoming) outline of various factors and related issues has important, substantive value in describing performance constraints on the TOEFL test. However, a more intensive and careful effort is needed in order to interpret fully the underlying issues in a more definitive and analytically useful fashion than is possible in this report.

Evaluation of the content of TOEFL items with regard to their academic and social naturalness leads to the conclusion that items are limited in how well they simulate authentic language situations that may be faced by examinees when attending North American colleges. This conclusion is to be expected given that individual test items and item stimuli are very abbreviated in comparison to language use in authentic communication contexts. The absence of information about a language use context, the inability of examinees to exchange language reciprocally, and the brevity of discourse-length texts are the most critical factors inducing judged lack of authenticity of TOEFL items. The item types showing the greatest authenticity—minitalks/extended conversations and reading comprehension—also involve the grammatically, lexically, and rhetorically richest discourse of all TOEFL items. Even these item types, however, can be judged as having limited authenticity because they retain an isolated character that renders them as fragments of extended discourse drawn in an *ad hoc* fashion from the range of all possible social–academic situations and academic content experiences that students might encounter in college. Strengthening the naturalness of language found on these TOEFL items by revising item content specifications is possible in principle, though there are a number of practical, psychometric, and operational issues that would mitigate this suggestion. This matter is addressed in the final section of the report.

Evaluation of the minimal ILR proficiency level required to solve items on various TOEFL sections led to the conclusion that the test is appropriate in difficulty for basic, intermediate, and advanced learners of English. Taken collectively, test items are capable of discriminating persons who might be rated at all but the highest ILR levels in a given modality of language use. The upper levels on the ILR scale for a given modality involve examinees' ability to produce or comprehend language with the same fluency, cultural appropriateness, and cognitive problem-solving ability as educated native speakers. Assessment of proficiency at these levels is not the purpose of the TOEFL test, but some items nonetheless are capable of assessing the English skills of highly proficient, near-native English speakers.

Considerable variation in the ILR proficiency level exhibited by different item types was noted. In general, consistent with other findings in this report, the minimal ILR level required to work item types correctly was directly related to the extent of discourse presented by an item type. The reading comprehension section of TOEFL seemed to require consistently the highest ILR proficiency levels.

The analysis of TOEFL that is summarized here at times might be interpreted as having a critical tone that may be misleading; research on the test has clearly demonstrated its value as an instrument for assessing the language proficiency of incoming foreign college students. The principal concern here is with understanding better the content nature of TOEFL items, and thereby some of the strengths and limits of the test in assessing language proficiency skills. A secondary goal was to suggest how TOEFL and other tests might be made more responsive to improved assessment needs that theoretical developments and research in applied linguistics permit us to describe. The weaknesses of TOEFL are not unique to this proficiency instrument, and the extensive review of the test from a communicative proficiency viewpoint provided here is unavailable currently for any similar commercial instrument. There is no reason to believe that any other similar, currently available language proficiency test would be evaluated any more favorably than the TOEFL test. However, a number of efforts are underway to develop proficiency tests based on a communicative approach to language testing (Wesche, 1981; Canale, in press). Communicative approaches to language proficiency assessment have raised new challenges to language test developers. The next section of the report discusses these challenges and ways in which they might be resolved in a manner leading to improved test use and benefits to examinees and institutions. Following this discussion, attention returns to TOEFL and to efforts that the TOEFL program could undertake to develop new item types and tests, and efforts that also would strengthen appropriate use of the existing TOEFL.

3.   Suggestions for Improving Language Testing

This section summarizes some recent views on general test design that suggest how language testing might be improved. First, there is a discussion of two guiding principles for improved test design. Next, an outline of four test design features consistent with these principles is presented.

3.1   Two Guiding Principles.   Most discussions of test design emphasize that a good test is characterized minimally by validity, reliability, and practicality. Many major language tests do seem to reflect careful attention to content and concurrent validity, to internal and test–retest reliability, and to practicality of test administration and scoring. Two further considerations, not always emphasized in test design or reflected well in many major language tests, are test acceptability and feedback potential. Acceptability, similar to the notion of face validity, concerns the extent to which a test task is accepted as fair, important, and interesting by both examinees and test users. Feedback potential concerns the extent to which a test task rewards both examinees and test users with clear, rich, relevant, and generalizable information. Both may be hidden in a test score.

While these two considerations may be acknowledged by many test developers, they are often accorded lower priority than are concurrent validity, reliability, and practicality concerns. As a result, one risks developing and tolerating language tests that may measure something well but be neither acceptable nor rewarding to examinees and test users. A rather extreme example, noted by Clark (1972) would be that a test of oral interaction skills that consisted of pencil-and-paper multiple-choice items that never required the examinee to face an interlocutor or to speak. No doubt such a test could be validated and used. However, this would be to ignore—almost to degrade—the interests of the examinee on the one hand, and, on the other, of the educator seeking to understand and improve the examinee's skills. While such testing practices may be more defensible when large numbers of examinees are involved, they unfortunately risk becoming the model for testing small numbers of examinees as well (e.g., in classroom testing).

To counter the risk of emphasizing only psychometric and practical concerns in test development, the following guiding principles are offered.

Principle 1: attempt to elicit the best performance from examinees by presenting tasks that are fair, important in themselves, and interesting in themselves. In Swain's (1982) terms, bias for best.

Principle 2: attempt to provide test tasks that reveal to examinees and educators clear, rich, relevant, and generalizable information—in our terms, bias for rewarding feedback.

These two principles are highlighted here not because they are the only ones worth considering but because they are often not represented adequately in language tests. Furthermore, these principles are certainly compatible with suggestions calling for close attention to the variety and quality of performance elicited by language tests as well as to the naturalness of tasks on such tests.

3.2   Four Test Design Features.   In keeping with these last comments, four general design features are worth considering to improve receptive language testing.

(a) *Thematic organization.* In contrast to a language test that might be organized according to linguistic criteria (e.g., a vocabulary section, a sentence structure section), skill areas (e.g., a sound discrimination section, a reading comprehension section), or other criteria, a thematically organized test would represent and group those tasks that provide a coherent, natural, and motivating structure to the overall test. Swain (1982) and colleagues provide an example of such a test, in which a variety of subthemes and language tasks are naturally linked to an overall theme, such as organizing a summer music festival or setting up a student job program. The soundness of this approach deserves more intensive examination since there would be a need to avoid item content bias that might be introduced.

(b) *Four stages in test administration.* In the Oral Interview of the U.S. Government, oral interaction skills are elicited in four stages, each of which has psychological, linguistic, and evaluative purposes. The warm-up is intended to put the examinee at ease and to familiarize him or her with the target language and with the interviewers. Next, the level check seeks to identify that proficiency level at which the examinee performs best (e.g., most comfortably and most satisfactorily). Then, at the probe stage, an effort is made to challenge the examinee with tasks thought to be just beyond this identified level, both to verify the examinee's maximum proficiency level and to demonstrate to the examinee what tasks he or she cannot yet perform. Finally, the wind-up presents tasks at the examinee's best performance level so that he or she finishes the test with a sense of accomplsihment. (For further discussion and references on these stages in administration of both productive and receptive language tests, see Canale, in press, and Lowe, 1981).

(c) *Adaptive testing procedures.* In contrast to a traditional test, in which a group of examinees is required to respond to the same items regardless of the individuals' varying abilities to do so, an adaptive test is tailored *during its actual administration* according to each examinee's level of performance on successive items or groups of items. The Oral Interview procedure just described is one example of an adaptive testing procedure. Adaptive tests may also be delivered by computer. For example, an examinee who performed poorly on the first, say, five items of a reading test could be automatically administered five items different (and presumably easier) from those items automatically administered to another examinee who performed well on the first five. Automatic presentation of further groups of items would depend on each examinee's performance on the second group of five, and so on, until a consistent (and here different) level of performance had been confirmed for each student. Measurement experts such as Green (1983) and Wainer (1983) argue that such adaptive testing is not only feasible from measurement and technological viewpoints, but is highly desirable for a variety of reasons. One important reason is that an adaptive test allows the examinee to work at his or her own pace and provides repeated measurements at his or her performance level, and hence less room for measurement error. Another is that examinees are likely to find adaptive tests less boring, frustrating, and tiring than traditional ones, since most items should correspond to the individual examinee's performance level and since there are fewer items and less emphasis on speed.

(d) *Criterion-referenced tests.* Whereas a norm-referenced test consists of tasks designed to maximize differences in performance among examinees, a criterion-referenced test consists of whatever tasks (or sample of tasks) examines must be able to perform for a given purpose and at a given proficiency level. In other words, a criterion-referenced test is designed to determine the extent to which a given examinee can or cannot perform a target (or criterion) task. Educational evaluation experts such as Popham (1975:134 ff.) often stress two main advantages of criterion-referenced tests over norm-referenced ones. First, the tasks on the former must represent, in a direct and theoretically sound manner, tasks that are crucial to performance of the criterion task; the tasks on a norm-referenced test need only produce scores that show a high correlation with scores on the criterion task. Thus, while one could conceive of a norm-referenced test of oral interaction skills in which no examinee was ever required to speak, such a criterion-referenced test would be inconceivable. Second, the scores on a criterion-referenced test are intended to be directly interpretable in terms of some actual criterion performance; scores on a norm-referenced test are intended only to indicate how each examinee stands in comparison to a larger group of examinees, with little or no clear feedback as to the reasons for such relative standing. While criterion-referenced testing also has certain disadvantages (e.g., in requiring new statistical techniques for computing reliability estimates) and is not suitable or desirable in all testing situations (cf. Allen and Yen, 1979), it is nonetheless a worthwhile consideration in the testing of both productive and receptive language skills.

4. Implications for TOEFL Program Activities

This section suggests some activities addressing issues missed by this report that might be considered by the TOEFL program. The intent of these suggestions is not to provide firm prescriptions, but rather to mention possible activities that are likely to have positive benefits for improving use of the existing TOEFL and for research and test development activities.

4.1 Study of the TOEFL Test Specifications and Continued Study of the Content Characteristics of TOEFL Items.

The research described in this report did not refer to the TOEFL test specifications. While the investigators had access to the specifications and, indeed, reviewed them briefly in preparation for the research, there was no opportunity to investigate how the conclusions drawn from this report might be useful in reviewing the existing test specfications. Such a review would seem to be an important next step in applying the findings of this report. Attention should focus on the overlap and lack of overlap between the description of the TOEFL test given here and in the specifications; one valuable goal would be to identify ways in which the specifications might be revised to increase the naturalness of discourse occurring in the test.

Parallel with review of the specifications, further research and test development activities aimed at describing TOEFL items using communicative approaches should be considered. This effort is important in order to understand how the content characteristics of TOEFL items are related to examinees' performance on items.

4.2 Development Research on Thematic Presentation of Items and on New Item Types.

The TOEFL program should consider ways for increasing the face validity and naturalness of language usage occurring in the TOEFL test. It is important to recognize that changes in the existing TOEFL cannot be undertaken in an abrupt fashion. Any changes that are considered need to be evaluated for their soundness with regard to several criteria, e.g., psychometric integrity of the test and implications for program operational procedures, including test development procedures, costs, and TOEFL score report use.

The first step in this process is to study alternative ways in which the face and content validity of the existing TOEFL might be improved. It ought to prove useful to consider ways in which the contents of existing item types might be made more thematically relevant to college life and academic experience. For example, a series of revised statement items might have contents that are related to a few general themes appropriate to college experiences, such as attending a lecture series, learning to use a library, and registering for course work.

It is important to note that a decision to use items with a shared thematic content may have disadvantages as well as advantages. Research would be needed to make sure that using items with shared thematic content would not lead to test content bias. By restricting the number of topics that items may refer to, it is possible that examinees' differential familiarity with these topics may have a systematic impact on differences in test scores.

A second step worth considering is the development of new item types that would feature more extended use of integrated proficiency skills. The results of the present review of the TOEFL test suggest that the breadth of language recognition competencies required of examinees is directly related to the length and textual complexity of TOEFL item stimuli. Accordingly, increasing the amount of language and the complexity of discourse in items is likely to benefit the range and nature of skills exercised in taking TOEFL. The process of suggesting new item types is nontrivial. The considerations raised by Bachman and Palmer (forthcoming) as factors influencing test performance will need to be considered. For example, increasing the amount of language in item stimuli and the number of questions, and hence distance between questions and stimuli, may have unexpected side effects on performance.

4.3 New Approaches to Assess Communicaiive Proficiency. The existing TOEFL, even with modifications, could not be expected to assess some important proficiency skills. For example, the test cannot test speaking ability or writing ability directly. Accordingly, efforts should be considered to map out additional competencies that may be tested by other instruments, such as the Test of Spoken English (TSE) and by prototype direct essay tasks currently being field tested. In addition, thought should be given to the desirability and feasibility of altogether new instruments to assess communicative skills not now tested.

4.4 Technology, Innovative Measurement, and Adaptive Testing. Another consideration raised here concerns the importance of evaluating how advances in technology might aid the TOEFL program in developing new items and tests capable of assessing new ranges of communicative skills. The TOEFL program should take steps to enhance its access to information concerning new technological advances, involving microcomputers, programming languages and software, video disks, voice synthesis, and other electronic technology, that could have an impact on development of new item types. It is important to note that some technologies, such as voice synthesis, are not yet feasible to implement easily on existing microcomputers because of memory limitations.

The interactive capabilities of microcomputers, plus the availability of video disks, may portend new possibilities for assessment of language proficiency skills not currently assessed by TOEFL. For example, it ought to prove feasible in technologically advanced countries to present examinees with video recordings of a person or persons conversing with each other, delivering a lecture, or asking questions of an examinee. One can envision an enhanced version of

Section 1 of the current TOEFL that could be delivered by video disk. The use of a visual medium for test presentation has the advantage that it is standardized over examinees and would permit a richer range of questions to be asked about a discourse. A disadvantage might be that it could prove difficult to ensure the security of video-based items to the extent now possible with printed items.

Other possibilities involving the interactive capabilities of computers in language testing should be explored. For example, is it possible to design innovative conversation items that would permit assessment of examinees' ability to display sociolinguistic, discourse, and strategic competence? Obviously, in considering such suggestions, beyond construct and content validity issues, operational constraints in administering a test must be kept in mind.

Computer adaptive testing using conventional or enhanced TOEFL items is still another possibility. This area is currently under active investigation by the TOEFL program.

4.5   Validity Research.   As this report demonstrates, it is possible to identify some ways in which the TOEFL examination resembles or differs from language use in authentic settings. A basic question that deserves research is how well the existing TOEFL, with its strengths and limitations, is capable of measuring language proficiency skills that are strongly related to performance in authentic language use situations. The skills required in taking TOEFL may or may not be predictive of a broader range of examinee language proficiency skills. This matter can only be resolved through empirical research on the question. An important step in pursuing such research will be to identify authentic, criterion language tasks and appropriate performance measures on these tasks. One valuable orientation toward the design of research studies of the sort that are needed can be found in the work of Bachman and Palmer (1981). These researchers have utilized a multitrait–multimethod approach to investigate the convergent and discriminant validity of batteries of proficiency tests designed to measure a variety of communicative proficiency skills.

4.6   Staying Abreast with the Assessment Field.   In closing this report, it is important to endorse the significant benefits that language proficiency test developers can derive from contact with new research in the language proficiency assessment field. The field is undergoing an evolution as a result of attempts to increase the breadth of language skills that instruments might test. It is to the obvious advantage of test producers that they stay informed of developments. Contact with the field and evaluation of its advances with regard to the validity and appropriate use of existing tests is not unidirectional. As this report illustrates, there is merit in evaluating a proficiency test in light of communicative approaches to language assessment. The fact that a communicative approach leads to identification of many important skills not reflected on a test does not imply that simple remedies are at hand to improve existing tests. Clearly, it is of fundamental importance to test use that improvements in testing be identified, but it is far easier to identify skills not assessed by a test than it is to devise practical and scientifically sound ways in which to legitimately assess skills that are not currently assessed. We should always expect that language assessment theory will be ahead of language assessment practice. Amidst all the leading theoretical developments in proficiency assessment, some issues and approaches to assessment will be more tractable than others. It is important that proficiency test developers contribute to the cutting edge of these concerns, even though there can be no guarantees that new theory and assessment approaches will necessarily always lead to improvement in testing practices. Many steps are involved in striving for the goal of improved tests. This report illustrates ways in which theory might help in evaluating and improving existing instruments and testing practices.

The ways in which testing programs such as the TOEFL program, respond to advances in language proficiency assessment theory will be of significance to language assessment research. The responses will inform researchers as to the gap that remains between theory and practice, and to the problems encountered in enacting testing practices that are responsive to advances in theory. This feedback may, in turn, contribute to the design of more adequate models for language proficiency assessment.

REFERENCES

Allen, M.J., & Yen, W.M. (1979). *Introduction to measurement theory*. Monterey, CA: Brooks-Cole.

Austin, J.L. (1962). *How to do things with words*. Cambridge, MA: Harvard University Press.

Bachman, L., & Palmer, A. (1981). A multitrait–multimethod investigation into the construct validity of six tests of speaking and reading. In A Palmer, P. Groot, & G. Trosper (Eds.), *The construct validation of tests of communicative competence*. Washington, DC: Teachers of English to Speakers of Other Languages (TOEFL).

Bachman, L., & Palmer, A. (forthcoming). *Basic concerns in language test validation*. Reading, MA: Addison-Wesley.

Bolinger, D., & Sears, D. (1981). *Aspects of language*. New York: Harcourt, Brace, Jovanovich.

Bruner, J. S. (1975). Language as an instrument of thought. In A. Davies (Ed.), *Problems of language and learning*. London: Heinemann.

Buros, O.K. (1977). Fifty years in testing: Some reminiscences, criticisms, and suggestions. *Educational Research, 6*, 9–15.

Burt, M.K., Dulay, H.C., & Hernandez-Chavez, E. (1976). *Bilingual syntax measure technical manual*. New York: Psychological Corp.

Canale, M. (1983a). On some dimensions of language proficiency. In J.W. Oller, Jr. (Ed.), *Issues in language testing research*. Rowley, MA: Newbury House Publishers.

Canale, M. (1983b). From communicative competence to communicative language pedagogy. In J.C. Richards and R. Schmidt (Eds.), *Language and communication*. London: Longman.

Canale, M. (1984). Testing in a communicative approach. In G.A. Jarvis (Ed.), *The challenge for excellence in foreign language education*. Middlebury, VT: The Northeast Conference.

Canale, M. (in press). Considerations in the testing of reading listening proficiency. *Foreign Language Annals*.

Canale, M., & Swain, M. (1980). Theoretical bases of communicative approaches to second language teaching and testing. *Applied Linguistics, 1,* 1–47.

Chomsky, N. (1965). *Aspects of the theory of syntax.* Cambridge, MA: MIT Press.

Clark, J.L.D. (1972). *Foreign language testing: Theory and practice.* Philadelphia, PA: The Center for Curriculum Development.

Clark, J.L.D. (Ed.). (1978). *Direct testing of speaking proficiency: Theory and application.* Princeton, NJ: Educational Testing Service.

Clark, J. (1980). Toward a common measure of speaking proficiency. In J. Frith (Ed.), *Measuring spoken language proficiency.* Washington, DC: Georgetown University Press.

Clark, H., & Clark, E. (1977). *Psychology and language.* New York: Harcourt Brace Jovanovich.

Clark, J.L.D., & Swinton, S.S. (1980). *The Test of Spoken English as a measure of communicative ability in English-medium instructional settings* (TOEFL Research Report 7). Princeton, NJ: Educational Testing Service.

Cummins, J. (1983). Language proficiency and academic achievement. In J.W. Oller, Jr. (Ed.), *Issues in language testing research.* Rowley, MA: Newbury House Publishers.

Cummins, J. (1984). Wanted: A theoretical framework for relating language proficiency to academic achievement among bilingual students. In C. Rivera (Ed.), *Language proficiency and academic achievement.* Clevedon, England: Multilingual Matters.

Deyhle, D. (1983). Between games and failure: A micro-ethnographic study of Navajo students and testing. *Curriculum Inquiry, 13*(4), 347–376.

Duran, R.P. (1984). Implications of communicative competence research for integrative proficiency testing. In C. Rivera (Ed.), *Communicative competence approaches to language proficiency assessment: Research and application.* Clevedon, England: Multilingual Matters.

Educational Testing Service. (1980). *Understanding TOEFL: Test Kit 1.* Test of English as a Foreign Language Program. Princeton, NJ.

Educational Testing Service. (1983). *Test and Score Manual, 1983 Edition.* Test of English as a Foreign Language Program. Princeton, NJ.

Fodor, J., Bever, T., & Garrett, M. (1974). *The psychology of language.* New York: McGraw-Hill.

Francis, W.N. (1958). *The structure of American English.* New York: The Ronald Press.

Garvin, P. (1978). An empirilist epistemology for linguistics. In M. Paradis (Ed.), *The Fourth LACUS Forum 1977.* Columbia, SC: Hornbeam Press.

Green, B. (1983). The promise of tailored tests. In H. Wainer & S. Messick (Eds.), *Principals of modern psychological measurement.* (A Festschrift for Frederic M. Lord.) Hillsdale, NJ: Erlbaum.

Gumperz, J.J. (1971). *Language in social groups. Essays by John J. Gumperz.* (Selected and introduced by Anwar S.D.L.). Stanford, CA: Stanford University Press.

Gumperz, J.J. (1982). *Discourse strategies.* Cambridge, England: Cambridge University Press.

Gumperz, J.J., & Kaltman, H. (1980). Prosody, linguistic diffusion and conversational inferences. *Proceedings of the Sixth Annual Meeting of the Berkeley Linguistics Society,* (pp. 44–65). Berkeley, CA: Berkeley Linguistics Society.

Halliday, M.A.K. (1973). *Explorations in the functions of language.* New York: Elsevier North-Holland.

Hatch, EM. (1983). *Psycholinguistics. A second language perspective.* Rowley, MA: Newbury House Publishers.

Hudson, R.A. (1980). *Sociolinguistics.* Cambridge: Cambridge University Press.

Hymes, D. (1974). *Foundations in sociolinguistics. An ethnographic approach.* Philadelphia: University of Pennsylvania Press.

Jones, R. (1983, March). *Current research in second language performance testing.* Keynote address presented at the Conference on Second Language Performance Testing, University of Ottawa and Carleton University, Ottawa, Ontario.

Joos, M. (1967). *The five clocks.* New York: Harcourt Brace Jovanovich.

Kaplan, R. (1966). Cultural thought patterns in intercultural education. *Language Learning, 16*, 1–20.

Krashen, S. (1982). *Principles and practice in second language acquisition.* Oxford: Pergamon.

Leech, G., & Svartvik, J. (1975). *A communicative grammar of English.* Singapore: Longman.

Lowe, P. (1981). Structure of the oral interview and content validity. In A.S. Palmer, P.J.M. Groot, & G.A. Trosper (Eds.), *The construct validation of tests of communicative competence.* Washington, DC: TESOL.

Lowe, P. (forthcoming). "The" question: A response to Michael Canale. *Foreign Language Annals,* (fall 1974).

Malinowski, B. (1944). *A scientific thory of culture and other essays.* Chapel Hill: The University of North Carolina Press.

Mathiot, M. (1970). The semantic and cognitive domains of language. In P. Garvin (Ed.), *Cognition: A multiple view.* New York: Spartan Books.

McLaughlin, B., Rossman, T., & McLeod, B. (1983). Second language learning: An information-processing perspective. *Language Learning, 33*(2), 135–158.

Messick, S. (1981). Evidence and ethics in the evaluation of tests. *Educational Researcher, 10*(9), 9–20.

Munby, J. (1978). *Communicative syllabus design.* Cambridge, England: Cambridge University Press.

Oller, J.W., & Spolsky, B. (1979). The Test of English as a Foreign Language (TOEFL). In B. Spolsky (Ed.), *Advances in language testing* (Vol. 1). Washington, DC: Center for Applied Linguistics.

Penfield, J. (1979). *Essay writing for the African world.* Unpublished manuscript.

Popham, W.J. (1975). *Educational evaluation.* Englewood Cliffs, NJ: Prentice-Hall.

Savignon, S. (1983). *Communicative competence: Theory and classroom practice.* Reading, MA: Addison-Wesley.

Scott, M., & Madsen, H. (1983). The influence of retesting on test affect. In J.W. Oller (Ed.), *Issues in language testing research.* Rowley, MA: Newbury House Publishers.

Shoemaker, D. (1980). Improving achievement testing. *Educational Policy Analysis, 2*(6), 37–49.

Spolsky, B. (1979). Linguistics and language testers. In B. Spolsky (Ed.), *Advances in language testing* (Vol. 1). Washington, DC: Center for Applied Linguistics.

Swain, M. (1982, December). *Large-scale communicative language testing: A case study.* Plenary paper presented at the International Symposium on Language Testing. Hong Kong: University of Hong Kong, Mimeo.

Vygotsky, L.S. (1962). *Thought and language.* Cambridge, MA: MIT Press.

Wainer, H. (1983). On item response theory and computerized adaptive tests. *The Journal of College Admissions, 28*(4) 9–16.

Wesche, M.B. (1981). Communicative testing in a second language. *The Canadian Modern Language Review, 37*(3), 551–571.

Yorio, C.A. (1980). Conventionalized language forms and the development of communicative competence. *TESOL Quarterly, 14*(4), 433–442.

APPENDIX A: SAMPLE TOEFL TEST

TEST OF ENGLISH AS A FOREIGN LANGUAGE

General Directions

This is a test of your ability to use the English language. It is divided into three sections, some of which have more than one part. Each section or part of the test begins with a set of specific directions that include sample questions. Be sure you understand what you are to do before you begin to work on a section.

The supervisor will tell you when to start each section and when to go on to the the next section. You should work quickly but carefully. Do not spend too much time on any one question. If you finish a section early, you may review your answers on that section only. You may not go on to the next section and you may not go back to a section you have already worked on.

You will find that some of the questions are more difficult than others, but you should try to answer every one. Your score will be based on the number of correct answers you give. If you are not sure of the correct answer to a question, make the best guess that you can. It is to your advantage to answer every question, even if you have to guess the answer.

Do not mark your answers in this test book. You must mark all of your answers on the separate answer sheet that is inside this test book. When you mark your answer to a question on your answer sheet, you must:

- Use the pencil you have been given or another medium-soft (#2 or HB) black lead pencil.
- Carefully and completely blacken the oval corresponding to the answer you choose for each question. Be sure to mark your answer in the row with the same number as the number of the question you are answering.
- Mark only one answer to each question.
- Completely fill the oval with a heavy, dark mark so that you cannot see the letter inside the oval. Light or partial marks may not be read properly by the scoring machine.
- Erase all extra marks completely and thoroughly. If you change your mind about an answer after you have marked it on your answer sheet, completely erase your old answer and then mark your new answer.

The examples below show you the correct and wrong ways of marking an answer sheet. Be sure to fill in the ovals on your answer sheet the correct way.

CORRECT	WRONG	WRONG	WRONG	WRONG

Some or all of the passages for this test have been adapted from published material to provide the examinee with significant problems for analysis and evaluation. To make the passages suitable for testing purposes, the style, content, or point of view of the original may have been altered in some cases. The ideas contained in the passages do not necessarily represent the opinions of the TOEFL Policy Council or Educational Testing Service.

679877
VV23P5.6 pp.25 qtn.150
Printed In U.S.A.

Print your
full name here _____
(last)   (first)   (middle)

TEST OF ENGLISH AS
A FOREIGN LANGUAGE

Read the directions on the back cover.

**Do not break the seals
until you are told to do so.**

This test book was used at the May 14, 1983,
TOEFL administration. It is distributed by the
TOEFL program office only to examinees who
took the test on May 14, 1983.

1 · 1 · 1 · 1 · 1 · 1 · 1

LISTENING COMPREHENSION

In this section of the test, you will have an opportunity to demonstrate your ability to understand spoken English. There are three parts to this section, with special directions for each part.

Part A

Directions: For each question in Part A, you will hear a short statement. The statements will be spoken just one time. They will not be written out for you, and you must listen carefully to understand what the speaker says.

After you hear a statement, read the four sentences in your test book, marked (A), (B), (C), and (D), and decide which one is closest in meaning to the statement you heard. Then, on your answer sheet, find the number of the question and blacken the space that corresponds to the letter of the answer you have chosen so that the letter inside the oval cannot be seen.

Example I

Sample Answer

You will hear:

● Ⓑ Ⓒ Ⓓ

You will read: (A) John does better in his studies than James.
(B) James is bigger than his brother John.
(C) John has only one brother.
(D) The teacher likes James better than John.

Sentence (A), "John does better in his studies than James," means most nearly the same as the statement "John is a better student than his brother James." Therefore, you should choose answer (A).

Example II

Sample Answer

You will hear:

Ⓐ Ⓑ ● Ⓓ

You will read: (A) The traffic isn't bad today.
(B) The trucks weigh a lot.
(C) There are a lot of trucks on the highway.
(D) The highway has been closed to heavy trucks.

Sentence (C), "There are a lot of trucks on the highway," is closest in meaning to the sentence "The truck traffic on this highway is so heavy I can barely see where I'm going." Therefore, you should choose answer (C).

1. (A) Go directly to the post office when class is over.
   (B) Let's first straighten up the classroom and then go to the post office.
   (C) That's the most direct way to the post office from our class.
   (D) The post office is straight ahead of the classroom building.

2. (A) I don't think that algebra is hard.
   (B) I like algebra better than geometry.
   (C) Geometry isn't difficult for me.
   (D) Geometry is easier for me than algebra.

GO ON TO THE NEXT PAGE

-2-

3. (A) Greg believed he could do it alone.
   (B) Greg thought he'd cut himself.
   (C) Greg thought he was selfish.
   (D) Greg alone believed it could be done.

4. (A) After it rained, he washed his car.
   (B) He was unable to wash his car because it was raining.
   (C) It began to rain right after he washed his car.
   (D) He had to finish washing his car in the rain.

5. (A) Don't make noise in the kitchen.
   (B) You may not cook here.
   (C) They were quiet when they ate.
   (D) These are homemade cookies.

6. (A) You should call Margaret soon.
   (B) Margaret will be better later on.
   (C) It's too late to call on Margaret now.
   (D) Margaret is the best person to tell.

7. (A) He never walks to the library at night.
   (B) There is only one librarian here at night.
   (C) The library is the only place to study.
   (D) He never works in the library in the daytime.

8. (A) How was your dinner?
   (B) Please have dinner with us.
   (C) We had dinner together.
   (D) Will there be four of us for dinner?

9. (A) Jerry dislikes the clothes he has.
   (B) Jerry doesn't like doing his laundry.
   (C) Jerry hates to take showers.
   (D) Jerry's clothes don't need ironing.

10. (A) Debbie checked with her son's doctor.
    (B) Debbie sent her son for a checkup.
    (C) Debbie paid her son's doctor.
    (D) Debbie wrote a note to the doctor's son.

11. (A) The pool was scheduled to open on Tuesday.
    (B) The pool is opening today.
    (C) The pool will open tomorrow.
    (D) The pool should be open on Saturday.

12. (A) Nelson Studios took the picture for my passport.
    (B) I studied the photograph of the port.
    (C) I took my passport to the studios.
    (D) I pass by Nelson Studios on my way to work.

13. (A) I told you to see a lot of museums.
    (B) You've taught me a great deal here.
    (C) People say that you know this place well.
    (D) Many museums are like this one, you know.

14. (A) I'd expected Linda to give a performance.
    (B) Linda hadn't been expecting to perform.
    (C) I'd expected Linda to do things differently.
    (D) Linda had expected me to be there.

GO ON TO THE NEXT PAGE ▶

15. (A) You'll probably finish in time to help Dorothy.
    (B) Dorothy would be a great help to you.
    (C) Dorothy won't finish without your help.
    (D) There's no time for Dorothy to help you.

16. (A) I have no supplies.
    (B) I just left the supply store.
    (C) I just found a supply.
    (D) I went out to get supplies.

17. (A) You don't think the seminar is fascinating, do you?
    (B) The seminar will continue while we are eating.
    (C) I find the seminar extremely interesting.
    (D) The dissemination of information is fast, isn't it?

18. (A) She didn't use the record player afterwards.
    (B) She didn't play all her old records.
    (C) She bought the same kind of record player.
    (D) She kept her old record player.

19. (A) The encyclopedias were on order.
    (B) The encyclopedias weren't checked out.
    (C) The encyclopedias weren't any good.
    (D) The encyclopedias were improperly arranged.

20. (A) We broke two cups.
    (B) We left at two o'clock.
    (C) We divided into two groups.
    (D) We met two people.

Part B

Directions: In Part B you will hear short conversations between two speakers. At the end of each conversation, a third voice will ask a question about what was said. The question will be spoken just one time. After you hear a conversation and the question about it, read the four possible answers in your test book and decide which one is the best answer to the question you heard. Then, on your answer sheet, find the number of the question and blacken the space that corresponds to the letter of the answer you have chosen.

Example I   Sample Answer

You will hear: Ⓐ Ⓑ Ⓒ ●

You will read: (A) Read a book.
                 (B) Write a composition.
                 (C) Talk about a problem.
                 (D) Listen to the radio.

From the conversation you know that the assignment is to listen to a radio program and be ready to talk about it. The best answer, then, is (D), "Listen to the radio." Therefore, you should choose answer (D).

GO ON TO THE NEXT PAGE

21. (A) In a department store.
    (B) In a bank.
    (C) At a tourist bureau.
    (D) At a hotel.

22. (A) Eat before seeing the movie.
    (B) See the movie immediately.
    (C) Get the first theater seat.
    (D) Stay in town for a while.

23. (A) The winter has just begun.
    (B) Once it starts, it'll snow a lot.
    (C) They're ready for the snow.
    (D) It has been snowing for some
        time.

24. (A) Traveling a lot.
    (B) Getting a lot of exercise.
    (C) Working too hard.
    (D) Waiting for the train.

25. (A) He can't find his new building.
    (B) He had a bigger apartment
        before.
    (C) He's not accustomed to the large
        building.
    (D) He's having a hard time finding
        an apartment.

26. (A) Find the trouble.
    (B) Carry the parts outside.
    (C) Practice working together.
    (D) Follow the directions.

27. (A) He fixes bicycles.
    (B) He raises sheep.
    (C) He sells chairs.
    (D) He's a gardener.

28. (A) It doesn't matter which color the
        man chooses.
    (B) It's a difficult decision.
    (C) She doesn't like either color.
    (D) The man should choose a
        different room.

29. (A) She'd like the store to send it
        to her.
    (B) It will arrive next week.
    (C) It must be wrapped quickly.
    (D) She'll take it with her to save
        trouble.

30. (A) They want to go downtown.
    (B) He wants to go to the park, but
        she doesn't.
    (C) He doesn't know where to park
        the car.
    (D) He wants to find out the
        location of the park.

31. (A) Try a new ribbon.
    (B) Help her type the paper.
    (C) Get another typewriter.
    (D) Change the paper.

32. (A) Tom is unable to hear well.
    (B) Tom didn't say anything at the
        meeting.
    (C) Tom doesn't listen to him.
    (D) Tom went out before the
        meeting was over.

33. (A) Help fill up the boxes.
    (B) Take some of the boxes.
    (C) Look for something else.
    (D) Make sure her hands are clean.

34. (A) He wants the others to follow
        him.
    (B) He must study the animals he
        caught.
    (C) He will catch up with them later.
    (D) He is behind in his schoolwork.

35. (A) You should believe everything
        you read.
    (B) She thinks the book is excellent.
    (C) She wonders which newspaper
        he reads.
    (D) Reaction to the book has been
        varied.

GO ON TO THE NEXT PAGE

Part C

Directions: In this part of the test, you will hear several short talks and conversations. After each talk or conversation, you will be asked some questions. The talks and questions will be spoken just one time. They will not be written out for you, so you will have to listen carefully to understand what the speaker says.

After you hear a question, read the four possible answers in your test book and decide which one is the best answer to the question you heard. Then, on your answer sheet, find the number of the question and blacken the space that corresponds to the letter of the answer you have chosen.

> Listen to this sample talk.

> You will hear:

> Now look at the following example.

> You will hear:

> You will read: (A) By plane.
> (B) By ship.
> (C) By train.
> (D) By bus.

Sample Answer

(A) ● (C) (D)

The best answer to the question "How did people generally arrive at Ellis Island?" is (B), "By ship." Therefore, you should choose answer (B).

> Now look at the next example.

> You will hear:

> You will read: (A) New immigrants.
> (B) International traders.
> (C) Fishermen.
> (D) Tourists.

Sample Answer

(A) (B) (C) ●

The best answer to the question "Who visits Ellis Island today?" is (D), "Tourists." Therefore, you should choose answer (D).

36. (A) At a telephone laboratory.
    (B) At the library.
    (C) On Martha's Vineyard.
    (D) In a lecture hall.

37. (A) It was settled more than
         300 years ago.
    (B) Alexander Graham Bell visited
         there.
    (C) A large number of its residents
         were deaf.
    (D) Each family living there had
         many children.

38. (A) They inherited deafness.
    (B) An epidemic struck the island.
    (C) The climate caused hearing loss.
    (D) It was an unlucky place.

39. (A) Two.
    (B) Seventeen.
    (C) Twenty-five.
    (D) Forty.

GO ON TO THE NEXT PAGE

78

40. (A) Establish his laboratory.
    (B) Have a vacation.
    (C) Study deafness among the families.
    (D) Visit members of his family.

41. (A) The patterns of marriage have changed.
    (B) Many deaf people have regained their hearing.
    (C) Most of the original population has left the island.
    (D) The island has become famous for its research facilities.

42. (A) San Francisco.
    (B) Forest fires.
    (C) Redwood trees.
    (D) Survival skills.

43. (A) In Muir Woods.
    (B) Near Los Angeles.
    (C) In San Francisco.
    (D) Along the northern California coast.

44. (A) It has no admission fee.
    (B) It is near San Francisco.
    (C) It has a good view of the coast.
    (D) It can be seen in one hour.

45. (A) 350 years.
    (B) 400 years.
    (C) 800 years.
    (D) 2,000 years.

46. (A) Absence of natural enemies.
    (B) Resistant bark and damp climate.
    (C) Coastal isolation.
    (D) Cool weather and daily fog.

47. (A) Book catalogers.
    (B) People shelving books.
    (C) People reading magazines.
    (D) Students doing research.

48. (A) Very shortly.
    (B) After everyone has finished.
    (C) Tomorrow night.
    (D) In a few days.

49. (A) Close their test books now.
    (B) Return the next day to finish.
    (C) Put books back where they belong.
    (D) Check to see if they have their books.

50. (A) They can be taken out overnight.
    (B) They will be held overnight.
    (C) They need to be returned now.
    (D) They are on a special shelf.

THIS IS THE END OF THE LISTENING COMPREHENSION SECTION OF THE TEST.

THE NEXT PART OF THE TEST IS SECTION 2. TURN TO THE
DIRECTIONS FOR SECTION 2 IN YOUR TEST BOOK,
READ THEM, AND BEGIN WORK.
DO NOT READ OR WORK ON ANY OTHER SECTION OF THE TEST.

STOP STOP STOP **STOP** STOP STOP STOP

SECTION 2

STRUCTURE AND WRITTEN EXPRESSION

Time—25 minutes

This section is designed to measure your ability to recognize language that is appropriate for standard written English. There are two types of questions in this section, with special directions for each type.

Directions: Questions 1-15 are incomplete sentences. Four words or phrases, marked (A), (B), (C), and (D), are given beneath each sentence. You are to choose the one word or phrase that best completes the sentence. Then, on your answer sheet, find the number of the question and blacken the space that corresponds to the letter of the answer you have chosen so that the letter inside the oval cannot be seen.

Example I

Mt. Hood ------- in the state of Oregon.

(A) although
(B) and
(C) is
(D) which

Sample Answer

Ⓐ Ⓑ ● Ⓓ

In English, the sentence should read, "Mt. Hood is in the state of Oregon." Therefore, you should choose (C).

Example II

------- most important event in San Francisco's history was the disastrous earthquake and fire of 1906.

(A) The
(B) It was the
(C) That the
(D) There was a

Sample Answer

● Ⓑ Ⓒ Ⓓ

In English, the sentence should read, "The most important event in San Francisco's history was the disastrous earthquake and fire of 1906." Therefore, you should choose (A).

As soon as you understand the directions, begin work on the questions.

1. Conifers first appeared on the Earth ------- the early Permian period, some 270 million years ago.

(A) when
(B) or
(C) and
(D) during

2. There are very few areas in the world ------- be grown successfully.

(A) where apricots can
(B) apricots can
(C) apricots that can
(D) where can apricots

3. ------- a baby turtle is hatched, it must be able to fend for itself.

(A) Not sooner than
(B) No sooner
(C) So soon that
(D) As soon as

GO ON TO THE NEXT PAGE

4. Tungsten, a gray metal with the
   -------, is used to form the wires in
   electric light bulbs.

   (A) point at which it melts is the
       highest of any metal
   (B) melting point is the highest of
       any metal
   (C) highest melting point of any
       metal
   (D) metal's highest melting point
       of any

5. Rattan comes from ------- of different
   kinds of palms.

   (A) its reedy stems
   (B) the reedy stems
   (C) the stems are reedy
   (D) stems that are reedy

6. At thirteen ------- at a district school
   near her home, and when she was
   fifteen, she saw her first article in
   print.

   (A) the first teaching position that
       Mary Jane Hawes had
   (B) the teaching position was Mary
       Jane Hawes' first
   (C) when Mary Jane Hawes had her
       first teaching position
   (D) Mary Jane Hawes had her first
       teaching position

7. Vitamin C, discovered in 1932, -------
   first vitamin for which the molecular
   structure was established.

   (A) the
   (B) was the
   (C) as the
   (D) being the

8. The behavior of gases is explained by
   ------- the kinetic theory.

   (A) what scientists call
   (B) what do scientists call
   (C) scientists they call
   (D) scientists call it

9. Ironically, sails were the salvation of
   many steamships ------- mechanical
   failures.

   (A) they suffered
   (B) suffered
   (C) were suffered
   (D) that had suffered

10. ------- some mammals came to live in
    the sea is not known.

    (A) Which
    (B) Since
    (C) Although
    (D) How

11. ------- their nests well, but also build
    them well.

    (A) Not only brown thrashers
        protect
    (B) Protect not only brown
        thrashers
    (C) Brown thrashers not only
        protect
    (D) Not only protect brown
        thrashers

12. The name Nebraska comes from the
    Oto Indian word "nebrathka," -------
    flat water.

    (A) to mean
    (B) meaning
    (C) it means
    (D) by meaning

13. Biochemists use fireflies to study
    bioluminescence, -------.

    (A) the heatless light given off by
        certain plants and animals
    (B) certain plants and animals give
        off the heatless light
    (C) which certain plants and animals
        give off the heatless light
    (D) is the heatless light given off by
        certain plants and animals

14. Rich tobacco and champion race
    horses have ------- of Kentucky.

    (A) long been symbols
    (B) been long symbols
    (C) symbols been long
    (D) long symbols been

15. Today's libraries differ greatly from
    -------.

    (A) the past
    (B) those of the past
    (C) that are past
    (D) those past

GO ON TO THE NEXT PAGE

-10-

81

Directions: In questions 16-40 each sentence has four words or phrases underlined. The four underlined parts of the sentence are marked (A), (B), (C), and (D). You are to identify the one underlined word or phrase that should be corrected or rewritten. Then, on your answer sheet, find the number of the question and blacken the space that corresponds to the letter of the answer you have chosen.

Example I

Much federal and industrial experts
  A
are certain that meat shortages will
     B   C
cause an enormous increase in the
           D
consumption of fish and other

sea products.

Sample Answer

● Ⓑ Ⓒ Ⓓ

Answer (A), the underlined word much, would not be accepted in carefully written English; the word many is used with the plural experts. Therefore, the sentence should read, "Many federal and industrial experts are certain that meat shortages will cause an enormous increase in the consumption of fish and other sea products." To answer the question correctly, you would choose (A).

Example II

It was during the 1920's that the
            A
friendship between Hemingway and
      B
Fitzgerald reached their highest point.
         C   D

Sample Answer

Ⓐ Ⓑ ● Ⓓ

Answer (C), the underlined word their, would not be accepted in carefully written English; the singular form its should be used because friendship is singular. Therefore, the sentence should read, "It was during the 1920's that the friendship between Hemingway and Fitzgerald reached its highest point." To answer the question correctly, you should choose (C).

As soon as you understand the directions, begin work on the questions.

16. Edna Ferber told the story of her life in two book.
              A   B   C   D

17. The period of a quarantine depends to the amount of time necessary for protection
          A   B   C
against the spread of a particular disease.
   D

18. By 1642 all towns in the colony of Massachusetts was required by law to have schools.
   A   B   C   D

GO ON TO THE NEXT PAGE

19. The bobwhite is the kind only of quail native to the area east of the Mississippi River.
      ___A___ ___B___   ___C___ ___D___

20. June bugs they often cause damage by stripping the young leaves from trees and shrubs.
             ___A___   ___B___   ___C___   ___D___

21. Since beginning of photography, inventors have tried to make photographs that duplicate
      ___A___   ___B___ ___C___
natural colors.
   ___D___

22. Artificial rubies and sapphires have the same hard and composition as the real stones.
   ___A___   ___B___ ___C___   ___D___

23. Although they sleep most of the winter, chipmunks are very active in summer when they
   ___A___   ___B___
gather and carry food in their cheek pouches and storing it underground.
                        ___C___   ___D___

24. Manufacturers use both chemical or mechanical methods to obtain clear glue.
   ___A___   ___B___   ___C___   ___D___

25. The eel larva looks alike a thin willow leaf and is as transparent as glass.
                     ___A___   ___B___ ___C___   ___D___

26. The sun has always been a important guide to direction.
   ___A___ ___B___   ___C___   ___D___

27. The manner in which fuel enters a diesel engine is the primary factor that affects its
                  ___A___   ___B___   ___C___
efficiently.
   ___D___

28. Traces of radon are found in the air in various amounts, according the weather.
                  ___A___   ___B___ ___C___   ___D___

29. Basic knowledge of mathematic and electronics was used to develop the high-speed
   ___A___   ___B___   ___C___
electronic computer.
   ___D___

30. The field of guidance and counseling was still in its infancy in 1914 when Orie Hatcher
                        ___A___   ___B___   ___C___
entered them.
        ___D___

GO ON TO THE NEXT PAGE

31. There are vineyards in California that product some of the best wine in the world.
    A   B   C   D

32. The formation of snow must be occurring slowly, in calm air, and at a temperature
                          A   B
    near the freezing point.
     C   D

33. Thomas Jefferson skillfully organized his supporter in Congress into a strong
                     A   B   C   D
    political group.

34. The greenest and plentifulest leaves are the leaves of grasses.
        A   B   C   D

35. W. H. Auden's subtle use of everyday "nonpoetic" language and conversational
                               A   B
    rhythms great influenced modern poetry.
          C   D

36. Long before the dawn of recorded history, humans celebrated to harvest their crops.
    A   B   C   D

37. In 1931, Duke Ellington broke the traditional three-minutes time limit set for commercial
                            A   B   C   D
    records.

38. The basilisk lizard can run on the hind legs at speeds up to seven miles per hour.
                        A   B   C   D

39. Dairy farm is carried on in all parts of the United States.
         A   B   C   D

40. Duckbill platypuses eat to half their weight each day, and at times even more.
                        A   B   C   D

THIS IS THE END OF SECTION 2

IF YOU FINISH BEFORE TIME IS CALLED, CHECK YOUR WORK
ON SECTION 2 ONLY.
DO NOT READ OR WORK ON ANY OTHER SECTION OF THE TEST.
THE SUPERVISOR WILL TELL YOU WHEN TO BEGIN
WORK ON SECTION 3.

SECTION 3

READING COMPREHENSION AND VOCABULARY

Time—45 minutes

This section is designed to measure your ability to understand various kinds of reading materials, as well as your ability to understand the meaning and use of words. There are two types of questions in this section, with special directions for each type.

<u>Directions:</u> In questions 1-30 each sentence has a word or phrase underlined. Below each sentence are four other words or phrases, marked (A), (B), (C), and (D). You are to choose the one word or phrase that <u>best keeps the meaning</u> of the original sentence if it is substituted for the underlined word or phrase. Then, on your answer sheet, find the number of the question and blacken the space that corresponds to the letter you have chosen so that the letter inside the oval cannot be seen.

Example

The <u>ordinary</u> land snail moves at the rate of about two inches per minute.

Sample Answer

Ⓐ Ⓑ ● Ⓓ

(A) expert
(B) active
(C) common
(D) colorful

The best answer is (C) because "The common land snail moves at the rate of about two inches per minute" is closest in meaning to the original sentence, "The ordinary land snail moves at the rate of about two inches per minute." Therefore, you should choose answer (C).

As soon as you understand the directions, begin work on the questions.

1. In masculine rhyme, the <u>end</u> sounds of stressed syllables are repeated.

(A) dominant
(B) vowel
(C) hard
(D) final

2. About a <u>quarter</u> of the workers in the United States are employed in factories.

(A) third
(B) fourth
(C) tenth
(D) fifteenth

3. Bats are extremely <u>shy</u> creatures and avoid humans if at all possible.

(A) timid
(B) clean
(C) private
(D) noisy

4. Many kinds of seaweed grow along the Rhode Island <u>seashore.</u>

(A) bank
(B) coast
(C) canal
(D) gulf

5. Academic records from other institutions often become part of a university's official file and can neither be returned to a student nor <u>duplicated.</u>

(A) borrowed
(B) purchased
(C) copied
(D) rewritten

GO ON TO THE NEXT PAGE

6. Ammonia, one of the earliest known nitrogen compounds, was originally produced by distilling organic <u>materials</u>.

(A) masses
(B) fabrics
(C) substances
(D) liquids

7. Loud noises can be <u>annoying</u>.

(A) hateful
(B) painful
(C) unnerving
(D) irritating

8. The <u>sensation</u> of a "lump in one's throat" arises from an increased flow of blood into the tissues of the pharynx and larynx.

(A) explanation
(B) disease
(C) feeling
(D) unpleasantness

9. The <u>apparently</u> homogeneous Dakota grasslands are actually a botanical garden of more than 400 types of grasses.

(A) seemingly
(B) comparatively
(C) dazzlingly
(D) strangely

10. Photojournalist Margaret Bourke-White became famous for her <u>coverage</u> of significant events during the Second World War.

(A) usage
(B) camouflage
(C) collage
(D) reportage

11. Almost all economists agree that nations <u>gain</u> by trading with one another.

(A) cooperate
(B) profit
(C) become more stable
(D) become more dependent

12. The Cheyenne Indians were considered spectacular riders and fierce <u>warriors</u>.

(A) hunters
(B) defenders
(C) enemies
(D) fighters

13. It has been suggested that people who watch television <u>incessantly</u> may become overly passive.

(A) seriously
(B) skeptically
(C) constantly
(D) arbitrarily

14. While serving in the Senate in the early 1970's, Barbara Jordan supported legislation to <u>ban</u> discrimination and to <u>deal with</u> environmental problems.

(A) list
(B) forbid
(C) handle
(D) investigate

15. Aneroid barometers are able to show much <u>slighter</u> changes in the atmosphere than mercury barometers.

(A) smaller
(B) thinner
(C) more sudden
(D) more narrow

16. In a bullfight, it is the movement, not the color, of objects that <u>arouses</u> the bull.

(A) confuses
(B) excites
(C) scares
(D) diverts

GO ON TO THE NEXT PAGE

17. Sleep is associated with characteristic electrical <u>rhythms</u> in the brain.

    (A) cells
    (B) cues
    (C) shocks
    (D) patterns

18. Philip Roth was <u>hailed</u> as a major new author in 1960.

    (A) published
    (B) challenged
    (C) acclaimed
    (D) guided

19. Below 600 feet, ocean waters range from <u>dimly</u> lit to completely dark.

    (A) perversely
    (B) erratically
    (C) faintly
    (D) sufficiently

20. During their <u>heyday</u>, showboats were popular and <u>generally</u> prosperous.

    (A) golden age
    (B) infancy
    (C) summer voyages
    (D) revivals

21. Light rays are <u>turned aside</u> by the intense <u>gravitational field</u> surrounding a black hole.

    (A) heightened
    (B) deflected
    (C) rotated
    (D) created

22. The gar is a fish with a long, <u>slender</u> body and scales as hard as flint.

    (A) flat
    (B) straight
    (C) slim
    (D) fragile

23. Francis Scott Key wrote the words to "The Star-spangled Banner" after <u>witnessing</u> the unsuccessful attack on Fort McHenry.

    (A) participating in
    (B) observing
    (C) hearing about
    (D) resisting

24. Human facial expressions differ from those of animals in the degree to which they can be <u>deliberately</u> controlled and modified.

    (A) both
    (B) noticeably
    (C) intentionally
    (D) absolutely

25. If wool is submerged in hot water, it tends to <u>shrink</u>.

    (A) smell
    (B) fade
    (C) unravel
    (D) contract

26. The Constitution's <u>vague</u> nature has given it the flexibility to be adapted when circumstances change.

    (A) imprecise
    (B) diffuse
    (C) unpolished
    (D) elementary

GO ON TO THE NEXT PAGE

27. In the eighteenth century the heading of "natural philosophy" encompassed all of the sciences.

    (A) category
    (B) teachings
    (C) ideology
    (D) leaders

28. By today's standards, early farmers were imprudent because they planted the same crop repeatedly, exhausting the soil after a few harvests.

    (A) unwise
    (B) stubborn
    (C) tiresome
    (D) unscientific

29. The first step in planning a marketing strategy for a new product is to analyze the breakdown of sales figures for competitive products.

    (A) decrease in
    (B) reordering of
    (C) itemization of
    (D) collapse in

30. Georgia was colonized by a group of debtors from British prisons.

    (A) discovered
    (B) explored
    (C) settled
    (D) visited

GO ON TO THE NEXT PAGE

Directions: The rest of this section is based on a variety of reading material (single sentences, paragraphs, and the like) followed by questions about the meaning of the material. For questions 31-60, you are to choose the one best answer, (A), (B), (C), or (D), to each question. Then, on your answer sheet, find the number of the question and blacken the space that corresponds to the letter of the answer you have chosen.

Answer all questions following a passage on the basis of what is stated or implied in that passage.

Read the following passage.

Despite all the atrocities falsely attributed to it, the gorilla is essentially a peace loving creature that would rather retreat than fight except when its life is threatened and retreat is impossible. In the wild it has never been seen eating meat, although some have learned to do so in captivity. Nor do gorillas seem to drink water in the wild; they apparently get what moisture they need from their diet of greenery and fruit.

Example I

Gorillas have been known to eat meat only when they are

Sample Answer

● Ⓑ Ⓒ Ⓓ

(A) in captivity
(B) in the wild
(C) engaged in fighting
(D) hiding from enemies

The passage says that some gorillas have learned to eat meat in captivity. Therefore, you should choose answer (A).

Example II

Gorillas obtain most of the moisture they need from

Sample Answer

Ⓐ ● Ⓒ Ⓓ

(A) meat
(B) leaves and fruit
(C) small streams
(D) raids

The passage says that gorillas "apparently get what moisture they need from their diet of greenery and fruit." Therefore, you should choose (B) as the best completion of the sentence.

As soon as you understand the directions, begin work on the questions.

GO ON TO THE NEXT PAGE

Questions 31-34

Each variety of mosquito has its favored kind of water accumulation for breeding, and almost every imaginable type of still water has been used by at least one kind of mosquito to lay its eggs. After the eggs hatch, the larvae continue to be closely associated with the water's surface, hanging from the surface film and getting air through tubes that breaks the water's surface at the tail ends of their bodies. Because the larvae develop this way, they are never found in the open water of lakes where they would merely serve as fish food, or in places where they would be damaged by wave action or water currents.

31. According to the passage, what is true about the breeding habits of mosquitoes?

(A) Different mosquitoes tend to have different kinds of breeding places.
(B) Each mosquito usually breeds in several different places in one season.
(C) A few mosquitoes constantly vary their breeding places.
(D) Most mosquitoes mate in the same place in which they were bred.

32. According to the passage, most mosquito larvae develop

(A) on plants near water
(B) near sources of food
(C) under waterproof sacs
(D) in bodies of still water

33. According to the passage, most mosquito larvae breathe with

(A) their wings
(B) special tubes
(C) their gills
(D) modified mouths

34. According to the passage, mosquito larvae are never found in open water because they cannot

(A) withstand much motion
(B) find sufficient food there
(C) obtain enough air there
(D) tolerate too much moisture

GO ON TO THE NEXT PAGE

Questions 35-42

Decades before the American Revolution of 1776, Jesse Fish, a native New Yorker, retreated to an island off St. Augustine, Florida, to escape an unpleasant family situation. In time he became Florida's first orange baron and his oranges were in great demand in London throughout the 1770's. The English found them juicy and sweet and preferred them to other varieties, even though they had thin skins and were hard to peel.

There would probably have been other successful commercial growers before Fish if Florida had not been under Spanish rule for some two hundred years. Columbus first brought seeds for citrus trees to the New World and planted them in the Antilles. But it was most likely Ponce de León who introduced oranges to the North American continent when he discovered Florida in 1513. For a time, each Spanish sailor on a ship bound for America was required by law to carry one hundred seeds with him. Later, because seeds tended to dry out, all Spanish ships were required to carry young orange trees. The Spaniards planted citrus trees only for medicinal purposes, however. They saw no need to start commercial groves because oranges were so abundant in Spain.

35. What is the main topic of the passage?

(A) The role of Florida in the American Revolution
(B) The discovery of Florida by Ponce de León in 1513
(C) The history of the cultivation of oranges in Florida
(D) The popularity of Florida oranges in London in the 1770's

36. Jesse Fish came from

(A) London
(B) St. Augustine
(C) the Antilles
(D) New York

37. Jesse Fish went to Florida to

(A) grow oranges commercially
(B) buy an island off St. Augustine
(C) get away from his family
(D) work for the British government

38. Londoners liked the oranges grown by Jesse Fish because they

(A) had a lot of juice
(B) were not too sweet
(C) were not hard to peel
(D) had thin skins

39. Oranges were most probably introduced to Florida by

(A) Jesse Fish
(B) Ponce de León
(C) Columbus
(D) British sailors

40. According to the passage, Spanish vessels began to bring orange tree seedlings to North America when

(A) the United States agricultural laws were revised
(B) ambitious sailors began to smuggle seeds
(C) doctors reported a lack of medical supplies
(D) authorities realized that seeds did not travel well

41. According to the passage, Florida oranges were valued by the Spanish primarily

(A) as a medium of exchange
(B) for their unusual seeds
(C) for their medical use
(D) as a source of food for sailors

42. The Spaniards did not grow oranges commercially in the New World because

(A) oranges tended to dry out during shipping
(B) Florida oranges were very small
(C) there was no great demand for oranges in Europe
(D) oranges were plentiful in their home country

GO ON TO THE NEXT PAGE ➤

Questions 43-46

The very success of communications satellite systems has raised widespread concern about their future. Some countries are already using satellites for domestic communications in place of conventional telephone lines on land. Although this technique is extremely useful for linking widely scattered villages in remote or mountainous regions, in heavily built-up areas where extensive telephone and telegraph systems already exist domestic satellites (or "domsats") are seen by the land-line networks as unfair competition. Despite such opposition, domsats are gaining support from many businesses and public interest groups in the United States and seem likely to be more widely utilized in the future.

43. The passage mentions which of the following as a major advantage of domsats?

(A) They are inexpensive to operate.
(B) They easily connect distant points.
(C) They can be directed by remote control.
(D) They can be built to be very light.

44. According to the passage, the use of domsats is especially valuable for which of the following?

(A) Mountain areas
(B) Busy cities
(C) Small countries
(D) Private businesses

45. Who objects to the use of domsats?

(A) Managers of international business groups
(B) People in small villages
(C) Operators of conventional communications systems
(D) Large public interest groups

46. According to the passage, future United States domsats will probably

(A) be produced competitively
(B) carry telephone messages only
(C) become a government monopoly
(D) increase in use

GO ON TO THE NEXT PAGE

Questions 47-53

Allelomimetic behavior may be defined as behavior in which two or more individual animals do the same thing, with some degree of mutual stimulation and coordination. It can only evolve in species with sense organs that are well enough developed so that continuous sensory contact can be maintained. It is found primarily in vertebrates, in those species that are diurnal, and usually in those that spend much of their lives in the air, in open water, or on open plains.

In birds, allelomimetic behavior is the rule rather than the exception, though it may occasionally be limited to particular seasons of the year as it is in the redwing blackbird. Its principal function is that of providing safety from predators, partly because the flock can rely on many pairs of eyes to watch for enemies, and partly because if one bird reacts to danger, the whole flock is warned.

Among mammals, allelomimetic behavior is very rare in rodents, which almost never move in flocks or herds. Even when they are artificially crowded together, they do not conform in their movements. On the other hand, such behavior is a major system among large hoofed mammals such as sheep.

In the pack-hunting carnivores, allelomimetic behavior has another function, that of cooperative hunting for large prey animals such as moose. Wolves also defend their dens as a group against larger predators such as bears.

Finally, allelomimetic behavior is highly developed among most primate groups, where it has the principal function of providing warning against predators, though combined defensive behavior is also seen in troops of baboons.

47. The main topic of the passage is the

    (A) value of allelomimetic behavior in vertebrate and invertebrate species
    (B) definition and distribution of allelomimetic behavior
    (C) relationship of allelomimetic behavior to the survival of the fittest
    (D) personality factors that determine when an individual animal will show allelomimetic behavior

48. According to the passage, the primary function of allelomimetic behavior in birds is to

    (A) defend nests against predators
    (B) look at each other
    (C) locate prey
    (D) warn others of predators

49. Which of the following places is the most likely setting for allelomimetic behavior?

    (A) A lake
    (B) A cave
    (C) An underground tunnel
    (D) A thick forest

50. According to the passage, what happens to the behavior of rodents when they are artificially crowded together?

    (A) Their allelomimetic behavior increases.
    (B) Continuous cooperation between them is maintained.
    (C) They become aggressive and attack each other.
    (D) They show little allelomimetic behavior.

GO ON TO THE NEXT PAGE

51. The author implies that allelomimetic behavior occurs most often among animals that

    (A) prey on other animals
    (B) are less intelligent than their enemies
    (C) move in groups
    (D) have one sense organ that dominates perception

52. Which of the following is most clearly an example of allelomimetic behavior?

    (A) Bears hunting for carnivores
    (B) Cattle fleeing from a fire
    (C) Horses running at a racetrack
    (D) Dogs working with police officers

53. Which of the following groups of human beings would probably show the greatest amount of allelomimetic behavior?

    (A) A group of students taking a test
    (B) Tennis players competing in a tournament
    (C) A patrol of soldiers scouting for the enemy
    (D) Drivers waiting for a traffic light to change

GO ON TO THE NEXT PAGE

Questions 54-60

Criticism of research lays a significant foundation for future investigative work, but when students begin their own projects, they are likely to find that the standards of validity in field work are considerably more rigorous than the standards for most library research. When students are faced with the concrete problem of proof by field demonstration, they usually discover that many of the "important relationships" they may have criticized other researchers for failing to demonstrate are very elusive indeed. They will find, if they submit an outline or questionnaire to their classmates for criticism, that other students make comments similar to some they themselves may have made in discussing previously published research. For example, student researchers are likely to begin with a general question but find themselves forced to narrow its focus. They may learn that questions whose meanings seem perfectly obvious to them are not clearly understood by others, or that questions which seemed entirely objective to them appear to be highly biased to someone else. They usually find that the formulation of good research questions is a much more subtle and frustrating task than is generally believed by those who have not actually attempted it.

54. What does the author think about trying to find weaknesses in other people's research?

(A) It should only be attempted by experienced researchers.

(B) It may cause researchers to avoid publishing good work.

(C) It is currently being done to excess.

(D) It can be useful in planning future research.

55. According to the passage, what is one major criticism students often make of published research?

(A) The research has not been written in an interesting way.

(B) The research has been done in unimportant fields.

(C) The researchers did not adequately establish the relationships involved.

(D) The researchers failed to provide an appropriate summary.

56. According to the passage, how do students in class often react to another student's research?

(A) They react the way they do to any other research.

(B) They are especially critical of the quality of the research.

(C) They offer unusually good suggestions for improving the work.

(D) They show a lot of sympathy for the student researcher.

GO ON TO THE NEXT PAGE

57. According to the passage, what do student researchers often learn when they discuss their work in class?

    (A) Other students rarely have objective comments about it.
    (B) Other students do not believe the researchers did the work themselves.
    (C) Some students feel that the conclusions are too obvious.
    (D) Some students do not understand the meaning of the researchers' questions.

58. According to the passage, student researchers may have to change their research projects because

    (A) their budgets are too high
    (B) their original questions are too broad
    (C) their teachers do not give adequate advice
    (D) their time is very limited

59. What does the author conclude about preparing suitable questions for a research project?

    (A) It is more difficult than the student researcher may realize.
    (B) The researcher should get help from other people.
    (C) The questions should be brief so that they will be understood.
    (D) It is important to follow formulas closely.

60. What does this passage mainly discuss?

    (A) The decreasing emphasis on library research
    (B) How to publish controversial questionnaires
    (C) The role of criticism in new research
    (D) How to submit an outline for criticism

THIS IS THE END OF SECTION 3

IF YOU FINISH BEFORE TIME IS CALLED, CHECK YOUR WORK
ON SECTION 3 ONLY.
DO NOT READ OR WORK ON ANY OTHER SECTION OF THE TEST.

STOP STOP STOP STOP STOP STOP STOP

NOTICE TO TOEFL EXAMINEES

If you took TOEFL on the test date shown below, you may order a copy of the answer key (a list of the correct answers for the questions in the test), a copy of your completed answer sheet, and a cassette recording of Section 1 (listening comprehension). These materials will be available for only a limited time after the test date; this service is subject to change without notice.

HOW TO ORDER

To order these materials, you must complete the order form and mailing slip below. PRINT or TYPE all the required information. The form will be returned to you if you do not give complete information or if you do not enclose the correct fee.

Detach the order form and mail it and the correct payment (or receipt, if you pay by bank draft) to TOEFL, Box 2877, Princeton, NJ 08541, USA. Your materials will be mailed to the address you give on the form.

Materials requested soon after the test date shown on the order form will be mailed about sixty days after that date (they cannot be mailed earlier). Orders received more than sixty days after the test date may take up to thirty additional days to be filled. This order form will not be accepted after:

SEPTEMBER 13, 1983.

FEE

If your mailing address is in the United States (including its territories and possessions), Puerto Rico, or Canada, the fee for the materials is US$10. For addresses in all other countries, the fee is US$12.

DETACH HERE.

- -

TOEFL Test Materials Order Form

This form may be used only for the following test date:

MAY 14, 1983

Enclosed:
☐ US$10
☐ US$12

Application
Number: _____

Test Center
Number: _____

Name: _____
       Family Name (Surname)   First Name   Middle Name

Birth Date: __/__/__ Signature: _____

Name: _____

Address: _____

_____

_____

Do Not Detach Mailing Slip.

TOEFL
Box 2877
Princeton, NJ 08541, USA

AIR MAIL
575-52

Your Name: _____

Your Address: _____

_____

_____

YOUR TOEFL TEST MATERIALS ARE ENCLOSED.

TEST OF ENGLISH AS A FOREIGN LANGUAGE
SCRIPT FOR THE LISTENING COMPREHENSION SECTION

(MA) In a moment, you are going to hear an introductory statement by the three people who recorded this test. The purpose of this introduction is to give the proctor an opportunity to adjust the recording equipment or make changes in your seating arrangement before the actual test begins. Now listen carefully to the statement by each of the speakers whom you will hear on the test.

(Spoken in turn by MB, W, and MA) Flight number 53 to Paris will depart from gate six at 9:30 p.m. Will all passengers holding tickets kindly proceed to gate six at this time. Thank you. (5 second pause).

Now open your test book. Read the directions in your test book as you listen to the directions on the recording. (8 seconds)

LISTENING COMPREHENSION

In this section of the test, you will have an opportunity to demonstrate your ability to understand spoken English. There are three parts to this section, with special directions for each part.

*Part A

Directions: For each question in Part A, you will hear a short statement. The statements will be spoken just one time. They will not be written out for you, and you must listen carefully to understand what the speaker says.

After you hear a statement, read the four sentences in your test book, marked (A), (B), (C), and (D), and decide which one is closest in meaning to the statement you heard. Then, on your answer sheet, find the number of the question and blacken the space that corresponds to the letter of the answer you have chosen so that the letter inside the oval cannot be seen.

Look at Example I.

You will hear: (W) John is a better student than his brother James.

You will read: (A) John does better in his studies than James.
(B) James is bigger than his brother John.
(C) John has only one brother.
(D) The teacher likes James better than John.

Sentence (A), "John does better in his studies than James," means most nearly the same as the statement "John is a better student than his brother James." Therefore, you should choose answer (A).

Look at Example II.

You will hear: (MB) The truck traffic on this highway is so heavy I can barely see where I'm going.

You will read: (A) The traffic isn't bad today.
(B) The trucks weigh a lot.
(C) There are a lot of trucks on the highway.
(D) The highway has been closed to heavy trucks.

Sentence (C), "There are a lot of trucks on the highway," is closest in meaning to the sentence "The truck traffic on this highway is so heavy I can barely see where I'm going." Therefore, you should choose answer (C).

Now let us begin Part A with question number one.

*Unless otherwise noted, all directions will be read by (MA).

1. (MA) After class. go straight to the post office. (12 seconds)
2. (MB) Geometry is hard for me, but algebra is harder. (12 seconds)
3. (MA) Greg thought he could do it himself. (12 seconds)
4. (W) No sooner had he finished washing his car than it started to rain. (12 seconds)
5. (MB) Cooking is not allowed in this dormitory. (12 seconds)
6. (MB) You'd better call Margaret before it gets too late. (12 seconds)
7. (W) He works in the library only at night. (12 seconds)
8. (MA) How about joining us for dinner? (12 seconds)
9. (MB) Jerry hates washing and ironing his own clothes. (12 seconds)
10. (MA) Debbie wrote a check for her son's doctor bill. (12 seconds)
11. (W) Today is Thursday and the swimming pool is supposed to open the day after tomorrow. (12 seconds)
12. (MB) I got my passport photo taken at Nelson Studios. (12 seconds)
13. (W) I was told that you know a lot about this museum. (12 seconds)
14. (MA) Linda's performance wasn't what I'd expected. (12 seconds)
Go on to the next page. (8 seconds)
15. (W) If Dorothy helped you. you'd finish in no time. (12 seconds)
16. (MB) I just ran out of supplies. (12 seconds)
17. (W) This seminar is fascinating. don't you think? (12 seconds)
18. (MB) She didn't sell her old record player after all. (12 seconds)
19. (W) The encyclopedias were out of order. (12 seconds)
20. (W) Our group broke up at two. (12 seconds)

This is the end of Part A. Now look at the directions for Part B as they are read to you.

Directions: In Part B you will hear short conversations between two speakers. At the end of each conversation. a third voice will ask a question about what was said. The questions will be spoken just one time. After you hear a conversation and the question about it, read the four possible answers in your test book and decide which one is the best answer to the question you heard. Then, on your answer sheet, find the number of the question and blacken the space that corresponds to the letter of the answer you have chosen.

Look at Example I.

You will hear: (MB) <u>Is there any assignment for next Tuesday?</u>

(W) <u>Nothing to read or write. But we're supposed to listen to a radio program and be ready to talk about it in class.</u>

(MA) <u>What have the students been asked to do before Tuesday?</u>

You will read: (A) Read a book.
(B) Write a composition.
(C) Talk about a problem.
(D) Listen to the radio.

From the conversation you know that the assignment is to listen to a radio program and be ready to talk about it. The best answer, then, is (D), "Listen to the radio." Therefore, you should choose answer (D).

Now let us begin Part B with question twenty-one.

21. (MB) Good morning, may I help you?

(W) Yes. I'd like to cash these traveler's checks first and then open a savings account.

(MA) Where does this conversation probably take place? (12 seconds)

22. (W) We really must go to the new movie in town.

(MB) Let's eat first.

(MA) What does the man want to do? (12 seconds)

23. (MB) I think it's starting to snow.

(W) <u>Starting</u> to snow! The ground's already covered!

(MA) What does the woman mean? (12 seconds)

24. (W) John seems to have lost a lot of weight recently.

(MA) Yes, he's been training hard with the soccer team.

(MB) What has John been doing? (12 seconds)

25. (W) How do you find your new apartment?

(MB) Well, it's quite nice, really, although I'm having a hard time getting used to such a big building.

(MA) What is the man's problem? (12 seconds)

26. (MA) Have you ever put one of these together before?

(MB) No, never, but I think if we carry out these instructions exactly, we won't have any trouble.

(W) What is it important for them to do? (12 seconds)

27. (MB) The front tire is flat and the seat needs to be raised.

(W) Why not take it to Mr. Smith?

(MA) What kind of work does Mr. Smith probably do? (12 seconds)

28. (MA) I haven't decided which color to paint my room—white or yellow.

(W) Isn't easy to choose, is it?

(MB) What does the woman mean? (12 seconds)

29. (MB) If you'd like to take the package with you, Miss, it won't take long to wrap.

(W) There's no rush. Could you please have it delivered this week?

(MA) What does the woman mean? (12 seconds)

30. (W)   The map shows that this street goes downtown.

   (MB)   Yes, but what we want to know is how to get to the park.

   (MA)   What does the man mean? (12 seconds)

31. (MA)   My typing isn't dark enough and the paper doesn't look good.

   (W)   Why not change the typewriter ribbon and see if that helps?

   (MB)   What does the woman advise the man to do? (12 seconds)

32. (W)   Didn't you tell Tom about the meeting?

   (MB)   Whatever I say to him goes in one ear and out the other.

   (MA)   What does the man mean? (12 seconds)

33. (W)   You look like you have your hands full. Do you need some help carrying those boxes?

   (MA)   I sure do!

   (MB)   What will the woman do? (12 seconds)

34. (W)   Are you coming with us?

   (MB)   No, I have to catch up on my zoology assignments.

   (MA)   What does the man mean? (12 seconds)

35. (MA)   I heard that the newspaper gave that book a terrible review.

   (W)   It depends on which newspaper you read. (pronounce "reed")

   (MB)   What does the woman mean? (12 seconds)

This is the end of Part B. Go on to the next page. (8 seconds) Now look at the directions for Part C as they are read to you.

Part C

Directions: In this part of the test, you will hear several short talks and conversations. After each talk or conversation, you will be asked some questions. The talks and questions will be spoken just one time. They will not be written out for you, so you will have to listen carefully to understand what the speaker says.

After you hear a question, read the four possible answers in your test book and decide which one is the best answer to the question you heard. Then, on your answer sheet, find the number of the question and blacken the space that corresponds to the letter of the answer you have chosen.

Listen to this sample talk.

You will hear: (W)   Ellis Island is closed now—to all but the tourists, that is. This island, in New York harbor, was once one of the busiest places in America. It was the first stop for all immigrants arriving by ship from Europe, Africa and western Asia. Normally, immigrants came to Ellis Island at the rate of 5,000 a day, but at times twice that many would land in a single day. Most were processed through and ferried to the mainland on the same day. A total of 15 million people came to America by way of Ellis Island. With the advent of air travel, the island fell into disuse. Today it serves only as a reminder to tourists of the heritage of modern America.

Now look at the following example.

You will hear: (MB)   How did people generally arrive at Ellis Island?

You will read: (A) By plane.
                     (B) By ship.
                     (C) By train.
                     (D) By bus.

The best answer to the question "How did people generally arrive at Ellis Island?" is (B), "By ship." Therefore, you should choose answer (B).

Now look at the next example.

You will hear: (MB) <u>Who visits Ellis Island today?</u>
You will read: (A) New immigrants.
                   (B) International traders.
                   (C) Fishermen.
                   (D) Tourists.

The best answer to the question "Who visits Ellis Island today?" is (D), "Tourists." Therefore, you should choose answer (D).

Now let us begin Part C with question number thirty-six.

(MA) <u>Questions 36-41</u> refer to the following lecture.

(W)   Good morning, students. I hope you have been able to read the two books about speech and hearing problems that I put in the library. Today's lecture deals with the presence of the unusually large deaf population that existed on the Massachusetts island of Martha's Vineyard for about three centuries. From the settlement of the island in the 1640's to the twentieth century, the people there, who were descended from only twenty-five or thirty original families, married mainly other residents of the island. They formed a highly inbred group, producing an excellent example of the genetic patterns for the inheritance of deafness. Indeed, in the late 1800's, one out of every twenty-five people in one village on the island was born deaf, and the island as a whole had a deafness rate at least seventeen times greater than that of the rest of the United States. Even Alexander Graham Bell, the inventor of the telephone and a prominent researcher into hearing loss, visited Martha's Vineyard to study the population, but because the principles of genetics and inheritance were still unknown, he was not able to explain the <u>patterns</u> of deafness, and why a deaf parent did not always have deaf children. In the twentieth century, the local population has mixed with people off the island, and the rate of deafness has fallen.

36. (MB) Where does this talk take place? (12 seconds)

37. (MB) What is unusual about the island of Martha's Vineyard? (12 seconds)

38. (MB) Why were so many people there deaf? (12 seconds)

39. (MB) The island's rate of deafness was how many times greater than that of the rest of the United States? (12 seconds)

40. (MB) What did Alexander Graham Bell hope to do when he went to the island? (12 seconds)

41. (MB) According to the talk, how has the island changed in the twentieth century? (12 seconds)

(MA) <u>Questions 42-46</u> refer to the following dialogue.

(MB)   Have you ever visited a redwood forest? I recently had a chance to go to Muir Woods National Monument north of San Francisco.

(W)   I've never seen a redwood tree. I really can't imagine how big they are.

(MB)   The coastal redwoods are the tallest living things; some are more than three hundred fifty feet high. But, none of the trees in Muir Woods is <u>that</u> tall. You have to go further north in California to see the tallest trees.

(W)   You said that Muir Woods is near San Francisco? I guess it must be quite a tourist attraction.

(MB)   Yes. It's less than an hour's drive away, so it's easy to get to.

(W)   I've heard that many redwood trees are thousands of years old. Are the ones in Muir Woods that old?

(MB)   The oldest documented age for a coastal redwood is more than two thousand years. The trees in Muir Woods are four hundred to eight hundred years old.

(W)   Why have they survived so long?

(MB)   They have remarkable resistance to forest fires. Their tough, thick bark protects the trees during a fire. The coastal redwoods also like a damp, foggy climate.

(W)   Then, since Muir Woods is near foggy San Francisco, it must be ideal for the trees' survival. I can't wait to

go there and see them!

42. (MA) What is the main subject of this conversation? (12 seconds)

43. (MA) Where can the tallest trees be found? (12 seconds)

44. (MA) Why do many tourists visit Muir Woods rather than other redwood forests? (12 seconds)

45. (MA) Approximately what is the oldest documented age for a redwood tree?   (12 seconds)

46. (MA) What has contributed most to the redwoods' survival? (12 seconds)

(MA) Questions 47-50 are based on the following announcement.

(MB)   May I have your attention please? We will be closing in a few minutes. Please return reference books

to their shelves. People who wish to check out reserve books for overnight use may do so now.

47. (W)   For whom is the announcement primarily intended? (12 seconds)

48. (W)   When will the building be closed? (12 seconds)

49. (W)   What does the man ask the people to do? (12 seconds)

50. (W)   What does the man say about reserve books? (12 seconds)

(MA) Stop work on Section 1.

End of Recording.

APPENDIX B: GENERAL OUTLINE OF COMMUNICATION SKILLS

April 1983

GENERAL OUTLINE OF COMMUNICATION SKILLS

Michael Canale, O.I.S.E., Toronto

(Prepared for the project "Discourse Skills and the TOEFL"
directed by Richard Duran, Educational Testing Service)

COMPETENCE AREA	RELEVANT MODE(S)

A. Grammatical competence

1. Pronunciation:

1.1. Lexical items in connected speech (at normal rate of speech) — L, S, R (oral)

1.2. Modifications to normal pronunciation of lexical items at word boundaries (e.g., liaison and elision) and in unstressed syllables (e.g., vowel and consonant reduction) — L, S

1.3. Normal word stress in connected speech — L, S, R (oral)

1.4. Emphatic or contrastive word stress (e.g., Mary is happy but Paul is unhappy.) — L, S. R (oral)

1.5. Normal intonation patterns in connected speech (e.g., for imperatives, interrogatives, etc.) — L, S

1.6. Emphatic of contrastive intonation patterns for different clause types (e.g., He has arrived? with rising intonation to signal an interrogative) — L, S. R (oral)

1.7. Normal pauses, loudness, and rate of speech — L, S

1.8. Modifications to normal pauses, loudness, and rate of speech for emphatic or contrastive purposes — L, S

2. Orthography:

2.1. Graphemes (individually and in sequence) — R, W

2.2. Spelling (including capitalization and diacritics) for individual lexical items — R, W

2.3. Spelling of compounds (e.g., use of hyphens, as in lion-like, level-headed and vice-president) — R, W

2.4. Spelling of contractions (e.g., can't) — R, W

2.5. Spelling of abbreviations (e.g., cont'd) — R, W

2.6. Spelling of possessive noun forms (e.g., John's) — R, W

2.7. Common punctuation conventions (e.g., capitalization at beginning of a sentence and use of commas, quotes, etc.) — R, W

105

2.8. Conventions for marking emphasis (e.g., underlining, italics, bold-face type, capitalization)   R, W

3. Vocabulary:

3.1. Literal meaning of common content words, in
context, related to academic and social topics   L, S, R, W

3.2. Literal meaning of common function words in
context (e.g., prepositions, articles)   L, S,. R, W

3.3. Meaning of idioms and formulaic expressions in
context (e.g., That test was her Little Big Horn;
Take care!)   L, S, R, W

3.4. Extended or figurative meaning of words in context
(e.g., metaphorical uses of words as in Marriage is
a business partnership)   L, S, R, W

3.5. Synonyms, antonyms, and homonyms of common content
words in context   L, S, R, W

4. Word formation:

4.1. Inflection, in context, of nouns for number   L, S, R, W

4.2. Inflection, in context, of demonstrative and
possessive adjective for number   L, S, R, W

4.3. Inflection, in context, of verbs for person,
number and tense   L, S, R, W

4.4. Agreement, in context, of pronouns with nouns   L, S, R, W

4.5. Agreement, in context, of demonstrative and
possessive adjectives with nouns and pronouns   L, S, R, W

4.6. Agreement, in context, of nouns and pronouns
with verbs (person and number for verbs,
case for pronouns)   L, S, R, W

4.7. Derivational relationships (e.g., among attacker
and attack as a verb or noun) in context   L, S, R, W

4.8. Variation at word boundaries in context (e.g.,
a and an)   L, S, R, W

5. Sentence formation:

5.1. Basic form of common sentence and subsentence
structures, in context, relevant to academic and
social language-use situation (e.g., subject -
verb - complement word order for a simple
declarative sentence)   L, S, R, W

5.2. Literal meaning of a sentence having a given
structure (with vocabulary), in context   L, S, R, W

B. Sociolinguistic competence

1. In academic and social situations that vary according
to sociolinguistic variables, such as number and status

of participants (e.g., peers, strangers, authorities), setting (e.g., formal/informal, public/private, familiar/ unfamiliar), channel (e.g., face-to-face, radio, letter, telephone), purpose (e.g., routine/unusual, open-ended/ fixed) and amount of shared information:

1.1. Grammatical forms (e.g., pronunciation, etc.) appropriate for different communicative functions, such as supplying or requesting information, persuading, seeking approval, inviting, promising, complaining, socializing   L, S, R, W

1.2. Formulaic expressions appropriate for different communicative functions (e.g., Hello/Goodbye on the telephone rather than in written communication)   L, S, R, W

1.3. Appropriate grammatical forms for signaling attitudes (e.g., politeness, sincerity, empathy, certainty, anger)   L, S, R, W

1.4. Grammatical forms as indicators of social and geographical background (e.g., dialect features)   L, S, R, W

C. Discourse competence

1. Cohesion in genres of discourse relevant to academic and social language use:

1.1. Lexical cohesion devices for:

conciseness: e.g., pronouns, synonyms

continuity: e.g., repetition of a vocabulary item

transition: e.g., logical connectors such as however

emphasis: e.g., choice of unexpected vocabulary   L, S, R, W

1.2. Grammatical cohesion devices for:

conciseness: e.g., ellipsis

continuity: e.g., parallel structures, lists

transition: e.g., transitional sentences to introduce ideas

emphasis: e.g., focusing structures, such as What is needed is...   L, S, R, W

2. Coherence in genres of discourse relevant to academic and social language use:

2.1. Conversational discourse patterns: turn-taking rules (as in a telephone conversation)   L, S

2.2. conversational discourse patterns: acceptable oganization of ideas (literal meanings and communicative functions) in conversation in terms of: development: e.g., sequencing and direction of ideas

continuity: e.g., relevance and consitency of ideas

balance: e.g., treamtent of main vs. supporting ideas

completeness: e.g., thorough discussion of a topic   L, S, R, W

2.3. nonconversational discourse patterns: acceptable organization of ideas (literal meanings and

communicative functions) in terms of:
development

continuity

balance

completeness   L, S, R, W

3. Transposing information in nonverbal/graphic form to
   and from oral and written discourse (e.g., diagrams,
   graphs, and tables)   L, S, R, W

D. Strategic competences

   1. Compensatory strategies for grammatical difficulties:

   1.1. Reference books (e.g., dictionary, grammar book)   R, W

   1.2. Reference centers (e.g., library, resource center),
        including use of index cards, knowledge of Dewey
        decimal system   R, W

   1.3. Phonetic spelling as a guide to pronunciation (e.g.,
        International Phonetic Alphabet)   S, R

   1.4. Grammatical and lexical paraphrase (e.g., use of
        general vocabulary items such as place, person,
        thing, way followed by a descriptive phrase; use
        of structures such as ask someone - infinitive
        rather than demand that - subjunctive)   L, S, R, W

   1.5. Form of requests for repetition, clarification,
        or slower speech   L, S

   1.6. Use of nonverbal symbols (e.g., gestures, drawings)   L, S, R, W

   1.7. Use of contextual clues for inferences about literal
        meaning of unfamiliar vocabulary and structures   L, S, R

   1.8. Use of word formation rules to draw inferences about
        literal meaning of unfamiliar vocabulary and structures
        (e.g., coinage of fish-house to express aquarium)   L, S, R, W

   1.9. Other (e.g., avoidance of unfamiliar topics,
        memorization of certain verbal repertoires)   L, S, R, W

   2. Compensatory strategies for sociolinguistic difficulties:

   2.1. Single grammatical form for different communicative
        functions (e.g., a declarative such as Dinner is at 5:00
        with varying in tonation to signal a statement, a
        question, a promise, an order, an invitation--all
        depending on sociolinguistic context)   L, S, R, W

   2.2. Use of sociolinguistically neutral grammatical forms
        when uncertain about appropriateness of other forms
        in a given sociolinguistic context (e.g., in meeting
        someone, omission of the person's name if unsure
        about using his or her first name versus title)   S, W

   2.3. Use of first language knowledge about appropriateness
        of grammatical forms or communicative functions in a
        given sociolinguistic context   L, S, R, W

2.4. Use of contextual clues for inferences about social
meaning (communicative function, etc.) in unfamiliar
sociolinguistic situations or when unfamiliar grammatical forms are used   L, S, R

3. Compensatory strategies for discourse difficulties:

3.1. Use of nonverbal symbols or of emphatic stress
and intonation to indicate cohesion and coherence
(e.g., use of drawings to indicate sequencing of
actions/ideas)   L, S, R, W

3.2. Use of first language knowledge about oral/written
discourse patterns when uncertain about such aspects
of discourse in second language   L, S, R, W

3.3. Use of contextual clues for inferences about
patterning of literal and social meanings in
unfamiliar discourse   L, S, R, W

4. Compensatory strategies for performance limitations:

4.1. Coping with background noise, interruptions,
frequent changes in topic/interlocutors, and other
distractions   L, S, R, W

4.2. Use of pause fillers (e.g., well, you know,
my, my) to maintain one's turn in conversation
while searching for ideas or grammatical forms or
while monitoring them)   L, S

5. Rhetorical enhancement strategies (noncompensatory):

5.1. In oral and written discourse, use of structures and
vocabulary for special effect (e.g., use of adverbial
phrase preposing, as in Out of the woods came...)   L, S, R, W

5.2. In oral discourse, use of slow, soft, deliberate
speech for special effect   L, S

5.3. In oral and written discourse, use of literary devices
(sentence rhythm, alliteration, literary references)   L, S, R, W

APPENDIX C: CHECKLIST OF COMPETENCE AREAS FOR EVALUATING TOEFL (DEVELOPED BY JOYCE PENFIELD, RUTGERS UNIVERSITY, AND RICHARD DURAN, EDUCATIONAL TESTING SERVICE; BASED ON APPENDIX B AND ADDITIONAL SOURCE MATERIALS)

A. GRAMMATICAL COMPETENCE

   1. Pronunciation

      1.1 Lexical items in connected speech in full phonemic form

      1.2 Lexical items modified in connected speech

          1.2.1 Vowel reduction/deletion or consonant cluster reduction

          1.2.2 Palatalization (e.g., wacha/for "what do you")

          1.2.3 Contraction

      1.3 Stress and intonation patterns marking neutral, nonemotive reference

      1.4 Stress and intonation patterns marking contrastive or emphatic meaning

      1.5 Tempo, range/height of pitch, or pauses marking emotive or attitudinal meaning

   2. Script (written symbols)

      2.1 Letters in sequence

          2.1.1 Inherent spelling pattern for words

          2.1.2 Modification of inherent spelling pattern of stem/root forms (e.g., "cried" from "cry")

      2.2 Graphic symbols used to mark structural groupings

          2.2.1 Sentences

          2.2.2 Clauses (e.g., to separate subordinate/main clause, a clausal list, or two main changes)

          2.2.3 Phrases (e.g., to mark introductory phrases, separate a list of items or dates, places)

      2.3 Use of graphic symbols to mark speech-based modifications (e.g., contractions)

      2.4 Use of graphic symbols to mark specific concepts

          2.4.1 Mathematical concepts or relationships (e.g., 1/300 or $5.20

          2.4.2 Identity (e.g., quotes to identify titles, newspapers, as in: "As Smith notes in 'Passages'....")

      2.5 Use of graphic symbols to mark emphatic or contrastive meaning

3. Lexicon (vocabulary)

   3.1 Literal use of content words in context

   3.2 Idiomatic expressions (i.e., words frozen together into a
       semantic whole whose meaning cannot be determined by
       combining the meanings of the parts)

       3.2.1 Compound nouns

       3.2.2 Compound verbs

       3.2.3 Others

   3.3 Metaphorical uses of words/expressions (i.e., unique
       extension of literal reference to nonliteral meaning)
       (e.g., "the flower of my life")

   3.4 Literal use of function words in context

       3.4.1 Location; direction (e.g., this/that, near, in)

       3.4.2 Specificity

             3.4.2.1 Definite

             3.4.2.2 Indefinite

       3.4.3 Quantity; amount (e.g., many, few)

       3.4.4 Time: frequency of occurrence and span (e.g., never,
             since)

       3.4.5 Instrument or means (e.g., he walks with a cane)

       3.4.6 Possession (e.g., the wheel of the car)

       3.4.7 Comparison/degree (e.g., more intelligent than)

       3.4.8 Negation

4. Morphology (word formation)

   4.1 Inflection

       4.1.1 Number (e.g., books)

       4.1.2 Possession (e.g. John's book)

       4.1.3 Person in third person present (e.g., he plays)

       4.1.4 Tense

             4.1.4.1 Present progressive (e.g. I'm coming)

             4.1.4.2 Simple past in regular and irregular form
                     (e.g., he walked/ he sang)

             4.1.4.3 Present perfect in regular and irregular
                     forms (e.g. he has walked / he has sung /
                     he has spoken)

             4.1.4.4 Past perfect (e.g. he had walked)

4.1.5 Comparative/superlative (e.g., sadd<u>er</u>, sadd<u>est</u>)

4.2 Derivational relationships <u>in context</u> (e.g., attack/attacker)

5. Sentence formation (ordering of logical constituents)

    5.1 Simple sentence word ordering

        5.1.1 Declarative, active statements

        5.1.2 Questions (yes-no or WH)

        5.1.3 Imperatives

        5.1.4 Passives (with or without a stated agent)

        5.1.5 Existential THERE statements (e.g., There is a rat in the room.)

    5.2 Compound sentence word ordering (coordinated main clauses)

    5.3 Complex sentence with subordinate clause outside main clause (e.g., <u>When he's ready</u>, he'll call.)

    5.4 Sentences with subordinate clause embedded in main clause

        5.4.1 Noun phrase (complementation or nominalization)

        5.4.2 Relative clause (possibly signaled by relative pronoun <u>who</u>, <u>which</u>, <u>that</u>, <u>whose</u>)

    5.5 Focus shifting, extraposition, or topicalization (e.g., "What I want is that you come." "That I've had plenty of.")

B. SOCIOLINGUISTIC COMPETENCE

1. Factors defining rules of appropriateness for language usage in a given communicative event

    1.1 Status/power relationships between participants

        1.1.1 Equal role relationship

        1.1.2 Subordinate/superordinate role relationship

    1.2 Topic

        1.2.1 Academic living

        1.2.2 Academic content topic

        1.2.3 Social naturalness

    1.3 Setting/scene

        1.3.1 Formal

        1.3.2 Informal

    1.4 Channel

        1.4.1 Spoken

        1.4.2 Written

1.5 Genre (format of communicative event)

    1.5.1 Lecture

    1.5.2 Conversation

    1.5.3 Letter

    1.5.4 Note

    1.5.5 Announcement

    1.5.6 Dated comments

    1.5.7 Written passage

    1.5.8 Limited functional interaction or segment there from

    1.5.9 Statement

2. Language used to accomplish communicative purposes

  2.1 Request information

    2.1.1 Direct

    2.1.2 Indirect

  2.2 Persuade

    2.2.1 Direct

    2.2.2 Indirect

  2.3 Seek approval

    2.3.1 Direct

    2.3.2 Indirect

  2.4 Request help or advice

    2.4.1 Direct

    2.4.2 Indirect

  2.5 Promise/assure

    2.5.1 Direct

    2.5.2 Indirect

  2.6 Invite

    2.6.1 Direct

    2.6.2 Indirect

  2.7 Complain

    2.7.1 Direct

    2.7.2 Indirect

  2.8 Express regret

2.19.1 Direct

2.19.2 Indirect

2.20 Give information

2.20.1 Direct

2.20.2 Indirect

2.21 Other

2.21.1 Direct

2.21.2 Indirect

3. Formulaic expressions in routine usage for phatic communication
(e.g.,"Good morning, class. Today's lecture is....")

4. Indirect perspective toward a communicative event (attitudinal
or emotive in nature)

4.1 Sarcasm

4.2 Ridicule

4.3 Defeat

4.4 Frustration

4.5 Criticism

4.6 Doubt

5. Linguistic forms or speech modes not typical in broadcast or
standard written English

C. DISCOURSE COMPETENCE

1. Cohesion: linguistic devices used to bind text together

1.1 Lexical cohesion devices

1.1.1 Pronoun reference

1.1.2 Synonymy

1.1.3 Word repetition

1.1.4 Endo-centric reference

1.1.5 Sequence markers: first, second

1.1.6 Use of phrasal conjoiners, e.g., and, or, but, for, etc.

1.2 Sentence level

1.2.1 Conciseness (e.g., ellipsis, clausal reduction)

1.2.2 Continuity: (e.g., parallel structures, lists)

115

1.2.3 Semantic relationships (e.g., conjunctive adverbs) between clauses

    1.2.3.1 Addition

    1.2.3.2 Contrast

    1.2.3.3 Illustration

    1.2.3.4 Similarity

    1.2.3.5 Result, conclusion

    1.2.3.6 Emphasis

    1.2.3.7 Time

    1.2.3.8 Place

    1.2.3.9 Condition

1.2.4 Emphasis: (e.g., extraposition)

2. Coherence

2.1 Conversational discourse patterns

    2.1.1 Initiating the discourse

    2.1.2 Maintaining the discourse

    2.1.3 Terminating the discourse

2.2 Structuring of ideas in planned texts

    2.2.1 Classification (class-inclusion relations used to discuss topic)

    2.2.2 Illustration (concrete examples or ancedote used to explain topic)

    2.2.3 Definition (synonymic/metaphonic relations or negative definition used)

    2.2.4 Process (event-order)

        2.2.4.1 Events narrated according to significance

        2.2.4.2 Events narrated according to chronological order

    2.2.5 Description (indirect descriptive statements used to establish affect)

    2.2.6 Comparison (semantic similarities and differences explored)

        2.2.6.1 Alternating order

        2.2.6.2 Sequential order

    2.2.7 Cause and effect

    2.2.8 Factual development (facts chained together by content progression)

APPENDIX D: SUMMARY OF CHECKLIST RESULTS

Entries are organized according to section and item type within section. Collapsed entries across item types within a section and across the entire test are also provided. Fractional entries represent the proportion of items manifesting a given characteristic at least once in either their language stimulus, question, or correct response option. Entries in parentheses are the decimal equivalents of fractions.

Competence Areas for Evaluating the TOEFL

A. GRAMMATICAL COMPETENCE

   1. Pronunciation

      1.1 Lexical items in connected speech in full phonemic form

I: 50/50 (1.00) Sta: 20/20 (1.00) D: 15/15 (1.00) M/EC: 15/15 (1.00)

II: 0/40 (0.00) Str: 0/15 (0.00) WE: 0/25 (0.00)

III: 0/60 (0.00) V: 0/30 (0.00) RC: 0/30 (0.00)

Total: 50/150 (0.33)

      1.2 Lexical items modified in connected speech

         1.2.1 Vowel reduction/deletion or consonant cluster reduction

I: 39/50 (0.78) Sta: 14/20 (0.70) D: 12/15 (0.80) M/EC: 11/15 (0.73)

II: 0/40 (0.00) Str: 0/15 (0.00) WE: 0/25 (0.00)

III: 0/60 (0.00) V: 0/30 (0.00) RC: 0/30 (0.00)

Total: 39/150 (0.26)

         1.2.2 Palatalization (e.g. wacha/for "what do you")

I: 1/50 (0.02) Sta: 1/20 (0.05) D: 0/15 (0.00) M/EC: 0/15 (0.00)

II: 0/40 (0.00) Str: 0/15 (0.00) WE: 0/25 (0.00)

III: 0/60 (0.00) V: 0/30 (0.00) RC: 0/30 (0.00)

Total: 1/150 (0.01)

         1.2.3 Contraction

I: 18/50 (0.36) Sta: 5/20 (0.25) D: 8/15 (0.53) M/EC: 5/15 (0.33)

II: 0/40 (0.00) Str: 0/15 (0.00) WE: 0/25 (0.00)

III: 0/60 (0.00) V: 0/30 (0.00) RC: 0/30 (0.00)

Total: 18/150 (0.12)

      1.3 Stress and intonation patterns marking neutral, non-emotive reference

I: 47/50 (0.94) Sta: 17/20 (0.85) D: 15/15 (1.00) M/EC: 15/15 (1.00)

II: 0/40 (0.00) Str: 0/15 (0.00) WE: 0/25 (0.00)

III: 0/60 (0.00)   V: 0/30 (0.00)   RC: 0/30 (0.00)

Total: 47/150 (0.31)

1.4 Stress and intonation patterns marking contrastive or emphatic meaning

I: 25/50 (0.50)   Sta: 10/20 (0.50)   D: 8/15 (0.53)   M/EC: 7/15 (0.47)

II: 0/40 (0.00)   Str: 0/15 (0.00)   WE: 0/25 (0.00)

III: 0/60 (0.00)   V: 0/30 (0.00)   RC: 0/30 (0.00)

Total: 25/150 (0.17)

1.5 Tempo, range/height of pitch, or pauses marking emotive or attitudinal meaning

I: 48/50 (0.96)   Sta: 18/20 (0.90)   D: 15/15 (1.00)   M/EC: 15/15 (1.00)

II: 0/40 (0.00)   Str: 0/15 (0.00)   WE: 0/25 (0.00)

III: 0/60 (0.00)   V: 0/30 (0.00)   RC: 0/30 (0.00)

Total: 48/150 (0.32)

2. Script (written symbols)

2.1 Letters in sequence

2.1.1 Inherent spelling pattern for words

I: 48/50 (0.96)   Sta: 18/20 (0.90)   D: 15/15 (1.00)   M/EC: 15/15 (1.00)

II: 40/40 (1.00)   Str: 15/15 (1.00)   WE: 15/25 (0.60)

III: 60/60 (1.00)   V: 30/30 (1.00)   RC: 30/30 (1.00)

Total: 148/150 (0.99)

2.1.2 Modification of inherent spelling pattern of stem/root forms (e.g., "cried" from "cry")

I: 5/50 (0.10)   Sta: 2/20 (0.10)   D: 1/15 (0.07)   M/EC: 2/15 (0.13)

II: 10/40 (0.25)   Str: 3/15 (0.20)   WE: 7/25 (0.28)

III: 39/60 (0.65)   V: 9/30 (0.30)   RC: 30/30 (1.00)

Total: 54/150 (0.36)

2.2 Graphic symbols used to mark structural groupings

2.2.1 Sentences

I: 49/50 (0.98)   Sta: 20/20 (1.00)   D: 15/15 (1.00)   M/EC: 14/15 (0.93)

II: 38/40 (0.95)   Str: 14/15 (0.93)   WE: 24/25 (0.96)

III: 56/60 (0.97)   V: 28/30 (0.93)   RC: 30/30 (1.00)

Total: 145/150 (0.97)

2.2.2 Clauses (e.g., to separate subordinate/main clause, a clausal list, or two main changes)

I: 0/50 (0.00) Sta: 0/20 (0.00)   D: 0/15 (0.00) M/EC: 0/15 (0.00)

II: 10/40 (0.25) Str: 8/15 (0.33) WE: 2/25 (0.08)

III: 33/60 (0.55)   V: 3/30 (0.10) RC: 30/30 (1.00)

Total: 43/150 (0.29)

2.2.3 Phrases (e.g., to mark introductory phrases, separate a list of items or dates, places)

I: 0/50 (0.00) Sta: 0/20 (0.00)   D: 0/15 (0.00) M/EC: 0/15 (0.00)

II: 6/40 (0.15) Str: 1/15 (0.07) WE: 5/25 (0.20)

III: 33/60 (0.55)   V: 7/30 (0.23) RC: 26/30 (0.87)

Total: 39/150 (0.26)

2.3 Use of graphic symbols to mark speech-based modifications (e.g., contractions)

I: 7/50 (0.14) Sta: 4/20 (0.20)   D: 3/15 (0.20) M/EC: 0/15 (0.00)

II: 6/40 (0.15) Str: 1/15 (0.07) WE: 1/25 (0.04)

III: 18/60 (0.30)   V: 5/30 (0.17) RC: 13/30 (0.43)

Total: 31/150 (0.21)

2.4 Use of graphic symbols to mark specific concepts

2.4.1 Mathematical concepts or relationships (e.g., 1/300 or $5.20)

I: 1/50 (0.02) Sta: 0/20 (0.00)   D: 0/15 (0.00) M/EC: 1/15 (0.07)

II: 1/40 (0.02) Str: 0/15 (0.00) WE: 1/25 (0.04)

III: 8/60 (0.13)   V: 0/30 (0.00) RC: 8/30 (0.27)

Total: 10/150 (0.07)

2.4.2 Identity (e.g., quotes to identify titles, newspapers as in: "As Smith notes in 'Passages'....")

I: 3/50 (0.06) Sta: 3/20 (0.15)   D: 0/15 (0.00) M/EC: 0/15 (0.00)

II: 14/40 (0.35) Str: 5/15 (0.33) WE: 9/25 (0.36)

III: 30/60 (0.50)   V: 11/30 (0.37) RC: 19/30 (0.63)

Total: 47/150 (0.31)

2.5 Use of graphic symbols to mark emphatic or contrastive meaning

I: 0/50 (0.00) Sta: 0/20 (0.00)   D: 0/15 (0.00) M/EC: 0/15 (0.00)

II: 0/40 (0.00) Str: 0/15 (0.00) WE: 0/25 (0.00)

III: 0/60 (0.00)   V: 0/30 (0.00) RC: 0/30 (0.00)

Total: 0/150 (0.00)

3. Lexicon (vocabulary)

3.1 Literal use of content words in context

I: 50/50 (1.00)   Sta: 20/20 (1.00)   D: 15/15 (1.00)   M/EC: 15/15 (1.00)

II: 40/40 (1.00)   Str: 15/15 (1.00)   WE: 25/25 (1.00)

III: 59/60 (0.98)   V: 29/30 (0.97)   RC: 30/30 (1.00)

Total: 149/150 (0.99)

3.2 Idiomatic expressions (i.e., words frozen together into a semantic whole whose meaning can not be determined by combining the meanings of the parts)

3.2.1 Compound nouns

I: 26/50 (0.52)   Sta: 5/20 (0.25)   D: 6/15 (0.40)   M/EC: 15/15 (1.00)

II: 17/40 (0.42)   Str: 7/15 (0.47)   WE: 10/25 (0.40)

III: 44/60 (0.73)   V: 14/30 (0.47)   RC: 30/30 (1.00)

Total: 87/150 (0.58)

3.2.2 Compound verbs

I: 20/50 (0.40)   Sta: 4/20 (0.20)   D: 6/15 (0.40)   M/EC: 10/15 (0.67)

II: 5/40 (0.12)   Str: 2/15 (0.13)   WE: 3/25 (0.12)

III: 21/60 (0.35)   V: 0/30 (0.00)   RC: 2/30 (0.70)

Total: 46/150 (0.31)

3.2.3 Others

I: 17/50 (0.34)   Sta: 8/20 (0.40)   D: 3/15 (0.20)   M/EC: 6/15 (0.40)

II: 2/40 (0.05)   Str: 1/15 (0.07)   WE: 1/25 (0.04)

III: 11/60 (0.18)   V: 4/30 (0.13)   RC: 7/30 (0.23)

Total: 30/150 (0.20)

3.3 Metaphorical uses of words/expressions (i.e., unique extension of literal reference to non-literal meaning) (e.g., "the flower of my life")

I: 1/50 (0.02)   Sta: 0/20 (0.00)   D: 1/15 (0.07)   M/EC: 0/15 (0.00)

II: 1/40 (0.02)   Str: 0/15 (0.00)   WE: 1/25 (0.04)

III: 0/60 (0.00)   V: 0/30 (0.00)   RC: 0/30 (0.00)

Total: 2/150 (0.01)

3.4 Literal use of function words in context

3.4.1 Location; direction (e.g., this/that, near, in)

I: 29/50 (0.58)   Sta: 6/20 (0.30)   D: 8/15 (0.53)   M/EC: 15/15 (1.00)

II: 14/40 (0.35)   Str: 5/15 (0.33)   WE: 9/25 (0.36)

III: 45/60 (0.75)   V: 15/30 (0.50)   RC: 30/30 (1.00)

Total: 88/150 (0.59)

3.4.2 Specificity

3.4.2.1 Definite

I: 43/50 (0.86) Sta: 13/20 (0.65)   D: 15/15 (1.00) M/EC: 15/15 (1.00)

II: 38/40 (0.95) Str: 14/15 (0.93) WE: 24/25 (0.96)

III: 52/60 (0.87)   V: 22/30 (0.73) RC: 30/30 (1.00)

Total: 130/150 (0.87)

3.4.2.2 Indefinite

I: 31/50 (0.62) Sta: 12/20 (0.60)   D: 4/15 (0.27) M/EC: 15/15 (1.00)

II: 24/40 (0.60) Str: 10/15 (0.67) WE: 14/25 (0.56)

III: 56/60 (0.93)   V: 26/30 (0.87) RC: 30/30 (1.00)

Total: 111/150 (0.74)

3.4.3 Quantity; amount (e.g., many, few)

I: 21/50 (0.42) Sta: 3/20 (0.15)   D: 3/15 (0.20) M/EC: 15/15 (1.00)

II: 15/40 (0.37) Str: 4/15 (0.27) WE: 11/25 (0.44)

III: 40/60 (0.67)   V: 10/30 (0.33) RC: 30/30 (1.00)

Total: 76/150 (0.51)

3.4.4 Time: frequency of occurrence and span (e.g., never, since)

I: 20/50 (0.40) Sta: 7/20 (0.35)   D: 4/15 (0.27) M/EC: 9/15 (0.60)

II: 4/40 (0.10) Str: 0/15 (0.00) WE: 4/25 (0.12)

III: 34/60 (0.57)   V: 4/30 (0.13) RC: 30/30 (1.00)

Total: 58/150 (0.39)

3.4.5 Instrument or means (e.g., he walks with a cane)

I: 0/50 (0.00) Sta: 0/20 (0.00)   D: 0/15 (0.00) M/EC: 0/15 (0.00)

II: 3/40 (0.07) Str: 0/15 (0.00) WE: 3/25 (0.12)

III: 5/60 (0.08)   V: 1/30 (0.03) RC: 4/30 (0.13)

Total: 8/150 (0.05)

3.4.6 Possession (e.g., the wheel of the car)

I: 23/50 (0.46) Sta: 7/20 (0.35)   D: 5/15 (0.33) M/EC: 11/15 (0.73)

II: 15/40 (0.37) Str: 8/15 (0.53) WE: 7/25 (0.28)

III: 32/60   (0.53)   V: 2/30 (0.07)   RC: 30/30 (1.00)

Total: 70/150 (0.47)

3.4.7 Comparison/degree (e.g., more intelligent than)

  I: 12/50   (0.24)   Sta: 1/20 (0.05)   D: 0/15 (0.00)   M/EC: 11/15 (0.73)

 II: 5/40   (0.12)   Str: 1/15 (0.07)   WE: 4/25 (0.11)

III: 13/60   (0.22)   V: 3/30 (0.10)   RC: 10/30 (0.33)

Total: 30/150 (0.20)

3.4.8 Negation

  I: 26/50   (0.52)   Sta: 7/20 (0.35)   D: 8/15 (0.53)   M/EC: 11/15 (0.73)

 II: 1/40   (0.02)   Str: 1/15 (0.07)   WE: 0/25 (0.00)

III: 28/60   (0.47)   V: 2/30 (0.07)   RC: 26/30 (0.87)

Total: 55/150 (0.37)

4. Morphology (word formation)

4.1 Inflection

4.1.1 Number (e.g., books)

  I: 23/50   (0.46)   Sta: 3/20 (0.15)   D: 5/15 (0.33)   M/EC: 15/15 (1.00)

 II: 29/40   (0.72)   Str: 11/15 (0.73)   WE: 18/25 (0.72)

III: 57/60   (0.95)   V: 27/30 (0.90)   RC: 30/30 (1.00)

Total: 109/150 (0.73)

4.1.2 Possession (e.g., John's book)

  I: 14/50   (0.28)   Sta: 2/20 (0.10)   D: 1/15 (0.07)   M/EC: 11/15 (0.73)

 II: 2/40   (0.05)   Str: 1/15 (0.07)   WE: 1/25 (0.04)

III: 15/60   (0.25)   V: 3/30 (0.10)   RC: 12/30 (0.40)

Total: 31/150 (0.21)

4.1.3 Person in third person present (e.g., he plays)

  I: 33/50   (0.66)   Sta: 6/20 (0.30)   D: 13/15 (0.87)   M/EC: 14/15 (0.93)

 II: 16/40   (0.40)   Str: 9/15 (0.60)   WE: 7/25 (0.28)

III: 30/60   (0.50)   V: 7/30 (0.23)   RC: 23/30 (0.77)

Total: 79/150 (0.53)

4.1.4 Tense

4.1.4.1 Present progressive (e.g., I'm coming)

  I: 3/50   (0.06)   Sta: 1/20 (0.05)   D: 2/15 (0.13)   M/EC: 0/15 (0.00)

 II: 0/40   (0.00)   Str: 0/15 (0.00)   WE: 0/25 (0.00)

III: 4/60 (0.06)   V: 0/30 (0.00) RC: 4/30 (0.13)

Total: 7/150 (0.05)

4.1.4.2 Simple past in regular and irregular form (e.g., he walked/he sang)

I: 24/50 (0.48) Sta: 11/20 (0.55) D: 2/15 (0.13) M/EC: 11/15 (0.73)

II: 16/40 (0.40) Str: 6/15 (0.40) WE: 10/25 (0.40)

III: 29/60 (0.48) V: 14/30 (0.47) RC: 15/30 (0.50)

Total: 69/150 (0.46)

4.1.4.3 Present perfect in regular and irregular forms (e.g., he has walked/he has sung/ he has spoken)

I: 15/50 (0.30) Sta: 1/20 (0.05) D: 3/15 (0.20) M/EC: 11/15 (0.73)

II: 3/40 (0.07) Str: 1/15 (0.07) WE: 2/25 (0.08)

III: 24/60 (0.40) V: 1/30 (0.03) RC: 23/30 (0.92)

Total: 42/150 (0.28)

4.1.4.4 Past perfect (e.g., he had walked)

I: 2/50 (0.04) Sta: 2/20 (0.10) D: 0/15 (0.00) M/EC: 0/15 (0.00)

II: 1/40 (0.02) Str: 1/15 (0.07) WE: 0/25 (0.00)

III: 8/60 (0.13) V: 0/30 (0.00) RC: 8/30 (0.27)

Total: 11/150 (0.07)

4.1.5 Comparative/superlative (e.g., sadder, saddest)

I: 12/50 (0.24) Sta: 1/20 (0.05) D: 0/15 (0.00) M/EC: 11/15 (0.73)

II: 1/40 (0.02) Str: 1/15 (0.07) WE: 0/25 (0.00)

III: 9/60 (0.15) V: 2/30 (0.07) RC: 7/30 (0.23)

Total: 22/150 (0.15)

4.2 Derivational relationships in context (e.g., attack/attacker)

I: 13/50 (0.26) Sta: 1/20 (0.05) D: 0/15 (0.00) M/EC: 11/15 (0.73)

II: 1/40 (0.02) Str: 1/15 (0.07) WE: 1/25 (0.04)

III: 24/60 (0.40) V: 2/30 (0.07) RC: 22/30 (0.88)

Total: 38/150 (0.25)

5. Sentence formation (ordering of logical constituents)

5.1 Simple sentence word ordering

5.1.1 Declarative, active statements

I: 49/50 (0.98) Sta: 19/20 (0.95) D: 15/15 (1.00) M/EC: 15/15 (1.00)

II: 31/40 (0.77) Str: 11/15 (0.73) WE: 20/25 (0.80)

III: 52/60 (0.87)   V: 22/30 (0.73) RC: 30/30 (1.00)

Total: 132/150 (0.88)

5.1.2 Questions (yes-no or WH)

I: 31/50 (0.62) Sta: 1/20 (0.05) D: 15/15 (1.00) M/EC: 15/15 (1.00)

II: 0/40 (0.00) Str: 0/15 (0.00) WE: 0/25 (0.00)

III: 14/60 (0.23)   V: 0/30 (0.00) RC: 14/30 (0.23)

Total: 45/150 (0.30)

5.1.3 Imperatives

I: 7/50 (0.14) Sta: 3/20 (0.15) D: 3/15 (0.20) M/EC: 1/15 (0.07)

II: 0/40 (0.00) Str: 0/15 (0.00) WE: 0/25 (0.00)

III: 0/60 (0.00)   V: 0/30 (0.00) RC: 0/30 (0.00)

Total: 7/150 (0.05)

5.1.4 Passives (with or without a stated agent)

I: 15/50 (0.30) Sta: 4/20 (0.20) D: 2/15 (0.13) M/EC: 9/15 (0.60)

II: 11/40 (0.27) Str: 7/15 (0.47) WE: 4/25 (0.11)

III: 42/60 (0.70)   V: 12/30 (0.40) RC: 30/30 (1.00)

Total: 68/150 (0.45)

5.1.5 Existential THERE statements (e.g., There is a rat in the room.)

I: 1/50 (0.02) Sta: 0/20 (0.00) D: 1/15 (0.07) M/EC: 6/15 (0.40)

II: 2/40 (0.05) Str: 1/15 (0.07) WE: 1/25 (0.04)

III: 8/60 (0.13)   V: 0/30 (0.00) RC: 8/30 (0.63)

Total: 11/150 (0.07)

5.2 Compound sentence word ordering (coordinated main clauses)

I: 7/50 (0.14) Sta: 0/20 (0.00) D: 1/15 (0.07) M/EC: 6/15 (0.40)

II: 3/40 (0.07) Str: 2/15 (0.13) WE: 1/25 (0.04)

III: 19/60 (0.32)   V: 0/30 (0.00) RC: 19/30 (0.63)

Total: 29/150 (0.19)

5.3 Complex sentence with subordinate clause outside main clause (e.g., When he's ready, he'll call.)

I: 16/50 (0.32) Sta: 2/20 (0.10) D: 2/15 (0.13) M/EC: 12/15 (0.80)

II: 4/40 (0.10) Str: 2/15 (0.13) WE: 2/25 (0.08)

III: 33/60 (0.55)   V: 3/30 (0.10) RC: 30/30 (1.00)

Total: 53/150 (0.35)

5.4 Sentences with subordinate clause embedded in main clause

5.4.1 Noun phrase (complementation or nominalization)

I: 3/50 (0.06) Sta: 1/20 (0.05)   D: 2/15 (0.13) M/EC: 0/15 (0.00)

II: 2/40 (0.05) Str: 1/15 (0.07) WE: 1/25 (0.04)

III: 3/60 (0.05)   V: 1/30 (0.03) RC: 2/30 (0.07)

Total: 8/150 (0.05)

5.4.2 Relative clause (possibly signalled by relative pronouns who, which, that, whose)

I: 14/50 (0.28) Sta: 1/20 (0.05)   D: 3/15 (0.20) M/EC: 10/15 (0.67)

II: 5/40 (0.12) Str: 2/15 (0.13) WE: 3/25 (0.12)

III: 32/60 (0.53)   V: 4/30 (0.13) RC: 28/30 (0.93)

Total: 51/150 (0.34)

5.5 Focus shifting, extraposition or topicalization (e.g., "What I want is that you come." "That I've had plenty of.")

I: 2/50 (0.04) Sta: 0/20 (0.00)   D: 1/15 (0.07) M/EC: 1/15 (0.07)

II: 0/40 (0.00) Str: 0/15 (0.00) WE: 0/25 (0.00)

III: 11/60 (0.18)   V: 1/30 (0.03) RC: 10/30 (0.33)

Total: 13/150 (0.09)

B. SOCIOLINGUISTIC COMPETENCE

1. Factors defining rules of appropriateness for language usage in a given communicative event

1.1 Status/power relationships between participants

1.1.1 Equal role relationship

I: 11/50 (0.22) Sta: 0/20 (0.00)   D: 6/15 (0.40) M/EC: 5/15 (0.33)

II: 0/40 (0.00) Str: 0/15 (0.00) WE: 0/25 (0.00)

III: 0/60 (0.00)   V: 0/30 (0.00) RC: 0/30 (0.00)

Total: 11/150 (0.07)

1.1.2 Subordinate/superordinate role relationship

I: 13/50 (0.26) Sta: 1/20 (0.05)   D: 2/15 (0.13) M/EC: 10/15 (0.67)

II: 0/40 (0.00) Str: 0/15 (0.00) WE: 0/25 (0.00)

III: 0/60 (0.00)   V: 0/30 (0.00) RC: 0/30 (0.00)

Total: 13/150 (0.09)

1.2 Topic

1.2.1 Academic living

I: $\overline{X} = 1.70$ Sta: $\overline{x} = 1.50$ D: $\overline{x} = 1.27$ M/EC: $\overline{x} = 2.33$

II: $\overline{X} = 1.52$ Str: $\overline{x} = 1.53$ WE: $\overline{x} = 1.52$

III: $\overline{X} = 1.98$ V: $\overline{x} = 1.97$ RC: $\overline{x} = 2.00$

1.2.2 Academic content topic

I: $\overline{X} = 1.28$ Sta: $\overline{x} = 1.05$ D: $\overline{x} = 1.00$ M/EC: $\overline{x} = 1.80$

II: $\overline{X} = 1.52$ Str: $\overline{x} = 1.53$ WE: $\overline{x} = 1.52$

III: $\overline{X} = 1.95$ V: $\overline{x} = 1.90$ RC: $\overline{x} = 2.00$

1.2.3 Social naturalness

I: $\overline{X} = 2.45$ Sta: $\overline{x} = 2.55$ D: $\overline{x} = 2.40$ M/EC: $\overline{x} = 2.40$

1.3 Setting/scene

1.3.1 Formal

I: 14/50 (0.28) Sta: 0/20 (0.00) D: 4/15 (0.27) M/EC: 10/15 (0.67)

II: 0/40 (0.00) Str: 0/15 (0.00) WE: 0/25 (0.00)

III: 0/60 (0.00) V: 0/30 (0.00) RC: 0/30 (0.00)

Total: 14/150 (0.09)

1.3.2 Informal

I: 17/50 (0.34) Sta: 5/20 (0.25) D: 7/15 (0.47) M/EC: 5/15 (0.33)

II: 0/40 (0.00) Str: 0/15 (0.00) WE: 0/25 (0.00)

III: 0/60 (0.00) V: 0/30 (0.00) RC: 0/30 (0.00)

Total: 17/150 (0.11)

1.4 Channel

1.4.1 Spoken

I: 50/50 (1.00) Sta: 20/20 (1.00) D: 15/15 (1.00) M/EC: 15/15 (1.00)

II: 0/40 (0.00) Str: 0/15 (0.00) WE: 0/25 (0.00)

III: 0/60 (0.00) V: 0/30 (0.00) RC: 0/30 (0.00)

Total: 50/150 (0.33)

1.4.2 Written

I: 46/50 (0.92) Sta: 16/20 (0.80) D: 15/15 (1.00) M/EC: 15/15 (1.00)

II: 40/40 (1.00) Str: 15/15 (1.00) WE: 25/25 (1.00)

III: 60/60 (1.00) V: 30/30 (1.00) RC: 30/30 (1.00)

Total: 146/150 (0.97)

126

1.5 Genre (format of communicative event)

1.5.1 Lecture

I:	6/50	(0.12)	Sta:	0/20 (0.00)	D:	0/15 (0.00)	M/EC:	6/15 (0.40)
II:	0/40	(0.00)	Str:	0/15 (0.00)	WE:	0/25 (0.00)		
III:	0/60	(0.00)	V:	0/30 (0.00)	RC:	0/30 (0.00)		
Total:	6/150	(0.04)						

1.5.2 Conversation

I:	19/50	(0.38)	Sta:	0/20 (0.00)	D:	14/15 (0.93)	M/EC:	5/15 (0.33)
II:	0/40	(0.00)	Str:	0/15 (0.00)	WE:	0/25 (0.00)		
III:	0/60	(0.00)	V:	0/30 (0.00)	RC:	0/30 (0.00)		
Total:	19/150	(0.13)						

1.5.3 Letter

I:	0/50	(0.00)	Sta:	0/20 (0.00)	D:	0/15 (0.00)	M/EC:	0/15 (0.00)
II:	0/40	(0.00)	Str:	0/15 (0.00)	WE:	0/25 (0.00)		
III:	0/60	(0.00)	V:	0/30 (0.00)	RC:	0/30 (0.00)		
Total:	0/150	(0.00)						

1.5.4 Note

I:	0/50	(0.00)	Sta:	0/20 (0.00)	D:	0/15 (0.00)	M/EC:	0/15 (0.00)
II:	0/40	(0.00)	Str:	0/15 (0.00)	WE:	0/25 (0.00)		
III:	0/60	(0.00)	V:	0/30 (0.00)	RC:	0/30 (0.00)		
Total:	0/150	(0.00)						

1.5.5 Announcement

I:	5/50	(0.10)	Sta:	1/20 (0.05)	D:	0/15 (0.00)	M/EC:	4/15 (0.27)
II:	0/40	(0.00)	Str:	0/15 (0.00)	WE:	0/25 (0.00)		
III:	0/60	(0.00)	V:	0/30 (0.00)	RC:	0/30 (0.00)		
Total:	5/150	(0.03)						

1.5.6 Dated comments

I:	0/50	(0.00)	Sta:	0/20 (0.00)	D:	0/15 (0.00)	M/EC:	0/15 (0.00)
II:	0/40	(0.00)	Str:	0/15 (0.00)	WE:	0/25 (0.00)		
III:	0/60	(0.00)	V:	0/30 (0.00)	RC:	0/30 (0.00)		
Total:	0/150	(0.00)						

1.5.7 Written passage

I:	0/50	(0.00)	Sta:	0/20 (0.00)	D:	0/15 (0.00)	M/EC:	0/15 (0.00)

II: 0/40   (0.00)   Str: 0/15 (0.00)   WE: 0/25 (0.00)

III: 30/60 (0.50)   V: 0/30 (0.00)   RC: 30/30 (1.00)

Total: 30/150 (0.20)

1.5.8 Limited functional interaction or segment there from

I: 34/50   (0.68)   Sta: 5/20 (0.25)   D: 15/15 (1.00)   M/EC: 14/15 (0.93)

II: 0/40   (0.00)   Str: 0/15 (0.00)   WE: 0/25 (0.00)

III: 30/60 (0.50)   V: 0/30 (0.00)   RC: 30/30 (1.00)

Total: 64/150 (0.43)

1.5.9 Statement

I: 34/50   (0.68)   Sta: 16/20 (0.80)   D: 4/15 (0.27)   M/EC: 14/15 (0.93)

II: 36/40   (0.90)   Str: 15/15 (1.00)   WE: 21/25 (0.84)

III: 37/60 (0.62)   V: 30/30 (1.00)   RC: 7/30 (0.23)

Total: 107/150 (0.71)

2. Language used to accomplish communicative purposes

2.1 Request information

2.1.1 Direct

I: 29/50   (0.58)   Sta: 0/20 (0.00)   D: 15/15 (1.00)   M/EC: 14/15 (0.93)

II: 0/40   (0.00)   Str: 0/15 (0.00)   WE: 0/25 (0.00)

III: 29/60 (0.48)   V: 0/30 (0.00)   RC: 29/30 (0.97)

Total: 58/150 (0.39)

2.1.2 Indirect

I: 0/50   (0.00)   Sta: 0/20 (0.00)   D: 0/15 (0.00)   M/EC: 0/15 (0.00)

II: 0/40   (0.00)   Str: 0/15 (0.00)   WE: 0/25 (0.00)

III: 0/60   (0.00)   V: 0/30 (0.00)   RC: 0/30 (0.00)

Total: 0/150 (0.00)

2.2 Persuade

2.2.1 Direct

I: 2/50   (0.04)   Sta: 0/20 (0.00)   D: 0/15 (0.00)   M/EC: 2/15 (0.13)

II: 0/40   (0.00)   Str: 0/15 (0.00)   WE: 0/25 (0.00)

III: 0/60   (0.00)   V: 0/30 (0.00)   RC: 0/30 (0.00)

Total: 2/150 (0.01)

2.2.2 Indirect

I: 0/50   (0.00)   Sta: 0/20 (0.00)   D: 0/15 (0.00)   M/EC: 0/15 (0.00)

II: 0/40 (0.00) Str: 0/15 (0.00) WE: 0/25 (0.00)

III: 0/60 (0.00)   V: 0/30 (0.00) RC: 0/30 (0.00)

Total: 0/150 (0.00)

2.3 Seek approval

2.3.1 Direct

I: 0/50 (0.00) Sta: 0/20 (0.00) D: 0/15 (0.00) M/EC: 0/15 (0.00)

II: 0/40 (0.00) Str: 0/15 (0.00) WE: 0/25 (0.00)

III: 0/60 (0.00)   V: 0/30 (0.00) RC: 0/30 (0.00)

Total: 0/150 (0.00)

2.3.2 Indirect

I: 1/50 (0.02) Sta: 0/20 (0.00) D: 0/15 (0.00) M/EC: 1/15 (0.00)

II: 0/40 (0.00) Str: 0/15 (0.00) WE: 0/25 (0.00)

III: 0/60 (0.00)   V: 0/30 (0.00) RC: 0/30 (0.00)

Total: 1/150 (0.01)

2.4 Request help or advice

2.4.1 Direct

I: 1/50 (0.02) Sta: 0/20 (0.00) D: 1/15 (0.07) M/EC: 0/15 (0.00)

II: 0/40 (0.00) Str: 0/15 (0.00) WE: 0/25 (0.00)

III: 0/60 (0.00)   V: 0/30 (0.00) RC: 0/30 (0.00)

Total: 1/150 (0.01)

2.4.2 Indirect

I: 2/50 (0.04) Sta: 0/20 (0.00) D: 2/15 (0.13) M/EC: 0/15 (0.00)

II: 0/40 (0.00) Str: 0/15 (0.00) WE: 0/25 (0.00)

III: 0/60 (0.00)   V: 0/30 (0.00) RC: 0/30 (0.00)

Total: 2/150 (0.01)

2.5 Promise/assure

2.5.1 Direct

I: 2/50 (0.04) Sta: 1/20 (0.05) D: 1/15 (0.07) M/EC: 0/15 (0.00)

II: 0/40 (0.00) Str: 0/15 (0.00) WE: 0/25 (0.00)

III: 0/60 (0.00)   V: 0/30 (0.00) RC: 0/30 (0.00)

Total: 2/150 (0.01)

2.5.2 Indirect

I: 1/50 (0.02) Sta: 0/20 (0.00) D: 1/15 (0.07) M/EC: 0/15 (0.00)

II: 0/40 (0.00) Str: 0/15 (0.00) WE: 0/25 (0.00)

III: 0/60 (0.00)   V: 0/30 (0.00) RC: 0/30 (0.00)

Total: 1/150 (0.01)

2.6 Invite

2.6.1 Direct

I: 1/50 (0.02) Sta: 1/20 (0.05)   D: 0/15 (0.00) M/EC: 0/15 (0.00)

II: 0/40 (0.00) Str: 0/15 (0.00) WE: 0/25 (0.00)

III: 0/60 (0.00)   V: 0/30 (0.00) RC: 0/30 (0.00)

Total: 1/150 (0.01)

2.6.2 Indirect

I: 2/50 (0.02) Sta: 0/20 (0.00)   D: 2/15 (0.13) M/EC: 0/15 (0.00)

II: 0/40 (0.00) Str: 0/15 (0.00) WE: 0/25 (0.00)

III: 0/60 (0.00)   V: 0/30 (0.00) RC: 0/30 (0.00)

Total: 2/150 (0.01)

2.7 Complain

2.7.1 Direct

I: 1/50 (0.02) Sta: 0/20 (0.00)   D: 1/15 (0.07) M/EC: 0/15 (0.00)

II: 0/40 (0.00) Str: 0/15 (0.00) WE: 0/25 (0.00)

III: 0/60 (0.00)   V: 0/30 (0.00) RC: 0/30 (0.00)

Total: 1/150 (0.01)

2.7.2 Indirect

I: 3/50 (0.06) Sta: 0/20 (0.00)   D: 3/15 (0.20) M/EC: 0/15 (0.00)

II: 0/40 (0.00) Str: 0/15 (0.00) WE: 0/25 (0.00)

III: 0/60 (0.00)   V: 0/30 (0.00) RC: 0/30 (0.00)

Total: 3/150 (0.02)

2.8 Express regret

2.8.1 Direct

I: 1/50 (0.02) Sta: 1/20 (0.05)   D: 0/15 (0.00) M/EC: 0/15 (0.00)

II: 0/40 (0.00) Str: 0/15 (0.00) WE: 0/25 (0.00)

III: 0/60 (0.00)   V: 0/30 (0.00) RC: 0/30 (0.00)

Total: 1/150 (0.01)

2.8.2 Indirect

I: 2/50 (0.04) Sta: 0/20 (0.00)   D: 2/15 (0.13) M/EC: 0/15 (0.00)

II: 0/40 (0.00) Str: 0/15 (0.00) WE: 0/25 (0.00)

III: 0/60 (0.00)   V: 0/30 (0.00) RC: 0/30 (0.00)

Total: 2/150 (0.01)

2.9 Insult

2.9.1 Direct

I: 0/50 (0.00) Sta: 0/20 (0.00)   D: 0/15 (0.00) M/EC: 0/15 (0.00)

II: 0/40 (0.00) Str: 0/15 (0.00) WE: 0/25 (0.00)

III: 0/60 (0.00)   V: 0/30 (0.00) RC: 0/30 (0.00)

Total: 0/150 (0.00)

2.9.2 Indirect

I: 1/50 (0.02) Sta: 0/20 (0.00)   D: 1/15 (0.07) M/EC: 0/15 (0.00)

II: 0/40 (0.00) Str: 0/15 (0.00) WE: 0/25 (0.00)

III: 0/60 (0.00)   V: 0/30 (0.00) RC: 0/30 (0.00)

Total: 1/150 (0.01)

2.10 Make a suggestion

2.10.1 Direct

I: 3/50 (0.06) Sta: 0/20 (0.00)   D: 3/15 (0.20) M/EC: 0/15 (0.00)

II: 0/40 (0.00) Str: 0/15 (0.00) WE: 0/25 (0.00)

III: 0/60 (0.00)   V: 0/30 (0.00) RC: 0/30 (0.00)

Total: 3/150 (0.02)

2.10.2 Indirect

I: 2/50 (0.04) Sta: 0/20 (0.00)   D: 2/15 (0.13) M/EC: 0/15 (0.00)

II: 0/40 (0.00) Str: 0/15 (0.00) WE: 0/25 (0.00)

III: 0/60 (0.00)   V: 0/30 (0.00) RC: 0/30 (0.00)

Total: 2/150 (0.01)

2.11 Warn

2.11.1 Direct

I: 2/50 (0.04) Sta: 2/20 (0.10)   D: 0/15 (0.00) M/EC: 0/15 (0.00)

II: 0/40 (0.00) Str: 0/15 (0.00) WE: 0/25 (0.00)

III: 0/60 (0.00)   V: 0/30 (0.00) RC: 0/30 (0.00)

Total: 2/150 (0.01)

2.11.2 Indirect

I:	0/50 (0.00)	Sta:	0/20 (0.00)	D:	0/15 (0.00)	M/EC:	0/15 (0.00)
II:	0/40 (0.00)	Str:	0/15 (0.00)	WE:	0/25 (0.00)		
III:	0/60 (0.00)	V:	0/30 (0.00)	RC:	0/30 (0.00)		
Total:	0/150 (0.00)						

2.12 Request permission

2.12.1 Direct

I:	0/50 (0.00)	Sta:	0/20 (0.00)	D:	0/15 (0.00)	M/EC:	0/15 (0.00)
II:	0/40 (0.00)	Str:	0/15 (0.00)	WE:	0/25 (0.00)		
III:	0/60 (0.00)	V:	0/30 (0.00)	RC:	0/30 (0.00)		
Total:	0/150 (0.00)						

2.12.2 Indirect

I:	0/50 (0.00)	Sta:	0/20 (0.00)	D:	0/15 (0.00)	M/EC:	0/15 (0.00)
II:	0/40 (0.00)	Str:	0/15 (0.00)	WE:	0/25 (0.00)		
III:	0/60 (0.00)	V:	0/30 (0.00)	RC:	0/30 (0.00)		
Total:	0/150 (0.00)						

2.13 Express impatience, annoyance

2.13.1 Direct

I:	2/50 (0.04)	Sta:	0/20 (0.00)	D:	2/15 (0.13)	M/EC:	0/15 (0.00)
II:	0/40 (0.00)	Str:	0/15 (0.00)	WE:	0/25 (0.00)		
III:	0/60 (0.00)	V:	0/30 (0.00)	RC:	0/30 (0.00)		
Total:	2/150 (0.01)						

2.13.2 Indirect

I:	2/50 (0.04)	Sta:	0/20 (0.00)	D:	2/15 (0.13)	M/EC:	0/15 (0.00)
II:	0/40 (0.00)	Str:	0/15 (0.00)	WE:	0/25 (0.00)		
III:	0/60 (0.00)	V:	0/30 (0.00)	RC:	0/30 (0.00)		
Total:	2/150 (0.01)						

2.14 Express preference

2.14.1 Direct

I:	1/50 (0.02)	Sta:	0/20 (0.00)	D:	0/15 (0.00)	M/EC:	1/15 (0.07)
II:	0/40 (0.00)	Str:	0/15 (0.00)	WE:	0/25 (0.00)		
III:	0/60 (0.00)	V:	0/30 (0.00)	RC:	0/30 (0.00)		
Total:	1/150 (0.01)						

2.14.2 Indirect

I:	1/50 (0.02) Sta: 0/20 (0.00)	D: 0/15 (0.00)	M/EC: 1/15 (0.07)
II:	0/40 (0.00) Str: 0/15 (0.00)	WE: 0/25 (0.00)	
III:	0/60 (0.00) V: 0/30 (0.00)	RC: 0/30 (0.00)	
Total:	1/150 (0.01)		

2.15 Advise

2.15.1 Direct

I:	3/50 (0.06) Sta: 2/20 (0.10)	D: 1/15 (0.07)	M/EC: 0/15 (0.00)
II:	0/40 (0.00) Str: 0/15 (0.00)	WE: 0/25 (0.00)	
III:	0/60 (0.00) V: 0/30 (0.00)	RC: 0/30 (0.00)	
Total:	3/150 (0.02)		

2.15.2 Indirect

I:	2/50 (0.04) Sta: 1/20 (0.05)	D: 0/15 (0.00)	M/EC: 1/15 (0.07)
II:	0/40 (0.00) Str: 0/15 (0.00)	WE: 0/25 (0.00)	
III:	0/60 (0.00) V: 0/30 (0.00)	RC: 0/30 (0.00)	
Total:	2/150 (0.01)		

2.16 Give an order

2.16.1 Direct

I:	1/50 (0.02) Sta: 1/20 (0.05)	D: 0/15 (0.00)	M/EC: 0/15 (0.00)
II:	0/40 (0.00) Str: 0/15 (0.00)	WE: 0/25 (0.00)	
III:	0/60 (0.00) V: 0/30 (0.00)	RC: 0/30 (0.00)	
Total:	1/150 (0.01)		

2.16.2 Indirect

I:	4/50 (0.08) Sta: 0/20 (0.00)	D: 0/15 (0.00)	M/EC: 4/15 (0.27)
II:	0/40 (0.00) Str: 0/15 (0.00)	WE: 0/25 (0.00)	
III:	0/60 (0.00) V: 0/30 (0.00)	RC: 0/30 (0.00)	
Total:	4/150 (0.03)		

2.17 Purchase/transact

2.17.1 Direct

I:	2/50 (0.04) Sta: 0/20 (0.00)	D: 2/15 (0.13)	M/EC: 0/15 (0.00)
II:	0/40 (0.00) Str: 0/15 (0.00)	WE: 0/25 (0.00)	
III:	0/60 (0.00) V: 0/30 (0.00)	RC: 0/30 (0.00)	
Total:	2/150 (0.01)		

2.17.2 Indirect

I: 0/50 (0.00) Sta: 0/20 (0.00) D: 0/15 (0.00) M/EC: 0/15 (0.00)

II: 0/40 (0.00) Str: 0/15 (0.00) WE: 0/25 (0.00)

III: 0/60 (0.00) V: 0/30 (0.00) RC: 0/30 (0.00)

Total: 0/150 (0.00)

2.18 Refuse assistance

2.18.1 Direct

I: 0/50 (0.00) Sta: 0/20 (0.00) D: 0/15 (0.00) M/EC: 0/15 (0.00)

II: 0/40 (0.00) Str: 0/15 (0.00) WE: 0/25 (0.00)

III: 0/60 (0.00) V: 0/30 (0.00) RC: 0/30 (0.00)

Total: 0/150 (0.00)

2.18.2 Indirect

I: 0/50 (0.00) Sta: 0/20 (0.00) D: 0/15 (0.00) M/EC: 0/15 (0.00)

II: 0/40 (0.00) Str: 0/15 (0.00) WE: 0/25 (0.00)

III: 0/60 (0.00) V: 0/30 (0.00) RC: 0/30 (0.00)

Total: 0/150 (0.00)

2.19 Deny

2.19.1 Direct

I: 0/50 (0.00) Sta: 0/20 (0.00) D: 0/15 (0.00) M/EC: 0/15 (0.00)

II: 0/40 (0.00) Str: 0/15 (0.00) WE: 0/25 (0.00)

III: 0/60 (0.00) V: 0/30 (0.00) RC: 0/30 (0.00)

Total: 0/150 (0.00)

2.19.2 Indirect

I: 0/50 (0.00) Sta: 0/20 (0.00) D: 0/15 (0.00) M/EC: 0/15 (0.00)

II: 0/40 (0.00) Str: 0/15 (0.00) WE: 0/25 (0.00)

III: 0/60 (0.00) V: 0/30 (0.00) RC: 0/30 (0.00)

Total: 0/150 (0.00)

2.20 Give information

2.20.1 Direct

I: 39/50 (0.90) Sta: 11/20 (0.55) D: 13/15 (0.87) M/EC: 15/15 (1.00)

II: 40/40 (1.00) Str: 15/15 (1.00) WE: 25/25 (1.00)

III: 60/60 (1.00) V: 30/30 (1.00) RC: 30/30 (1.00)

Total: 145/150 (0.93)

2.20.2 Indirect

I: 2/50 (0.04) Sta: 0/20 (0.00) D: 2/15 (0.13) M/EC: 0/15 (0.00)

II: 0/40 (0.00) Str: 0/15 (0.00) WE: 0/25 (0.00)

III: 0/60 (0.00)   V: 0/30 (0.00) RC: 0/30 (0.00)

Total: 2/150 (0.01)

2.21 Other

2.21.1 Direct

I: 7/50 (0.14) Sta: 0/20 (0.00) D: 2/15 (0.13) M/EC: 5/15 (0.33)

II: 0/40 (0.00) Str: 0/15 (0.00) WE: 0/25 (0.00)

III: 0/60 (0.00)   V: 0/30 (0.00) RC: 0/30 (0.00)

Total: 7/150 (0.05)

2.21.2 Indirect

I: 5/50 (0.10) Sta: 0/20 (0.00) D: 5/15 (0.33) M/EC: 0/15 (0.00)

II: 0/40 (0.00) Str: 0/15 (0.00) WE: 0/25 (0.00)

III: 0/60 (0.00)   V: 0/30 (0.00) RC: 0/30 (0.00)

Total: 5/150 (0.03)

3. Formulaic expressions in routine usage for phatic communication
(e.g.,"Good morning, class. Today's lecture is....)

I: 14/50 (0.93) Sta: 0/20 (0.00) D: 4/15 (0.27) M/EC: 10/15 (0.67)

II: 0/40 (0.00) Str: 0/15 (0.00) WE: 0/25 (0.00)

III: 0/60 (0.00)   V: 0/30 (0.00) RC: 0/30 (0.00)

Total: 14/150 (0.09)

4. Indirect perspective toward a communicative event (attitudinal
or emotive in nature)

4.1 Sarcasm

I: 2/50 (0.04) Sta: 0/20 (0.00) D: 2/15 (0.13) M/EC: 0/15 (0.00)

II: 0/40 (0.00) Str: 0/15 (0.00) WE: 0/25 (0.00)

III: 0/60 (0.00)   V: 0/30 (0.00) RC: 0/30 (0.00)

Total: 2/150 (0.01)

4.2 Ridicule

I: 0/50 (0.00) Sta: 0/20 (0.00) D: 0/15 (0.00) M/EC: 0/15 (0.00)

II: 0/40 (0.00) Str: 0/15 (0.00) WE: 0/25 (0.00)

III: 0/60 (0.00)   V: 0/30 (0.00) RC: 0/30 (0.00)

Total: 0/150 (0.00)

4.3 Defeat

I: 0/50 (0.00) Sta: 0/20 (0.00) D: 0/15 (0.00) M/EC: 0/15 (0.00)

II: 0/40 (0.00) Str: 0/15 (0.00) WE: 0/25 (0.00)

III: 0/60 (0.00)   V: 0/30 (0.00) RC: 0/30 (0.00)

Total: 0/150 (0.00)

4.4 Frustration

I: 2/50 (0.04) Sta: 0/20 (0.00) D: 2/15 (0.13) M/EC: 0/15 (0.00)

II: 0/40 (0.00) Str: 0/15 (0.00) WE: 0/25 (0.00)

III: 0/60 (0.00)   V: 0/30 (0.00) RC: 0/30 (0.00)

Total: 2/150 (0.01)

4.5 Criticism

I: 2/50 (0.04) Sta: 0/20 (0.00) D: 2/15 (0.13) M/EC: 0/15 (0.00)

II: 0/40 (0.00) Str: 0/15 (0.00) WE: 0/25 (0.00)

III: 0/60 (0.00)   V: 0/30 (0.00) RC: 0/30 (0.00)

Total: 2/150 (0.01)

4.6 Doubt

I: 1/50 (0.02) Sta: 0/20 (0.00) D: 1/15 (0.07) M/EC: 0/15 (0.00)

II: 0/40 (0.00) Str: 0/15 (0.00) WE: 0/25 (0.00)

III: 0/60 (0.00)   V: 0/30 (0.00) RC: 0/30 (0.00)

Total: 1/150 (0.01)

5. Linguistic forms or speech modes not typical in broadcast or standard written English

I: 1/50 (0.02) Sta: 0/20 (0.00) D: 1/15 (0.07) M/EC: 0/15 (0.00)

II: 0/40 (0.00) Str: 0/15 (0.00) WE: 0/25 (0.00)

III: 0/60 (0.00)   V: 0/30 (0.00) RC: 0/30 (0.00)

Total: 1/150 (0.01)

C. DISCOURSE COMPETENCE

1. Cohesion: linguistic devices used to bind text together

   1.1 Lexical cohesion devices

      1.1.1 Pronoun reference

I: 41/50 (0.82) Sta: 15/20 (0.75) D: 13/15 (0.87) M/EC: 13/15 (0.87)

II: 11/40 (0.27) Str: 3/15 (0.20) WE: 8/25 (0.32)

136

III: 37/60 (0.62)   V: 7/30 (0.28)   RC: 30/30 (1.00)
Total: 89/150 (0.59)

1.1.2 Synonymy

I: 12/50 (0.24) Sta: 0/20 (0.00)   D: 1/15 (0.07) M/EC: 11/15 (0.73)
II: 5/40 (0.12) Str: 2/15 (0.13) WE: 3/25 (0.12)
III: 33/60 (0.55)   V: 3/30 (0.10) RC: 30/30 (1.00)
Total: 50/150 (0.33)

1.1.3 Word repetition

I: 13/50 (0.26) Sta: 0/20 (0.00)   D: 2/15 (0.13) M/EC: 11/15 (0.73)
II: 5/40 (0.12) Str: 3/15 (0.20) WE: 2/25 (0.08)
III: 32/60 (0.53)   V: 2/30 (0.07) RC: 30/30 (1.00)
Total: 60/150 (0.40)

1.1.4 Endo-centric reference

I: 4/50 (0.08) Sta: 0/20 (0.00)   D: 3/15 (0.20) M/EC: 1/15 (0.07)
II: 1/40 (0.02) Str: 1/15 (0.07) WE: 0/25 (0.00)
III: 16/60 (0.27)   V: 1/30 (0.03) RC: 15/30 (0.50)
Total: 21/150 (0.14)

1.1.5 Sequence markers: first, second

I: 7/50 (0.14) Sta: 0/20 (0.00)   D: 7/15 (0.47) M/EC: 0/15 (0.00)
II: 2/40 (0.05) Str: 2/15 (0.13) WE: 0/25 (0.00)
III: 16/60 (0.27)   V: 1/30 (0.03) RC: 15/30 (0.50)
Total: 25/150 (0.17)

1.1.6 Use of phrasal conjoiners (e.g., and, or, but, for, etc.)

I: 12/50 (0.24) Sta: 1/20 (0.05)   D: 0/15 (0.00) M/EC: 11/15 (0.73)
II: 11/40 (0.27) Str: 1/15 (0.07) WE: 10/25 (0.40)
III: 35/60 (0.58)   V: 5/30 (0.17) RC: 30/30 (1.00)
Total: 58/150 (0.39)

1.2 Sentence level

1.2.1 Conciseness (e.g., ellipsis; clausal reduction)

I: 24/50 (0.48) Sta: 2/20 (0.10)   D: 8/15 (0.53) M/EC: 14/15 (0.93)
II: 12/40 (0.30) Str: 6/15 (0.40) WE: 6/25 (0.24)
III: 38/60 (0.63)   V: 8/30 (0.27) RC: 30/30 (1.00)
Total: 49/150 (0.74)

137

1.2.2 Continuity (e.g., parallel structures; lists)

I: 10/50 (0.20) Sta: 0/20 (0.00) D: 0/15 (0.00) M/EC: 10/15 (0.67)

II: 6/40 (0.15) Str: 2/15 (0.13) WE: 4/25 (0.16)

III: 30/60 (0.50) V: 6/30 (0.20) RC: 30/30 (1.00)

Total: 46/150 (0.31)

1.2.3 Semantic relationships (e.g., conjunctive adverbs)
between clauses

1.2.3.1 Addition

I: 10/50 (0.20) Sta: 1/20 (0.05) D: 3/15 (0.20) M/EC: 6/15 (0.40)

II: 3/40 (0.07) Str: 2/15 (0.13) WE: 1/25 (0.04)

III: 14/60 (0.23) V: 2/30 (0.07) RC: 12/30 (0.40)

Total: 27/150 (0.18)

1.2.3.2 Contrast

I: 14/50 (0.28) Sta: 1/20 (0.05) D: 2/15 (0.13) M/EC: 11/15 (0.73)

II: 2/40 (0.05) Str: 0/15 (0.00) WE: 2/25 (0.08)

III: 26/60 (0.43) V: 0/30 (0.00) RC: 26/30 (0.87)

Total: 42/150 (0.28)

1.2.3.3 Illustration

I: 0/50 (0.00) Sta: 0/20 (0.00) D: 0/15 (0.00) M/EC: 0/15 (0.00)

II: 0/40 (0.00) Str: 0/15 (0.00) WE: 0/25 (0.00)

III: 0/60 (0.00) V: 0/30 (0.00) RC: 0/30 (0.00)

Total: 0/150 (0.00)

1.2.3.4 Similarity

I: 0/50 (0.00) Sta: 0/20 (0.00) D: 0/15 (0.00) M/EC: 0/15 (0.00)

II: 0/40 (0.00) Str: 0/15 (0.00) WE: 0/25 (0.00)

III: 0/60 (0.00) V: 0/30 (0.00) RC: 0/30 (0.00)

Total: 0/150 (0.00)

1.2.3.5 Result; conclusion

I: 11/50 (0.22) Sta: 0/20 (0.00) D: 0/15 (0.00) M/EC: 11/15 (0.73)

II: 0/40 (0.00) Str: 0/15 (0.00) WE: 0/25 (0.00)

III: 21/60 (0.35) V: 2/30 (0.07) RC: 19/30 (0.63)

Total: 32/150 (0.21)

1.2.3.6 Emphasis

I: 0/50 (0.00) Sta: 0/20 (0.00) D: 0/15 (0.00) M/EC: 0/15 (0.00)

II: 0/40 (0.00) Str: 0/15 (0.00) WE: 0/25 (0.00)

III: 0/60 (0.00)   V: 0/30 (0.00) RC: 0/30 (0.00)

Total: 0/150 (0.00)

1.2.3.7 Time

I: 4/50 (0.08) Sta: 3/20 (0.15)   D: 0/15 (0.00) M/EC: 1/15 (0.07)

II: 4/40 (0.10) Str: 2/15 (0.13) WE: 2/25 (0.08)

III: 22/60 (0.37)   V: 2/30 (0.07) RC: 20/30 (0.67)

Total: 30/150 (0.20)

1.2.3.8 Place

I: 1/50 (0.02) Sta: 0/20 (0.00)   D: 0/15 (0.00) M/EC: 1/15 (0.07)

II: 0/40 (0.00) Str: 0/15 (0.00) WE: 0/25 (0.00)

III: 0/60 (0.00)   V: 0/30 (0.00) RC: 0/30 (0.00)

Total: 1/150 (0.01)

1.2.3.9 Condition

I: 4/50 (0.08) Sta: 1/2 (0.05)   D: 3/15 (0.20) M/EC: 0/15 (0.00)

II: 0/40 (0.00) Str: 0/15 (0.00) WE: 0/25 (0.00)

III: 17/60 (0.28)   V: 1/30 (0.03) RC: 16/30 (0.53)

Total: 0/150 (0.00)

1.2.4 Emphasis (e.g., extraposition)

I: 1/50 (0.02) Sta: 0/20 (0.00)   D: 0/15 (0.00) M/EC: 1/15 (0.07)

II: 0/40 (0.00) Str: 0/15 (0.00) WE: 0/25 (0.00)

III: 0/60 (0.00)   V: 0/30 (0.00) RC: 0/30 (0.00)

Total: 1/150 (0.01)

2. Coherence

2.1 Conversational discourse patterns

2.1.1 Initiating the discourse

I: 17/50 (0.34) Sta: 1/20 (0.05)   D: 11/15 (0.73) M/EC: 5/15 (0.33)

II: 0/40 (0.00) Str: 0/15 (0.00) WE: 0/25 (0.00)

III: 0/60 (0.00)   V: 0/30 (0.00) RC: 0/30 (0.00)

Total: 17/150 (0.11)

2.1.2 Maintaining the discourse

I: 20/50 (0.40) Sta: 0/20 (0.00)   D: 15/15 (1.00) M/EC: 5/15 (0.33)

II: 0/40 (0.00) Str: 0/15 (0.00) WE: 0/25 (0.00)

III: 0/60 (0.00)   V: 0/30 (0.00) RC: 0/30 (0.00)

Total: 20/150 (0.13)

2.1.3 Terminating the discourse

I: 5/50 (0.10) Sta: 0/20 (0.00)   D: 0/00 (0.00) M/EC: 5/15 (0.33)

II: 0/40 (0.00) Str: 0/15 (0.00) WE: 0/25 (0.00)

III: 0/60 (0.00)   V: 0/30 (0.00) RC: 0/30 (0.00)

Total: 5/150 (0.03)

2.2 Structuring of ideas in planned texts

2.2.1 Classification (class-inclusion relations used to discuss topic)

I: 0/50 (0.00) Sta: 0/20 (0.00)   D: 0/15 (0.00) M/EC: 0/15 (0.00)

II: 0/40 (0.00) Str: 0/15 (0.00) WE: 0/25 (0.00)

III: 0/60 (0.00)   V: 0/30 (0.00) RC: 0/30 (0.00)

Total: 0/150 (0.00)

2.2.2 Illustration (concrete examples or ancedote used to explain topic)

I: 0/50 (0.00) Sta: 0/20 (0.00)   D: 0/15 (0.00) M/EC: 0/15 (0.00)

II: 0/40 (0.00) Str: 0/15 (0.00) WE: 0/25 (0.00)

III: 0/60 (0.00)   V: 0/30 (0.00) RC: 0/30 (0.00)

Total: 0/150 (0.00)

2.2.3 Definition (synonymic/metaphonic relations or negative definition used)

I: 0/50 (0.00) Sta: 0/20 (0.00)   D: 0/15 (0.00) M/EC: 0/15 (0.00)

II: 0/40 (0.00) Str: 0/15 (0.00) WE: 0/25 (0.00)

III: 0/60 (0.00)   V: 0/30 (0.00) RC: 0/30 (0.00)

Total: 0/150 (0.00)

2.2.4 Process (event-order)

2.2.4.1 Events narrated according to significance

I: 6/50 (0.12) Sta: 0/20 (0.00)   D: 0/15 (0.00) M/EC: 6/15 (0.40)

II: 0/40 (0.00) Str: 0/15 (0.00) WE: 0/25 (0.00)

III: 12/60 (0.20)   V: 0/30 (0.00) RC: 12/30 (0.40)

Total: 18/150 (0.12)

2.2.4.2 Events narrated according to chronological order

I: 0/50 (0.00) Sta: 0/20 (0.00)   Γ: 0/15 (0.00) M/EC: 0/15 (0.00)

II: 0/40   (0.00)   Str: 0/15 (0.00)   WE: 0/25 (0.00)

III: 0/60   (0.00)   V: 0/30 (0.00)   RC: 0/30 (0.00)

Total: 0/150 (0.00)

2.2.5 Description (indirect descriptive statements used to establish affect)

I: 0/50   (0.00)   Sta: 0/20 (0.00)   D: 0/15 (0.00)   M/EC: 0/15 (0.00)

II: 0/40   (0.00)   Str: 0/15 (0.00)   WE: 0/25 (0.00)

III: 0/60   (0.00)   V: 0/30 (0.00)   RC: 0/30 (0.00)

Total: 0/150 (0.00)

2.2.6 Comparison (semantic similarities and differences explored)

2.2.6.1 Alternating order

I: 0/50   (0.00)   Sta: 0/20 (0.00)   D: 0/15 (0.00)   M/EC: 0/15 (0.00)

II: 0/40   (0.00)   Str: 0/15 (0.00)   WE: 0/25 (0.00)

III: 0/60   (0.00)   V: 0/30 (0.00)   RC: 0/30 (0.00)

Total: 0/150 (0.00)

2.2.6.2 Sequential order

I: 1/50   (0.02)   Sta: 0/20 (0.00)   D: 1/15 (0.07)   M/EC: 0/15 (0.00)

II: 0/40   (0.00)   Str: 0/15 (0.00)   WE: 0/25 (0.00)

III: 0/60   (0.00)   V: 0/30 (0.00)   RC: 0/30 (0.00)

Total: 1/150 (0.01)

2.2.7 Cause and effect

I: 0/50   (0.00)   Sta: 0/20 (0.00)   D: 0/15 (0.00)   M/EC: 0/15 (0.00)

II: 0/40   (0.00)   Str: 0/15 (0.00)   WE: 0/25 (0.00)

III: 0/60   (0.00)   V: 0/30 (0.00)   RC: 0/30 (0.00)

Total: 0/150 (0.00)

2.2.8 Factual development (facts chained together by content progression)

I: 0/50   (0.00)   Sta: 0/20 (0.00)   D: 0/15 (0.00)   M/EC: 0/15 (0.00)

II: 0/40   (0.00)   Str: 0/15 (0.00)   WE: 0/25 (0.00)

III: 18/60   (0.30)   V: 0/30 (0.00)   RC: 18/30 (0.60)

Total: 18/150 (0.12)

APPENDIX E: INTERAGENCY LANGUAGE ROUNDTABLE SKILL LEVEL DESCRIPTIONS

Preface

The following descriptions of proficiency levels 0, 1, 2, 3, 4, and 5 characterize spoken-language use. Each higher level implies control of the previous levels' functions and accuracy. The designation 0+, 1+, 2+, etc. will be assigned when proficiency substantially exceeds one skill level and does not fully meet the criteria for the next level. The "plus-level" descriptions, therefore, are subsidiary to the "base-level" descriptions.

A skill level is assigned to a person through an authorized language examination. Examiners assign a level on a variety of performance criteria exemplified in the descriptive statements. Therefore, the examples given here illustrate, but do not exhaustively describe, either the skills a person may possess or situations in which he/she may function effectively.

Statements describing accuracy refer to typical stages in the development of competence in the most commonly taught languages in formal training programs. In other languages, emerging competence parallels these characterizations, but often with different details.

Unless otherwise specified, the term "native speaker" refers to native speakers of a standard dialect.

"Well-educated," in the context of these proficiency descriptions, does not necessarily imply formal higher education. However, in cultures where formal higher education is common, the language-use abilities of persons who have had such education is considered the standard. That is, such a person meets contemporary expectations for the formal, careful style of the language, as well as a range of less formal varieties of the language.

These descriptions may be further specified by individual agencies to characterize those aspects of language-use performance which are of insufficient generality to be included here.

S-0 NO PROFICIENCY

Unable to function in the spoken language. Oral production is limited to occasional isolated words. Has essentially no communicative ability.

S-0+ MEMORIZED PROFICIENCY

Able to satisfy immediate needs using rehearsed utterances. Shows little real autonomy of expression, flexibility, or spontaneity. Can ask questions or make statements with reasonable accuracy only with memorized utterances or formulae. Attempts at creating speech are usually unsuccessful.

Examples: The S-0+'s vocabulary is usually limited to areas of immediate survival needs. Most utterances are telegraphic; that is, functors (linking words, markers, and the like) are omitted, confused, or distorted. An S-0+ can usually differentiate most significant sounds when produced in isolation, but, when combined in words or groups of words, errors may be frequent. Even with repetition, communication is severely limited even with persons used to dealing with foreigners. Stress, intonation, tone, etc. are usually quite faulty.

S-1 ELEMENTARY PROFICIENCY
(Base Level)

Able to satisfy minimum courtesy requirements and maintain very simple face-to-face conversations on familiar topics. A native speaker must often use slowed speech, repetition, paraphrase, or a combination of these to be understood by an S-1. Similarly, the native speaker must strain and employ real-world knowledge to understand even simple statements/questions from the S-1. An S-1 speaker has a functional, but limited proficiency. Misunderstandings are frequent, but the S-1 is able to ask for help and to verify comprehension of native speech in face-to-face interaction. The S-1 is unable to produce continuous discourse except with rehearsed material.

Examples. Structural accuracy is likely to be random or severely limited. Time concepts are vague. Vocabulary is inaccurate, and its range is very narrow. The S-1 often speaks with great difficulty. By repeating, such speakers can make themselves understood to native speakers who are in regular contact with foreigners but there is little precision in the information conveyed. Needs, experience, or training may vary greatly from individual to individual; for example, S-1s may have encountered quite different vocabulary areas. However, the S-1 can typically satisfy predictable, simple, personal and accommodation needs; can generally meet courtesy, introduction, and identification requirements; exchange greetings; elicit and provide, for example, predictable and skeletal biographical information. An S-1 might give information about business hours, explain routine procedures in a limited way, and state in a simple manner what actions will be taken. The S-1 is able to formulate some questions even in languages with complicated question constructions. Almost every utterance may be characterized by structural errors and errors in basic grammatical relations. Vocabulary is extremely limited and characteristically does not include modifiers. Pronunciation, stress, and intonation are generally poor, often heavily influenced by another language. Use of structure and vocabulary is highly imprecise.

S-1+ ELEMENTARY PROFICIENCY
(Higher Level)

Can initiate and maintain predictable face-to-face conversations and satisfy limited social demands. The S-1+ may, however, have little understanding of the social conventions of conversation. The interlocutor is generally required to strain and employ real-world knowledge to understand even some simple speech. An S-1+ may hesitate and may have to change subjects due to lack of language resources. Range and control of the language are limited. Speech largely consists of a series of short, discrete utterances.

Examples: An S-1+ is able to satisfy most travel and accommodation needs and a limited range of social demands beyond exchanges of skeletal biographic information. Speaking ability may extend beyond immediate survival needs. Accuracy in basic grammatical relations is evident, although not consistent. May exhibit the commoner forms of verb tenses, for example, but make frequent errors in formation and selection. While some structures are established, errors occur in more complex patterns. The S-1+ typically cannot sustain coherent structures in longer utterances or unfamiliar situations. Ability to describe and give precise information is limited. Person, space, and time references are often used incorrectly. Pronunciation is understandable to natives used to dealing with foreigners. Can combine most significant sounds with reasonable comprehensibility, but has difficulty in producing certain sounds in certain positions or in certain combinations. Speech will usually be labored. Frequently has to repeat utterances to be understood by the general public.

S-2 LIMITED WORKING PROFICIENCY
(Base Level)

Able to satisfy routine social demands and limited work requirements. Can handle routine work-related interactions that are limited in scope. In more complex and sophisticated work-related tasks, language usage generally disturbs the native speaker. Can handle with confidence, but not with facility, most normal, high-frequency social conversational situations including extensive, but casual conversations about current events, as well as work, family, and autobiographical information. The S-2 can get the gist of most everyday conversations but has some difficulty understanding native speakers in situations that require specialized or sophisticated knowledge. The S-2's utterances are minimally cohesive. Linguistic structure is usually not very elaborate and not thoroughly controlled; errors are frequent. Vocabulary use is appropriate for high-frequency utterances, but unusual or imprecise elsewhere.

Examples: While these interactions will vary widely from individual to individual, an S-2 can typically ask and answer predictable questions in the workplace and give straightforward instructions to subordinates. Additionally, the S-2 can participate in personal and accommodation-type interactions with elaboration and facility; that is, can give and understand complicated, detailed, and extensive directions and make non-routine changes in travel and accommodation arrangements. Simple structures and basic grammatical relations are typically controlled; however, there are areas of weakness. In the commonly taught languages, these may be simple markings such as plurals, articles, linking words, and negatives or more complex structures such as tense/aspect usage, case morphology, passive constructions, word order, and embedding.

S-2+ LIMITED WORKING PROFICIENCY
(Higher Level)

Able to satisfy most work requirements with language usage that is often, but not always, acceptable and effective. An S-2+ shows considerable ability to communicate effectively on topics relating to particular interests and special fields of competence. Often shows a high degree of fluency and ease of speech, yet when under tension or pressure, the ability to use the language effectively may deteriorate. Comprehension of normal native speech is typically nearly complete. An S-2+ may miss cultural and local references and may require a native speaker to adjust to his/her limitations in some ways. Native speakers often perceive the S-2+'s speech to contain awkward or inaccurate phrasing of ideas, mistaken time, space, and person references, or to be in some way inappropriate, if not strictly incorrect.

Examples: Typically an S-2+ can participate in most social, formal, and informal interactions; but limitations either in range of contexts, types of tasks, or level of accuracy hinder effectiveness. The S-2+ may be ill at ease with the use of the language either in social interaction or in speaking at length in professional contexts. An S-2+ is generally strong in either structural precision or vocabulary, but not in both. Weakness or unevenness in one of the foregoing, or in pronunciation, occasionally results in miscommunication. Normally controls, but cannot always easily produce general vocabulary. Discourse is often incohesive.

S-3 GENERAL PROFESSIONAL PROFICIENCY
(Base Level)

Able to speak the language with sufficient structural accuracy and vocabulary to participate effectively in most formal and informal conversations on practical, social, and professional topics. Nevertheless, an S-3's limitations generally restrict the professional contexts of language use to matters of shared knowledge and/or international convention. Discourse is cohesive. An S-3 uses the language acceptably, but with some noticeable imperfections; yet, errors virtually never interfere with understanding and rarely disturb the native speaker. An S-3 can effectively combine structure and vocabulary to convey his/her meaning accurately. An S-3 speaks readily and fills pauses suitably. In face-to-face conversation with natives speaking the standard dialect at a normal rate of speech, comprehension is quite complete. Although cultural references, proverbs, and the implications of nuances and idiom may not be fully understood, the S-3 can easily repair the conversation. Pronunciation may be obviously foreign. Individual sounds are accurate; but stress, intonation, and pitch control may be faulty. **Examples:** Can typically discuss particular interests and special fields of competence with reasonable ease. Can use the language as part of normal professional duties such as answering objections, clarifying points, justifying decisions, understanding the essence of challenges, stating and defending policy, conducting meetings, delivering briefings, or other extended and elaborate informative monologues. Can reliably elicit information and informed opinion from native speakers. Structural inaccuracy is rarely the major cause of misunderstanding. Use of structural devices is flexible and elaborate. Without searching for words or phrases, an S-3 uses the language clearly and relatively naturally to elaborate concepts freely and make ideas easily understandable to native speakers. Errors occur in low-frequency and highly complex structures.

S-3+ GENERAL PROFESSIONAL PROFICIENCY (Higher Level)

Is often able to use the language to satisfy professional needs in a wide range of sophisticated and demanding tasks. **Examples:** Despite obvious strengths, may exhibit some hesitancy, uncertainty, effort, or errors which limit the range of language-use tasks that can be reliably performed. Typically there is particular strength in fluency and one or more, but not all, of the following: has breadth of lexicon, including low- and medium-frequency items, especially socio-linguistic/cultural references and nuances of close synonyms; employs structural precision, with sophisticated features that are readily, accurately, and appropriately controlled (such as complex modification and embedding in Indo-European languages); has discourse competence in a wide range of contexts and tasks, often matching a native speaker's strategic and organizational abilities and expectations. Occasional patterned errors occur in low frequency and highly-complex structures.

S-4 ADVANCED PROFESSIONAL PROFICIENCY (Base Level)

Able to use the language fluently and accurately on all levels normally pertinent to professional needs. An S-4's language usage and ability to function are fully successful. Organizes discourse well, employing functional rhetorical speech devices, native cultural references, and understanding. Language ability only rarely hinders him/her in performing any task requiring language; yet, an S-4 will seldom be perceived as a native. Speaks effortlessly and smoothly and is able to use the language with a high degree of effectiveness, reliability, and precision for all representational purposes within the range of personal and professional experience and scope of responsibilities. Can serve as an informal interpreter in a range of unpredictable circumstances. Can perform extensive, sophisticated language tasks, encompassing most matters of interest to well-educated native speakers, including tasks which do not bear directly on a professional specialty. **Examples:** Can discuss in detail concepts which are fundamentally different from those of the target culture and make those concepts clear and accessible to the native speaker. Similarly, an S-4 can understand the details and ramifications of concepts that are culturally or conceptually different from his/her own. Can set the tone of interpersonal official, semi-official, and non-professional verbal exchanges with a representative range of native speakers (in a range of varied audiences, purposes, tasks, and settings). Can play an effective role among native speakers in such contexts as conferences, lectures, and debates on matters of disagreement. Can advocate a position at length, both formally and in chance encounters, using sophisticated verbal strategies. Can understand and reliably produce shifts of both subject matter and tone. Can understand native speakers of the standard and other major dialects in essentially any face-to-face interaction.

S-4+ ADVANCED PROFESSIONAL PROFICIENCY (Higher Level)

Speaking proficiency is regularly superior in all respects, usually equivalent to that of a well-educated, highly articulate native speaker. Language ability does not impede the performance of any language-use task. However, an S-4+ would not necessarily be perceived as culturally native. **Examples:** An S-4+ organizes discourse well, employing functional rhetorical speech devices, native cultural references and understanding. Effectively applies a native speaker's social and circumstantial knowledge. However, cannot sustain that performance under all circumstances. While an S-4+ has a wide range and control of structure, an occasional non-native slip may occur. An S-4+ has a sophisticated control of vocabulary and phrasing that is rarely imprecise, yet there are occasional weaknesses in idioms, colloquialisms, pronunciation, cultural reference or there may be an occasional failure to interact in a totally native manner.

S-5 FUNCTIONALLY NATIVE PROFICIENCY

Speaking proficiency is functionally equivalent to that of a highly articulate well-educated native speaker and reflects the cultural standards of the country where the language is natively spoken. An S-5 uses the language with complete flexibility and intuition, so that speech on all levels is fully accepted by well-educated native speakers in all of its features, including breadth of vocabulary and idiom, colloquialisms, and pertinent cultural references. Pronunciation is typically consistent with that of well-educated native speakers of a non-stigmatized dialect.

INTERAGENCY LANGUAGE ROUNDTABLE
LANGUAGE SKILL LEVEL DESCRIPTIONS
LISTENING

L-0 NO PROFICIENCY

No practical understanding of the spoken language. Understanding is limited to occasional isolated words with essentially no ability to comprehend communication.

L-0+ MEMORIZED PROFICIENCY

Sufficient comprehension to understand a number of memorized utterances in areas of immediate needs. Slight increase in utterance length understood but requires frequent long pauses between understood phrases and repeated requests on the listener's part for repetition. Understands with reasonable accuracy only when this involves short memorized utterances or formulae. Utterances understood are relatively short in length. Misunderstandings arise due to ignoring or inaccurately hearing sounds or word endings (both inflectional and non-inflectional), distorting the original meaning. Can understand only with difficulty even persons such as teachers who are used to speaking with non-native speakers. Can understand best those statements where context strongly supports the utterance's meaning. Gets some main ideas.

L-1 ELEMENTARY PROFICIENCY
(Base Level)

Sufficient comprehension to understand utterances about basic survival needs and minimum courtesy and travel requirements. In areas of immediate need or on very familiar topics, can understand simple questions and answers, simple statements and very simple face-to-face conversations in a standard dialect. These must often be delivered more clearly than normal at a rate slower than normal, with frequent repetitions or paraphrase (that is, by a native used to dealing with foreigners). Once learned, these sentences can be varied for similar level vocabulary and grammar and still be understood. In the majority of utterances, misunderstandings arise due to overlooked or misunderstood syntax and other grammatical clues. Comprehension vocabulary inadequate to understand anything but the most elementary needs. Strong interference from the candidate's native language occurs. Little precision in the information understood owing to tentative state of passive grammar and lack of vocabulary. Comprehension areas include basic needs such as: meals, lodging, transportation, time and simple directions (including both route instructions and orders from customs officials, policemen, etc.). Understands main ideas.

L-1+ ELEMENTARY PROFICIENCY
(Higher Level)

Sufficient comprehension to understand short conversations about all survival needs and limited social demands. Developing flexibility evident in understanding into a range of circumstances beyond immediate survival needs. Shows spontaneity in understanding by speed, although consistency of understanding uneven. Limited vocabulary range necessitates repetition for understanding. Understands commoner time forms and most question forms, some word order patterns but miscommunication still occurs with more complex patterns. Cannot sustain understanding of coherent structures in longer utterances or in unfamiliar situations. Understanding of descriptions and the giving of precise information is limited. Aware of basic cohesive features, e.g., pronouns, verb inflections, but many are unreliably understood, especially if less immediate in reference. Understanding is largely limited to a series of short, discrete utterances. Still has to ask for utterances to be repeated. Some ability to understand the facts.

L-2 LIMITED WORKING PROFICIENCY
(Base Level)

Sufficient comprehension to understand conversations on routine social demands and limited job requirements. Able to understand face-to-face speech in a standard dialect, delivered at a normal rate with some repetition and rewording, by a native speaker not used to dealing with foreigners, about everyday topics, common personal and family news, well-known current events, and routine office matters through descriptions and narration about current, past and future events; can follow essential points of discussion or speech at an elementary level on topics in his/her special professional field. Only understands occasional words and phrases of statements made in unfavorable conditions, for example through loudspeakers outdoors. Understands factual content. Native language causes less interference in listening comprehension. Able to understand the facts, i.e., the lines but not between or beyond the lines.

L-2+ LIMITED WORKING PROFICIENCY
(Higher Level)

Sufficient comprehension to understand most routine social demands and most conversations on work requirements as well as some discussions on concrete topics

145

related to particular interests and special fields of competence. Often shows remarkable ability and ease of understanding, but under tension or pressure may break down. Candidate may display weakness or deficiency due to inadequate vocabulary base or less than secure knowledge of grammar and syntax. Normally understands general vocabulary with some hesitant understanding of everyday vocabulary still evident. Can sometimes detect emotional overtones. Some ability to understand between the lines (i.e., to grasp inferences).

L-3 GENERAL PROFESSIONAL PROFICIENCY (Base Level)

Able to understand the essentials of all speech in a standard dialect including technical discussions within a special field. Has effective understanding of face-to-face speech, delivered with normal clarity and speed in a standard dialect, on general topics and areas of special interest; understands hypothesizing and supported opinions. Has broad enough vocabulary that rarely has to ask for paraphrasing or explanation. Can follow accurately the essentials of conversations between educated native speakers, reasonably clear telephone calls, radio broadcasts, news stories similar to wire service reports, oral reports, some oral technical reports and public addresses on non-technical subjects; can understand without difficulty all forms of standard speech concerning a special professional field. Does not understand native speakers if they speak very quickly or use some slang or dialect. Can often detect emotional overtones. Can understand between the lines (i.e., grasp inferences)

L-3+ GENERAL PROFESSIONAL PROFICIENCY (Higher Level)

Comprehends most of the content and intent of a variety of forms and styles of speech pertinent to professional needs, as well as general topics and social conversation. Ability to comprehend many sociolinguistic and cultural references. However, may miss some subtleties and nuances. Increased ability to comprehend unusually complex structures in lengthy utterances and to comprehend many distinctions in language tailored for different audiences. Increased ability to understand native speakers talking quickly, using nonstandard dialect or slang; however, comprehension not complete. Some ability to understand "beyond the lines" in addition to strong ability to understand "between the lines."

L-4 ADVANCED PROFESSIONAL PROFICIENCY (Base Level)

Able to understand all forms and styles of speech pertinent to professional needs. Able to understand fully all speech with extensive and precise vocabulary, subtleties and nuances in all standard dialects on any subject relevant to professional needs within the range of his/her experience, including social conversations; all intelligible broadcasts and telephone calls; and many kinds of technical discussions and discourse. Understands language specifically tailored (including persuasion, representation, counseling, and negotiating) to different audiences. Able to understand the essentials of speech in some non-standard dialects. Has difficulty in understanding extreme dialect and slang, also in understanding speech in unfavorable conditions, for example through bad loudspeakers out doors. Understands "beyond the lines" all forms of the language directed to the general listener, (i.e., able to develop and analyze the argumentation presented).

L-4+ ADVANCED PROFESSIONAL PROFICIENCY (Higher Level)

Increased ability to understand extremely difficult and abstract speech as well as ability to understand all forms and styles of speech pertinent to professional needs, including social conversations. Increased ability to comprehend native speakers using extreme non-standard dialects and slang as well as to understand speech in unfavorable conditions. Strong sensitivity to sociolinguistic and cultural references. Accuracy is close to that of the well-educated native listener but still not equivalent.

L-5 FUNCTIONALLY NATIVE PROFICIENCY

Comprehension equivalent to that of the well-educated native listener. Able to understand fully all forms and styles of speech intelligible to the well-educated native listener, including a number of regional and illiterate dialects, highly colloquial speech and discourse distorted by marked interference from other noise. Able to understand how natives think as they create discourse. Able to understand extremely difficult and abstract speech.

INTERAGENCY LANGUAGE ROUNDTABLE
LANGUAGE SKILL LEVEL DESCRIPTIONS
READING

Preface

In the following descriptions a standard set of text-types is associated with each level. The text-type is generally characterized in each descriptive statement. The word "read," in the context of these proficiency descriptions, means that the person at a given skill level can thoroughly understand the communicative intent in the text-types described. In the usual case the reader could be expected to make a full representation, thorough summary, or translation of the text into English.

Other useful operations can be performed on written texts that do not require the ability to "read," as defined above. Examples of such tasks which persons of a given skill level may reasonably be expected to perform are provided, when appropriate, in the descriptions.

R-0 NO PROFICIENCY

No practical ability to read the language. Consistently misunderstands or cannot comprehend at all.

R-0+ MEMORIZED PROFICIENCY

Can recognize all the letters in the printed version of an alphabetic system and high-frequency elements of a syllabary or a character system. Able to read some or all of the following: numbers, isolated words and phrases, personal and place names, street signs, office and shop designations. The above often interpreted inaccurately. Unable to read connected prose.

R-1 ELEMENTARY PROFICIENCY
(Base Level)

Sufficient comprehension to read very simple connected written material in a form equivalent to usual printing or typescript. Can read either representations of familiar formulaic verbal exchanges or simple language containing only the highest frequency structural patterns and vocabulary, including shared international vocabulary items and cognates (when appropriate). Able to read and understand known language elements that have been recombined in new ways to achieve different meanings at a similar level of simplicity. Texts may include simple narratives of routine behavior; highly predictable descriptions of persons, places or things; and explanations of geography and government such as those simplified for tourists. Some misunderstandings possible on simple texts. Can get some main ideas and locate prominent items of professional significance in more complex texts. Can identify general subject matter in some authentic texts.

R-1+ ELEMENTARY PROFICIENCY
(Higher Level)

Sufficient comprehension to understand simple discourse in printed form for informative social purposes. Can read material such as announcements of public events, simple prose containing biographical information or narration of events, and straightforward newspaper headlines. Can guess at unfamiliar vocabulary if highly contextualized, but with difficulty in unfamiliar contexts. Can get some main ideas and locate routine information of professional significance in more complex texts. Can follow essential points of written discussion at an elementary level on topics in his/her special professional field.

In commonly taught languages, an R-1+ may not control the structure well. For example, basic grammatical relations are often misinterpreted, and temporal reference may rely primarily on lexical items as time indicators. Has some difficulty with the cohesive factors in discourse, such as matching pronouns with referents. May have to read materials several times for understanding.

R-2 LIMITED WORKING PROFICIENCY
(Base Level)

Sufficient comprehension to read simple, authentic written material in a form equivalent to usual printing or typescript on subjects within a familiar context. Able to read with some misunderstandings straightforward, familiar, factual material, but in general insufficiently experienced with the language to draw inferences directly from the linguistic aspects of the text. Can locate and understand the main ideas and details in material written for the general reader. However, persons who have professional knowledge of a subject may be able to summarize or perform sorting and locating tasks with written texts that are well beyond their general proficiency level. The R-2 can read uncomplicated, but authentic prose on familiar subjects that are normally presented in a predictable sequence which aids the reader in understanding. Texts may include descriptions and narrations in contexts such as news items describing frequently occurring events, simple biographical information, social notices, formulaic business letters, and simple technical material written for the general reader. Generally the prose that can be read by an R-2 is predominantly in straightforward/high-frequency sentence patterns. The R-2 does not have a broad active vocabulary (that is, which he/she recognizes immediately on sight), but is able to use contextual and real-world cues to understand the text. Characteristically, however, the R-2 is quite slow in performing such a process. Is typically able to answer factual questions about authentic texts of the types described above.

R-2+ LIMITED WORKING PROFICIENCY
(Higher Level)

Sufficient comprehension to understand most factual material in non-technical prose as well as some discussions on concrete topics related to special professional interests. Is markedly more proficient at reading materials on a familiar topic. Is able to separate the main ideas and details from lesser ones and uses that distinction to advance understanding. The R-2+ is able to use linguistic context and real-world knowledge to make sensible guesses about unfamiliar material. Has a broad active reading vocabulary. The R-2+ is able to get the gist of main and subsidiary ideas in texts which could only be read thoroughly by persons with much higher proficiencies. Weaknesses include slowness, uncertainty, inability to discern nuance and/or intentionally disguised meaning.

R-3 GENERAL PROFESSIONAL PROFICIENCY
(Base Level)

Able to read within a normal range of speed and with almost complete comprehension a variety of authentic prose material on unfamiliar subjects. Reading ability is not dependent on subject matter knowledge, although it is not expected that an R-3 can comprehend thoroughly subject matter which is highly dependent on cultural knowledge or which is outside his/her general experience and not accompanied by explanation. Text-types include news stories similar to wire service reports or international news items in major periodicals, routine correspondence, general reports, and technical material in his/her professional field; all of these may include hypothesis, argumentation,and supported opinions. Misreading rare. Almost always able to interpret material correctly, relate ideas, and "read between the lines," (that is, understand the writers' implicit intents in texts of the above types). Can get the gist of more sophisticated texts, but may be unable to detect or understand subtlety and nuance. Rarely has to pause over or reread general vocabulary. However, may experience some difficulty with unusually complex structure and low frequency idioms.

R-3+ GENERAL PROFESSIONAL PROFICIENCY
(Higher Level)

Can comprehend a variety of styles and forms pertinent to professional needs. Rarely misinterprets such texts or rarely experiences difficulty relating ideas or making inferences. Able to comprehend many sociolinguistic and cultural references. However, may miss some nuances and subtleties. Able to comprehend a considerable range of intentionally complex structures, low frequency idioms, and uncommon connotative intentions; however, accuracy is not complete. The S-3+ is typically able to read with facility, understand,

and appreciate contemporary expository, technical, or literary texts which do not rely heavily on slang and unusual idioms.

R-4 ADVANCED PROFESSIONAL PROFICIENCY
(Base Level)

Able to read fluently and accurately all styles and forms of the language pertinent to professional needs. The R-4's experience with the written language is extensive enough that he/she is able to relate inferences in the text to real-world knowledge and understand almost all sociolinguistic and cultural references. Able to "read beyond the lines" (that is, to understand the full ramifications of texts as they are situated in the wider cultural, political, or social environment). Able to read and understand the intent of writers' employment of nuance and subtlety. An R-4 can discern relationships among sophisticated written materials in the context of broad experience. Can follow unpredictable turns of thought readily in, for example, editorial, conjectural, and literary texts in any subject matter area directed to the general reader. Can read essentially all materials in his/her special field, including official and professional documents and correspondence. Recognizes all professionally relevant vocabulary known to the educated non-professional native, although may have some difficulty with slang. Can read reasonably legible handwriting without difficulty. Accuracy is often nearly that of a well-educated native reader.

R-4+ ADVANCED PROFESSIONAL PROFICIENCY
(Higher Level)

Nearly native ability to read and understand extremely difficult or abstract prose, a very wide variety of vocabulary, idioms, colloquialisms, and slang. Strong sensitivity to and understanding of sociolinguistic and cultural references. Little difficulty in reading less than fully legible handwriting. Broad ability to "read beyond the lines" (that is, to understand the full ramifications of texts as they are situated in the wider cultural, political, or social environment) is nearly that of a well-read or well-educated native reader. Accuracy is close to that of the well-educated native reader, but not equivalent.

R-5 FUNCTIONALLY NATIVE PROFICIENCY

Reading proficiency is functionally equivalent to that of the well-educated native reader. Can read extremely difficult and abstract prose; for example, general legal and technical as well as highly colloquial writings. Able to read literary texts, typically including contemporary avant-garde prose, poetry, and theatrical writing. Can read classical/archaic forms of literature with the same degree of facility as the well-educated, but non-specialist native. Reads and understands a wide variety of vocabulary and idioms, colloquialisms, slang, and pertinent cultural references. With varying degrees of difficulty, can read all kinds of handwritten documents. Accuracy of comprehension is equivalent to that of a well-educated native reader.

W-0 NO PROFICIENCY

No functional writing ability.

W-0+ MEMORIZED PROFICIENCY

Writes using memorized material and set expressions. Can produce symbols in an alphabetic or syllabic writing system or 50 of the most common characters. Can write numbers and dates, own name, nationality, address, etc., such as on a hotel registration form. Otherwise, ability to write is limited to simple lists of common items such as a few short sentences. Spelling and even representation of symbols (letters, syllables, characters) may be incorrect.

W-1 ELEMENTARY PROFICIENCY
(Base Level)

Has sufficient control of the writing system to meet limited practical needs. Can create by writing statements and questions on topics very familiar to him/her within the scope of his/her very limited language experience. Writing vocabulary is inadequate to express anything but elementary needs; writes in simple sentences making continual errors in spelling, grammar and punctuation but writing can be read and understood by a native reader used to dealing with foreigners attempting to write his/her language. Writing tends to be a loose collection of sentences (or fragments) on a given topic and provides little evidence of conscious organization. While topics which are "very familiar" and elementary needs vary considerably from individual to individual, any person at this level should be able to write simple phone messages, excuses, notes to service people and simple notes to friends. (800-1000 characters controlled.)

W-1+ ELEMENTARY PROFICIENCY
(Higher Level)

Sufficient control of writing system to meet most survival needs and limited social demands. Can create sentences and short paragraphs related to most survival needs (food, lodging, transportation, immediate surroundings and situations) and limited social demands. Can express fairly accurate present and future time. Can produce some past verb forms but not always accurately or with correct usage. Can relate personal history, discuss topics such as daily life, preferences and very familiar material. Shows good control of elementary vocabulary and some control of basic syntactic patterns but major errors still occur when expressing more complex thoughts. Dictionary usage may still yield incorrect vocabulary or forms, although the W-1+ can use a dictionary to advantage to express simple ideas. Generally cannot use basic cohesive elements of discourse to advantage (such as relative constructions, object pronouns, connectors, etc.). Can take notes in some detail on familiar topics, and respond to personal questions using elementary vocabulary and common structures. Can write simple letters, summaries of biographical data and work experience with fair accuracy. Writing, though faulty, is comprehensible to native speakers used to dealing with foreigners.

W-2 LIMITED WORKING PROFICIENCY
(Base Level)

Able to write routine social correspondence and prepare documentary materials required for most limited work requirements. Has writing vocabulary sufficient to express himself/herself simply with some circumlocutions. Can write simply about a very limited number of current events or daily situations. Still makes common errors in spelling and punctuation but shows some control of the most common formats and punctuation conventions. Good control of morphology of language (in inflected languages) and of the most frequently used syntactic structures. Elementary constructions are usually handled quite accurately and writing is understandable to a native reader not used to reading the writing of foreigners. Uses a limited number of cohesive devices.

W-2+ LIMITED WORKING PROFICIENCY
(Higher Level)

Shows ability to write with some precision and in some detail about most common topics. Can write about concrete topics relating to particular interests and special fields of competence. Often shows surprising fluency and ease of expression but under time constraints and pressure language may be inaccurate and/or incomprehensible. Generally strong in either grammar or vocabulary but not in both. Weaknesses or unevenness in one of the foregoing or in spelling result in occasional miscommunication. Areas of weakness range from simple constructions such as plurals, articles, prepositions and negatives to more complex structures such as tense usage, passive constructions, word order and relative clauses. Normally controls general vocabulary with some misuse of everyday vocabulary evident. Shows a limited ability to use circumlocutions. Uses dictionary to advantage to supply unknown words. Can take fairly accurate notes on material presented orally and handle with fair accuracy most social correspondence. Writing is understandable to native speakers not used to dealing with foreigners' attempts to write the language, though style is still obviously foreign.

W-3 GENERAL PROFESSIONAL PROFICIENCY (Base Level)

Able to use the language effectively in most formal and informal written exchanges on practical, social and professional topics. Can write reports, summaries, short library research papers on current events, on particular areas of interest or on special fields with reasonable ease. Control of structure, spelling and general vocabulary is adequate to convey his/her message accurately but style may be obviously foreign. Errors virtually never interfere with comprehension and rarely disturb the native reader. Punctuation generally controlled. Employs a full range of structures. Control of grammar good with only sporadic errors in basic structures, occasional errors in the most complex frequent structures and somewhat more frequent errors in low frequency complex structures. Consistent control of compound and complex sentences. Relationship of ideas is consistently clear.

W-3+ GENERAL PROFESSIONAL PROFICIENCY (Higher Level)

Able to write the language in a few prose styles pertinent to professional/educational needs. Not always able to tailor language to suit audience. Weaknesses may lie in poor control of low frequency complex structures, vocabulary or the ability to express subtleties and nuances. May be able to write on some topics pertinent to professional/educational needs. Organization may suffer due to lack of variety in organizational patterns or in variety of cohesive devices.

W-4 ADVANCED PROFESSIONAL PROFICIENCY (Base Level)

Able to write the language precisely and accurately in a variety of prose styles pertinent to professional/

educational needs. Errors of grammar are rare including those in low frequency complex structures. Consistently able to tailor language to suit audience and able to express subtleties and nuances. Expository prose is clearly, consistently and explicitly organized. The writer employs a variety of organizational patterns, uses a wide variety of cohesive devices such as ellipsis and parallelisms, and subordinates in a variety of ways. Able to write on all topics normally pertinent to professional/educational needs and on social issues of a general nature. Writing adequate to express all his/her experiences.

W-4+ ADVANCED PROFESSIONAL PROFICIENCY (Higher Level)

Able to write the language precisely and accurately in a wide variety of prose styles pertinent to professional/educational needs. May have some ability to edit but not in the full range of styles. Has some flexibility within a style and shows some evidence of a use of stylistic devices.

W-5 FUNCTIONALLY NATIVE PROFICIENCY

Has writing proficiency equal to that of a well-educated native. Without non-native errors of structure, spelling, style or vocabulary can write and edit both formal and informal correspondence, official reports and documents, and professional/educational articles including writing for special purposes which might include legal, technical, educational, literary and colloquial writing. In addition to being clear, explicit and informative, the writing and the ideas are also imaginative. The writer employs a very wide range of stylistic devices.

21 November 1983

These descriptions were approved by the Interagency Language Roundtable, consisting of the following agencies.

Department of Defense
Department of State
Central Intelligence Agency
National Security Agency
Department of the Interior
National Endowment for the Humanities
National Institutes of Health
National Science Foundation
Department of Agriculture
Drug Enforcement Administration

Federal Bureau of Investigation
ACTION/Peace Corps
Agency for International Development
Office of Personnel Management
Immigration and Naturalization Service
Department of Education
US Customs Service
US Information Agency
Library of Congress

CHAPTER 2

Cognitive Analyses of Verbal Aptitude Tests*

Mary E. Curtis

Harvard University, Cambridge, MA

Aptitude testing has long been one of the ways in which the skills of a learner have been considered in educational practice. As a consequence, much research activity has been directed over the years to issues of predictive validity, test reliability, and item construction. With more recent attempts to unify psychological testing with other areas of psychology (e.g., see Carroll, 1978; Cronbach, 1957), however, there has also been an increasing interest in the nature and locus of the individual differences that underly the scores on the tests. In this paper, I describe some of the ways in which cognitive psychologists have attempted to characterize the processes, strategies, and knowledge that contribute to success on verbal aptitude tests. Much of this work is still only in its beginning stages—it requires further validation and understanding. However, it will be argued that viewing individual differences in terms of cognitive functioning can provide us with a basis for moving beyond the prediction of success in school to the design of instruments and environments that maximize the learner's potential for success.

The discussion is organized in terms of three aspects of cognitive functioning that research has shown to be related to verbal aptitude test performance: efficiency in information processing; strategies for processing information; and the nature and extent of semantic knowledge. Within each of these aspects, I attempt to provide a framework for the issues that have been addressed, and to point to those issues that need to be further examined.

EFFICIENCY IN INFORMATION-PROCESSING

The relationship between verbal aptitude and speed of processing has intrigued cognitive psychologists ever since Hunt and his colleagues first asked the question, "What does it mean to be high verbal?" (Hunt, Lunneborg, & Lewis,

* The research reported herein was supported by the Learning Research and Development Center (LRDC), University of Pittsburgh. The LRDC is supported in part as a research and development center by funds from the National Institute of Education (NIE). The opinions expressed do not necessarily reflect the position or policy of NIE and no official endorsement should be inferred.

1975). In their pioneering work in this area, these researchers (see also Hunt, 1978; Hunt, Frost, & Lunneborg, 1973) found that differences in the rate of performing laboratory-developed tasks such as letter-name matching (Posner & Mitchell, 1967) were related to individual differences in scores on verbal ability tests. These differences in the facility with which information was accessed and manipulated in memory led Hunt (1978) to propose that verbal performances are dependent on efficiency in executing the mechanistic (or information-free) processes that activate knowledge in memory. In particular, Hunt argued that inefficiency in the rate at which knowledge is accessed can affect performance on tasks that require access to previously stored verbal information, as well as success in acquiring and applying new information.

The approach taken by Hunt and others to the study of individual differences in aptitude has since been identified as a "cognitive correlates" approach (Pellegrino & Glaser, 1979). That is, conclusions about what aptitude tests measure are made on the basis of skill differences in the performance of basic information-processing tasks. The logic of this kind of approach, as well as its focus on speed in executing very basic cognitive processes, have both been questioned (e.g., Carroll, 1981; Hogaboam & Pellegrino, 1978; Pellegrino & Glaser, 1979; Sternberg & Powell, 1983). More specifically, concerns have been voiced over (a) conclusions about processing differences on aptitude test tasks drawn post hoc from individual differences data, and (b) the modest size of the correlations that have been reported (typically around .3).

An alternative approach, called the "cognitive components" approach (Pellegrino & Glaser, 1979), differs from the previous one in that it begins instead with analyses of the kinds of tasks used on aptitude tests. From these analyses, laboratory tasks are developed which require the processes that underlie the test tasks. Comparisons are then made between the performances of high- and low-aptitude individuals on these laboratory tasks. (The work of Sternberg (1977) and Mulholland, Pellegrino, & Glaser (1980) are examples of this kind of approach).

In a cognitive components approach to verbal aptitude test tasks, access to word name codes in memory would be viewed as a component process that is required for item solution. And if, as the cognitive correlates approach has suggested, efficiency in activating this information in memory is related to verbal aptitude, test performance should then be related to speed in executing this process.

Our preliminary work in this area suggests that this is not, in fact, the case. On the basis of performance on a multiple-choice vocabulary test, we selected a group of high- and low-verbal college undergraduates and a set of target words for further study. The students had Verbal Scholastic Aptitude Test (VSAT) scores either above 600 or below 400. Among the words, two-thirds were from items that were cognitively interesting—that is, both skill groups had either gotten all of the items correct on the test or all of them incorrect. The remaining one-third of the words were taken from items that were psychometrically interesting as well—that is, the high-verbal individuals had gotten all of the items correct on the test while the low-verbal group had missed them all.

We then assessed speed of accessing word name codes in memory with a vocalization task in which the students were asked to read each word aloud as soon as they had identified it. Consistent with the previous findings, speed of accurate word decoding was significantly related to both vocabulary test scores (r = .69) and VSAT scores (r = .65). However, in neither of the skill groups was there a significant difference between the time it took to accurately decode those words taken from correctly answered items and those taken from incorrectly answered items (1.24 ms vs. 1.27 ms in the low-verbal group, and 0.97 ms vs. 0.98 ms in the high-verbal group). Thus, the difference in speed of decoding was related overall to verbal aptitude scores, but not to specific verbal aptitude item performances.

Since it is possible, particularly for skilled readers like those who participated in the study, to vocalize the names of words even when name "codes" do not exist in memory, the vocalization task must be viewed as only a rough assessment of facility in accessing memory information. However, these results do suggest some interesting conclusions about efficiency in information processing and verbal aptitude. First, it appears that word name vocalization is consistent with Hunt's (1978) definition of a mechanistic process. That is, speed in executing it was not affected by the amount of semantic knowledge associated with the particular words. Second, although the relationship between mechanistic processing speed and verbal ability seems to be a very stable one, the nature of that relationship is still not very clear. It seems unlikely that this correlation stems solely from the shared emphasis on speed in both the laboratory and aptitude test tasks, since vocalization speed was not so much related to Quantitative Scholastic Aptitude Test scores (r = .3) as it was to the verbal scores (r = .6). Instead, it may be that facility in accessing word names is related to skill in reading (e.g., see Curtis, 1980; Lesgold & Perfetti, 1981). Since readers who are slow at decoding individual words can experience difficulty in getting meaning out of what they have decoded, individual differences in verbal coding speed could reflect differences in reading ability, and as a consequence, correlate with verbal aptitude test performance.

In summary, the speed at which basic information processes are executed appears to be related, but in only a very general way, to variation in verbal aptitude test scores. Individual differences in success on particular items do not seem to be related to differences in the efficiency in carrying out mechanistic, or information-free, processes. In the following section, research that suggests an alternative source for variation in verbal aptitude test performance will be examined, one that is based instead on skill differences in the kinds of processes that are used in solution of test items.

STRATEGIES FOR PROCESSING INFORMATION

Processing time has been a variable of interest in research that examines variation in the processes that individuals use in dealing with verbal information. In this case, however, the goal has been to discover whether *qualitative* rather than quantitative differences exist in the cognitive processes that underlie aptitude test performances. An example of a qualitative look is Sternberg's (1977) use of latency data to derive values for the processes involved in analogical reasoning. Four such processes were identified: encoding, inferencing, mapping, and decision making. The encoding process was defined by Sternberg as the identification of the semantic attributes of the words in a problem. And, in a laboratory task designed to examine this initial processing, he found that skilled analogical reasoners spent a *greater* proportion of their total solution time in encoding than did the less-skilled reasoners.

Thus, in contrast to the results discussed in the previous section, high-verbal individuals were characterized by more relative time being spent on a particular cognitive process than low verbals. This difference in the use of time during problem solution can be interpreted as a strategy difference between skilled and less-skilled verbal problem-solvers. In particular, Sternberg hypothesized that the more complete initial encoding of the high-verbal individuals allowed them to complete the inferencing, mapping, and decision-making processes in a more efficient manner.

The component processes specified by Sternberg were examined with solution latencies on correct items. As such, only easy analogies were used in this research. However, a very different picture of skill differences in processing time allocation can emerge when the items that are studied are more similar to those used on standardized tests of verbal aptitude. Our own work in this area has involved collection of eye movement data while high- and low-verbal adults (Verbal SATs either above 600 or below 400) are presented with verbal analogy problems and simply asked to solve them. In one of these studies (Gitomer & Curtis, 1983), three types of verbal analogies were used. The first kind consisted of only very easy items—that is, items in which the majority of our subjects were able to successfully solve the analogy without the benefit of the answer terms. The second and third kinds of items were more difficult ones to solve—the second kind because the relationship between the words was difficult to infer or because more than one answer was possible, and the third kind because the meaning of one or more of the words in the items was unfamiliar to the subjects.

In terms of solution accuracy, the high-skill group was more accurate overall than the low-skill group. The third kind of analogy was most difficult for both groups (49% correct for the high-skill group and 21% correct for the low-skill group). The skill group difference was smallest on the easiest items (91% and 84% correct for the high and low verbals on type 1 items; 76% and 48% correct on the type 2 items).

In examining solution processes, we looked at both total solution time and the number of fixations on each kind of item for the skill groups. On the easy problems (type 1), the high-verbal individuals were faster than individuals of the low-verbal group, although both groups made the same number of word fixations. This is consistent with the results on skill differences in efficiency in information processing. Also, in agreement with Sternberg's results, the proportion of total solution time spent on encoding the stem words (or first three words in the analogy) was greater for the high-verbal group than for the low group.

On the more difficult problems (types 2 and 3), both of the groups increased their total time to solution and number of word fixations. Total time to solution on type 2 problems (familiar words but difficult relation) was the same for both groups, but the high skill individuals made more fixations than did the low skill ones. On type 3 problems (unfamiliar vocabulary), the high verbals not only made many more word fixations than the low verbals did, they were also somewhat slower than the low verbals to solve the problems.

According to Sternberg's explanation, it would be expected that the additional time for problem solution (on type 3 items) and the increased number of word fixations (on types 2 and 3) taken by the high-verbal group should have been on the initial encoding of the stem words in the analogy (i.e., before the answer terms had been considered). But this was not the case. The proportion of total solution time spent on initially encoding the first three words was greater for the low-verbal group than for the high verbals on the more difficult items. In contrast to their strategy on the easy items, the high-verbal individuals tended to "look over" the more difficult items, going back and forth between the stem and answer terms many times before selecting their answer.

Thus, item difficulty seems to be a significant influence on the processes that individuals use in solving verbal analogies. Our eye movement data, along with protocol studies of analogical reasoning (e.g., Heller, 1979), suggest that high verbals engage in an "interactive" solution strategy on more difficult problems. This interactive strategy involves much reencoding of the stem and answer terms, and can be contrasted with their strategy on easy items—one in which the initial encoding of the stem allows an answer term to be selected. Low-verbal individuals also seem to use an interactive strategy, but to a much lesser extent and with less success. More often, low-verbal individuals do not seem to differentiate between easy and difficult analogies (based on their total solution times and number of fixations), treating each problem as if it can be solved on the basis of the initial encoding of the stem words and their relation.

This failure of low-skill individuals to engage in the more extensive processing necessary to solve more difficult analogies may be related to limitations of the kind discussed in the previous section. That is, less efficient lower-level processes may take up some of the processing resources that are necessary for higher-level strategies. In addition, however, the differential use of processes by skilled and less-skilled problem-solvers may be related to differential knowledge about the meanings of the words in the analogy items. In the section that follows, research that examines the differences in the semantic knowledge of high- and low-verbal individuals will be discussed.

NATURE OF SEMANTIC KNOWLEDGE

Knowledge of a word's meaning is rarely, if ever, an all-or-none phenomenon, and a considerable amount of research activity has been directed toward establishing the various ways in which a word's meaning can be known. This issue is an important one for studying growth in word knowledge, since the way in which word meaning is measured can influence estimates of vocabulary size (Dale, 1965; Lorge & Chall, 1963). In addition, however, it affects our understanding of individual differences in verbal aptitude, since the ability to perform well on verbal test tasks can be a function of how well one needs to know the meanings of the words. For example, consider the difference in word knowledge that is required by the following two multiple-choice items (from Curtis & Glaser, 1983):

1. *Desist:*   (A) stop   (B) consider   (C) review   (D) debate
2. *Desist:*   (A) pause   (B) halt   (C) prevent   (D) discontinue

Whereas in the first item, a minimal degree of semantic knowledge is necessary to pick the correct answer, the second item requires that a more precise semantic discrimination is made among the answer options.

Although a substantial body of literature exists on the different ways of knowing a word's meaning (e.g., Anderson & Freebody, 1979; Carroll, 1971; Cronbach, 1942) and the interrelationships that exist among various types of vocabulary measures (e.g. Berwick, 1959; Marshalek, 1981; Seashore & Eckerson, 1940), comparatively little work has been done on the nature of the knowledge assessed by verbal aptitude tests. We have recently completed some preliminary work in this area, and in this section, I summarize some of the differences among individuals and item formats that we have identified.

We began by asking the adults who participated in the word vocalization study to define the words that they had read (Curtis, Gitomer, Collins & Glaser, April 1983). As a first step in analyzing these definitions, we sorted them into one of two categories: known versus unknown words. Known words were those that the students were able to recall any accurate semantic information about, regardless of the precision of that information. For example, both of the following definitions were placed in the known category:

3. *"Confiscate* would be like smuggling—they confiscate it from you when they find it."
4. *"Vacillation* means wavering."

Unknown words, on the other hand, were those that the students either gave incorrect information about (e.g., "*Vacillation* probably means the same as vaccination."), or they were unable to define at all.

Although this initial sorting of the definitions represented a very "loose" criterion for knowing the meaning of a word, it corresponded very well with the students' performances on the previously administered vocabulary test. On those items that both the high- and low-verbal groups got correct on the test, the majority of definitions were sorted into the known word category (98% for the high group and 89% for the low). On the psychometrically discriminating items—that is, those that the high group got correct and the low group missed— 84% of the words were scored as known for the high group, while only 20% were known for the low verbals. Finally, on those items that both groups missed on the test, 52% were known for the high group and 22% for the low. Thus, it is apparent even with a very liberal criterion for knowing a word that the low-verbal individuals had *no* accurate semantic information about the majority of the words that they had missed on the vocabulary test.

We were also interested in comparing the quality of the definitions that were generated by the high- and low-verbal groups for the words that they knew. In order to increase the pool of "known" words for each group, we also had the students give us definitions for some of the answer options that had appeared on the test. Using the known/unknown criterion again, 87 out of a possible 96 words (91%) were known to the high-verbal individuals, and 72 words (75%) were known to the low-verbal individuals. In making comparisons between the skill groups on the definitions that were generated for known words, we found an interesting difference. The low-verbal group tended more often than the high group to tie their definitions to specific contexts in which the words could occur (20% vs. 10%). For example, the definition of *confiscate* (example 3 above) would be classified as a contextually tied definition, as were the following:

5. "*Surveillance* is what the police do in crime situations."
6. "*Contempt*—I think of someone being in contempt, like contempt of court—doing something they shouldn't be doing."

The high-verbal group, on the other hand, was more likely than the low verbals to give definitions that considered the word's meaning apart from a context in which it could occur (67% vs. 52%).

Our conclusions from this work thus far are as follows. High-verbal individuals are less likely than low-verbal individuals to include contextualized information in their definitions of words. It is possible, but seems unlikely, that high verbals do not have contextual information available in memory. Instead, what the difference suggests to us is that contextualized information may sometimes be the only information that is available to the low-skill group. Vocabulary tests, in their current form, do not make apparent this qualitative difference in what is known about a word. Since the tests require only a minimal degree of semantic knowledge, they seem to "work" by measuring differences between no knowledge and some knowledge about the meanings of words.

In contrast to vocabulary tests, performance on verbal analogy items can be more directly related to the ability to make precise semantic discriminations among the meanings of words. Although analogies can be difficult because of a lack of knowledge about the meanings of one or more of the words in the item, difficulties can also occur when more than one possible relation exists between words in the stem. We have observed several instances of this in the protocols of low-verbal individuals during solution of analogy problems. For example, consider the following analogy from the Cognitive Abilities Test (Thorndike & Hagen, 1971):

feather: fur:: robin:

When shown this problem, high-verbal college students indicate that, since robins have feathers, the name of any animal with fur will complete the analogy. Many low-verbal students, on the other hand, have told us the *bird* completes this analogy. They base their choice on shared semantic features between the first and second terms (e.g., "Feathers are like fur, and a robin is a bird."). When asked to then select a completion term from the following set of possible answers:

(A) worm   (B) egg   (C) fly   (D) rabbit

they often have a difficult time choosing among the first three answers. *Rabbit,* on the other hand, is easy to eliminate because "rabbits are totally different from birds."

Thus, the kind of information activated about words whose meanings are known can significantly influence the way that high- and low-verbal individuals solve analogy problems. In general, low-skill individuals are more likely to use their initial understanding of the analogical rule as the basis for evaluating the answer options. On items in which an answer "matches" the answer that they generate, they select and justify that answer on the basis of a rule. When an answer does not match their answer, however, they often make a choice on the basis of the word that is semantically closest to it (e.g., "Birds fly."). High-skill individuals, on the other hand, are much more likely to modify their initial understanding of the relation on the basis of the answer options. As indicated in both our protocol and eye movement data, they engage in an increasingly detailed specification of the analogical rule, and continually consider alternative possibilities for that rule. Moreover, in contrast to the low-verbal group, they consistently attend to the nature of the relation rather than violate the constraints of the task by selecting a nonaligned, although semantically related, alternative.

SUMMARY AND CONCLUSIONS

I have described three aspects of cognitive functioning that are related to individual differences in verbal aptitude. The first was efficiency in activating verbal information in memory. Research on this factor indicates that, although a consistent relationship between measures of mechanistic processing speed and verbal aptitude is found, rate of processing information does not seem to be directly related to variations in test performances. Instead, it may be that facility in accessing verbal information is a consequence rather than a source of the variation in knowledge and skills assessed by verbal aptitude tests.

The second aspect of cogitive functioning discussed was the nature and kinds of processes used to solve verbal test tasks. The research reported suggests that high- and low-verbal individuals use different kinds of processes to reach problem solution, particularly on more difficult items. As in the case of information-processing efficiency, however, the sources of these differences remain unclear. Although strategies may be more directly related to aptitude test scores than rate of processing, research on strategic differences is also more descriptive than explanatory of individual differences in test performances.

The third aspect concerned differences in knowledge about word meanings and their relationships. Research on this factor suggests that high- and low-verbal individuals differ in their semantic knowledge in at least two significant ways. First, high-verbal individuals know the meanings of more words than do low-verbal individuals. This difference seems to be the one indicated by scores on most vocabulary tests. Second, high-verbal individuals have more precise knowledge about the meanings of the words that they are familiar with than do low-verbal individuals. Although not directly measured by verbal aptitude test items, the nature of the knowledge associated with words whose meanings are known does seem to be a factor in verbal analogy item performance.

What are the advantages of viewing verbal aptitude in terms of these three factors? First, I think that the cognitive analyses completed thus far point to some interesting directions for future research. Skill differences in the nature and extent of semantic knowledge make it more likely that low verbal individuals will need to engage in more extensive processing. And yet, skill differences in both efficiency at lower-level processing and the kinds of processes used suggest that they are less able or less likely to do this. Rather than competing hypotheses about the sources of individual variation in verbal aptitude, future research must consider the interactions among these interrelated factors. For example, how do these skill differences in semantic knowledge come about in the first place (e.g., see Sternberg & Powell, 1983)? What is the relation between differential knowledge about words and skill differences in the nature and efficiency of verbal information processing?

Second, I believe that these three aspects of cognitive functioning can help us in understanding the predictive power of verbal aptitude tests. For example, facility in verbal coding, including access to semantic information, has been identified as a source of skill differences in reading comprehension. Furthermore, theoretical links among strategies for processing information, the nature and organization of the knowledge base, and comprehension are assumed in current models of the reading process (e.g., see Carpenter & Just, 1981; Rumelhart & Ortony, 1977). Continued research on how these factors influence verbal aptitude test performance should better inform us about how the tests are related to the criterion performances that they predict.

Finally, viewing verbal aptitude in terms of these factors should aid us in designing tests that can be diagnostically informative as well as predictive of success in school. Vocabulary tests would be a good place to begin. Forty years ago, Cronbach (1942, 1943) argued that existing tests of vocabulary knowledge were not indicative of the degree to which understanding of a word's meaning is complete. Perhaps recent cognitive analyses of vocabulary tests can help us now to realize the wisdom of his words.

REFERENCES

Anderson, R.C., & Freebody, P. (1979). *Vocabulary knowledge* (Tech. Rep. No. 136). Urbana-Champaign: University of Illinois, Center for the Study of Reading.

Berwick, M. (1959). The semantic method for testing vocabulary. *Journal of Experimental Education, 28,* 124–141.

Carpenter, P.A., & Just, M.A. (1981). Cognitive processes in reading: Models based on readers' eye fixations. In A.M. Lesgold & C.A. Perfetti (Eds.), *Interactive processes in reading.* Hillsdale, NJ: Lawrence Erlbaum Assoc.

Carroll, J.B. (1971). Development of native language skills beyond the early years. In C.E. Reed (Ed.), *The learning of language.* New York: Appleton-Century-Crofts.

Carroll, J.B. (1978). On the theory-practice interface in the measurement of intellectual abilities. In P. Suppes (Ed.), *Impact of research on education: Some case studies.* Washington, DC: National Academy of Education.

Carroll, J.B. (1981). Ability and task difficulty in cognitive psychology. *Educational Researcher, 10,* 11–21.

Cronbach, L.J. (1942). An analysis of techniques for diagnostic testing in vocabulary. *Journal of Educational Research, 36,* 206–217.

Cronbach, L.J. (1943). Measuring knowledge of precise word meanings. *Journal of Educational Research, 36,* 528–534.

Cronbach, L.J. (1957). The two disciplines of scientific psychology. *American Psychologist, 12,* 671–684.

Curtis, M.E. (1980). Development of components of reading skill. *Journal of Educational Psychology, 72,* 656–669.

Curtis, M.E., Gitomer, D.H., Collins, J., & Glaser, R. (1983, April). *Word knowledge influences on comprehension.* Paper presented at the American Educational Research Association meeting, Montreal.

Curtis, M.E., & Glaser, R. (1983). Reading theory and the assessment of reading achievement. *Journal of Educational Measurement, 20,* 133–147.

Dale, E. (1965). Vocabulary measurement: Techniques and major findings. *Elementary English, 42*, 895–901, 948.

Gitomer, D.H., & Curtis, M.E. (1983, April). *Individual differences in verbal analogy problem solving*. Paper presented at American Educational Research Association meeting, Montreal.

Heller, J.I. (1979). *Cognitive processes in verbal analogy solution*. Unpublished doctoral dissertation, University of Pittsburgh.

Hogaboam, T.W., & Pellegrino, J.W. (1978). Hunting for individual differences in cognitive processes: Verbal ability and semantic processing of pictures and words. *Memory and Cognition, 6*, 189–193.

Hunt, E. (1978). Mechanics of verbal ability. *Psychological Review, 85*, 109–130.

Hunt, E., Frost, N., & Lunneborg, C. (1973). Individual differences in cognition: A new approach to intelligence. In G. Bower (Ed.), *The psychology of learning and motivation* (Vol. 7). New York: Academic Press.

Hunt, E., Lunneborg, C., & Lewis, J. (1975). What does it mean to be high verbal? *Cognitive Psychology, 7*, 194–227.

Lesgold, A.M., & Perfetti, C.A. (1981). *Interactive processes in reading*. Hillsdale, NJ: Lawrence Erlbaum Assoc.

Lorge, I., & Chall, J.S. (1963). Estimating the size of vocabularies of children and adults: An analysis of methodological issues. *Journal of Experimental Education, 32*, 147–157.

Marshalek, B. (1981). *Trait and process aspects of vocabulary knowledge and verbal ability* (Tech. Rep. No. 15). Stanford, CA: Stanford University.

Mulholland, T.M., Pellegrino, J.W., & Glaser, R. (1980). Components of geometric analogy solution. *Cognitive Psychology, 12*, 252–284.

Pellegrino, J.W., & Glaser, R. (1979). Cognitive correlates and components in the analysis of individual differences. *Intelligence, 3*, 187–214.

Posner, M.I., & Mitchell, R. (1967). Chronometric analysis of classification. *Psychological Review, 74*, 392–409.

Rumelhart, D.E., & Ortony, A. (1977). The representation of knowledge in memory. In R.C. Anderson, R.J. Spiro, & W.E. Montagu (Eds.), *Schooling and the acquisition of knowledge*. Hillsdale, NJ: Lawrence Erlbaum Assoc.

Seashore, R.H., & Eckerson, L.D. (1940). The measurement of individual differences in general English vocabularies. *Journal of Educational Psychology, 31*, 14–38.

Sternberg, R.J. (1977). *Intelligence, information processing, and analogical reasoning*. Hillsdale, NJ: Lawrence Erlbaum Assoc.

Sternberg, R.J., & Powell, J.S. (1983). Comprehending verbal comprehension. *American Psychologist, 38*, 878–893.

Thorndike, R.L., & Hagen, E. (1971). *Cognitive abilities test*. Boston: Houghton-Mifflin.

CHAPTER 3

An Exploratory Study of the Relative Difficulty of TOEFL's Listening Comprehension Items[1]

Roy O. Freedle
Educational Testing Service, Princeton, NJ
Christiane Fellbaum
Westminster Choir College, Princeton, NJ

INTRODUCTION

The purpose of this exploratory language study is to analyze the structure and content of test items so as to reveal in greater detail what discriminations are required by test takers in selecting the correct option and avoiding the incorrect options. A secondary purpose is to demonstrate that, once a more detailed description of the structures and contents of test items of a given language test is available, this information can be used to account for relative difficulty among items.

A section of the Test of English as a Foreign Language (TOEFL) called Listening Comprehension was selected for our current purposes because the items involve readily scorable language texts. Typically one sentence is used in the item stem and one sentence is used in each of the response options. A typical example follows.

(The test taker listens to the following sentence):

"John wanted to leave the house." (This part is called the *item stem*)
(1)   John needed a house.
(2)   John intended to get away from the house.
(3)   John wanted Ted to lease the house.
(4)   Leave the house now.

The test taker's task is to pick the response option that best captures the meaning of the item stem. Because such texts are brief and because the manner in which these items were constructed often seems quite apparent, the Listening Comprehension section of TOEFL was thought to be an ideal place to demonstrate

---
[1] This work was funded by the TOEFL Research Committee of ETS, Princeton, N.J. This paper is based upon a 1981 report which was revised and accepted by the research committee in 1982.

that knowledge of these more elementary parts of test items can be used to account for relative difficulty. Having such an analysis of which elementary parts contribute to guiding a test taker's choices can be regarded as a necessary first step in developing a more complete information-processing account of how people respond to verbal test items.

METHODS AND PROCEDURES

This paper represents a first step in developing a set of language measures which most efficiently discloses the critical information found in one section of TOEFL. The reasoning we used to discover what critical language elements are present in each item was as follows. We took a small sample of items and examined each response option for each item. We asked, "What elements does this response option have in common with the item stem and in what ways is it different from the stem?" By using this type of process we quickly isolated what we felt were the crucial structural and content elements which lie behind the construction of these items. Such an exploratory approach to defining our linguistic scoring categories seemed preferable to arbitrarily selecting some existing scoring system (e.g., such as the cohesion system developed by Halliday & Hasan, 1976) and applying it to the data in the hope that it might adequately capture the critical elements which influence response selections (and hence influence item difficulty). Because there was no a priori reason for selecting any existing language scoring system over any other, the pragmatic approach described above seemed preferable. Also it was hypothesized that the pragmatic approach would increase the likelihood that the two goals of this project would be achieved: by selecting just those language measures which appear necessary to distinguish correct from incorrect responses, one would more likely be able to say what elementary language discriminations are being tested by this particular language competency test (i.e., the Listening Comprehension section of TOEFL) and one would more likely be able to identify why one test item is harder than another.

Materials Used

This project focused upon 100 test items taken from five Listening Comprehension sections of TOEFL (20 items times five forms = 100 items). A scoring system using eight language measures was developed and applied to these 100 items and the results were correlated with the percentage of individuals that got each item correct.

Additional analyses examined the relative difficulty of each item for each of five ability groups. These ability groups were automatically computed in TOEFL reports of item statistics which were made available to us. A description of how these five ability groups were defined is given in the footnote of Table 1. The number of people who responded to each test administration and other relevant information concerning the five test forms is also provided in Table 1.

Table 1. Number of People Who Responded to Each of Five Test Forms

No. Items Used from Section A	Test Form	No. Students	No. Students in Each of Five Ability Groups[a]
20	1	2,635	527
20	2	1,680	336
20	3	1,935	387
20	4	1,970	394
20	5	2,105	421
100 items total			

[a]The five ability groups for each test form were determined as follows. The total test score for each student was found. Those students in the top 20% were assigned to the top ability group, those students in the next 20% were assigned to the second ability group, and so on down to the lowest-ability group which consisted of those students who received the lowest total test scores on TOEFL.

Language Measures Used

Eight language measures were developed to score each of the 100 items from the Listening Comprehension sections. After scanning many items from such tests, eight critical measures were finally isolated which appear to exhaust most of the variations found among such items. They fall into four general categories:

a. Phonological (to be described below),
b. Word and phrase level,
c. Sentence level (or clause level), and
d. Suprasentential level (involving two or more clauses).

The Phonological Level. At this level two measures were defined. One is called a *similar pair* and the other *homonymity*.

1. A phonologically similar pair measure establishes a sound relationship between one or more words in the item stem and one or more words in a response option, for example, "He looked *sick*" versus "He looked at the *thick*ening fog." The correspondence is between *sick* and *thick*. Another example would be "The *hostess* is alone" and "*Most es*timates are low." The correspondence is now between *hostess* and *most-es* (note that the latter spans two words to establish the sound correspondence with *hostess*). Our notion of a similar pair can reduce to the more typical idea of a minimal pair when a single word in the item stem is separated by a single phonemic contrast with a word in a response option, for example, "I *found* it" versus "I *bound* it." For economy's sake, we grouped all these relationships under the single category of a similar pair.

Suppose the item stem asserted "She needed a *rest*" and one of the incorrect response options was "She needed to be *dressed.*" In order to reject this option as a close paraphrase of the stem, one must have sufficient command of English to notice this phonological (and graphemic) distinction—the stem is presented aurally whereas the response options are presented in printed form; thus one actually is dealing with a phonological versus a graphemic contrast in comprehension. It was hypothesized that the lowest ability students would show a significant attraction for distractors involving similar pairs whereas the choices of progressively higher scoring individuals would show a decreasing correlation with this measure. One should note at this point that many of the categories to be scored below can have more than one occurrence of the same category for any given response option. For example, if the stem was "His *mouth* needed a *rest*" and the response option under consideration was "His *mouse* needed a *nest,*" then there are two occurrences of the similar pair category for this particular response option vis-a-vis the item stem.

2. The measure called homonymity is more familiar. If the stem asserts "There were *two* cars present" and one of the response options is "There were *too* many cars present," we see that *two* and *too* represent an occurrence of the homonym category linking this response option with the item stem. We hypothesized that if this measure proved to be significantly associated with item difficulty, then the lowest scoring individuals (the lowest of the five ability groups) would be more likely to select options involving homonyms than would the higher scoring groups.

The Word (Lexical) and Phrase Level. Four scores reflected the lexical and phrasal levels in comparing an item stem with each of the options: *morphology, lexical synonymity, lexical inference,* and *lexical repetition.*

1. One morphological variation is illustrated by the following. Suppose the item stem asserts "Her *friend* was pleasant" and one of the options is "The *friendly* person was present." *Friend* is a noun whereas *friendly* is an adjective and both derive from a common lexical stem; hence this would be scored in our morphology category. This particular example also would be scored for an occurrence of the similar pair category since the stem and option share a phonologically similar pair of words (e.g., *pleasant* and *present*).

2. An example of our lexical synonymity category would be the use of the word *car* in the item stem and *automobile* in a response option. Both words mean roughly the same thing. The same would apply for the words *incorrect* and *wrong.*

3. An example of our category of lexical inference would be as follows. Suppose the item stem asserts "She loves bright colors" and a response option asserts "She likes red." *Color* and *red* are related in a superordinate/subordinate manner. Also, in this same item *love* and *like* would be inferentially connected at the lexical level. This category represents a more sophisticated command of English and hence we might expect higher scoring students to show a significant

correlation in correctly selecting a response option that involves the ability to make a lexical inference.

4. The last measure used at the lexical (or phrasal) level is called lexical repetition. This category is used when a repetition between words in the item stem is found in a particular response option, providing the words have a similar meaning and referent (see scoring manual in the appendix for further details). Small variations in plurality (e.g., doll/dolls and car/cars) were ignored in matching lexically repeated items in stem and response options. For example, a repetition occurs when the item stem asserts "Those cars upset me" and the response option asserts "The car upset me." This example also repeats the words *upset* and *me* across stem and response option so the total number of entries for the lexical repetition category for this response option would be 3. Only content words were considered in scoring this category.

Sentence or Clausal Level.   At this level we have a category called *case*. This refers to the semantic role that a noun or noun phrase or pronoun occupies in a sentence (see scoring manual in the appendix for further details). For example, if the stem asserts "*He* cut the grass" and the option is "The grass was cut *by him*" then they share the agent case even though one word (*he*) is in the subject position while the phrase *by him* is in the predicate. For simplicity of scoring, Fillmore's (1968) categories were adopted from his early work along with two categories from his later word (Fillmore, 1971) which replaced the dative case with two other cases—the beneficiary and experiencer (see Appendix A for details). The reader should carefully note that our use of Fillmore's case system is strictly pragmatically based rather than theoretically based. It is used here because in the exploratory study of listening comprehension items, it was found that many items use, for example, the same agent case in the item stem and response option, but that the verb type does not necessarily match. For example, comparing the sentences "Mary performed" and "Mary hit the ball," it seemed desirable to capture the fact that *Mary* plays a similar agent role in the two sentences (in addition to being recorded as a lexical repetition) even though the verb in the first sentence is intransitive and in the second is transitive. It would be more accurate then for the reader to regard our case scoring as a pragmatic device deriving its inspiration from Fillmore's early work, rather than as an accurate reflection of ongoing work in linguistic case theory (see, e.g., Cook, 1972). The seven case roles which were used are as follows: agent, experiencer, beneficiary, factitive, objective, locative, and instrumental (see appendix for examples and definitions). Because of the subtlety of the case category, we might expect that only higher ability students would be able to make this distinction among the item stem and response options.

Suprasentential Level.   There is only one category which occurs at the suprasentential level; it is called logical inference. This category appears to be the most difficult discrimination of all to make. It involves relating the meaning of one sentence in the stem with another whole sentence in a response option. For example, if the stem asserts ''She cut her finger,'' then an inferentially related sentence among the response options might be ''She injured part of her hand because of carelessness.'' While *finger* and *part of her hand* are linked at a lower category level (e.g., lexical inference), it is still the case that one must realize that the entire information in the response option is consistent with the information in the item stem; because none of the other categories can fully convey such information, we would score this particular example as illustrating an occurrence of the logical inference category. To be absolutely clear about this example we want to point out that *injured* and *cut* would also be scored as an occurrence of lexical inference and *she* would be scored as a repeated case across stem and option. Nevertheless there is a substantial part of the option (i.e., . . . *because of carelessness*) that is consistent with the information in the stem but does not seem to be scorable by the seven other categories. The logical inference category is used to cover special information of this type. Our hypothesis is that if this category helps to discriminate item difficulty, only the higher ability individuals will be able to use information of this type. (Note: A fully scored example is given in Appendix B using all 8 categories.)

Each of the 100 test items from the Listening Comprehension section had four response options. Every such option was scored for the frequency of occurrence of each of these eight language measures. Hence 400 response options were scored (100 correct options and 300 incorrect options) for each of the eight language measures.

RESULTS AND DISCUSSION

Stability of Language Measures Across Test Forms
The mean occurrence of each of the eight language measures for each of the five test forms is shown in Table 2. It is obvious that the frequency of use of each of the eight measures is relatively constant across the five test forms. If we examine the right-most column which averages the use of these measures across the five test forms we see that the category called lexical repetition is the one most frequently used. Next most frequent in use is the case category followed by lexical inference. The category called logical inference is the least used among the eight measures.

The simplest way to check the stability of any given measure is to use the standard deviation which is listed in parentheses to the right of each mean frequency. For example, the largest mean frequency for the lexical repetition category is 2.012 and the smallest is 1.612. We would like to know if this difference indicates whether the two test forms from which these means were taken are very different from each other. The difference between 2.012 and 1.612 equals .400. This amount is much smaller than each of the standard deviations listed to the right of each frequency in the lexical repetition row (e.g., .400 is

Table 2. Mean Frequency of Use (and Standard Deviation) of Each Language Measure for Each of Five Test Forms

Language Measure	Form 1	Form 2	Form 3	Form 4	Form 5	Mean Freq. for All Five Forms
Log. Inf.	.125 (.333)	.112 (.318)	.112 (.318)	.112 (.318)	.112 (.318)	.115
Case	.712 (.750)	1.025 (.842)	.688 (.628)	.900 (.686)	.938 (.643)	.853
Lex. Rep.	1.612 (.934)	1.800 (.999)	2.000 (1.091)	2.012 (.974)	1.662 (.795)	1.817
Synony.	.287 (.556)	.325 (.591)	.362 (.648)	.262 (.522)	.462 (.635)	.340
Lex. Inf.	.637 (.661)	.412 (.650)	.563 (.653)	.287 (.482)	.438 (.613)	.467
Morph.	.200 (.403)	.063 (.244)	.125 (.333)	.162 (.371)	.162 (.371)	.142
Homony.	.087 (.284)	.100 (.302)	.175 (.444)	.100 (.302)	.162 (.404)	.125
Sim. Pr.	.188 (.424)	.438 (.592)	.438 (.672)	.425 (.632)	.262 (.497)	.350

smaller than .934, .999, 1.091, .974, and .795, respectively). Because it is smaller, the observed difference can in effect be discounted.

A Comparison of the Eight Language Scores for Correct and Incorrect Options

This section will examine whether the eight language scores occur equally often for the correct response options as compared to the incorrect options. The next set of tables helps to answer this issue. First consider Table 3.

In Table 3 are presented the mean frequency of use of the eight language scores for the correct as well as the incorrect response options. Several differences be!ween the two sections of the table are evident. For example, a mean of zero occurs for the use of logical inference when incorrect options are examined (except for one instance of a mean of .05) Correct options tend to have nonzero entries for logical inference. Some other obvious differences between correct and incorrect options are the zero entries for homonymity and similar pairs that occur among the correct options for each of the five test forms. Incorrect options by contrast have entries larger than zero for these same two language categories.

These differences make a good deal of sense. It would be difficult (but not impossible) to construct correct options that used homonyms and/or similar pair contrasts; it is easy to use similar pairs and homonyms among incorrect options.

Table 3. Mean Frequency of Occurrence of Eight Language Scores for Each of Five Parallel Forms (Section I, Part A)

Name of Category[a]	Form 1	Form 2	Form 3	Form 4	Form 5
Only correct options scored for five parallel forms					
Log. Inf.	.500	.400	.450	.450	.450
Case	.950	1.100	.750	.950	1.200
Lex. Rep.	1.750	1.850	1.650	2.000	1.900
Synony.	.600	.700	.950	.650	.750
Lex. Inf.	.600	.500	.500	.450	.500
Morph.	.150	.100	.000	.150	.050
Homony.	.000	.000	.000	.000	.000
Sim. Pr.	.000	.000	.000	.000	.000
Only incorrect options scored for five parallel forms					
Log. Inf.	.000	.167	.000	.000	.000
Case	.633	.983	.667	.900	.850
Lex. Rep.	1.583	1.766	1.483	1.967	1.583
Synony.	.183	.200	.167	.133	.367
Lex. Inf.	.650	.367	.600	.233	.417
Morph.	.217	.050	.167	.167	.200
Homony.	.117	.133	.233	.133	.217
Sim. Pr.	.250	.583	.583	.567	.350

Similarly, a logical inference is difficult (but not impossible) to construct for incorrect options but is a very natural category to use for correct options. The fact that there are differences in category use for correct versus incorrect options is not disturbing for these particular categories. However, the next category which we shall discuss (that of synonymity) is perhaps less easily justified. A large difference in frequency of use can be seen between correct and incorrect options. A mean of .73 occurrence per correct option is found as contrasted with a mean of only .21 per incorrect option. Thus correct options use more than three times as many synonyms as do the incorrect options. Should this category turn out to be highly correlated with item difficulty it would suggest that people notice which option has at least one synonym in it and choose that option over the remaining options (the incorrects) which happen to have virtually no synonyms. While later analyses will reveal that this is not quite the case, we discuss the possibility of such an outcome for several reasons. One is that it shows how one might hypothesize what decision strategy test takers might use in order to select which of several response options is the best one. Another is that it points out the virtue of performing very detailed linguistic analyses of test items—one can detect patterns that might otherwise have eluded the test writers attention, and, once a discrepancy is found one has the option of deciding whether this is serious enough to warrant changing how new items are written. In the present case the discrepancy is not really serious because (as we shall see) the synonym category does not play a very significant role in influencing choices among response options (and hence plays little role in item difficulty).

The discrepancy noted above concerning the absence of homonyms and similar pairs for the correct options, and a relatively heavy use of these for the incorrect options is actually a desirable difference to maintain. A good user of English will notice the "play" on sound that occurs among many of the incorrect options and will use this knowledge to avoid choosing those options. Similarly, the ability to notice the occurrence of a logical inference—which tends to occur only for some of the correct response options—reflects an appropriate language capability for helping one make an informed decision about which option is the best or closest paraphrase of the item stem. The reason the synonym category seemed to provide a more difficult result for us is that a strategy based on such a minor discrimination (as the main rule for deciding which option is the correct one) would tend to trivialize what is otherwise a perfectly good language capability—namely, the ability to detect close paraphrases among sentences. If one were really interested in a student's ability to detect only synonyms, the best way to test this would be in a simple vocabulary test. Fortunately, the results which will be presented later in this report indicate that synonym detection do not play a strong role in guiding choices among alternative options.

The analyses presented below are intended to determine which combination (if any) of these language scores is significantly related to the ability to identify the correct option for each test item. Before investigating this, however, two additional issues will be addressed: the percentage of occurrence of each of the seven Fillmore cases and the reliability of each of the eight language scores.

Percent Use of Each of the Seven Scored Semantic Cases for Correct and Incorrect Response Options

Of the eight language scores, only the measure involving case matches consisted of subcategories, here the seven scored cases consisting of agentive, experiencer, beneficiary, factitive, objective, locative, and instrumental (see Appendix A for definitions). Of the 100 correct response options, 75% involved case matches; that is, the item stem and the correct option had at least one case in common for 75% of the items. For the remaining 25% no case matches were found. On the other hand, when the 300 incorrect response options were examined, only 63.7% involved at least one case match with the item stem (and 39.3% involved no case match with the item stem). Clearly, a correct option is more likely to involve case matching than an incorrect option.

If one restricts the sample to just those items that involve at least one case match with the item stem, the differences between correct and incorrect options disappear with respect to the relative frequency of use for each of the seven cases. For example, among the 75 correct options that involve at least one case match one has the following percentage of use for the seven cases: 69.0% for the agentive case, 0.0% for the experiencer case, 2.0% for the beneficiary case, 15.5% for the factitive case, 0.0% for the objective case, 13.3% for the locative case, and 0.0% for the instrumental case. The corresponding percentages for just those incorrect options that had at least one case match with their item stems are as follows: 61.8% for the agentive case, 7.4% for the experiencer case, 1.2% for the beneficiary case, 12.0% for the factitive case, 6.2% for the objective case, 10.8% for the locative case, and 0.4% for the instrumental case.

One sees that the most frequently used case is the agentive (69.0% for correct options and 61.8% for incorrect options). The second most frequently used case is the factitive (15.5% for correct and 12.0% for incorrect options). The third most frequently used case is the locative (13.3% for correct options and 10.8% for the incorrect options). By and large the case types tend to be used at about the same overall percentage level for correct and incorrect response options, provided our calculations are restricted to just those items that involve at least one case match with their respective item stems.

Reliability of the Eight Language Scores

Table 4 presents the interrater reliability of each of the eight language scores. Two judges experienced in language analysis scored 80 response items in a first round of training. This was followed by a discussion of differences between the two scorers which led to minor refinements in the scoring manual. Finally,

Table 4. Interrater Reliability for Each of Eight Language Measures

Name of Language Measure	Reliability
Similar Pair	.884
Homonymity	.711
Morphology	.948
Lexical Inference	.815
Synonymity	.669
Lexical Repetition	.936
Case	.925
Logical Inference	.233

another 80 response items were scored and this second group provided the basis for the reported reliabilities.[2] In Table 4 one sees that the reliabilities are, in general, quite high. For example, a high reliability was obtained for the most frequently occurring category of lexical repetition ($r = .936$). Case, the second most frequently used category, was also high in reliability ($r = .925$).

The third most frequently used category, lexical inference, also produced a moderately high reliability ($r = .815$). Similar pairs, the next most frequently used category, yielded a moderately high reliability of .884. Synonymity, the next most frequent category, yielded a value of .669. The three least occurring categories were morphology, homonymity, and logical inference; their reliabilities were .948, .711, and .233, respectively. The only extremely low reliability was for logical inference; however, since this category is not productively used among the 100 test items (i.e., has the lowest frequency of use), this reliability is not a troublesome matter. (In fact, as will be seen below, this score was not a significant predictor in accounting for item difficulty.)

Correlation of an Item's Eight Language Scores with the Percentage of Students Passing an Item

In all subsequent results the five test forms will be combined into a single sample of 100 items (20 items from each of the five forms). The concern of this section is whether the language scores are significantly correlated with item difficulty,

---

[2] The reliabilities are based on two types of correlation coefficients. The variable called "logical inference" can assume one of two values—either '0' or '1'. This means that either the response option has the desired characteristic or it doesn't; correlations based on data obtained from such a condition are called "point biserials" (see McNemar, 1962, p. 112). For the remaining language measures, the correlation coefficient is based on the Pearson product moment correlation. In this case the values from each judge's judgments can assume any integer value from '0' to any arbitrarily large integer value.

and, whether the five ability groups show different patterns of correlation with the eight language scores. (The percentage of students who identified the correct option was correlated with the frequency of use of each category for each of the 100 items.)

The correlations for the correct options and the frequency of use of each category for each of five ability groups is given in Table 5.

Table 5 is quite interesting. It indicates that lexical repetition is positively correlated with getting an item correct; this is especially true of the lowest-ability groups. (A psychological interpretation will be given to this finding momentarily.) The correlational results also suggest that lexical synonymity may be playing a slightly significant role in discriminating among the ability groups, but only at the lower levels of ability. (Later it will be argued, following a presentation of the regression results,[3] that there may not be any real contribution made by lexical synonymity; hence a simple examination of the correlational patterns is not in itself a sufficient way to determine how the language scores combine to predict performance on these items.)

The correct option correlated with the frequency of use of each of the eight language measures has just been presented. A similar correlation can be computed for the incorrect options. These are presented in Table 6 below. In this table 100 test items are still represented. The three incorrect options have been summed for each of the eight language measures, and the number of entries per correlation coefficient is still 100. These frequencies were correlated with the percent who passed each item in order to facilitate comparisons across Tables 5 and 6.

In Table 6 it is again seen that lexical repetition plays a significant role in accounting for each ability group's performance. For the lowest ability group three language scores account for all the significant correlational effects: lexical repetition ($r = -.22$), lexical inference ($r = -.20$), and similar pair ($r = .26$). The negative correlations here mean the following: The more lexical repetitions that occur among the incorrect options, the more likely the low-ability students will be to select a wrong option; hence, the lower will be their score on percent corrects. A similar analysis is applied to lexical inference. It is seen that low-ability students are attracted to wrong options whenever there are lexical inferences present; this attraction was not in evidence for choosing the correct option, however. A positive correlation is found for similar pairs and the proba-

---

[3] The reason a simple correlational result may not give us a fully accurate picture of what combination of variables is most predictive of test performance is as follows. Suppose two variables both show a very high correlation with performance. Call these variables A and B. Ordinarily one might think that a combination of both these variables would yield an even better prediction of performance than each alone would give. But for this to be true, we would have to show that A and B are not correlated with each other. If they are very highly correlated, then one is just a "substitute" for the other; a regression analysis partials out the effects of intercorrelations among the predictor variables in determining which combination of variables is the best set of predictors.

Table 5. Correlation of Percent Passing an Item with the Frequency of Use of Each Language Measure (Correct Option Only)

Language Measure	The Five Ability Groups					Correlation for All Five Ability Groups
	A (Lowest)	B	C	D	E (Highest)	
Log. Inf.	−.06	−.05	−.06	−.05	−.04	−.05
Case	.12	.16	.17	.11	.02	.13
Lex. Rep.	.35**	.37**	.37**	.29**	.16	.34**
Synony.	−.19*	−.19*	−.18	−.12	−.10	−.17
Lex. Inf.	−.07	−.12	−.12	−.11	.01	−.09
Morph.	.00	.05	.05	.07	.03	.05
Homony.	—	—	—	—	—	— tends not to occur
Sim. Pr.	—	—	—	—	—	— for the correct option

Note: There are always 100 items compared for each correlation; the only thing that changes over ability groups is the percentage of individuals who passed the item.

*The correlation is significant at the .05 level of probability.

**The correlation is significant at the .01 level of probability.

Table 6. Correlation of Percent Passing an Item with the Frequency of Use of Each Language Measure (Calculated for Sum of Incorrect Options Only)

Language Measure	The Five Ability Groups					Correlation for All Five Ability Groups
	A (Lowest)	B	C	D	E (Highest)	
Log. Inf.	−.12	−.12	−.11	−.11	−.07	−.11
Case	−.10	−.04	−.03	−.06	−.13	−.07
Lex. Rep.	−.22*	−.14	−.12	−.12	−.18	−.16
Synony.	−.08	−.08	−.09	−.10	−.09	−.09
Lex. Inf.	−.20*	−.16	−.16	−.14	−.16	−.17
Morph.	.00	.04	.03	.04	.06	.04
Homony.	.07	.03	.07	.06	.09	.07
Sim. Pr.	.26**	.18	.13	.08	.10	.16

*The correlation is significant at the .05 level of probability.
**The correlation is significant at the .01 level of probability.

bility of choosing a correct option! This suggests that low-ability students try to avoid incorrect options by noticing when there is a similar/pair. This means that low ability students try to *avoid* incorrect options by noticing when there is a similar pair present across item stem and response option. Thus the correlational results seem to suggest that low-ability students may pick their correct options in the following way: They notice which option has many lexical repetitions; among these, they restrict their choice to that option which does not contain any similar pairs. Needless to say, this is not a very workable set of strategies to use in finding the correct paraphrase of the stem since one is at the vagaries of whether an item happens to use similar pairs anywhere among its incorrect options. Also one is never sure that the correct option has more lexical repetitions than the incorrect options. Nevertheless, use of these strategies might enable these students to attain better than a chance score.

The evidence for these strategies is indirect. But one can see that the correlational results must be taken to imply something different about the behavior of high- and low-ability groups. By definition, the fact that the low-ability groups do not do well means—for the listening comprehension part, at least—that they do not often identify the correct paraphrase of the whole item stem. If they do not comprehend the whole sentence (or sentences) of the stem, then there is always the possibility that they have tried to comprehend the parts of the sentence(s). But these part scores are precisely what most of our language measures consist of. Hence, the fact that these language scores do show a significant correlation with the performance of the lower ability groups (and fail to show a strong result for the higher ability groups) is the basis for our deduction that these results reflect the existence of a psychological strategy for comprehending the test items.

It was noted that lexical repetition plays an important role in choosing a correct option and in selecting an incorrect option. This is especially so when one examines the lowest-ability groups. These two results together suggest the following application: *There are at least two ways to make an item easy:* Increase the lexical repetitions in the correct option, and/or decrease the lexical repetitions among the incorrect options. A corollary of this is that there are at least two ways to make any new test item from the listening comprehension section hard: Decrease the lexical repetitions in the correct option, and/or increase the lexical repetitions occurring among the incorrect options.

Numerically, if an item had a 70% chance of being correct, it was determined that the addition of a single lexical repetition to the correct option increased the chance of a correct response to 80%: likewise, if one increased the number of lexical repetitions by 1 anywhere among the incorrect options, the chance of a correct response decreased by a similar amount (from 70% to 60%).

Regression Analysis

In addition to the simple correlational analysis presented above we can also examine the relationship of item difficulty (percent who get item correct) as a *joint* function of the eight language scores for the correct as well as the incorrect options. Regression analysis was used to examine this joint influence. The following general format was used:

$$\frac{\text{Independent variable}}{\underset{\text{(\% correct for each of 100 items)}}{y}} = \frac{\text{Dependent variables}}{ax_1 + \cdots + hx_8 + ix_9 + \cdots + px_{16} + q}$$

where
x_1 through x_8 equal the frequencies of use of the eight language scores for the correct option;
a through h are the numerical weights estimated by the regression routine that best fits the % correct score for each item;
x_9 through x_{16} equal the frequencies of use of the eight language scores summed over the three incorrect response options for a particular item;
i through p represent the numerical weights that best fit the % correct score for each item; and
q represents an added constant.

The reason we group all three distractor options together in this regression analysis is as follows. Items differ in the composition of each distractor with respect to our language scores. For example, an item may have a clearly wrong option involving, say, a similar pair while the remaining two distractors may involve homonyms. Another item may have two clearly wrong options involving similar pairs and may have one distractor using a homonym. There is no simple way to combine all types of items that differ so widely in their distractor patterns except to sum all distractor characteristics together into a single group of variables. By doing so, such a regression analysis can tell whether the percent correct is in any way associated with just the characteristics of the correct option, or whether it is some more complex function of both the correct option characteristics and all distractor characteristics.

Table 7 below presents the results of a stepwise regression analysis for each of the five ability groups. Only the significant predictors are listed. (In each case the first three stepwise variables were significant for each ability group.)

One can see that the strongest predictor is almost always the lexical repetition score that occurs for the correct response option and the second most important predictor (in terms of magnitude of its F score) is typically lexical repetitions for the incorrect options. The third most important predictor is lexical inference for just the incorrect options.

These results are fairly consistent with what was found for the simple correlations, except that now we are able to combine all the important variables into a single equation that optimizes the fit of the observed language scores to the

Table 7. Results of a Step-Wise Regression Analysis

Ability Group	Best Predictors	F Value	Beta Weight	Multiple Regression	Percent Variance Accounted for	
A (lowest)	Lexical Rep. (correct)	32.8	11.6	.57	31	(adjusted)
	Lexical Rep. (incorrect)	25.8	−4.0			
	Lexical Inf. (incorrect)	5.0	−3.0			
	q = added constant		37.4			
B	Lexical Rep. (correct)	28.2	12.9	.52	25	"
	Lexical Rep. (incorrect)	15.3	−3.7			
	Lexical Inf. (incorrect)	2.9	−2.7			
	q = added constant		46.7			
C	Lexical Rep. (correct)	26.2	13.1	.50	23	"
	Lexical Rep. (incorrect)	12.9	−3.5			
	Lexical Inf. (incorrect)	2.6	−2.7			
	q = added constant		55.8			
D	Lexical Rep. (correct)	16.0	10.2	.42	15	"
	Lexical Rep. (incorrect)	8.8	−2.9			
	Lexical Inf. (incorrect)	2.0	−2.3			
	q = added constant		69.0			
E (highest)	Lexical Rep. (correct)	6.7	4.5	.35	10	"
	Lexical Rep. (incorrect)	8.7	−2.0			
	Lexical Inf. (incorrect)	3.0	−1.9			
	q = added constant		89.9			
All groups combined	Lexical Rep. (correct)	25.2	10.6	.51	23	"
	Lexical Rep. (incorrect)	15.5	−3.2			
	Lexical Inf. (incorrect)	3.1	−2.4			
	q = added constant		59.2			

percent correct score for each of the 100 test items. For example, if we use the results for the lowest-ability group, we would write the regression equation as follows:

$y = 11.6$ (lex.rep.) $- 4.0$ (lex.rep.;incorrects) $- 3.0$ (lex.inf.; incorrects) $+ 37.4$.

When such results are calculated for each of the 100 items for the lowest-ability students the overall agreement between observed and predicted percent correct yields a multiple correlation of $r = .57$. This accounts for 31% of the variance in the observed percent correct score.

In general, the regression analysis best predicts the lower-ability students and predicts only a moderate amount of the variance for the highest-ability group (10%). For all groups combined, the overall variance accounted for is 23%.

These regression results suggest the hypothesis that for low-ability students (and to a lesser degree for higher-ability students) the following response strategies are in effect: *Choose that option which tends to repeat most of the same words as used in the item stem and avoid those options which use lexical inference.*

One can use the regression equations to predict how any *new* test item will fare when exposed to a population similar to the one who took TOEFL in 1980. First, select the most important predictor variables and score the new item for its frequency of use of each of these critical predictors. Then, place the resulting frequencies into the regression equation. The result is the predicted percentage of students who will get this new item correct.

Intercorrelations Among the Eight Language Scores for Correct and Incorrect Options

It was noted earlier that there are some puzzling aspects that result from both the correlational and regression analyses that are difficult to explain. In particular it is hard to see why lexical inferences play a significant role when they appear among the incorrect options but fail to play a significant role when they appear among the correct options. One way to try to understand this result is to look in more detail at the correlations that exist among the predictor variables themselves. A set of detailed intercorrelations are presented in Appendix B; the interested reader is referred to these results. The gist of the argument presented there is that the source of the asymmetry is due primarily to the fact that there is a nonsignificant correlation which links the number of lexical inferences among the correct option to the number of lexical inferences that occur among the incorrect options of each item. Furthermore, the correlation patterns of lexical inferences among the eight language measures is different when just the correct responses are intercorrelated as compared with the incorrect responses. Given these differences in intercorrelation patterns, it is hardly surprising that the number of lexical inferences among the incorrect responses proves to be a significant predictor of item difficulty whereas the number of lexical inferences used for the correct responses does not prove to be significant. (See Appendix C for a detailed discussion of these patterns.)

CONCLUSION

Phase 1 of this project has intensively analyzed 100 test items from the Listening Comprehension section of TOEFL. The major results are as follows:

1. Five parallel forms from the Listening Comprehension section of TOEFL were found to be very similar in their underlying language patterns; each scored category was within 1 standard deviation of every other test form. Thus high consistency was found in the underlying language factors that were used to generate the listening comprehension test.
2. In terms of the most frequently used language patterns, listening comprehension items use lexical repetition most frequently, followed next by semantic case and lexical inference.
3. Correlational and regression analyses suggest a functional rule that may operate in determining which test items will be difficult and which easy. The functional rule singles out *lexical repetition* as the main factor determining item difficulty and also suggests a smaller contribution stemming from use of *lexical inference*.
4. The five ability groups analyzed appear to make differential use of this functional rule such that the lowest-ability students rely upon it most heavily, while successively higher-ability groups rely upon it less heavily.
5. Generally high reliability coefficients apply to our scoring procedure for eight language measures.
6. The regression equations were shown to be useful in predicting how difficult any new item might be in advance of administering the item. In general, it was argued that a new test item can be made more difficult by increasing the number of lexical repetitions among its incorrect options and/or decreasing the number of lexical repetitions in the correct option. Also the new item can be made more difficult if more lexical inferences are added to the incorrect response options. In corollary fashion, a new item can be made easier by decreasing lexical repetitions among its distractors and/or increasing them within the correct option. And it can be made increasingly easier by deleting lexical inferences among the distractor options.

As illustrated by the other chapters in this volume, this work falls into a general family of work now being pursued by a few psychologists and linguists who seek to understand the various discriminations that test-takers make when answering multiple-choice questions. Although the present work has purposefully chosen to analyze language items which appear to have a simple structure and content, the quantitative approach which has been advanced demonstrates the feasibility of carrying out a detailed analytic approach to language comprehension items and has demonstrated the feasibility of initially identifying several possible response strategies that examinees may bring to the language task.

A more detailed extension of this work could proceed in two directions. First, an experimental approach could be initiated in order to study the time it takes each examinee to respond to each item. One might consider studying eye scan movements in order to gain more information about what particular aspects of test items are being compared over successive units of time prior to the test-taker making a final choice from among the response options. Second, one could study a more complex set of language items such as that contained in three-person interactions or that contained in reading passages in TOEFL; this can be done in order to study whether the quantitative techniques used in this present study naturally extend to these more complex language materials. Of course, included in this second approach, one could pursue a more experimental approach by also studying eye scan movements and response times for these more complex language materials. These new approaches would enlarge one's understanding of the contribution that psychology can make to analyzing the various discriminations that people make to language competency test items.

Another set of implications of this work exists for people engaged in test item construction. It should be fairly clear that analyzing in greater depth the structures and contents contained in language competency items has sometimes brought to light some minor discrepancies between the frequency with which different language measures occur for the correct as opposed to the incorrect response options. In most cases, improvement in the quality of control of such test items can be attained by applying such language analyses as a final stage in the construction of new test forms; that is, the slight biases can easily be removed by increasing the number of case matches between item stem and the incorrect response options. This is done by rewording one or more of the response options. Similarly, the slight discrepancy in frequency of occurrence between correct and incorrect options for the language measure dealing with synonymity can also readily be adjusted. This shows the practical consequences of carrying out a more detailed analysis of item structure and content.

A word of caution is also in order, however. It was pointed out in several places that the empirical evidence suggests that lower-ability students may be using strategies that substitute for a complete understanding of the test item. That is, if language competence is low, the student appears to rely upon a more piecemeal approach to responding to a given language item in the hopes that this piecemeal strategy may help him/her obtain a slightly higher score than his/her language competency skills would warrant. Thus the language strategies considered here signal poor language competence. The temptation might be to *instruct* students in the language strategies mentioned herein; this would represent a serious mistake. Not only would it inhibit the student's determination to improve his/her total comprehension of the language represented in the test items, but it also is likely to place a greater cognitive burden on the student who must not only first try to understand the test items as fully as possible but would then also feel constrained to consciously apply *each* of the strategies that had been taught. Pursuit of such a course of action probably will lead to poorer test results than if the students are left to their own devices.

The approach we have developed in this paper explores one small part of what a more complete theory would look like. For example, we have developed categories which express a relationship between the stem and each option. Let us develop a notation system to express this: C(stem, response), where C represents a particular category, and the two terms enclosed in parentheses indicates that the category expresses some relationship between the stem and the response. Now we have argued in this paper that it is useful to separate the contribution of the correct options from the incorrect options when examining what categories are contributing to item difficulty. So, let's agree to let C(stem, response$_c$) and C(stem, response$_i$) to reprsent the relationships of the correct and incorrect responses, respectively.

There are two other sources that contribute to item difficulty though. We might want to develop categories that reflect how the structure of the item stem can contribute to difficulty. This could happen if we are dealing with a whole paragraph of information in the item stem (as opposed to the relatively simple sentences which were used in the paraphrase task analyzed in this report). A paragraph, for example, that contrasted two main ideas may prove to be more difficult to comprehend than one which describes just one main idea. If so, then we would like to add the contribution of such categories to our regression equation in order to improve our ability to predict which items will be hard and which easy. Another source of difficulty which we have yet to develop involves the relationship among the response options. It can easily happen that a regression equation might show that each of the response options seems to be the correct one; when this happens, it seems likely that the person will have developed some decision procedure for making a final choice among these options. A full theory of what affects item difficulty should incorporate such a component and add this to the regression equation.

REFERENCES

Cook, W.A. (1972). *Languages and linguistics: Working papers No. 6.* Washington, DC: Georgetown University Press.

Fillmore, C.J. (1968). The case for case. In E. Bach & R.T. Harms (Eds.), *Universals in linguistic theory.* New York: Holt, Rinehart and Winston.

Fillmore, C.J. (1971). Some problems for case grammar. In R. O'Brien (Ed.), *Georgetown University Monograph Series on Language and Linguistics Number 24.* Washington, DC: Georgetown University Press.

Halliday, M.A.K., & Hasan, R. (1976). *Cohesion in English.* London: Longman.

McNemar, Q. (1962). *Psychological statistics.* New York: Wiley.

APPENDIX A: SCORING MANUAL FOR EIGHT LANGUAGE CATEGORIES

Set up a matrix, where each column represents a particular type of problem that the student may face when choosing or discarding an option. For example, one of the columns below entitled "synonymity" gives information on whether a response option contains an item(s) that is (are) synonymous with an item(s) in the stimulus text. Each row represents information on one particular response option, so that by reading along a row across the columns, the option is fully characterized in terms of the features that may distinguish it (crucially) from the item stem.

The eight columns of features to be scored fall into four general categories: (a) suprasentential, (b) sentential, (c) lexical or phrasal, and (d) phonological (and/or graphemic). The eight scores which will be described below were designed primarily for the listening comprehension items of TOEFL. This part of TOEFL is likely to test the students' aural abilities at primarily the lexical and phonological levels. It appears likely that Part B of the Listening Comprehension section, which deals with three-person interactions, will place increasing emphasis on the semantic comprehension of the student for short spans of sentences. The Reading Comprehension section of TOEFL appears likely to place very strong emphasis on higher level inferencing ability since it deals with comprehension of long reading passages. Hence the most immediate use of the present language categories is probably for the comprehension of single sentences.

General Procedure for Evaluating Item Stems and Response Options

For a given option, indicate the relevant information in each column either by checking the presence or absence of a feature by a 0 or 1, respectively (e.g., for the category called "logical inference"), or by giving the appropriate numerical information (e.g., indicate the number of "case matches" that occurred between the item stem and the particular response option). In every instance, use of 0, 1, or some larger numerical entry indicates the relationship that the item stem has with the particular response option that is under current examination. Thus for the particular language category called "homonyms" an entry of 0 reflects no discernible homonyms between the item stem and a particular response option, while an entry of 2 would mean that two homonyms were found in common between the item stem and a particular response option.

Also note that the information given by the various columns is not of the same kind. The homonyms column typically indicates the presence or absence of an incorrect distractor, while others, such as the logical inference column, reveal decisions that are necessary to identify the correct option. Thus, a 1 in one column may mean an entry associated with a typically wrong option, while a 1 in another column might be associated with a typically correct option. Note also that while most response options can be clearly characterized as either "false" or "true" (or "wrong" or "right"), some are correct by degrees.

Category A/Column 1 (Suprasentential/Logical Inference)

As mentioned above, this category is the most difficult one in that it places both linguistic and cognitive demands on the student. Matching decisions are made independent of linguistic abilities, though the latter are a prerequisite and thus necessary, but not sufficient. The subject must use his/her world knowledge in a reasonable way. For example: If the stimulus text (sometimes called the item stem) asserts "She cut her finger" and the response option states "She hurt part of her hand because of carelessness," one must use world knowledge to realize that carelessness is an appropriate extension of the information in the item stem. None of the other categories which are described below capture this type of relationship of semantic extension.

Category B/Column 1 (Sentential/Case)

In this column, enter the number of nouns in the response option that are in the same case as the corresponding nouns in the item stem. We will adopt the system originally proposed by Fillmore (1968) and later slightly modified by him (Fillmore, 1971) so that the dative case is here represented by the experiencer and beneficiary cases.

Case Name	Definition	Examples
(a) Agentive	The case of the typically animate perceived instigator of the action identified by the verb	He cut the grass. The grass was cut by him. She hid. John opened the door.
(b) Experiencer	The one who experiences the sensation, emotion, or cognition identified by the verb	Mary was surprised. John thought a lot. I heard the thunder.
(c) Beneficiary	The one who is in the state of possession or one who undergoes loss or gain in the transfer of an object	He got a car. Dad gave him a car. The wind benefits us all.
(d) Factitive	The object or being resulting from the action or state identified by the verb	Dad gave me a car. She brushed her hair. He cleaned the dog.
(e) Objective	The semantically most neutral case, the case of anything representable by a noun whose role in the action or state identified by the verb is identified by the semantic interpretation of the verb itself; conceivably the concept should be limited to things which are affected by the action or state identified by the verb	He took a bite. She gave a gasp. I took a swim.

| (f) Locative | The case which identifies the location or spatial orientation of the state or action identified by the verb | You put it <u>on the shelf</u>.
 <u>The bus</u> seats 30.
 Thirty can be seated <u>in the bus</u>.
 <u>The Sahara</u> is hot. |
| (g) Instrumental | The case of the inanimate force causally involved in action or state identified by the verb | <u>The stone</u> hit me.
 <u>The hammer</u> broke the window.
 <u>A car</u> knocked her down. |

We scored for a case match regardless of modifying words. For example, compare "The *boy* cried" versus "The small *boy* cried." The noun *boy* would be scored as a case match. It helps in deciding on case matches to convert all pronouns into nouns (if possible); for example, "Rose left home" versus "She went home." Convert *she* into its full noun referent *Rose*. This yields "*Rose* left home" versus "*Rose* went home." Now it is obvious that *Rose* represents a case match. Notice in the last example that we do not require the same verb to be present in both sentences in order for a case match to occur; we do require, though, that the nouns bear the same case relation to their respective verbs in order to be counted as a case match. *Category C, Column 1* (Lexical/Lexical repetition).

This is the most easily identifiable category. Check for words that are simple repetitions of the stimulus material (the item stem) that have the same phonological shape and the same meaning and referent (apply this matching for content words only, not function words). Small variations are to be disregarded in noticing a lexical match (i.e., ignore singular/plural variation, ignore verb tense variations). Significant morphological derivations, however, are not to be checked in this column (e.g., none of the following pairs are considered lexical repetitions: dry - dryer; vary - variation; divine - divinity; to house a friend - the house is clean). Also, superficial identities that do not exist on the semantic level must be ruled out (for example, *hard* (adj.) - *hardware; hard* (adj.) - *hardhat;* these would not be scored as lexical repetitions). Do count compounds whose one member is lexically and phonologically identical to the comparison word, as in, *house - housewife. Category C/ Column 2* (Lexical/ Synonymity)

In this column, check all words or phrases that have the same meaning but a different phonological shape, as in, *car - automobile, incorrect - wrong, female - woman*, etc.

Category C/ Column 3 (Lexical/ Lexical Inference)

In this column, check for words/phrases, whose "semantic distance" is larger than that of synonyms, but which can nevertheless be related by some justifiable and reasonable inference. Their relation can be one of whole–part (e.g., *car – bumper*), one of association (*doorbell – ringing*), or antonyms (*enter – leave*). It should be noted that this column deals with strictly lexical inference only; that is, the relation between the two items must be on the word or phrase level. We also include here words of generic/specific type (e.g., *book – dictionary; music – symphony*).

It makes a difference whether one moves from stimulus text information to a response option or vice versa; it makes a difference with respect to what category gets scored. For example, if the stimulus asserts "Person *x* deals with money orders, savings accounts, and checking accounts" and one of the response options states that "Person *x* is a banker," then moving from the stimulus text to the response option, tends to focus the material at the suprasentential category level. But if we focus first on the response option and move back to the stimulus text, then we are more likely to categorize the result under the category of lexical inference (e.g., we would notice the lexical item *banker* and associate it back to a part of the stimulus text such as *savings accounts* etc.) We shall agree to limit our search for the appropriate categorization by first focusing upon response options and then noting what relationship exists with respect to the stimulus text.

Before we move on to the next category we should clarify a possible source of confusion between lexical inference and our earlier category of synonymity. Strictly speaking, synonymity does not exist since any two words are never precisely alike in what they denote or connote. Given this, one would be forced to always classify any two similar words as an example of lexical inference. But this is too strong a distinction. We can still retain both categories if we follow the decision rule given below. If two words can be *substituted* for each other in a sentence without changing the basic meaning of that sentence, then these words are synonyms. For example, "There were a lot of (*disagreements/differences*) in their marriage" where *disagreements* and *differences* are categorized as synonyms because they are substitutable in this sentence. However, in the next example "I drove (*the car/the bumper*) to school" the two words *car* and *bumper* are not synonyms because the sentence does not have the same basic meaning when one is substituted for the other. Therefore *car* and *bumper* would be classified as an instance of the lexical inference category.

Category C/ Column 4 (Lexical/ Morphology)

In this column, check words with the same morphological stem or derived from the same stem with the same meaning, but belonging to different grammatical categories and with different pronunciations; for example, *vary* (V) – *variation* (N); *hunt* (V) – *hunting* (N); *house* (V) – *house* (N); *half* (N) – *halve* (V); *enter* (V) – *entrance* (N), etc. (Remember, when two words differ only in singular/plural aspect they are to be scored under lexical repetition.) Notice that identify of the word stem is crucial here; thus we would disregard prefixes or suffixes for this category. For example, *re-enter* (V) – *entrance* (N) would be scored as an instance of morphological variation since both words share the same stem (*enter*). Also in this category indicate the presence of word pairs whose one member is a compount containing an additional morpheme, as in *house – housing complex.*

Cateogry D/ Column 1 (Phonological/ Homonymity)

In this column write the number of word pairs that have the same phonological shape but different meanings; for example, *hard*$_1$ (not soft to the touch) – *hard*$_2$ (difficult); *two – too.* Include word pairs of different grammatical categories with different meanings (e.g., *foot*$_n$ – *foot*$_v$ (as in, to foot the bill); *interest*$_n$ (at a bank) – *interested*$_v$; also include verb/noun pairs whose stress patterns differ (e.g., *compound*$_v$ – *compound*$_n$; *transfer*$_v$ – *transfer*$_n$). Include idiomatic meanings. Count also compounds, as in, *hard* (not easy) – *hardhat.*

Special note: Regional differences in pronunciation will often alter whether a given word pair will get scored as a homonym category or as a similar/minimal pair category (see category below). For example, sometimes the following pairs will be perceived as belonging to the homonym category and sometimes to the similar/minimal pair category: *do – due; been – bin; oil – Earl; to – two,* and so on. When such a distinction becomes difficult to justify, combine the homonym and similar/minimal pair categories, or, enter the same word pair under both categories.

Category D/ Column 2 (Phonological/ Similar Pair)

Check the number of word pairs that differ from each other by one (or possibly two) phonemes; for example, *mouse – mouth; sick – thick; twin – win.* Include also pairs that differ from each other in the presence or absence of additional syllables; for example, *wind – window; rest – abreast; abreast – interest.* Occasionally one will need to use the similar pair category in order to capture a relationship across several words (e.g., *sickly – thick meat*) where successive syllables across words in a response option can be found to match or rhyme with another string of syllables in the item stem.

APPENDIX B: AN ILLUSTRATION OF A FULLY SCORED ITEM FOR EACH OF FOUR RESPONSE OPTIONS AND AN ILLUSTRATION OF HOW THIS INFORMATION IS PREPARED FOR INPUT TO A REGRESSION ANALYSIS

To illustrate a full scoring of an item, consider one presented in the main text:

"John wanted to leave the house."
1. John needed a house.
2. John intended to get away from the house.
3. John wanted Ted to lease the house.
4. Leave the house now.

The frequency of use of each of the eight language categories is considered for each of the response options as illustrated as follows:

The Eight Language Categories

Relation Scored	Lex. Rep.	Syn.	Lex. Inf.	Case	Morph.	Homon.	Sim. Pr.	Inf.
1st option and stem	2	1	0	1	0	0	0	0
2nd option and stem	2	2	0	2	0	0	0	0
3rd option and stem	3	0	0	1	0	0	1	0
4th option and stem	2	0	0	1	1	0	0	0

The correct option is option 2. The sum of the incorrect options for the eight categories respectively is as follows: 7, 1, 0, 3, 1, 0, 1, 0. Suppose we are listing the data for the lowest ability group and we know that only 20% passed this particular item. The percent passed is out criterion score; there will be 16 predictor categories (the eight scores for the correct option and the eight scores representing the sum of the eight categories for the three incorrect options). Hence the data for this item will be entered as follows:

Criterion Score	The Eight Scores for the Correct Option								The Eight Scores for the Summed Incorrect Options							
20	2	2	0	2	0	0	0	0	7	1	0	3	1	0	1	0

Since there are 99 other items scored in a similar fashion, there would be a total of 100 data lines listed in the regression analysis.

For each ability group the percent who pass each item will change in every regression analysis; however, the predictor variables will remain the same regardless of which ability group is being analyzed.

In the more complete model which was sketched in the main body of this report it was mentioned that there are at least three other sources which can affect the percentage who pass each item. These other sources were: A set of categories reflecting the structure of the item stem, a set of categories reflecting how decisions are made when two or more response options look equally likely to be the correct one. A new regression analysis which reflected all these components (old and new) can be sketched as below:

Criterion score = (the 8 scores reflecting the relationship between the item stem and the correct option)
  + (the 8 scores reflecting the relationship between the item stem and the sum of the incorrect options)
  + (the set of scores reflecting important structural features of the item stem)
  + (the set of scores reflecting what weights are to be at-

tached if two or more of the response options looks equally good).

The gist of the full model of analysis has been given, but of course the details of expressing how one is to resolve differences among the options (given some apparent "tie") might turn out to be much more complex than expressed above.

APPENDIX C: INTERCORRELATIONS AMONG THE EIGHT LANGUAGE SCORES

It was noted in the main body of this report that there are some puzzling aspects that result from both the correlational and regression analyses that are difficult to explain. In particular, it is hard to see why lexical inferences play a significant role when they appear among the incorrect options but fail to play a significant role when they appear among the correct options. One way to try to understand this result is to look in more detail at the correlations that exist among the predictor variables themselves (the predictor variables are the eight language measures).

Table 8 presents the intercorrelations among the eight language measures for the correct options only. This table suggests the following (we focus on just the significant correlations below): When a correct option is written, the *more lexical repetitions* it has, the *more semantic cases* it has (correlation = .515). Also the more *lexical repetitions* it has, the *fewer synonyms* it tends to have (correlation = −.294). Also the *more lexical inferences* it has, the *fewer synonyms* it has (correlation = −.246). One should ignore any significant correlations that occur for the logical inference measure because it was not sufficiently reliable to warrant further comment.

The correlations that were significant when the incorrect options are examined will now be compared. These are presented in Table 9. The results of Table 9 depict a strong correlation between number of lexical repetitions that occur and the number of semantic cases that occur (correlation = .652). This agrees so far with what was found for the correct options. None of the remaining correlations that were found to be significant for the correct options, however, are significant for the incorrect options. Thus one does *not* see a close relationship (whether positive or negative) between lexical repetition and synonymity or between lexical inference and synonymity. Thus the constraints that operate when correct options are written do not appear to be very similar to the constraints that operate when incorrect options are written, with the exception of the strong positive correlation between lexical repetition and case.

Given this result, it is not puzzling to find in the regression analysis that lexical inferences relate differently to the criterion variable (the percent who pass an item) across the correct and incorrect options. Another piece of evidence that

Table 8. Intercorrelations among the Eight Language Measures for the Correct Options Only

Name of Language Measure	Name of Language Measure							
	Log. Inf.	Case	Lex. Rep.	Synony.	Lex. Inf.	Morph.	Homony.	Sim. Pr.
Log. Inf.	1.000							
Case	−.043	1.000						
Lex. Rep.	.063	.515**	1.000					
Synony.	−.535**	−.022	−.294**	1.000				
Lex. Inf.	−.028	−.050	−.177	−.246*	1.000			
Morph.	.137	.044	.022	.019	−.132	1.000		
Homony.	—	—	—	—	—	—	—	
Sim. Pr.	—	—	—	—	—	—	—	—

*The correlation is significant at the .05 level of probability.
**The correlation is significant at the .01 level of probability.

Table 9. Intercorrelations among the Eight Language Measures for the Incorrect Options Only

Name of Language Measure	Name of Language Measure							
	Log. Inf.	Case	Lex. Rep.	Synony.	Lex. Inf.	Morph.	Homony.	Sim. Pr.
Log. Inf.	1.000							
Case	.219*	1.000						
Lex. Rep.	.182	.652**	1.000					
Synony.	.047	−.095	−.177	1.000				
Lex. Inf.	−.115	−.175	−.108	−.018	1.000			
Morph.	−.070	−.028	−.029	.014	−.089	1.000		
Homony.	−.070	−.085	−.118	.026	−.212*	.123	1.000	
Sim. Pr.	−.102	−.149	−.334**	−.321**	−.161	−.193*	−.132	1.000

*The correlation is significant at the .05 level of probability.
**The correlation is significant at the .01 level of probability.

Table 10. Intercorrelations among the Eight Language Measures for the Correct vs the Incorrect Options

Name of Language Measure for the Incorrect Options	Name of Language Measure (for the Correct Option)							
	Log. Inf.	Case	Lex. Rep.	Synony.	Lex. Inf.	Morph.	Homony.	Sim. Pr.
Log. Inf.	−0.091	.139	.020	.035	.072	−.032	—	—
Case	.075	.563**	.345**	.075	−.092	.090	—	—
Lex. Rep.	.143	.438**	.426**	.129	−.030	.218	—	—
Synony.	−.085	−.075	−.152	.336**	−.021	−.117	—	—
Lex. Inf.	.081	−.088	−.108	.136	.155	.081	—	—
Morph.	.041	−.071	−.032	−.242	.096	.086	—	—
Homony.	−.014	−.048	−.008	.009	−.072	−.073	—	—
Sim. Pr.	−.160	−.027	.006	−.020	.080	−.142	—	—

appears to agree with the foregoing observations is the correlations among the correct and incorrect options for each of the eight language measures. These correlations are presented in Table 10.

Only five correlations are significant in Table 10. Two of them one would expect to be significant from what was found in Tables 8 and 9; in particular, the correlation between lexical repetition (among the incorrects) and semantic case (for the corrects) is .438, and the correlation between lexical repetition (among the corrects) and semantic case (for the incorrects) is .345. The other three significant correlations show the following. The more semantic case overlap is used among the incorrects, the more semantic case overlap also tend to be used among the correct options (here, the correlation is .563). Similarly, the more lexical repetitions that are used among the incorrects, the more lexical repetitions are used among the correct option (for the very same item); here, the correlation is .426. Also the more synonyms that are used among the incorrects for a given time, the more synonyms there are among the correct option of that item; here, the correlation is .336. Perhaps, what is most interesting is the failure of the lexical inference category to be significant ($r = .155$) across correct and incorrect options. This helps to explain why there is a significant regression predictor for lexical inference among the incorrect options but why one fails to get a similar effect for the correct options. Thus, the best explanation for the asymmetrical regression result regarding the different strengths of the language measures to be significant across corrects and incorrects appears to lie in the *patterning* of the language measures at the time the response options are generated.

CHAPTER 4

A Preliminary Analysis of Cognitive-Linguistic Aspects of Sentence Completion Tasks

Christiane Fellbaum

Westminster Choir College
Princeton, NJ

INTRODUCTION

The goal of this paper is to investigate the nature of certain sentence completion tasks appearing on the Scholastic Aptitude Test (SAT). These items require a number of cognitive-linguistic operations and processes which we shall isolate, classify, and analyze. We shall elucidate some sentence processing strategies and ways in which the reader makes use of the given structural, lexical, and morphological information. Some of the necessary processing operations are correlated with the difficulty level of the given item(s).

MATERIAL

The items analyzed here appear in the Verbal section of the SAT form.[1] They call for the completion of a sentence with one or two gaps. The following are illustrative examples:

1. He was suddenly thrown into a fit of despair, his faith in himself infirm, his self-confidence _____.
   (A) shattered (B) soaring (C) unassailable
   (D) inflated (E) delayed

2. Although its publicity has been _____, the film itself is intelligent, well acted, handsomely produced, and altogether _____.
   (A) tasteless . . . respectable (B) extensive . . . moderate
   (C) sophisticated . . . amateur (D) risque . . . crude
   (E) perfect . . . spectacular

Each gap must be filled with either one word or a phrase consisting of two words such as a preposition and a noun. The student is given five options from which

---

[1] The specific materials used here are SAT forms published and released by the Educational Testing Service, Princeton, New Jersey. They are Form Code 1B (administered April 1981); Form Code 0B023 (administered March 1980); the booklet *Taking the SAT: A Guide to the SAT* (1981); and a practice booklet containing six SAT forms (no title, 1982).

s/he must choose the correct one (multiple choice). The gapped words are adjectives, nouns, verbs, and verb-derived constituents.[2] The incomplete sentences usually are complex ones consisting of an independent or main clause (MC) and one or more dependent or subordinate clause (SC), in any of the orders that are logically permissible and grammatically possible. Occasionally, two MCs occur, connected by a colon or a semicolon. Simple MCs are relatively infrequent. All sentences are declarative.

On each test form, items occur in groups of five. Most groups have three items with one gap each and two items with two gaps each. The difficulty level increases gradually from the first to the fifth item. Of the 120 items that were analyzed, the percentages of correct answers given during a particular administration were available for 30 items. With rising difficulty, they decreased from around 90% correct answers (for the first, i.e., easiest items) to as low as 13% (for the fifth, i.e., hardest items). The difficulty level of the 90 items for which no statistics were available can thus be estimated by their position within the group. The percentage figures or the position of the items, then, can give us an objective measure for the degree of difficulty which is used to correlate our findings concerning syntactic and semantic difficulties.[3]

LEVELS OF DIFFICULTY

Structural Properties as Potential Sources of Difficulty

A perfectly legitimate starting assumption might be one stating that the difficulty level of an item may be determined, at least in part, by factors having nothing to do with syntactic or semantic properties but rather with superficial structural features of the item. However, no correlation between such criteria and the difficulty degree of an item could be found.

To begin with, the total number of words per item is independent of the item's difficulty, as is the number of clauses: Both very easy and very hard items could be short (15 words) or long (15–30 words). The number of clauses varied from one to four, with multiple embeddings. Thus, complexity cannot be measured only in terms of length. The number of gaps (one or two) does not correlate with difficulty, either.

---

[2] That is, the missing words are content words rather than function words such as articles. This is, of course, not surprising given the assumption that it is not primarily the student's facility with grammar that is being tested, but rather his/her comprehension of the entire sentence.

[3] Note, however, that while within each group the level of difficulty is rising from item 1 to 5, the level of difficulty of two items in the same position can vary considerably across groups. The 30 items for which actual percentage figures were available consisted of six groups of five items each. The percentage of correct answers for the first (i.e., easiest) items varied from 68 to 92%; for the second items from 84 to 50%; for the third items from 54 to 31%; for the fourth items from 46 to 24%; and for the fifth (i.e., hardest) items from 42 to 13%. Note the considerable overlap.

No relation exists between an item's difficulty and the number of words preceding the (first) gap, following the (last) gap, or occurring between the two gaps. This is true only for the item as a whole; we did not consider individual clauses within the item. In a two-clause sentence with two gaps, the location of both gaps in the same clause versus one gap in each clause has no bearing on the item's difficulty. The difficulty level, furthermore, cannot be correlated with the nature of the gapped word(s), that is, no discrimination exists between words that represent different parts of speech. The most frequently gapped words were predicate adjectives, verbs, and subject noun phrases, followed by attributive adjectives and object noun phrases or other noun phrases; adverbs were gapped least frequently. Even though the most commonly missing constituents are those that appear to be most crucial to the comprehension of a sentence (i.e., those belonging to the basic syntactic categories sentence (S), verb phrase (VP)), their absence does not automatically result in a high degree of difficulty. This indicates that it is the lexical and semantic properties of the gapped item and its lexical and semantic relations to the remaining constituents in the sentence that determine the correct choice, rather than the purely syntactic relations among the sentence elements. In other words, it appears likely that the correct word or words is/are chosen on the basis of the compatibility of its or their meaning with that of the rest of the sentence.

Next let us test the assumption that a gap or gaps in one type of clause is harder to fill than in another clause type. For example, one might hypothesize that the meaning of incomplete SCs is easier to guess than that of incomplete MCs, reasoning that SCs usually contain given, nonfocused background information.

The items were grouped into three sentence types: MC, MC–MC, (MC–SC)/(SC–MC) (no difference in the difficulty level was found between the two kinds of complex clauses in the last group).

3. Her _____ media coverage of Hispanic affairs in Los Angeles led Francisca Flores to publish a newsletter aimed at informing the Hispanic community of _____ events (MC)

4. The author includes very little _____ of the dragon: monsters are more fearful if pictured in the imagination. (MC–MC)

5. Although William the Conqueror preserved whatever institutions of the Anglo-Saxon regime suited his purpose, innovation was more evident than the maintenance of _____ during his reign. (SC–MC)

6. Modern physicists are inclined to believe in the validity of general relativity for _____ reasons, because it is mathematically so elegant and philosophically so _____. (MC–SC)

Table 1.   MC-SC and SC/MC

Gap(s) in MC Only		Gap(s) in SC Only
10	Hard	7
2	Medium	7
5	Easy	11
17	Total	25

We found that about half of the MC and MC–MC items were difficult ones (10 out of 24 and 14 out of 28, respectively). Out of the 61 sentences with either MC–SC or SC–MC structures, 21 were hard, 14 medium-hard, and 26 were easy items. Seventeen had a gap(s) in the MC only, and 25 had a gap(s) in the SC only. The findings in Table 1 show the relation between the difficulty level and the location of the gap(s). Even though the numbers are too small to permit any reliable conclusions, they seem to indicate that an MC is harder to complete than an SC, and/or that a complete SC supplies less vital information for sentence comprehension than an MC. The data also agree with those for MC and MC–MC sentences given above, of which about half were hard and the remaining half were medium-hard or easy. These findings will be evaluated later on and brought into perspective.

Syntactic Sources of Difficulty

The previous section has shown that the purely superficial structural properties of an item do not contribute to its difficulty level. However, the clause type does seem to play a role, and it is this clue that we shall pursue here.

First, we noted that simple MC and, especially, MC–MC sentences were somewhat harder than those containing both an MC and an SC. This was true independent of the location of the gap(s) as well as of the total number of words per item, so that increased information and context do not seem to play a crucial role.[4]

In most of the MC–MC sentences, the two clauses are connected either by a semicolon or by a conjunction such as *and, so, similarly*. That is to say, no "logical" connection other than one of addition or consequence is made; each of the clauses virtually stands by itself and must be comprehended by itself.[5]

---

[4] It should be noted here that our procedure of isolating structural, syntactic, and lexical/semantic components is misleading in that most items present difficulties from more than one of these groups. That is, a structurally complex item may also contain words of low frequency in English that are known to relatively few students only and which therefore contribute greatly to the item's difficulty, in addition to the structural difficulty. Due to their number and the complexity of interaction among these variables, however, we must analyze each one in isolation.

[5] We are not considering here MCs joined by conjunctions expressing antonymy such as *but* and *however;* they will be dealt with later in this chapter.

Thus, these constructions are really quite similar to single MCs, which likewise express a proposition that is not directly connected to any other one. As stated above, both MC–MC and MC sentences tend to be more difficult items, generally, than SC–MC or MC–SC sentences where, in many cases, a subordinating conjunction creates a logical connection (causal, concessive, contrastive, etc.) between the two clauses. We suggest that it is precisely the presence of such a conjunction that facilitates comprehension of a complex sentence, while, on the other hand, its absence renders the task of sentence completion more difficult.

One supporting piece of evidence is the fact that MC–SC or SC–MC sentences with logical conjunctions are generally much less difficult than MCs followed by SCs introduced by the complementizer *that* (six out of nine MC–*that*–SC sentences are hard items.) The latter kind of complex sentence is similar to the MC–MC one in that no temporal, causal, and so on connection between the two clauses exists. In fact, it is easy to reformulate such sentences as two MCs that are connected by a colon instead of by *that*. The *that*-clauses are assertions or propositions whose contents cannot always be verified against, or related to, any background information given elsewhere in the sentence; thus the student, in order to complete the item, has to recreate a plausible proposition.

Let us now look in some more detail at complex sentences containing subordinate conjunctions. Among the 120 items we analyzed, no SCs introduced by *where, when,* and so on occurred. After all the conjunctions were listed, it became obvious that they fell into two basic categories: those introducing an SC whose contents were "parallel" to, or in agreement with, those of the MC, and those conjunctions heading SCs with "antonymic" or "opposing" contents (see Table 2).

As can be seen from Table 2, opposing conjunctions occurred far more often than parallel ones: There were 12 of the latter and 23 of the former. Among these, *although* was by far the most common conjunction, occurring 15 times

Table 2.

Parallel	Opposing
because	whereas
whereby	(even) though
even	although
so . . . that	if not . . . then[a]
if . . . then[a]	yet[a]
since	but[a]
while	nevertheless[a]
(just) as . . . (so)	however[a]

[a]These conjunctions introduce MCs, not SCs, but are listed and considered here because they are very similar in nature to those introducing SCs of the kind we are interested in.

(out of a total of 23). Furthermore, the *although* items were mostly easy ones (9 easy ones vs. 4 difficult ones); the same was true for the other conjunctions in this group. If we add the sentences with an antonymic MC (introduced by *but, however, yet, nevertheless*), the picture becomes still clearer, for all these items are easy (in fact, these constitute most of the exceptions to our earlier finding that the MC–MC structures were generally hard.)

The sentences containing a parallel SC were too few to permit any conclusions (out of 13, 7 were hard, 2 were medium-hard, and 4 were easy), but if we include all those MC–MC sentences that are conjoined by a parallel conjunction (such as *thus, therefore, and so*, etc.) and that were all difficult, we can state more safely that the parallelism tends to make an item more difficult.

The results so far, then, seem to be these:

1. Single MCs or MC–MC constructions are more difficult to complete than MC–SC or SC–MC sentences.
2. Two propositions connected by a causal, concessive, or similar conjunction are easier to complete than two propositions without such a connector.
3. Of the "logical" conjunctions, those expressing antonymy make for easier items; those expressing parallelism create more difficult items.

We suggest, therefore, that the parallelism–opposition distinction is an important one for sentence comprehension and completion. It is important to note here that among the options from which the students must choose, there is always at least one whose meaning is antonymic to the correct one. That is to say, the options are not all the same with regard to the polarity of the sentence meaning and, therefore, they allow for the student to find at least one choice that would be compatible with his or her erroneous interpretation of the relation between the two clauses.

Parallelism.   Let us now look in some more detail at various forms of parallelism (or synonymity[6]) in meaning as they occur in the test items.

The subordinating conjunctions discussed above link two clauses whose contents are similar or related in meaning, in a noncontradictory sense. Such parallelism can also be expressed on the single-clause level. For example, a very common form of this is represented by an item type that might be called "definitional," where a gapped word is defined by a preceding or following noun phrase (which often dominates a relative clause). For example:

7. Like all reformers, Wood is _____ who believes that the world can be changed by good people promoting right deeds.

---

6 Even though we shall occasionally use the term "synonymity" in connection with, or substituting for, "parallelism," we do not mean to suggest that the meanings of the words or phrases they refer to are synonymous in a strict sense. The term will be used very loosely but, we believe, in agreement with the reader's intuitive judgment.

Of the five options,

(A)   a statistician   (B)   a prodigal   (C)   a legislator
(D)   an opportunist   (E)   an optimist

only (E) can be considered to be a definition of the relative clause (although, of course, *optimist* can be defined in many other ways as well).

Other items are based on the same definitional relation between the gapped word and a clause, though the form may be subtle. For example:

8.   Meteors become _____ only after they enter the atmosphere, for it is then that they begin to burn and leave a luminous trail.

The correct option, *incandescent,* can be chosen only if the synonymous relation between it and the verb phrase in the *for*-clause is recognized.

Another example is the following:

9.   The _____ of the Navajos is reflected in the fact that many have retained their language and ancient customs.

While the word *reflect* does not express direct synonymity, it implies that the noun phrases or clauses it links (i.e., A and B in A *reflects B*) are somewhat close in meaning.

The difficulty levels of definitional items range from very easy to very hard. We suspect that this is not due to their rather straightforward structure, but to the student's familiarity with the gapped word or words in the item. Thus, examples 7 and 9 are medium-hard items, while example 8 is very hard. We shall return to this question later in a section dealing with lexical difficulty.

One of the easiest and most obvious forms of parallelism on the lexical level is a list of words, joined by a comma(s) or *and,* or a similar connector. Thus we have several items of the following form:

10. $\left.\begin{array}{l} \text{Adj.(P)} \\ \text{V(P)} \\ \text{N(P)} \end{array}\right\}$ $\left.\begin{array}{l} as\ well\ as \\ and \end{array}\right\}$ _____

or

11.   _____ $\left.\begin{array}{l} and \\ as\ well\ as \end{array}\right\}$ $\left.\begin{array}{l} \text{Adj.(P)} \\ \text{V(P)} \\ \text{NP(P)} \end{array}\right\}$

The gapped word is always the same part of speech as the word on the other side of the connector. These items are almost always easy ones (seven easy ones, two medium-hard ones—due to lexical difficulty). Intensifying or augmenting connectors, such as *even, especially, like,* between two constituents also occur in relatively easy items.

The parallelism can be more subtly expressed, and therefore less easily recognized, when it exists not between two constituents of the same grammatical category, but involves across-clausal relations between different parts of speech. A case in point is the following example:

12. Good health is _____ with a high degree of resistance to bacterial attack; any influence that lowers one's general health also _____ one's resistance to such an attack.

The key word is *also* in the second clause, for it indicates that the second gap must have a close meaning relation to *lowers*. This, in turn, leads to the completion of the first sentence, where *good health* and *high degree of resistance* must be close in meaning (the correct option is *synonymous . . . reduces.*) The general form of example 12 is

13. A is [*synonymous*] with B; if A is lowered, B is also [*reduce(d)*].

The relations here are fairly complex, and the item was correctly answered by only 48% of the test-takers.

To sum up, we found that parallelism in meaning is expressed on the sentential level across clauses be certain conjuctions, or by one clause "defining" another; on the clausal level, they are expressed by a noun phrase (usually heading a clause) defining another noun phrase, and on the phrase level, by noun phrases or other constituents linked by *and, as well as,* and so on. More complex items contain parallelisms of several kinds, often distributed across clauses or sentences.

Opposition

Opposition, or antonymy,[7] too, occurs on several levels. Across clauses, as we saw earlier, it is expressed by subordinate or coordinate conjunctions such as *(al)though, even though, despite the fact that, but, however,* and so on. We noted that antonymy in these forms appears to make an item easier rather than harder. On the phrase level, prepositions and adverbs expressing opposition in meaning include *despite, in spite of, though, save (NP), rather than, unlike, without, heretofore, previously(Adj.).* Without counting plain negation (*no, not, never,* etc.), there were more antonymic structures in the test that were easy items (10) than hard ones (5). (Of course, these figures are too small to permit any conclusions but indicate the direction for a future large-scale study.) The *rather than* construction occurs relatively frequently (four times) and is always easy. The relatively hard items have adverbs or phrases containing an implicit opposition like *heretofore* and *were there not,* which are somewhat bookish and

---

[7] Once more, we use this term loosely to refer to constituents or propositions whose meanings are opposed to one another or are in some kind of contrastive relationship.

less frequently used in the spoken language and, thus, possibly less comprehensible than the more common *unlike, despite,* and so on.

The definitional form of an item is also used in conjunction with antonymy: Rather than having an equational form, such items are "inequalities." For example:

14. The instructor added the restriction that all projects had to be ＿＿＿＿ : no student could research an area that had been investigated previously by anyone else.

In order to make the correct selection, *original,* the student must choose the word that agrees in meaning with the second clause which is under a negative sign. Like their "parallel" counterparts, these kinds of items are easy ones unless they are made harder by lexical factors.

By far the most common—and more subtle—antonymy is the lexicalized kind expressed either by morphological prefixes (*in-, un-, dis-,* etc.) or in words like *lack, lose, contrast with, deny, reject, different from, rare, little.* and so on. They build into the sentence an opposition or contradiction that the student must catch, for it is almost always precisely this opposition that is crucial for the choice of the correct option. For example:

15. The article claimed that unlike words, which can be ＿＿＿＿ context, the essential expressions of music are unchanging, no matter in what musical context they appear.

The student must note the negative sign of *unlike* and *unchanging* (possible also that of *no matter in what*) before s/he can choose the correct option, *transformed by* (in itself a word implying change and, possibly, connecting words with opposing meanings).

When an item contains two or more antonymic constituents, the student must keep track of all of them and "keep score" as each may cancel the preceding one and thus reverse the sign of the sentence as processed so far. A case in point is the following item:

16. Luard implies that rising state centralization is ＿＿＿＿ as well as detestable, and, so, nowhere sets out a strategy for ＿＿＿＿ it.

(The correct option is *inevitable . . . defeating.*) This item is fairly complex (and the hardest in its group): The gapped adjective and participle are dependent on one another in that one cannot identify one without the other, and, at the same time, they are somewhat opposed in meaning (you cannot defeat what is inevitable); they also contrast with the parallel-structured adjective *detestable* which would make one expect a connector like *yet* or *even though,* rather than the correct one *and, so.*

Similarly, the item

17. Polls are so _____ in our society that it is almost impossible to go out in public
    without being _____ by an opinion seeker.

has an overall parallel structure expressed by *so that;* yet the two negations
contained in *impossible* and *without* cannot be overlooked if the student wants to
choose the correct option (*pervasive . . . accosted*): The two negatives cancel
each other out.

Again, we cannot draw any definite conclusions as to the relationship between
(multiple) negation(s) and oppositions, and the difficulty level of an item; but
this might be an interesting direction to be explored with more data.

Lexical Aspects

The main reason that we did not get completely clear-cut correlations between
the syntactic and structural makeup and the difficulty level of a given item is that
we have so far ignored the difficulties presented by the lexical components of the
item. The student may be unfamiliar with one or more words in the item itself or
in the options offered for choice. He or she may guess the meaning of such words
from the context, but often the lexically harder words are precisely the key words
in an item, that is, those words on which the entire interpretation of the sentence
hinges and whose mutual relationship is crucial for the comprehension of the
item. While we cannot guess whether any given word is known to the average
high-school senior, a look at any of our 24 groups of items shows that the most
evident increase in difficulty from the first to the fifth item in a group is clearly
lexical in nature.

For example, in the following first-ranking item, probably most, if not all the
words, are known to the average college-bound student:

18. Rather than (*attacking*) wagons and (*hindering*) the pioneer's [*sic*] movement west-
    ward, many American Indians acted as guides and companions.

    Contrast this with a fifth-ranking item such as

19. Although Spalding (*deprecated*) the importance of the physical necessities of life,
    her most successful endeavor was the (*alleviation*) of the condition of the
    impoverished.

Here, not only are the gapped words less common, less frequently used ones,
but possibly also *endeavor* and *impoverished* may be unfamiliar to many
students.

We compiled a list of all the gapped words in our 120 items. We found eight
words (disregarding minor morphological changes) that were used more than
once, that is, in two different items. Although the structure and syntax of the
items thus paired differed in almost all cases, the difficulty level was the same in
the case of five pairs, and nearly the same in the pairs. Thus we may speculate
that it is the particular gapped word that largely determines the degree of diffi-

culty. The word *exacerbate,* for example, when gapped, always occurred in a very hard item. *Comprehensive* was gapped in two very different items, both of which were easy. *Justify* and *esthetic* each occurred in two medium-hard items that were otherwise very different from each other.

If we assume that difficulty or unfamiliarity of a word is strongly related to its frequency or occurrence in the language, a word frequency list should confirm this relation. We used Kučera and Francis' *Computational Analysis of Present-Day American English* (1967) which lists word frequencies for a body of over one million words drawn from writings of 15 different genres (such as *Learned Scientific Writing* and *Fiction: Romance and Love Story.*) In the entire corpus, *exacerbate(s)(d)* occurs only seven times, while *comprehensive(ly)* was found 21 times. *Justify* and *esthetic* occurred 62 and 6 times, respectively. *Increase(s)(d),* which was gapped in two different, very easy items, occurred 413 times in the corpus. This indicates that, indeed, frequency of occurrence has a direct bearing on the familiarity of a lexical item and hence on the degree of difficulty in comprehending or completing a sentence containing it.

Semantic Aspects

Linguists and philosophers who study semantics have often noted that the meaning of a word depends, in part, on its context. This assumes that a word can have several different meanings or a whole ''field'' of meaning, only part of which is applicable in a given context. Thus, Miller (1978) states that every word participates in making up several conceptual fields, which may be very different from one another. Only a selective number of features of a given word are part of a given conceptual field, created by the particular context. Miller postulates certain cognitive precesses that scan the context of the word for clues as to which concept is intended on a given occasion of the use of the word, so that the meaning of the word in its context can be understood. While Miller was probably interested primarily in the cognitive preocesses necessary for language comprehension, we can relate his ideas to the situation of our student who is given a context and must select a word from among five, often close, options to fit this context. It seems reasonable to assume that the cognitive processes involved in this task are essentially the same as those postulated by Miller; they certainly are the same for the student's initial comprehension of the item as it is given to him with the gap(s). Given the assumption that the student, on the basis of the incomplete item, postulates a lexical/conceptual field into which the missing word(s) must fit, we can guess that the student then tries out each option to see whether its semantic makeup includes conceptual features that are appropriate to the conceptual field already established, that is, each option is decomposed into (some of) its features and the student then tries to match them with features that have constructed the context. For example, in the structure

20. _____ and [Adj]

the correct option probably shares some features with the adjective given, assuming that both adjectives modify the same noun or nouns. They may have the same sign (i.e., plus or minus) with regard to a certain feature.[8] (This is, of course, just another way of defining on the word level what we called earlier parallelism.) For example, they may share the feature [-short], as do the adjectives *long* and *protracted*. However, they may also differ with respect to the sign even when sharing the same feature, like the adjectives in the phrase

21. All creatures great and small

or those in the item

22. This _____ painter was but _____ pianist . . . . (virtuoso . . . a mediocre)

Of course, adjectives that modify the same noun(s) may not share any features at all; yet they must each have features that can be used to describe the same noun(s). Our guess is that when the two adjectives share nothing more than that each can relate to the given noun(s), the task of matching these two adjectives is harder than in the cases described above, where the adjectives share a common feature(s). Thus, the prediction is that the adjectives in example 22 or in

23. Eastlake is a colorful and _____ commentator . . . (*versatile*)

are easier targets than the adjectives in, for example,

24. Ms. Warner supplements her selection of Queen Victoria's drawings with a text as idiosyncratic as it is _____ , for she can be _____ as well as a scholarly writer. (*accurate . . . an unconventional*)

An item may be difficult because there are two options that are semantically similar. Consider the following example:

25. Although most people have one explanation or another for what happened, the event remains _____ .

The correct option is *mysterious,* which is, undoubtedly, very felicitous. However, another option, *frightening,* cannot be ruled out a priori. The missing word clearly must be one whose meaning is somewhat antonymic to the phrase *have an explanation for;* this is dictated by the concessive conjunction *although* in the first clause. *Frightening* has, or can have, at least one such meaning, namely, when it refers to fright or fear of something inexplicable and unknown that cannot be made less fearsome by being given a rational explanation. Put differently, *mysterious* can share, for example, the features [confusing], [bewildering] with *frightening; mysterious* can even have the feature

---

[8] It is not clear whether such conceptual features are binary or not. To begin with, there does not exist, to the best of our knowledge, a definite list of semantic features; it is not even clear which features should be considered to be more basic than others.

[frightening], just as *frightening* can have, in certain conceptual contexts, the feature [mysterious]. Thus, *frightening* might be chosen by the student who is unfamiliar with (all the meanings of) the word *mysterious* yet who has constructed a perfectly "correct" conceptual field on the basis of the given context.

DIRECTION OF SENTENCE PROCESSING

Finally, we shall tentatively explore one aspect of how an item is comprehended: This is the direction in which it is processed.

An item with a gap at or near its end can be processed in a "forward" (i.e., left-to-right) direction, because all the information needed to fill the gap precedes it. An item whose gap is at or near the beginning can usually only be completed by storing at least the items in the immediate environment of the gap in the memory, proceeding to the end of the item, and then returning back to the part with the gap, which can now be filled on the basis of the information following it. Note that the sense of direction is not always the same for the entire item; often the forward or backward direction is confined to that clause or phrase containing the gap. We stated earlier that the location of the gap(s) within the entire item appeared to have no bearing on the difficulty level of that item, but a future study should examine the effect of the direction of processing within each meaning unit, that is, within a clause or phrase. In any case, the relative processing time for forward versus backward items should be measured. One might also guess that, due to the time pressure under which the student has to operate, more backward items are simply skipped when the student recognizes that they require too much time for rereading the item or parts of it.

More interesting even is the direction of processing in an item with two gaps; that is, the order in which the two gaps can be filled. It turns out that there exist not only cases where the first gap can be filled before the second and vice versa, but also where both gaps are dependent on one another and where the options have to be considered with both gaps being tested or tried out simultaneously. The following are examples.

Forward:

26. Although the designers have not yet been able to solve the emission problem in the new automobile, their lack of _____ so far cannot be interpreted as final _____.

The first word, *success*, can be supplied on the basis of all the preceding material (in fact, *lack of success* sums up the contents of the *although*-clause); the last gap is easily filled with the correct option, *failure*, for similar reasons.

Backward:

27. In poetry intended for presentation to large audiences with _____ expectations, there can be no place for _____ or for strained subtleties of any kind.

The first gap needs a key word, that is, one that will give an evaluative interpretation to the sentence. It cannot be filled on the basis of the preceding material which gives no clue as to this interpretation. As for the second gap, we know only that its meaning must be somewhat opposed to that of the first gap, but this is of course not sufficient. Reading on to the end of the sentence, we find the clue in the last noun phrase which is connected to the second gap by *or,* indicating possible similarity in meaning. The option whose second word is *preciosity* is then selected. Its first word is *unsophisticated* which fulfills the criterion of being in an antonymic relationship with the second option; it can now be filled in.

Simultaneous:

28. Unlike Professor Stark, who is openly _____ about the value of cell research, Dr. Gorman favors _____ the already sizeable funds allocated to the project.

Again, the first gapped word is crucial in that it lends an evaluative interpretation to the clause, but no clues are provided by the clause itself. The same is essentially true for the second gap, although the context suggests a word such as *increasing* or *trimming* (which are exact opposites here in this context). The overall structure of the entire sentence demands that the two gaps be opposed in meaning, and this is the only clue for selecting the correct option (*skeptical . . . augmenting*). Note that an antonymic pair with the opposition reversed would render an equally fitting interpretation.

Due to many other factors (structural, syntactic, lexical), no pattern relating direction of processing and difficulty level could be discerned, but a future study might control for these unwanted variables and establish such a pattern.

SUMMARY AND CONCLUSIONS

The linguistic analysis of 120 sentence completion items showed that the test taker is faced with the following tasks:

1. comprehension of the meaning of all words in the item as well as in the options (lexical/semantic),
2. comprehension of the syntactic ("grammatical") relations among the sentence constituents (syntactic),
3. recognition and retention during the sentence processing of lexically or morphologically expressed antonymic relations (lexical/semantic),
4. syntactic relations across clauses, in particular as expressed by conjunctions such as *even though* (syntactic/lexical).

The foregoing summarizes the cognitive–linguistic knowledge that the student must apply in order to complete the sentences. In addition, he or she must use this knowledge in ways that require more or less complex cognitive processes. For example, the antonymic markers referred to in task 3, after being recognized, must be stored in the memory and the student must keep track of each one and its effect on the preceding one (e.g., a cancellation). Relations that are not antonymic in character, too, must be recognized and extracted from the sentence in order to make the correct option selection that expresses this relation best.

The direction of processing varies among the items. Our guess is that if it is not simply from left to right, comprehension is more difficult.

All items tap several of the types of linguistic knowledge listed above and require several of the cognitive processes mentioned, but they can do so with varying degrees.

The following are the major results of our preliminary investigation: Purely structural features of the items, such as number and location of the gap(s) and length of the item, were found to be unrelated to the difficulty of the item. Clause type seemed to be related to difficult in the following way: MC or MC–MC constructions made for harder items than MC–SC or SC–MC structures. The reason seems to be that the conjunction introducing an SC (and lacking in MC–MC sentences) provides some clue, in the form of parallelism or antonymy, for the semantic relationship between the gapped word and other constituents in the item. It turned out that antonymic relations made for easier items than parallel ones; this was true both on the phrase level and the single clause level, and across clauses.

Although these correlations between the makeup of items and their difficulty levels could be discerned, clear-cut relations are hard to obtain due to the fact that all items require several kinds of cognitive–linguistic tasks that interact within the item-solving process. A future study where the individual tasks are controlled for should yield more clear-cut and revealing results.

REFERENCES

Kučera, H., & Francis, N.(1967). *Computational analysis of present-day American English.* Providence, RI: Brown University Press.

Miller, G.A. (1978). Semantic relations among words. In M. Halle, J. Bresnan, & G. Miller (Eds.), *Linguistic Theory and Psychological Reality* (pp. 60–118). Cambridge, MA: MIT Press.

CHAPTER 5

Three Properties of the Ideal Reader*

Paul Kay

Department of Linguistics
University of California, Berkeley

INTRODUCTION: THE IDEAL READER

One way to study the acquisition of the ability to read is to compare the fledgling reader's attempts at reading with the performance of a hypothesized ideal reader. An approach of this kind has been developed by a research project of which I am a part and on whose collective work I report here. The present essay does not attempt a full report of our project to date, nor even a full characterization of the concept "ideal reader" (for which see Fillmore, 1981). Rather I sketch only the bare outlines of the concept and then concentrate on three important properties of the ideal reader.

The ideal reader is defined in terms of a particular text and a particular interpretation of that text. Given the text and an interpretation, the ideal reader is a device that is possessed of just the knowledge and skills required to extract that interpretation from that text. The ideal reader knows what the text presupposes and is able to learn what the text is designed to convey. The ideal reader thus conceived is not to be confused with the mature competent reader; rather the ideal reader may be instantiated by a mature, competent reader of a well-constructed text with a straightforward interpretation. The distinction is illustrated by text (1), with the intended interpretation given in single quotes.

(1)   When Pat and Leslie met she smiled but the other didn't smile back.
      'When they met, Pat smiled but Leslie didn't smile back.'

---

* Coprincipal investigators on the project, supported by NIE Grant No. G-790121 Rev. 1, are Charles Fillmore and myself. Reading specialist Judith Langer has participated, as have graduate student assistants Robert Aronowitz, Karen Carroll, Linda Coleman, Katherine Kovacic, Thomas Larsen, and Mary Catherine O'Connor. Welcome advice has been received from Mary Sue Ammon, Kjell Madsen, John R. Ross, and Patrizia Violi.

Some of the material in this paper was presented at a session of the 1981 Georgetown Roundtable on Languages and Linguistics chaired by Ulla Connor. An earlier version of the paper was presented at the Universidade Estadual de Campinas (Brasil) in 1982, where the comments of Marcelo Dascal were particularly helpful. Comments by members of Robert Wilensky's seminar on text processing in the winter of 1982, at the University of California, Berkeley, are also gratefully acknowledged. The influence of Charles Fillmore is present throughout.

Since the ideal reader is defined with respect to a text and interpretation, the ideal reader of (1) will by definition achieve the interpretation given. But of course mature, competent readers (or hearers) will not unambiguously assign this interpretation to text (1). Thus, as well as providing a standard against which the performances of real readers can be judged, the concept of ideal reader gives us a basis for criticizing texts. If a text makes unrealistic or undesirable demands on its reader—for example, that the ideal reader for this text be clairvoyant or that it be content to believe contradictions, demands that we think are not made on actual, mature and competent readers by well-constructed texts—we judge the text on that account to be deficient.[1] The main thing an ideal reader does as it reads a text is construct an "envisionment" of that text, a term we have borrowed from John Seely Brown. The envisionment is the representation in the reader's mind of the content of the text. The envisionment grows, and sometimes changes, as the reader (or hearer of a monologue) progresses through the text.[2] According to this view, the ideal reader, as it reads a text, not only updates and supplements its envisionment of the world the text is describing, but also—in the service of building this envisionment—formulates hypotheses, asks questions, notes evidence and in general, accomplishes a variety of processing operations (Fillmore & Kay, 1980, pp. 22–49). These processing operations will not be discussed here. Rather, two of the properties of the ideal reader that I shall discuss have to do with the structure of the envisionment, and the third concerns the embedding of both the envisionment itself and the processing operations that directly produce it in higher-order processes. Instead of attempting further abstract characterization of these properties of the ideal reader, I will proceed directly to examples that illustrate the notions I have in mind.

LEVELS OF ENVISIONMENT

The first property of the ideal reader is that it does not invest in every part of its envisionment the same degree of confidence. The ideal reader does a lot of

---

[1] The texts with which our project is primarily concerned are the items on tests of reading comprehension given to third and fifth graders. An alarming number of these texts are deficient in the sense of requiring an ideal reader that corresponds either to no real reader (no matter how proficient) or to a real reader that it is unreasonable to expect a third or fifth grader to approximate. Some examples of such texts are given by Fillmore (1981), who also discusses the role that the concept ideal reader plays in our empirical procedures for studying the interaction between third and fifth graders and these texts.

[2] Reading is probably easier to model in this way than hearing is because reading lacks the interactive phenomena, such as negotiation of interpretive context, back channel signaling, and the like, that are the bread and butter of the conversational analyst. Nevertheless, reading is hard enough. In the remainder of this paper I talk about reading, but to the extent the model we are developing is correct, it should be useful in the understanding of the text semantics of spoken language as well. Written language also differs from spoken language in other ways, such as the imperfect substitution of punctuation for intonation, stress, and prosody.

reading between the lines. But the ideal reader also knows that it must place less trust in those parts of its envisionment that arise from reading between the lines than in those parts that come from reading the lines themselves. The ideal reader in fact distinguishes many levels of confidence within the envisionment. Consider the two text fragments:

(2) The Orioles' shortstop bunted the ball right to the first baseman, who grabbed it and tagged the batter out.

(3) The Orioles' shortstop threw the ball right to the first baseman, who grabbed it and tagged the batter out.

Let us catalogue several inferences the ideal reader will draw from these texts, that is, several items that ought to become part of the ideal reader's envisionment of these texts. In particular, we want to look at relations of coreference between pairs of noun phrases in the two texts. First of all, we note that in both (2) and (3) the pairs of noun phrases (*the ball, it*) and (*the first baseman, who*) are coreferential, which facts are summarized in Table 1. Facts (a) and (b) reflect directly the grammar of the texts, and nothing more. This may be seen by considering text (4), which is parallel in grammatical structure to both texts (2) and (3) (which themselves are grammatically parallel, differing only in the alternation between the lexical items *bunt* and *throw*), but in which nonsense words are substituted for the content items.

(4) The Wimbats' glurb slunked the wint to the girfman, who critched it and . . .

The reader will appreciate that the grammar of (4) determines that the relations of coreference must be as shown in (5), which accord with those of Table 1.

(5) The Wimbats' glurb$_i$ slunked the wint$_j$ to the girfman$_k$, who$_k$ critched it$_j$ and . . .

Thus inferences (a) and (b) are not dependent on any knowledge or skill the reader may possess beyond his or her knowledge of English grammar. In particular, no knowledge of the game of baseball is required. Also, and more importantly, it is impossible to imagine a continuation of text (2) or (3) that could overthrow these inferences. For example, if we load the content to make conflicting inferences regarding coreference more plausible, the result is not a switch of perceived relations of coreference but a judgment of incoherence. Thus in (6) we rig the content to try to get the relative pronoun *who* to be coreferential, not with

Table 1.

Text (2)	Text (3)
(a) *the ball = it*	(a) *the ball = it*
(b) *the first baseman = who*	(b) *the first baseman = who*

Table 2.

Text (2)	Text (3)
(a) *the ball = it*	(a) *the ball = it*
(b) *the first baseman = who*	(b) *the first baseman = who*
(c) *the Orioles' shortstop = the batter*	(c) *the Orioles' shortstop ≠ the batter*

the immediately preceding noun phrase but with the initial noun phrase; the attempt fails.

(6)   *The batter$_i$ grounded to the shortstop$_j$, who$_i$ was thrown out easily.

In short, the reader need know nothing about baseball and, in particular, need know nothing about the meanings of the words *shortstop, bunt, first baseman,* and so on, to infer the facts given in Table 1. Further, there is no way in which subsequent developments of the text (2) or (3) can induce the English-speaking reader to change his mind about the inferences (a,b) of Table 1.

Inferences (a) and (b) were the same for texts (2) and (3). There are inferences of the same general kind in which the two texts differ. In particular, in text (2) the Orioles' shortstop is the batter while in text (3) the Orioles' shortstop is not the batter. Table 2 adds these inferences in those of Table 1.

But now we note that these new inferences (c) are in part dependent on schematic knowledge of the game of baseball. In particular, they are dependent on the knowledge that *shortstop* is the name of a fielding position; that batters may be referred to by their fielding positions; that *bunting* is something that batters (not fielders) do; that throwing is something that fielders (not batters) do; that *the Orioles* is the name (or could be the name) of a baseball team; and so on (the list is not complete). The reader who has absolutely no knowledge of baseball will notice that he or she was unable to derive inferences (c).[3]

It is not impossible to imagine a continuation of the texts (2) and (3) that could vitiate inferences (c). We can imagine a game that is generally like baseball except the offensive player is not equipped with a bat but rather attempts to catch the pitch and throw it out into the playing field. The defensive players, on the other hand, are equipped with bats and are required to hit or bunt the ball to the basemen to put the batters out. A skilled writer might be able to build a text that

---

[3] Readers who doubt that inferences (c) require some knowledge of baseball should consult an acquaintance who lacks all such knowledge. To make the point I am making here, it has been necessary to select an example from a domain about which knowledge is widespread but not ubiquitous among English speakers. Those who lack knowledge of baseball at the requisite level will have either to take my word for it or consult someone who has such knowledge. No affront to either knowers or nonknowers of baseball is intended.

took (2) or (3) as the initial fragment and develop it along these lines so that the reader would ultimately reject his or her initial inference of type (c) and arrive at a final envisionment of a game of the sort just suggested. A text that began with fragments (2) or (3) and caused us to overthrow inferences (c) might seem farfetched, perhaps some kind of literary tour de force. Nevertheless, such a text is possible in English. In this important respect inferences of type (c) differ from those like (a) and (b), although one suspects that with regard to actual texts and actual readers the analytical distinction is unlikely to make much practical difference. Nonetheless, in thus distinguishing inferences (a,b) from (c), we have detected what we may call two *levels* of envisionment: the (a,b) level being absolutely ordained by the text and the (c) level being strongly—though not absolutely—determined by the text. The point, which we shall now pursue, is that items of the envisionment may be warranted by the text to varying degrees and therefore to varying degrees may be cancellable by further development of the text without discomfort to the ideal reader.

Consider now the inferences, obvious enough to those fairly familiar with baseball, that in text (2) the first baseman is not an Oriole while in text (3) the first baseman is an Oriole. These inferences require grammatical knowledge and the knowledge of baseball (and the lexicon of baseball) of the kinds already considered. In addition, they are based on the world knowledge that the players on one team of a given game normally belong to one ball club while the players on the other team belong to another ball club. That is, we normally think of baseball games which are known to involve players on regularly organized, league ball clubs as being regular league games, in which the players represent the teams of which they are regular members. There are, however, regularly occurring, if less frequent, events in American culture in which these conditions do not hold, for example, all-star games. The rosters of all-star teams are necessarily composed of players from a variety of teams. If the game being described in text (2) or (3) turns out to be an all-star game, then the text provides no warrant for the inferences just mentioned, which are given as (d) in Table 3.[4]

Inferences (d), although perfectly natural to draw from these texts are, as we have just seen, relatively easily suspendable under culturally nonfarfetched, contextual assumptions; this is the same as saying that they are easily suspendable under relatively nonfarfetched continuations of the same texts. We want to say, therefore, that inferences of types (a,b), (c) and (d) belong to increasingly "higher" levels of envisionment, where the lower the level the more direct and absolute the textual warrant for the inference and the higher level of envisionment the more contingent and revisable the inference is. Roughly speaking, if a text requires revision of something in the envisionment at the lowest level we say that the text is inconsistent, self-contradictory, or incoherent; if the text requires revision of something at a "medium" level of envisionment we are inclined to say that the text is surprising; if we find that the text requires revision of something we have at a very high level of envisionment we are inclined to

Table 3.

Text (2)		Text (3)	
(a)	*the ball = it*	(a)	*the ball = it*
(b)	*who = the first baseman*	(b)	*who = the first baseman*
(c)	*the Orioles' shortstop = the batter*	(c)	*the Orioles' shortstop ≠ the batter*
(d)	*the first baseman ≠* an Oriole	(d)	*the first baseman =* an Oriole

attribute no particular property to the text. Rather, we may register surprise that we as readers have populated our envisionment of a text with some item that lacks textual warrant.

For example, suppose the reader envisioned the Orioles' shortstop as right-handed. This would be reasonable as, not only are the majority of people right-handed, but the exigencies of baseball play are such that very few, if any, professional shortstops are left-handed.[5] The reader who envisioned the Orioles' shortstop as right-handed would have a right to be mildly surprised if it turned out later in the text that he wasn't, and the entitlement to surprise would increase with the length of text that intervened between the introduction of the shortstop and the revelation of his left-handedness. Compared to the (d) inferences about which team the first baseman is on, this inference about handedness is less directly warranted by the text and more by background knowledge of baseball; it also seems less likely to figure in coherence relations of the kind we will discuss under the parsimony principle below. For these reasons, we may with fair confidence add it to our table as representing a still more tenuous level of inference.

At a level of inference or imagination more tenuous yet, suppose some reader forms an image of the shortstop with a mustache. If it turns out later that the shortstop is clean-shaven, any reader who experiences surprise is not, we think, entitled to account for this experience by saying that the text is surprising. Hence we do not add this kind of inference to the ideal reader's envisionment at any level.

The ideal reader will thus make inferences regarding the content world of the text at a variety of levels. As we have noted, the reader who cannot or will not read between the lines is not a good reader, and the reader who is unable or unwilling to distinguish what he or she has been told from what he or she has inferred or imagined is also less than ideal. The latter ability, to distinguish what is directly warranted by the text from that which is less directly warranted (even to the point of what is not warranted at all by the text but is merely contributed idiosyncratically to the envisionment), is most obviously necessary to the reader

---

[4] There are other plausible continuations of texts (2) and (3) in which inferences (d) need not—in some cases cannot—hold; examples include sandlot games and intra-squad games.

[5] Left-handedness is common at other positions, for example, pitcher and first baseman.

Table 4.

Text (2)	Text (3)
(a) *the ball = it*	(a) *the ball = it*
(b) *who = the first baseman*	(b) *who = the first baseman*
(c) *the Orioles' shortstop = the batter*	(c) *the Orioles' shortstop ≠ the batter*
(d) *the first baseman ≠ an Oriole*	(d) *the first baseman = an Oriole*
(e) the Orioles' shortstop is right-handed	(e) the Orioles' shortstop is right-handed

of informational texts, or, more exactly, to the reader who approaches a text for the purpose of assimilating the information it contains.[6]

We have seen that the reader of informational texts—or the reader of texts in the informational mode—must keep straight the levels of his or her envisionment. The informational mode is the mode of reading taught initially in our grammar schools, and some educational critics would claim that it is the only mode of reading ever taught in our society, even in college literature courses. It might be thought, and has indeed been argued, that this kind of self-awareness in the reader—this ability of the ideal reader to reflect upon its own processing and recognize those parts of the envisionment that derive from distinct sorts of processing routines—is relevant only, or primarily, to the informational mode of reading. In the coming section I argue that reflexive self-awareness of the reader's internal processing is equally important in expressive-aesthetic kinds of reading, and that literary and rhetorical effects, including humor, may require just such awareness on the part of the reader of his or her own processing of the text.

THE TRUSTING IDEAL READER

We have seen that in order to study the interaction of young readers and the texts they encounter on tests of reading comprehension we must postulate an ideal reader with the degree of sophistication necessary to distinguish appropriate levels of the envisionment. There is another kind of sophistication possessed by real, mature readers that it is for the most part *not* necessary to impute to the ideal reader with which beginning readers are compared. This impoverished kind of

---

[6] Some texts—for example, assembly instructions—seem inherently informational while others—for example, poems—seem inherently intended to arouse aesthetic experiences rather than to impart objective information. It is, however, possible and perfectly normal to approach a text in a way that departs from the author's intention. Such is the case, for example, when the literature student reads a play or poem to learn its content and structure rather than to experience its aesthetic values. There is, of course, much more to the subject of what functions a text may fulfill than is suggested by the simple contrast "impart objective information" versus "arouse aesthetic experience."

ideal reader is one that lacks the capacity to reflect upon the history of its own processing of a text. The *trusting* ideal reader is literal minded. If it forms a hypothesis and then encounters evidence that leads to rejection of that hypothesis, it doesn't ask second-order questions such as, ''Why would the author have put in the information that led me to the first hypothesis if he or she were only to give me conflicting information later? Is there some kind of literary trick going on here?'' The trusting ideal reader is artless in the sense that it does not produce secondary interpretations of a text by reflecting upon the processing it has done in producing the primary interpretation. The trusting ideal reader does not construct an image of the author of the text it is processing and does not reflect upon this author's possible motivations.

The best illustration I can think of for the concept of the trusting ideal reader involves a text intended, not primarily to be read, but rather to be heard, a bit of doggerel that my peers and I in junior high school found amusing:

(7)   Of all the things I'd rather be,
      I'd rather be a bass.
      I'd climb up to the top of trees.
      And slide down on my hands and knees.

Part of the intended humorous effect of the text depends on the whimsical image of fish climbing trees; we will leave this matter for the moment and return to it later. For the rest, the addressee who gets the point and intended humor of the text incorporates the trusting addressee and reflects upon the results of this very trustingness in arriving at the intended rhetorical effect.

From the point of view of the trusting addressee the analysis of (7) goes in part as follows. At the end of the third line, one has noted that the rhyme scheme is so far *a b c* (or perhaps *a b a,* depending on whether *trees* is heard as an imperfect rhyme for *be*), and with regard to meter that all three lines are perfectly iambic, having four, three, and four feet, respectively. The pattern of rhyme and meter so far perceived is

(8)   ⌣′ ⌣′ ⌣′ ⌣′
      ⌣′⌣′~[bæs]
      ⌣′ ⌣′ ⌣′ ⌣′

One therefore contracts the expectation that the next (i.e., the fourth) line will 1) end in a stressed syllable concluding with [æs] to rhyme with *bass,* and 2) contain three iambic feet, completing the pattern given in (7) which is the basic ballad form, an extremely familiar genre in our culture.[7]

---

[7] One of many familiar quatrains that might be cited is from Oscar Wilde's ''*Ballad of reading gaol*'':

For each man kills the thing he loves;
Let this all be heard.
Some do it with a bitter look.

(9)   ∪ / ∪ / ∪ / ∪ /
      ∪ / ∪ / ∪ x̌
      ∪ / ∪ / ∪ / ∪ /
      ∪ / ∪ / ∪ x̌

At the end of the word *my* in the fourth line—with one syllable left to go—these hypotheses are still working perfectly. We lack only a single stressed syllable to complete the ballad form (4, 3, 4, 3 iambs), and there is a monosyllabic word which rhymes with *bass,* which names a part of the body one can slide on, thereby making as much semantic sense as one may hope for in a text containing the whimsy of bass climbing trees, and which, above all, provides the satisfaction of completing the pattern of rhyme, meter, and meaning with a tabooed word. For these reasons the trusting ideal hearer expects that word at this point.

When line 4 continues *hands and knees* the trusting addressee cancels his expectation without further thought and notes with simple satisfaction that the poem has been successfully concluded with a rhyme scheme *a b c c* and a matching meter of 4, 3, 4, 4 iambs. The trusting ideal addressee does not *reflect* upon the fact that his expectations have been violated, he merely revises them. He therefore doesn't appreciate that a trick has been played on him: that he has been led to contract an expectation for a tabooed word on the basis of the rhythmic, metric, and semantic pattern, but that that pattern has been completed satisfactorily without the use of the tabooed word. The sophisticated addressee, on the other hand, appreciates that a joke has been played on her in that she has been convicted in her own mind of "dirty-mindedness" for having supplied the tabooed word before it was produced, only to find that the poem was successfully completed without it.

What we want to note here is that the sophisticated ideal reader incorporates the trusting ideal reader. The sophisticated ideal reader gets the joke by virtue of noticing how the trusting reader inside of her or him has been led up the garden path. It seems a useful working hypothesis that many, if not all, texts that require something more than our trusting ideal reader to appreciate their full rhetorical effect require as one component of their sophisticated ideal reader a trusting ideal reader. Insofar as this hypothesis is correct, any theory that aims to explain the processes used by sophisticated readers in interpreting literary texts that rely on complex rhetorical strategies will need to *include* a theory of a trusting ideal reader. We therefore have grounds to hope that what we learn about the reading process by positing a trusting ideal reader who is competent to read very simple texts may be of use in understanding the workings of sophisticated readers who are able to interpret more complex texts successfully.

Some with a flattering word.

Note the rhyme of *heard* and *word.*

Linda Coleman, of our project, has drawn attention to examples, such as the following, which illustrate simultaneously both the levels-of-envisionment property and the trusting-versus-sophisticated-ideal-reader property. In a science fiction novel, Ursula LeGuin introduces a character as the Terran ambassador (i.e., the ambassador from Earth). Some time later, after this character has played a minor but not insignificant role in the proceedings for a while, we are allowed to learn that the Terran ambassador is a black woman. This comes as a shock to those readers, probably all, who have envisioned the ambassador from Earth as a white man. But, there is a double shock because the reader is shocked at being shocked. The initial shock is connected with feelings that the author is skating dangerously close to incoherence by allowing such a strongly warranted inference to stand this long before correction. The second shock comes with the rapid realization that the very strength of the inference is based on the strength of racial and sexual stereotypes that the reader of this kind of literature probably thinks that he or she doesn't have in the first place. And then the sophisticated reader envisions the rhetorical-political purposes of the author, who has foreseen all this processing going on in her readers' minds and intended it to happen just this way. By having kept straight his or her levels of envisionment, the naive reader is able to reject the image of a white man in the envisionment and substitute that of a black woman without imaging a contradiction. Further reflections on his or her own stereotyped behavior, racism, sexism, or on images of a clever author nondidactically pointing these out, belong to the sophisticated readers' reflection on the trusting reader inside her or him, who was able to effect the substitution "black woman" for "white man" but appreciated nothing of its significance.

THE PARSIMONY PRINCIPLE

In the first section of this paper, where we considered the necessity of keeping track of the different levels of certainty of the envisionment, we perforce considered the ideal reader's ability to read between the lines of a text, that is, to draw inferences that are not directly warranted by the grammar and lexicon of the text but that are nonetheless necessary to derive a coherent envisionment. For example, from a text such as (10), the reader who fails to draw inferences such as (11 a–f) will not be an ideal reader.

(10)   One day a chef went to Fisherman's Wharf and bought some fish from a fisherman.

(11)(a)   The chef will cook the fish at his restaurant.[8] He will not, for example, take it home to his wife.

---

[8] For simplicity we assume here that chefs are employed only in restaurants, though it is of course true that chefs are sometimes employed in the homes of the rich. Another assumption we have made tacitly, that has perhaps been noticed by some readers, but probably not many, is that the chef is a

(b)   The fisherman caught the fish. For example, he is not selling it for an electrician friend who happened to buy too much fish at the supermarket.

(c)   The fisherman is a commercial fisherman, and he caught the fish in order to sell it. He is not, for example, a lucky sports fisherman who just happened to be opportuned by the chef.

(d)   The money the chef gave the fisherman was not his own money but the restaurant's.

(e)   The purpose of the chef's visit to Fisherman's Wharf was to buy fish, not, say, to visit the Wax Museum.

(f)   The transaction took place at Fisherman's Wharf. Compare: "One windy day Charlotte went to the hairdresser's and bought a bandana from a street vendor."

Each of the inferences of (11) is of the between-the-lines type, that is, the inference is not absolutely warranted by the grammar and lexicon of the text. In each case the contrasting possibility mentioned is not what we immediately infer but is something that could turn out to be what the author had in mind. Inferences (11 a–f) are like the middle level inferences (c, d, and perhaps e) in our baseball example (2, 3); the ideal reader of this text would draw these inferences but would also remember them as, in varying degrees, subject to suspension by possible later developments. If they are suspended by later developments, the reader will be entitled to a reaction of surprise; the longer the delay, the greater the surprise.[9] So far we have discussed things that happen to the ideal reader's

---

man. Such inferences from stereotypes are a major target of various kinds of language reform; no doubt something of this reformist spirit motivated the novelist LeGuin when she constructed the Terran ambassador text mentioned above.

[9] Inferences (11 a–f) by no means exhaust what the ideal reader should extract from this text. In particular, the ideal reader will construct several little histories for the various participants in this story and know the temporal points of their relation to each other. Thus the money that paid for the fish probably originally came from customers in the restaurant who paid for food there and may well end up being paid out for bait or gasoline or other fishing supplies. The catching of the fish by the fisherman took place before the commercial event, while the cooking by the chef will take place subsequently, and the eating by the customers of the restaurant later still. Some, but not all, of the relevant historical understanding is represented diagrammatically in Figure 1.

At $time_1$ the chef has not got hold of this particular money and the fisherman is not yet in possession of the fish. Sometime later the money and the chef have become associated and the fish and the fisherman have become associated; this is represented by the picture at $time_2$. The commercial event takes place at $time_3$, briefly bringing all four participants into spatio-temporal contiguity. Following this, at $time_4$, the four participants divide into novel pairings, fish with chef and money with fisherman. Eventually, $time_5$, these pairings dissolve as the fish is eaten and the money spent or invested.

The relations depicted at times 2, 3, and 4 follow from our knowledge of the commercial event schema itself, while those at earlier and later points in the history, represented by times 1 and 5, depend on our schematic knowledge of the kinds of participants involved in the particular commercial event portrayed in this text. For example, with reference to $time_1$, it follows from our knowledge of FISHING (not of commercial events) that the fish and the fisherman were not always associated. If we consider a commercial event with different kinds of participants, we are not led to imagine an earlier time when the seller and the goods have not yet become associated. For example in O. Henry's

Figure 1

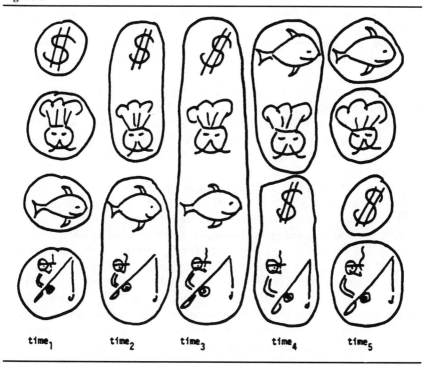

time₁   time₂   time₃   time₄   time₅

inferences after they are drawn, but we have not talked about how they are drawn in the first place. A full theory of the ideal reader will be concerned with the latter quite as much as the former. Although a complete theory of the ideal reader, one which predicts the actual inferences drawn from a text without

---

"Gift of the Magi" the sale of the young matron's beautiful hair does not invite us to imagine an earlier time when hair and matron enjoyed separate existences. Similarly, the ideal reader who encounters a commercial event in which someone buys an artificial limb or a pacemaker will not foresee a future time when the purchaser and his acquisition have become separated.

Of the relations depicted at times 1 and 5 in Figure 1, the separation of fish and fisherman at time₁ seems to have the more direct warrant in the text, in the form of a fishing schema which insists that fishermen catch fish they didn't previously have. (An activity, otherwise like fishing, that takes place in a bucket or a bathtub is probably not real fishing and surely not prototypical fishing.) In the actual analysis of any text, one always reaches a point at which the inferences that different competent analysts attribute to the ideal reader diverge. For example, some might wish to say that the separateness of the money and the chef at time₁ is something that the reader is supposed to get out of this text, while others will say that this is a plausible imagining, consistent with the text, but not something that would cause us to say that a reader had missed something if he or she failed to come to it. The methodological point is that for any text there are many things that all analysts agree in attributing to the ideal reader and also things about which they will disagree. These latter define those levels of envisionment where what is ordained by the text shades imperceptibly into what is permitted by the text.

making use of the human judgment of the analyst, seems distant from the present state of the art, perhaps there are a few steps we can take in this direction. Let us proceed inductively in the analysis of text (10) and the inferences (11) to which it gives rise, first discovering the background schemata that seem necessary and then investigating how these schemata are employed in reaching these inferences.

First, the word *chef* evokes a RESTAURANT schema. We have already noted (footnote 8) that chefs may not always occur in restaurants and we may at times wish to speak of a CHEF schema per se. Hence: In semantic memory schemata may intersect each other in a variety of ways: the CHEF schema is itself an (optional) *element* of the RESTAURANT schema and is also an *instance* of an OCCUPATIONAL schema.

There is also a FISHING schema evoked by our text. In fishing there is a person who attempts to catch fish, sometimes succeeds, may own fishing equipment, may ride in a boat, and so on. There are two principal kinds of fishermen: commercial fishermen and sports fishermen. One way to give theoretical recognition to this observation is to say that the fishing schema has two subschemata, sport and commercial. A contrasting way is to say that the fishing schema itself instantiates two distinct *families* of schemata: OCCUPATIONS and AVOCATIONS. A formal theory of semantic memory, one that specifies not only its constituent schemata but also the relations among them, would presumably have to take a position on issues such as this. For present purposes we are content to discover some of the elements of such a theory without specifying their interrelations.

The well-known COMMERCIAL EVENT schema (Fillmore, 1977) is of course involved in text (10).

We have made use in a casual way of the concept *family* of related schemata. In the present case, we may note that for all their many dissimilarities the FISHING and COMMERCIAL EVENTS schemata have something in common. They both involve purposeful actions and hence each involves at least one goal.

There is also a schematization of the time relations of actions involved in this, as in any text. (The temporal schematization of (10) is discussed in footnote 9.)

We would like now to say something about *how* these schemata are employed in drawing the between-the-lines sorts of inferences listed in (11). As a preliminary, let us consider how schemata are involved in drawing ground-level, unsuspendable inferences from our text (10). One such unsuspendable inference is:

(12)   The person who went to Fisherman's Wharf is the same as the one who bought the fish.

We can put this more long-windedly but in a way that better reveals our theoretical preconceptions, as follows: The grammar of (10) guarantees that the entity who fills the TRAVELER slot of the JOURNEY schema evoked by the first clause is the same entity as the one that fills the BUYER slot of the

COMMERCIAL EVENT schema evoked by the second clause; the TRAVELER participant in the JOURNEY scenario that forms the first part of our envisionment and the BUYER participant in the COMMERCIAL EVENT scenario that forms the second part of our envisionment are the same. We are talking here of *schemata* as structures in semantic memory that are employed on particular occasions to build the *scenarios* that constitute an envisionment. We speak of schemata as containing *slots* and of the things that fill these slots in a particular scenario as *participants*. Often, the slots in schemata that are filled by participants in scenarios are matched by noun phrases in the grammatical structure and the question whether two participants in different scenarios are the same often corresponds to the question whether two noun phrases are coreferential. We see thus that the main thing happening in inference (12) is that a single participant, the chef, connects two scenarios (going to Fisherman's Wharf, buying a fish) by filling distinct slots (traveler, buyer) in the schemata (JOURNEY, COMMERCIAL EVENT) that underlie the two scenarios. The two little scenarios are thereby joined into one larger scenario, giving the text coherence.

We have already noticed that, unlike the inferences of (11) with which we are primarily concerned here, the inference of (12) is forced by the grammar. If we consider a text of parallel grammar but which lacks an intuitive semantic support for an inference comparable to (12), we see that such an inference (14) is forced anyway.

(13)   One day a chef went to Fisherman's Wharf and sprained his ankle.

(14)   The person who went to Fisherman's Wharf is the one who sprained his ankle.

That is, unlike the inferences (11), the grammar forces the inference of (12) from (10) as it does the inference of (14) from (13).

This aspect of sentence semantics seems directly related to a principle of text semantics that we call the ''parsimony principle.'' The parsimony principle is this: *Whenever it is possible to link two separate scenarios into a single larger scenario by imagining them as sharing a common participant, the ideal reader does so.* Let us turn directly to our examples (11) to see how this principle works out in practice. In (15 a–f) the inferences (11 a–f) are repeated and each is followed by an explanation of how it arises from (10) via the parsimony principle.

(15)(a)   The chef will cook the fish at his restaurant. The food participant in the restaurant scenario and the goods participant in the commercial event scenario are the same.

(b)   The fisherman caught the fish. The fish participant in the fishing scenario is the same as the goods participant in the commercial event scenario.

(c)   The fisherman caught the fish in order to sell it and he is a commercial fisherman. The entire commercial event scenario is the goal participant of the fishing scenario. In the commercial fishing schema (or subschema) the fisherman is also a fish seller. If the commercial fishing schema is chosen, then the seller slot of the commercial fishing scenario can be accompanied by the same participant as the seller slot of the commercial event scenario. (This requires something beyond the parsimony principle as baldy stated; we will come back to this point.)

(d)   The money the chef gave the fisherman was not his own but the restaurant's. The restaurant schema has a slot for money, since restaurants are profit-seeking enterprises. The money slot in the restaurant schema can be made to share a participant with the money slot in the commercial event schema.

(e)   The goal of the chef's visit to Fisherman's Wharf was to buy fish. The entire commercial event scenario can serve as the goal participant of the journey scenario.

(f)   The transaction took place at Fisherman's Wharf. The destination participant of the journey scenario is inferred to be the same as the (optional) location slot of the commercial event scenario and the (optional) home-port slot of the fishing scenario.

These equations of participants across scenarios are displayed graphically in Figure 2 by the vertical arrows with single shafts. (Only the double-shafted arrows correspond to equations directly mandated by the language of the text and therefore requiring no potentially suspendable inferences.) Words in italics indicate words of the actual text. The words following these in capitals are the names of schemata that are evoked by the words of the text. Following the name of a schema is a series of names of slots in underlined lower case. Following the name of each slot, after a colon, is a word in ordinary print intended to indicate the identity of the participant of that slot in the particular scenario created by this text. For example, the arrow marked ''a'' indicates that the goods participant of the COMMERCIAL EVENT scenario is the same as the food participant of the RESTAURANT scenario; the fact that this arrow is single shafted indicates that this is a suspendable inference and the fact that it is marked ''a'' indicates that this inference corresponds to the inference labeled (11)a and (15)a in the text. The list of slots appearing for a given schema is not intended to represent a comprehensive analysis of that schema but only to portray those slots whose participants are identified with the participants of scenarios based on other schemata in the envisionment of this particular text (by the ideal reader). The inferences indicated by single arrows a–f on the figure are instances of the parsimony principle in action.

The examples of the parsimony principle so far considered have had the following structure: (a) Words of the text evoke schemata; (b) these schemata contain slots that need to be filled by participants in the text-specific scenarios that instantiate them; (c) the parsimony principle enjoins the ideal reader to keep the number of distinct participants to a minimum, hence to equate participants in distinct scenarios whenever possible; (d) this results in the entwining of the various small scenarios, creating out of them one large, reticulate scenario. I

Figure 2

word evokes   SCHEMA contains   *slot:* instantiated by participant (indicated by a word from the text when possible)

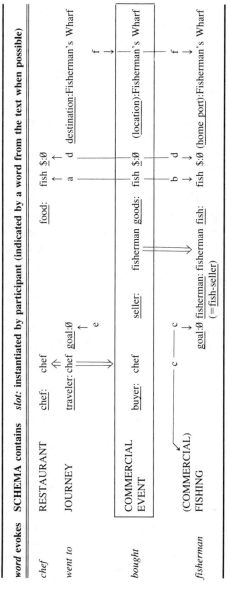

chef   RESTAURANT

went to   JOURNEY

bought   COMMERCIAL
              EVENT

              (COMMERCIAL)
              FISHING

fisherman

Schemata are evoked by words of the text. Schemata contain slots. Scenarios are instantiations of schemata in which the slots are filled by particular envisioned participants. The grammar and lexicon of the text and, particularly, the parsimony principle, create equations among participants in different scenarios, binding these individual scenarios into the larger scenario that is the envisionment.

223

would suggest that this reticulation of the overall scenario (i.e., of the envisionment) is an important part of our intuition of textual coherence.[10]

We have concentrated on examples in which the words of the text evoke
schemata and the parsimony principle then goes to work on these. But we have
also noted in passing certain examples where the parsimony principle does even
more: It helps to direct the initial choice of relevant schemata or subschemata.
One such example involves the choice of the commercial fishing subschema over
the sport fishing subschema. We note that if we choose the commercial fishing
subschema, then we might get a tighter schematic fit between two participants
who must be matched anyway on account of strict grammatical schemata. Recall
that the grammar ordains that the fisherman participant of the fishing scenario
and the seller participant of the commercial event scenario be the same. By
choosing the commercial fishing subschema, in which fishermen are fish sellers,
we achieve a matching in semantic schematization of participants who are anyway identified with each other by the grammar of the text. Here we see that the
parsimony principle not only matches participants for schemata that are already
evoked but leads the ideal reader in his selection of the content schemata themselves. This suggests a sort of metaprinciple for schema selection: *Select schemata in such a way as to give the parsimony principle the widest possible scope
of operation.* We might dub this metaprinciple the "parsimony promotion principle." Much more empirical work is obviously needed to delineate the details of
the operation of the closely related parsimony and parsimony promotion principles, but even the very preliminary examples discussed here suggest that these
principles are real and play an important role in both ideal readers' and competent real readers' interpretation of texts.

RFFERENCES

Fillmore, C.J. (1977). Topics in lexical semantics. In R. Cole (Ed.), *Current Issues in Linguistic
    Theory.* Bloomington: Indiana University Press.
Fillmore, C.J., & Kay, P. (1980). *Progress report: Text semantic analysis of reading comprehension
    tests.* Unpublished manuscript.
Fillmore, C.J. (1981). Ideal readers and real readers. *Proceedings of the 32nd Georgetown Roundta-
    ble on Languages and Linguistics.* Washington, DC: Georgetown University Press.

---

[10] The present statement of the parsimony principle can only be a first approximation because the
universal quantification *whenever* is too broad and will have to be constrained in a realistically
predictive theory. For example, if the chef-fisherman text (10) were to continue with the chef
returning to his restaurant and later a customer coming in, the ideal reader would not presume that the
customer and the previously mentioned fisherman were the same. But that inference is dictated by the
unconstrained version of the parsimony principle given in the text. I am indebted to Yigal Arens,
David Evans, and Peter Norvig for this observation.

CHAPTER 6

The Construction of Meaning and the Assessment of Comprehension: An Analysis of Reader Performance on Standardized Test Items*

Judith A. Langer

Stanford University

BACKGROUND

The study discussed here used a text semantic approach to investigate the processes readers used to construct an understanding of test items selected from among the norm referenced standardized reading comprehension tests most frequently used by schools across the United States. The broad goals of the project were (a) to identify aspects of test language and structure that might interfere with comprehension, (b) to describe the skills and knowledge necessary for a reader to comprehend each passage, and (c) to examine the extent to which young readers have that knowledge and those skills. Every aspect of the project—the formulation of research questions, the system of text analysis, and the interpretation of the data—was deeply influenced by a view of reading comprehension as a dynamically constructive process (Anderson, 1977; Bartlett, 1932; Goodman & Goodman, 1978; Polanyi, 1966; Rumelhart, 1977; Schank & Abelson, 1977).

The inquiry was conducted in two phases. The first phase focused on the development of a systematic procedure for the text semantic analysis of test items. The analysis codifies the lexical, syntactic, and rhetorical structures occurring in a specific text as well as the linguistic and conceptual demands these structures presumably pose for a reader (Fillmore, 1981b). It also tracks the manner in which the genre, the content, and the linguistic material of the text shape the developing meaning.

This system of text analysis served as the basis for the next phase of the study, an investigation of readers' comprehension and question-answering strategies.

---

* The work reported here was supported, in part, by the National Institute of Education under grant number G-790121 Rev: 1, "Text Semantic Analysis of Reading Comprehension Tests." Coprincipal investigators were Charles J. Fillmore and Paul Kay; research team members were Karen Carroll, Linda Coleman, Katherine Kovacic, and Mary Catherine O'Connor. Welcome advice was received from Mary Sue Ammon, Kjel Madsen, Haj Ross, and Patrizia Violi.

Using a variety of interview procedures and metacognitive probes, data were gathered which permitted analysis of aspects of test items (each consisting of a paragraph and accompanying multiple-choice questions) that posed difficulties for actual readers. We compared readers as meaning-integrators with readers as question-answerers in order to determine whether the test items examined identified as high scorers the same students who were identified as successful meaning-makers.

The project itself can be characterized as a series of descriptive studies carried out in the tradition of linguistic inquiry whereby our observations of readers' performance were used to inform our developing analyses of texts and readers, and these in turn were validated using other test items and other readers. All generalizations, therefore, are an outgrowth of these repeated, in-depth observations.

Ideal and Actual Readers

The analysis of a particular text proceeds linearly, tracing the changing interpretations that an "ideal reader" could justifiably make in the process of comprehending the text. The system conveys a dynamic and idealized version of reader-text interaction in that it codifies a finite number of cognitive expectations and integrations warranted by a particular text; these interpretations constitute a comprehensively developing envisionment of text meaning up to any specific point within the text.

The ideal reader, then, is an abstraction of that knowledge and those skills required for a particular interpretation of a particular text. The ideal reader is equipped with the array of schematic knowledge that the text presupposes for its interpretation, and lacks (but is prepared to learn) the material that the text introduces—material that the reader is not yet presumed to know. The kinds of schemata or knowledge structures utilized by the ideal reader for any particular text are evoked by (a) the concepts or ideas expressed, (b) the overall structure and organization, which may rely on such devices as conversational inference, indirect speech acts, and a story grammar, and (c) the internal language (the grammar in its broadest sense, including the lexicon). Analysis of the envisionment constructed by the ideal reader portrays the manner in which these knowledge structures operate and interact in the developing meaning of a passage.

This notion of ideal reader is not to be confused with a "mature" or "real" reader. Every reading experience, even among fully competent readers, is somewhat idiosyncratic, especially since good readers may use somewhat different processing operations to arrive at a range of acceptable interpretations. Real-life reading experiences also differ from our "ideal" in that readers have varying ways of interacting with text depending on their purpose for reading. For example, an actual reader does not necessarily want to make a complete interpretation when quickly reading a "whodunnit" mystery, but most certainly does want to make a fuller interpretation when preparing for an essay examination. Our analysis does not account for such alternative purposes for reading (although theoretically it could). The ideal reader we have created for this project is a very specific idealized reader designed to exemplify the kinds of cognitive operations deemed appropriate and useful in processing specific texts. (For a more complete examination of the ideal-reader concept, see Fillmore, 1981a, and Kay, 1981.)

The procedures for text analysis focus on the lexical, syntactic, and rhetorical structures that occur in consecutive meaning segments, the structures that contribute to the developing "envisionment" of the meaning of that particular passage. Codification permits location of the schemata and the schematic links an ideal reader draws upon or needs to construct in order to envision what is happening at any point in the text. Through this procedure we are also able to see where these processes are interrupted or thwarted by the text. When the ideal reader is left with unanswered questions, our theory judges the text to be defective—in some way incoherent or inadvertently misleading. In turn, we can use the analysis to compare how real readers depart from the ideal reader in developing an envisionment of the meaning of a particular passage; we can identify gaps in a reader's world knowledge or strategic knowledge—gaps that have inhibited comprehension of the text.

The System of Analysis

As a passage is processed, schemata are evoked and then integrated as the processing continues. Meaning derived from any given portion of the text is shaped by how earlier segments were interpreted and continues to develop and change in light of later segments. These changing "envisionments" are a record of the "text internal" world that is constructed by the reader while processing the text. These envisionments are the primary "dynamics" through which the reader experiences the "message." (See Langer, 1986, for further discussion of envisionment.) The system of analysis keeps track of the envisionments throughout the reading experience. It also keeps track of the cognitive processes executed in the reader's effort to construct these envisionments.

Since any text includes some concepts that are explicitly stated and many others that require varying degrees of inference, we distinguish among a variety of levels of envisionment that correspond to the degree of text-based or reader-based influence. Although greater or fewer distinctions are possible in categorizing levels of envisionment, we have most recently been working with four levels:

E_0 = the most literal level of the envisionment, including only those elements that are directly warranted by what the text says.

E_1 = that level which requires text-based inferences to be made.

E_2 = that level which requires inferences triggered by the text, but which is based on personal knowledge or assumptions.

E_3 = that level of the reader's "text world" that is not warranted by the text but represents the idiosyncratic embellishments of an actual reader. (E_3 by definition does not occur in the analysis of the ideal reader.)

Our analysis of a text keeps track of the changing levels of envisionment constructed by the ideal reader. It also specifies the schemata an ideal reader might use to construct, at a particular point in time, an acceptable envisionment. We can also follow the envisionments by actual readers to compare these with ideal readers' constructions.

For the analysis we have distinguished three sources—*domains of analysis*— which simultaneously influence the developing envisionment: genre, content, and text.

Genre (Gn) concerns itself with readers' hypotheses about the kind of text they are reading. A genre hypothesis is generally made early in the reading experience (as early as the first sentence) and influences a reader's expectations about what the text will "say" and how it will "end."

Content (Co) refers to the evolving base of information and events.

Text (Tx) refers to the grammatical and rhetorical aspects of the text; these features create relationships that help readers raise questions and resolve hypotheses.

In responding to elements in these three domains, readers perform a number of different types of cognitive operations in the process of generating meaning. Our system of analysis tracks six general operations:

1. Questions (Q)—uncertainties the reader has at any point during reading.
2. Hypotheses (H $\downarrow$)—predictions the reader makes about what the genre is, about what the function of a particular piece of text is, or about the answer to a question, based on a specific portion of the text.
   (H$\rightarrow$)—predictions the reader makes about what will be "said" in succeeding portions of the text.
3. Assumptions (Ass)—meanings the reader takes for granted without textual evidence.
4. Schemata (Sch)—basic memory structures evoked about genre, content, or text.
5. Conclusion (Con)—information which substantiates a hypothesis.
6. Validation (Val)—proof that a hypothesis (H $\downarrow$) was correct or (H$\rightarrow$) fulfilled.

Additional processes were identified in some of our notations and our system was refined as the project progressed. For a detailed presentation of our system of analysis and notation see Fillmore (1981; a, b), Kay (1981), and Langer (1985).

Figure 1 contains an abbreviated example of the opening segment of one test passage annotated using our system. The left column presents the ideal reader analysis of the text segment, tracing in detail the sources of the developing envisionments. In turn, this detail allowed us to develop a comprehensive set of questions to probe the developing envisionments of real readers confronted with these texts. The questions generated for this particular segment are listed in the right-hand column in Figure 1.

Figure 1. Bronco Buster

---

(1) **If a bronco buster wants to win a rodeo contest,**
LO(1)   If-clause, present tense, indefinite articles

Text Analysis	Related Interview Questions
1. Sch (Co) <u>CONTEST</u> PARTICIPANTS, DESIRE TO WIN, COMPETI- TION, RULES, CRITERIA FOR DECIDING ON WINNERS . . .	1. What do you think happens in a contest?
2. Sch (Co) <u>RODEO</u> CONTESTANTS, AUDIENCE, EVENTS, RIDING, ROPING, TYING . . .	2. What kinds of things happen in a rodeo?
3. SCHEMATIC LINKS a RODEO presents a number of CONTESTS	
4. Sch (Tx) <u>N + N COMPOUND</u> N^1 identifies a type of N^2	4. What do you think they meant by "rodeo contest"?
5. Sch (Co) <u>BRONCO BUSTING</u> HORSE: WHEN WILD WILL TRY TO THROW RIDER RIDER: RIDES WITHOUT GETTING THROWN, BY BREAKING WILL OF HORSE RENDERS HORSE TRAINABLE	5. What is a bronco buster? What does a bronco buster do?
6. SCHEMATIC LINKS BRONCO BUSTING is one of the kinds of events in a RODEO	
7. Sch (Tx) <u>N + V-er COMPOUND</u> compound designates someone who V's and N's	7. ("What does somebody who is a pig-washer do? What about a mailbox painter?")
8. Sch (Tx) CONDITIONAL SENTENCE ANTECEDENT, CONSEQUENT	
9. H↓ (Gn) GENRE-EXPOS PROSE	9. What kind of passage do you think this is? Do you think it might be the kind of thing you might read in a story book? . . . etc.
10. H↓ (Th) THEME-WINNING RODEO CONTEST	10. What do you think this passage is going to be about?
11. H→ (Tx) the next clause will be a modal clause, expressing obligation	11. What do you think the next cou- ple of words are going to be?
12. H↓ (Tx) the two noun phrases "a bronco buster" and "a rodeo contest" are to be interpreted as generic	12. From what we know so far, is this story going to be about how to be a bronco buster or about one bronco buster in particular?
13. Ass (Co) <u>E</u>^{1} when bronco busters choose to enter rodeos, they do so because they want to win	13. If bronco busters decide to be in a rodeo contest do you think they want to win, or doesn't it make a difference?

PROCEDURES

Subjects

During the two years of this study, many texts were selected from an array of standardized tests and analyzed using the procedures described above. Readers of a variety of ages were then interviewed following the general format described below. Over the course of the study, a continuing pattern of text analysis followed by observation of real readers was used to refine both the text analysis system and the interview procedures. This effort also provided a wide range of examples of how envisionments develop (or go astray) across a text; these shaped our interpretation of the specific set of data reported below, and will be drawn upon in some detail in the general discussion of results.

The major analyses to be reported here are based on intensive study of the developing envisionments of 26 third graders in response to the test item "Bronco Buster" (Figure 2). The students were selected from a middle-class elementary school in Oakland, California and had a varied ethnic and home language background. Because our focus was on comprehension of test items, students with decoding problems were not included in our sample. Results of the comprehensive Test of Basic Skills, Grade 3, were available for all students. Their percentile mean for the vocabulary subtest was 70.5; their comprehensive mean was 73.3.

Interviews

The text was presented to students in meaning segments corresponding to those used in describing the developing envisionment of the ideal reader. After a student had read a segment, questions such as those in the right-hand column of Figure 1 were asked. Because readers derived some meaning from clues in the prior text, and from such features as sentence length, paragraph length, and text length, each segment appeared with all previously read segments showing, and unread segments indicated but concealed. When reading the second segment of "Bronco Buster," for example, the students were presented with the item illus-

Figure 2. Bronco Buster

> If a bronco buster wants to win a rodeo contest, he must observe the contest rules. One of these rules is that the rider must keep one hand in the air. A rider who does not do this is disqualified.

1. A bronco buster who ignores the rules is
   A. skillful   B. disqualified   C. chosen   D. winner

2. In a rodeo contest a bronco buster must keep one hand
   A. under   B. still   C. free   D. hold

Figure 3.   Bronco Buster

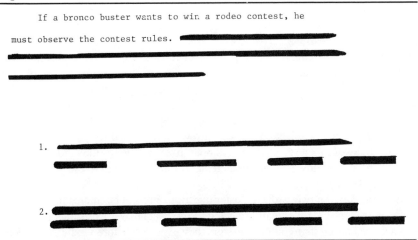

If a bronco buster wants to win a rodeo contest, he must observe the contest rules.

trated in Figure 3. This procedure necessitated that each short text be presented in a packet of several pages before it could be completely revealed.

Since text segmentation of this type may introduce variables that differ from those a student might encounter when reading the same text in an unmutilated version, two different interview procedures were developed. Half the students began by reading an unmutilated version of the text, followed by an oral retelling. They were then presented with the mutilated version and its accompanying questions, segment by segment. The other half of the students began with the segmented text and accompanying questions, without the opportunity to read and retell the text as a whole. Interviews for both groups began with a training session to familiarize the students with the mutilated text format, and ended with a general question about the main point of the story. Results from the two procedures were essentially identical and will be discussed together in the sections below.

Each interview session lasted between 45 minutes and one hour. Each session was taped and transcribed. The transcripts were coded in terms of specific aspects of the reader's developing envisionment, and evaluated to determine each student's overall ability to construct a reasonable, evolving envisionment of the meaning of the text. These analyses permitted us to make comparisons across groups of children as well as to describe in depth the performance of individuals.

RESULTS AND DISCUSSION

The data will be reported and discussed under two general headings: (a) observations about test takers, and (b) observations about tests. A final section will highlight some problems to consider when writing or taking tests, or when using their results.

Responses to Questions

This section will contain a review of the Bronco Buster questions and responses: what answers the students expected, what answers they chose, and why (see Figure 2 for the complete test item). After reading each passage segment by segment, students were asked to read and answer the first question, without being shown the multiple-choice selections. They were then shown the choices and asked to make a selection. Also, they were requested to explain why they "liked" the word they selected and did not "like" the words they did not select. (For an analysis of how test questions relate (or do not relate) to the passage, see Coleman, 1982.)

Responses to the two Bronco Buster questions present an interesting contrast: of the 26 students, 20 eventually selected the correct answer from among the four alternatives in each item, but the answers they expected before seeing the choices were quite different.

Question 1: A bronco buster who ignores the rules is
    A. skillful   B. disqualified   C. chosen   D. winner

For the first question, even before seeing the choices, 14 students (54%) antici-pated that "disqualified" would be the correct response, 8 were unable to answer, and 4 gave other responses. All 14 who anticipated "disqualified" also selected it as the correct response, as did another 6 students who had not original-ly anticipated that response. Of the 6 who selected incorrect responses to this item, 4 chose "winner" and 2 chose "skillful."

Because our interview questions are keyed to important aspects of the reader's developing envisionment, we can locate quite precisely the comprehension pro-cesses that led some readers to select the wrong responses. In this case, most of the problems stemmed from lack of knowledge of two words: "disqualified" (which appears in this passage and in the question) and "ignores" (which ap-pears only in the question). Although the 14 children who anticipated "dis-qualified" were familiar with its meaning, those who selected it from among the other choices had difficulty pronouncing it, were uncertain of its meaning, and selected it either because it seemed to be a key word in the passage or simply due to the visual match from passage to response. Of the four students who chose "winner," two explained that if you do not follow the rules you'll cheat and thereby increase your likelihood of winning. Although they did not know what "disqualified" meant, a combination of context clues and world knowledge led them to construct a reasonable rationale for "winner" as the correct response. The remaining four students were not familiar with either "ignore" or "dis-qualified" and chose "skillful" or "winner" based on their knowledge of a bronco buster's prowess. For at least those four readers, uncertainty about the meaning of the question was an obvious impediment to their selection of the correct response.

If the test-maker intended the question to measure students' ability to gain the meaning of a difficult word (''disqualified'') from the context of the passage, the inclusion of another difficult word (''ignores'') in the question thwarted this goal.

Question 2:   In a rodeo contest a bronco buster must keep one hand
   A. under   B. still   C. free   D. hold

After reading the stem to the second question, 17 students (65%) anticipated that ''in the air'' would be the response, a plausible conclusion to the stem although it does not appear as one of the choices. Five students who anticipated ''in the air'' got this question wrong when forced to select from the alternatives given: four chose ''hold'' and one chose ''still.'' (The other incorrect response was also ''hold''—by a student who did not offer any anticipated response.)

For this test item, the students' explanations about the plausibility of each response are especially revealing. Although finally rejecting it, two children explained that ''under'' was a logical response, reasoning that the bronco buster has to keep one hand *in the air* and the other hand *under* the rope. Four children considered selecting the word ''still,'' reasoning that if you do not hold your hand *still* you will fall off. One child stated that if you hold one hand *in the air* the other one has to be *still*. Eight students considered the word ''hold'' at some point, because if you don't hold you'll fall off. Two youngsters reasoned that if you keep one hand *in the air* you'll have to *hold* with the other one. The 26 readers did not all have a complete envisionment of the passage. Some did not know what a bronco buster was (interpreting bronco as a model name for an automobile), some confused the person with the animal, and still others were uncertain as to the kind of animal (cow, bull) a bronco was. However, all youngsters demonstrated some understanding that a bronco buster keeps one hand in the air and holds on to something with the other hand (in the interview they were asked to act this out). All of their explanations of possible responses indicated an understanding of this concept, even when they got the question itself wrong.

It seems, in this case, that the youngsters who selected an incorrect response did so for reasons reflecting an accurate construction of the meaning of this part of the passage. The range of possible responses permitted at least three semantically defensible selections. Of course, the issue of grammaticality needs to be addressed. In choosing among the alternatives provided, the readers we observed in this study focused more of their attention on selecting a word with appropriate meaning than on appropriate grammaticality within the sentence. Students sometimes admitted their selections didn't ''sound right'' but selected them anyway because they had the ''right meaning.'' C. J. Fillmore (discussion during project meetings, 1981) suggests that young children and second language learners may

Table 1.   Relationship between Incorrect Test Responses and
Envisionment Rating

Envisionment	Number of Students	Number with Incorrect Responses	Mean % Incorrect Responses
good	9	1	6
okay	11	5	23
fair	3	2	33
poor	3	2	67

be accustomed to hearing constructions with which they are unfamiliar and
therefore, even when aware of the ''ungrammaticality'' of a response, may be
less inhibited by that aspect than by imprecise meaning in choosing a response.

After the taped interviews were transcribed and analyzed, a coding sheet was
completed for each student. At least two raters reviewed the categories to which
each response was assigned and also supplied a holistic rating of each student's
envisionment on a four-point scale. Table 1 compares these envisionment ratings
(based on detailed understanding of the passages) with performance on the questions that followed. The results suggest that there is a fairly high association
between good envisionment and response accuracy as well as between poor
envisionment and poor test performance; the trend is in the right direction.

From these analyses it becomes apparent that individual readers may select
incorrect test item responses based on interpretations that are contextually acceptable; these readers never have the opportunity to demonstrate their understanding of the passage. Sometimes this is because the questions miss central
aspects of the envisionment; in other cases, it is a function of the idiosyncratic
array of response items. However, those readers who are better meaning inte-
grators also tend to be those who select the predetermined correct responses.
Findings from the analyses suggest that although the test questions themselves do
not measure the integration of meaning, the ability to develop a good envisionment and the ability to select a correct response are in some way related. (Further
studies of the relationship between test questions and reader response can be
found in Langer, 1985.)

Considerate and Inconsiderate Test Items

A test item is inconsiderate if it makes unwarranted demands on a reader, if it
creates great cognitive demands without corresponding conceptual payoff. This
is not to suggest that all difficult texts are inconsiderate and all easy ones
considerate, but that the effort put forth in reading a hard text needs to be
rewarded. It also suggests that the cognitive demands must be reasonable for the
intended audience, the implied purpose, and the particular topic. This section
will present five aspects of inconsiderate tests, aspects that have been apparent in
both our ''ideal reader'' text analyses and our analyses of real readers reading

real test items. In general, inconsiderate test items create gaps between the reader and the text that are not directly related to how well the reader constructs meaning, but are inherent instead in the way the test-maker composed the passage or presented the question. Although the five factors are presented as discrete categories, in actual tests any number of them may be interwoven; one inconsiderate feature often leads to the emergence of another.

1. Density of Ideas. Test items can be inconsiderate in the number of ideas that are presented and the frequency with which these ideas change. The brief passages used in test items sometimes provide too little elaboration of one concept before another concept is introduced. The ideas are too short-lived and change too quickly for the reader to develop any adequate envisionment. "Strange Machine" (Figure 4) is an example of such a text (Comprehensive Test of Basic Skills, 1974). The ideal reader analysis of this item portrays a rapid succession of new schemata introduced without any integration into a larger schematic whole. This density is deliberate in this passage, inherent in the riddle format and postponed answer about the identity of the strange machine. The reader is asked to envision a mouthpiece, which is associated with a range of possible schemata. Before the schema relevant to this text can be reinstantiated, another concept, "handle," is introduced. The ideal reader questions the array of possible "meanings," $Q(Co)$, and forms a rapid succession of hypotheses, $H \downarrow (Co)$, about the relationships between the parts of the machine. Rather than

Figure 4.   The Strange Machine

In 1877 a machine appeared which surprised many people. Can you guess the name of this strange new machine?

As you spoke into the mouthpiece and turned the handle, a tube covered with a thin piece of tin moved around. As the tube moved, a needle pressed deep lines into the tin. As you turned the handle once more, the needle touched against the same lines and played back your words.

This was the first phonograph! How different from the hi-fi of today!

— —

9. About how many years ago did the machine first appear?
   1) 25   2) 50   3) 100   4) 200
10. How did people feel when they saw this new machine?
   5) angry   6) astonished
   7) worried   8) frightened
11. As the handle was turned, which part of the machine moved?
   1) tube   2) needle
   3) press   4) mouthpiece
12. As the needle pressed lines into the tin, it was
   5) giving a shot
   6) recording a voice
   7) painting a picture
   8) sewing a piece of material

finding resolutions to these hypotheses and questions, the density of the text continues to build and the "riddle" remains unsolved until the answer is provided at the end of the passage.

While the ideal reader notation portrays a series of unresolved questions and hypotheses, real readers make judgments more rapidly even when little assistance is provided by the text. In our interviews, some children (third graders) developed an initial envisionment of the "mouthpiece" and clung to it, forcing each bit of new information into their initial envisionment. One reader envisioned a Coke machine with a "mouthpiece" for the coins and a "handle" as the drink selector. The "tube" (introduced next in the passage) became the round slot from which the tin Coke can was ejected. Others tried to change their envisionments to accommodate the new concepts, but created a series of disconnected images instead. One reader envisioned a mailbox, then turned it into a garage mail slot (with the slot as mouthpiece), and when this no longer worked, envisioned a lawnmower with the grass catcher as mouthpiece, the switch as the handle, and the blades as the tube and needle. Still others moved from concept to concept without even attempting to integrate the content.

The density of the ideas introduced without elaboration is counterproductive to the development of a cohesive envisionment. Hypotheses about the nature of the strange machine (which would integrate the various separate schema) are thwarted by another aspect of the text. The ideal reader assumes, when the riddle is posed at the end of the second sentence, that the "strange machine" will be similar enough to its modern version to be guessable, Ass(Gn). In fact, the early version of the machine is not at all like the present version, as the last line of the passage emphasizes. The assumption of similarity contributes to a series of resolutions, (Res), which invalidate earlier hypotheses—for example, that the strange machine is a tape recorder, since the machine recorded and played back your words. This particular test item was inconsiderate due to the density of ideas, and the lack of resemblance between the early prototype and present phonograph rendered the passage even more difficult for the reader.

2. Overreliance on Assumptions and Hypotheses. During our investigation we encountered several test items which required the ideal reader to make a large number of assumptions, (Ass), (Co), (Tx), and hypotheses, (H→), (H↓), (Co), (Tx), without corroborating textual evidence to permit their validation. The envisionment is constructed from implications drawn from the ideal reader's instantiation of unarticulated referents and knowledge of social conventions. While this can be a powerful stylistic device that works well for texts such as mysteries and gothic romances, the device requires space as well as a hospitable setting. When many assumptions and unresolved hypotheses are presented in a text, uncertainty builds as new suppositions are linked with old ones, and the reader is induced to conjure up a strained envisionment of vague images.

The text in Figure 5 (Cooperative English Tests, 1960), for example, may at

Figure 5

"Alice!" called a voice.

The effect on the reader and her listener, both of whom were sitting on the floor, was instantaneous. Each started and sat rigidly intent for a moment; then, as the sound of approaching footsteps was heard, one girl hastily slipped a little volume under the coverlet of the bed, while the other sprang to her feet and in a hurried, flustered way pretended to be getting something out of a tall wardrobe.

Before the one who hid the book had time to rise, a woman of fifty entered the room and, after a glance, cried "Alice! How often have I told you not to sit on the floor?"

"Very often, Mommy," said Alice, rising meekly, meantime casting a glance at the bed to see how far its smoothness had been disturbed.

"And still you continue such unbecoming behavior."

"Oh, Mommy, but it is so nice," cried the girl. "Didn't you like to sit on the floor when you were fifteen?"

— —

1. Alice's companion was
   A. A girl
   B. Her brother
   C. The family dog
   D. A doll

---

first glance appear simple for a fifteen-year-old to integrate. Yet, to build an envisionment of the meaning of this passage, the reader must rely on many assumptions and unresolved hypotheses. The ideal reader must make hypotheses about the antecedents for many referents throughout the passage, beginning in the very first sentence with "a voice," in the second sentence with "the reader" and "her listener," and so on throughout the text. An assumption must be made, based on social conventions, that the teenage girls were reading a "dirty" book of which they feared the mother would disapprove. An assumption must also be made that the girl and her mother are talking across each other, each concerned with different issues: the girl with her forbidden book, and the mother with the girl's forbidden floor-sitting. The reader must also infer that the girl is about fifteen. The actions (reading the book, hiding it, rising, glancing at the bed) are all linked by inference. This text type is inconsiderate due to the many premature hypotheses the reader must make; usual and appropriate inference strategies become tentative and strained.

3. Imitation Genre. There are a variety of genres that consistently appeared in the standardized reading tests we reviewed: stories, personal accounts, folk tales, letters, poems, and expository passages containing information about social studies, science, or health. Their inclusion seems based on the view that a reading comprehension test should include items from the variety of text types that students normally encounter in school. However, our analysis of the items disclosed that the passages sometimes violated the conceptual or structural patterns typically associated with the genres they were meant to reflect. In our analyses, both of the ideal reader and of real readers, this led to genre-based hypotheses, H ↓ (Gn), that were later invalidated. Although sometimes the effects on the envisionment were minor, in other cases the deviations from expected genre patterns caused major interference. For example, a short humorous story generally ends with its punchline. If any written material follows the punchline, it is likely to elaborate the "joke"; it can be read quickly, for embellishment. The reader familiar with this genre knows this convention and does not expect important information to follow. However, some test items place key information after the punchline, or ask questions dealing with what may take place afterward; because this violates a convention of the genre, the reader with knowledge of that convention is placed at a disadvantage. Figure 6 is an example of this test and question type (SRA Achievement Series, 1978). Instead of completing the action with the punchline, this test item requires the reader to predict what Fritz will do next. This caused some readers to doubt their interpretation of the punchline and therefore to select response A instead of B.

The passage in Figure 7 (Comprehensive Test of Basic Skills, 1974) is another example of a test item constructed to imitate a real genre, in this case expository prose. Unlike the genre the passage is imitating, however, there is no introduction to help the reader make a link from personal knowledge to new information, and the passage ends abruptly without a statement tying the passage together—all conventions of informational genre. Here, the departures from normal genre conventions do not mislead readers, but leave them without needed context for constructing an envisionment. The reader must begin with some quickly accessible knowledge about nose cones and rockets in order to even attempt to develop a cohesive envisionment. There is not a sharing of information about rockets from writer to reader, but a simple "listing" of key points. The reader who is familiar with the topic will be able to recognize these points, elaborate and connect them, and make sense of the passage, while the reader who

Figure 6

Fritz lived in a neighborhood with many interesting people. But Fritz felt out of place. He felt that he was ordinary. In fact, he felt so ordinary that he thought nobody noticed him. Today I'll be different, he thought. I'll wear an extra hat.

Then he went for a walk. People smiled at him. But no one spoke. At last he asked a neighbor, "Don't you see something unusual about me today?"

"Yes," the neighbor said, "You're wearing three hats instead of your usual two."

What will Fritz probably do next?
A. Ask more people if they think his hat looks different
B. Realize that people have always noticed him
C. Go to the store and buy some more hats
D. Stop going for walks in his neighborhood

Figure 7

The nose cone of a rocket carries the payload. The payload is anything men wish to send into space.

The payload can be a satellite. A satellite is a small object that travels around a larger object in space. The rocket travels fast to carry the satellite away from the earth.

The payload can be a camera. It can take pictures of the earth or the moon. The payload may be a man, shooting through space.

— — — — — — — — — — — — — — — — — — —

16. Which of the following can a space camera be used for?
    5) to take pictures of friends
    6) to measure the temperature
    7) to take pictures of the moon
    8) to measure the speed of rockets

17. The nose cone carried the
    1) fuel
    2) payload
    3) rocket
    4) airplane

18. A small object that travels around a larger one is called a
    5) camera
    6) satellite
    7) payload
    8) nose cone

is not already familiar with the topic will be at a loss. (Here we see again how one kind of problem, based on the use of an abbreviated genre form, creates another, the kind of density of ideas discussed earlier.)

We can see how this can interfere with a developing envisionment in the responses of a third grader interviewed as he read the passage. In the first sentence, he knew what rockets looked like (from television) and thought he knew what a nose cone was. He was not certain, but expected that it would be elaborated later in the text. He had no schematic links between rockets and payload, although he knew from the sentence structure that they must have some connection. In the third sentence, he recognized the word ''satellite'' and knew it had something to do with outer space, but he had no further knowledge of it. The fourth sentence did not help him because he could not envision what an object in outer space would be like.

Although this student was trying to make meaning from the passage and had a good idea of the information he would need to know in order to comprehend, in this case the text was uncooperative; it did not contain the kinds of structure and elaboration generally provided in informational texts. It could make sense only to a reader who already knew enough about rockets, satellites, and payloads to make the relevant connections among them.

A test item is not a literary work nor an actual piece of informational writing.

Test writers seem to have other goals in mind than trade book authors; their purposes and constraints are different. Test items must comply with a particular reading level, be topically appropriate for specific age groups, contain information which can be answered by specific questions, be inoffensive to all possible groups, and so on. In an attempt to mimic the variety of genres encountered in school and also to meet these "testing" constraints, test passages might be thought of as "imitation" genre, almost genre unto themselves with conventions of their own. It is this "imitation" which renders them inconsiderate: they invoke conventions which they do not follow.

4. Assertions Contrary to Readers' Beliefs. Yet another aspect of inconsiderate text occurs when test items make assertions contrary to readers' beliefs without acknowledging differences or providing schematic links from reader knowledge to textual content. Instead, some texts we analyzed required the ideal reader to make immediate hypotheses (H $\downarrow$, H→) based on an acceptance of the discordant assertion.

Figure 8 (Stanford Achievement Test, 1972) is an example of such a test item, from a fifth-grade test. In the ideal reader notation of the text segment "while attendance at baseball games has been falling off," there is a content hypothesis, H $\downarrow$ (Co), that falling attendance implies loss in popularity. There is also a text hypothesis, H $\downarrow$ (Tx), that "while" contrasts baseball's falling attendance with football, basketball, and ice hockey which are gaining in popularity. There are neither schematic nor text links elaborating this idea. The next text segment ("This is largely because") goes on to explore explanations of the loss in popularity. In this segment the ideal reader makes two hypotheses: H $\downarrow$ (Tx) that "this" refers to baseball's falling attendance, and H $\downarrow$ (Tx) that "largely" suggests more than one reason for the falling attendance. This is followed by a hypothesis H $\downarrow$ (Tx) in the next text segment that baseball is "slower" than other games.

Real readers interviewed with this text found the assertion about baseball's loss in popularity jarring. Since children see baseball games and baseball players in a wide variety of media contexts, they assume it is a very popular game. During an interview, one fifth-grade reader exhibited well-developed passage envisionment. However, when choosing the response to a question about the decrease in baseball's attendance, he said angrily, "I know people are going to come to baseball games. I've gone to other people's houses and they watch. And I've seen the stands just stuffed. They can barely cram another person in." Another reader knew the individual word meanings of "popularity" (like a movie star, very common), "falling off" (not coming to), and "attendance" (to come to). Despite this, his envisionment was poorly integrated. It wavered between baseball's gaining and not gaining in popularity, and therefore baseball's relation to the other games also wavered. Both readers appeared unable, on their own, to consistently link the text assertion with their personal beliefs about

Figure 8

Games of great speed and constant motion, such as football, basketball, and ice hockey, have been gaining in popularity, while attendance at baseball games has been falling off. This is largely because the game of baseball is slower and its action irregular. That is, the game alternates between great moments of high drama and excitement—such as when the bases are loaded and the batter hits a home run—and extended periods of comparative inactivity, such as when a batter takes full count, two strikes, and three balls, and then is walked on the last pitch. Many ideas are being explored for making baseball a faster game. One possibility, for example, might be to increase the distance between the pitcher and the batter, thereby allowing a split second more for the batter to judge the pitch and connect with the ball. This could produce more hits, thereby making baseball more of a running rather than a pitching game.

---

baseball attendance. This form of inconsiderate text results when the author fails to acknowledge the conflicting ideas that might arise, and the text fails to encourage the reader to question personally held ideas or beliefs that are contrary to those assumed in the text.

5. Contextual Discontinuity by Deceptive Simplicity. The fifth type of inconsiderate text occurs when a concept with which a reader is unfamiliar is presented bit by bit in a sequence of seemingly familiar details. In the ideal reader analysis, integration of the details leads to an envisionment of the whole concept. The notation of the "Strange Machine" test item (see Figure 4) is an example. In this passage, the strange machine is described bit by bit and the parts can be integrated as follows (partial notation):

As you spoke into the machine and turned the handle,
E_1—the clause describes the use of the machine in 1877
Sch(Co) mouthpiece: part of machine to do with the voice
Sch(Co) handle: part of machine—helps it to function when turned
Schematic link—machine with mouthpiece and handle, something to do with voice communication

a tube covered with a thin piece of tin moved around.
Q (Co) what is relationship of tube to mouthpiece and handle?
Q (Tx) how is the tube moving around?
H (Co) the tube is also part of the machine
E_0—in the strange machine, as you speak into the mouthpiece and turn the handle, the tube turns

As the tube moved, a needle pressed deep lines into the tin.
H ↓ (Co) the deep lines are related to the voice function
Schematic links—the machine has a needle, mouthpiece, handle, and a voice-related function
H ↓ (Co) the lines are pressed to record a message

As you turned the handle once more
H ↓ (Co) the machine does more than press lines
E_0—to make the machine work properly the handle must be turned at least twice

the needle touched against the same lines and played back your words.
Sch(Co) voice recording
Val—a voice recording is made
Val—the lines have a role in the machine's functioning
Con E_0—this strange machine allowed people in 1877 to record their voices
H ↓ (Co) this was a tape recorder? record player?

This was the first phonograph!
Con—the parts described are similar enough to the modern-day phonograph to call
it the first phonograph

How different from the hi-fi of today!
Con—both the phonograph and hi-fi play back sounds and are thereby related to
the strange machine

As we have already seen in discussing density of ideas, this passage leaves the reader with a high level of unintegrated detail. To further complicate the matter, the vocabulary is kept deceptively simple, deceptively because the concepts introduced have a wide range of possible referents (e.g., crank, bar, switch, lip for handle) and can therefore be attributed to a large number of schemata. Because the conceptual whole is not provided by the text, the reader must develop an envisionment by relating the bits of attributes which are part of an existing textually plausible schema. However, an integration problem occurs if the reader does not already have (or is unable to access) an appropriate schema, if the text concept is so remote that it cannot reasonably be related to known schemata, or if the text does not provide clues to help the reader select among the possible schematic choices.

This problem was evident in our interviews when it became apparent that, although the students were familiar with tape recorders, the handle, tube, and needle did not fit into their notion of a prototype tape recorder. And although they were familiar with record players, their notion of a prototype record player did not include a personal voice-recording function. Further, the third graders we interviewed were not familiar with either phonographs or hi-fi's although they were quite knowledgeable about stereos and record players. In the absence of an apparently useful schematic structure, many students clung to their first image, accommodating as necessary to new information. For example, one student envisioned (E_3) a robot with a mouth (mouthpiece), hands (handles), and a tube with wheels to move. The tube was covered with tin "so you won't get a shock." It also pressed lines "so you can see what he says. He draws letters." In this instance, these apparently simple text segments evoked schemata which were totally reader based. This reader did not have the benefit of either text or knowledge structures to validate his hypotheses. Therefore, lack of familiarity with the larger whole to which the "simple" parts relate precludes knowledgeable selection of appropriate schemata from among the array of those which, in an abstract sense, are potentially possible.

DISCUSSION

This study has examined some of the consequences of test language and its relationship to comprehension. It has also analyzed test passages in terms of the demands test items make on readers. The two preceding sections identify some of the complexities which may severely confound results obtained from standardized tests, complexities which pose processing or question-answering problems unrelated to students' ability to construct meaning.

These data suggest the need for caution when considering the purposes for the administration of tests and what it is that is being tested. If the goal is to make large-scale discriminations between better and poorer school achievers, reliance on linguistic and conceptual "puzzles" may suffice. However, if the purpose is to measure reading comprehension, to discriminate among the range of more and less successful users of meaning construction strategies, a test specifically designed to examine these strategies must be devised. These data indicate that although the reading comprehension tests examined do discriminate good from poor reading, the strategies required for success on these items do not bear a strong relation to the processes involved in constructive meaning-making. Standardized reading tests do not measure the processes involved in the construction of meaning from a text nor do they evaluate an individual's ability to manage those processes.

REFERENCES

Anderson, R.C. (1977). The notion of schemata and the educational enterprise. In R.C. Anderson, R.J. Spiro, & W.E. Montague (Eds.), *Schooling and the acquisition of knowledge*. Hillsdale, NJ: Lawrence Erlbaum Assoc.

Bartlett, F.C. (1932). *Remembering*. Cambridge: Cambridge University Press.

Coleman, L. (1982). *Answering test questions: Idealized readers in new test situations*. Working paper, Reading Project, Language Behavior Research Laboratory, University of California, Berkeley.

Cooperative English Tests. (1960). Princeton, NJ: Educational Testing Service.

CTB/McGraw-Hill. (1974). *Comprehensive Test of Basic Skills (Level 1, Form S)*, Monterey, CA: Author.

Fillmore, C.J. (1981a). *Ideal readers and real readers*. Washington, DC: Georgetown University Round Table.

Fillmore, C.J. (1981b). *On monitoring and describing the reading process*. Paper presented at National Reading Conference, Dallas, TX.

Goodman, K.S., & Goodman, Y.M. (1978). *Reading of American children whose language is a stable rural dialect of English or is a language other than English*. Final report to the National Institute of Education.

Kay, P. (1981). *Three properties of the ideal reader.* Washington, DC: Georgetown University Round Table.

Langer, J.A. (1985). Levels of questioning: An alternative view. *Reading Research Quarterly,* 20, 5, 586–602.

Langer, J. A. (1986). *Children reading and writing: Structures and strategies.* Norwood, NJ: Ablex.

Polanyi, M. (1966). *The tacit dimension.* Garden City, NY: Doubleday.

Rumelhart, D.E. (1977). Toward an interactive model of reading. In S. Dornick (ed.), *Attention and performance* IV. London: Academic Press.

Schank, R.C., & Abelson, R.P. (1977). *Scripts, plans, goals and understanding.* Hillsdale, NJ: Lawrence Erlbaum Assoc.

Science Research Assoc. (1972). *SRA Achievement Series* (Level E Form 1), Chicago, IL: Author.

Stanford Achievement Test (Intermediate II Form A), (1972). New York: Harcourt Brace Jovanovich.

CHAPTER 7

A Study of the Degrees of Reading Power Test*

Cecilia Freeman

University of California, Berkeley

INTRODUCTION

This report presents the results of a descriptive and evaluative study of the Degrees of Reading Power (DRP) Test. The DRP is a test of reading comprehension which is used in the state of New York as part of the Regents Competency Testing Program. A specified level of performance on the DRP Test is required for receiving a high school diploma in New York as of June 1981. The test is also administered in lower grades to identify students in need of remedial reading instruction. Grade-level promotion may be tied to test performance, and the test is intended to provide a measure of schools' effectiveness (The College Board, 1980, 1983a; *College Board News,* 1981; Lott, 1980).

The DRP is a modified form of cloze test. One test consists of a series of approximately 12 passages, ordered to represent increasing steps of reading difficulty. Specifications for test passages and items are designed to control the test task in such a way that a student's performance will indicate the most difficult level of prose he or she can read with a given level of comprehension (State of New York Education Department, 1978a, 1978b, 1979a). (See Appendices A and B for a description of the DRP and a sample passage.)

Development of the DRP Test began in the early 1970s and has continued with support from the Carnegie Corporation of New York. In 1979, the New York State Board of Regents assigned rights to the test to the College Entrance Examination Board, which is continuing development of the methodology and plans national distribution of the test. Extensive experimental research and quantitative analysis of test scores have been carried out by the developers of the DRP, Touchstone Applied Science Associates of Elmsford, New York. In the present study, which has been supported by a grant from the Ford Foundation, the test has been examined from a different perspective. We have analyzed

---

* This work was carried out at the Center for Applied Linguistics in Washington, DC, under a grant from the Ford Foundation, with the guidance and support of project officer Marjorie Martus. The active collaboration of Arnold Zwicky is gratefully acknowledged; his insights and contributions to the study are reflected throughout this report.

245

language properties of 12 passages at graduated levels of difficulty, constituting one DRP Test form. In this analysis we have focused on the comprehension tasks associated with each item in the test, thus in a sense adopting the point of view of a reader, in order to delineate the skills required for successful completion of the test.

In taking this approach, we are not concerned with the abstract representation of text meaning, text structure, or of the reader's knowledge. We are concerned with the actual language of the text, which works in systematic ways to convey the communicative intent of the writer—to make the intended meaning accessible to a reader. The language forms and organization of a written passage can be viewed as a system of "clues" which a reader must use (consciously or not) to reconstruct meaning. Through examination of language content, structure and organization in test passages, we see what kind of guidance it provides the reader/test-taker and what he or she must know and do in order to complete test items correctly. This information can then serve as the basis of an evaluation of the DRP as a measure of reading comprehension.

A study of this nature raises questions of theoretical interest, such as the relationship between the linguistic structure and organization of text, and reading difficulty. However, our primary goal in this work has been to address issues concerning the nature and use of the test. Does it measure reading ability, as intended, or does it depend on other independent skills as well? What sorts of abilities might be lacking in students who get low test scores? Does the test embody a standard which is fair to all students? Are the abilities needed to meet that standard the same abilities which people agree a high school graduate should possess? Can the test be used to improve reading instruction or to distribute good instruction more effectively?

Because this study is directed toward eventual answers to questions of this nature, the discussion is not intended to be exhaustive in descriptive detail, nor to present a thorough examination of theoretical issues relevant to the linguistic analysis. Instead, it is intended to present an array of information which will be useful to those who want to understand, for one purpose or another, how the DRP Test works.

This work has been carried out within certain practical limitations. First, only 12 test passages have been made available for review (out of more than 60 which exist). This means, on the one hand, that where quantitative data are presented in describing test properties, the numbers are sometimes too small to indicate clear patterns. When that is the case, statements will be made which can be confirmed or disconfirmed on the basis of examining a greater number of passages. On the other hand, the relatively small number of passages released does not limit our ability to address the central questions of the study, because of the way the test is designed: New passages are continually written for the test, according to a specific set of instructions; these criteria are intended to control the difficulty of prose, thus ensuring that any passage at a given difficulty level will be representative of the prose found in other passages at that level, in terms of the demands it places on the reader. Regardless of whether that requirement is strictly satisfied or not, the investigation of the 12 passages at hand yields evidence about the entire test: To the extent that this investigation raises questions about one test form's ability to measure reading comprehension unambiguously, it raises questions about the test in general. Therefore, conclusions supported by our study of these passages can be taken as general hypotheses about the DRP Test amenable to more extensive evaluation.

A second restriction affecting this report has to do with the amount of prose quoted from test passages. For purposes of this report, we cite no more than two items from any one passage and no more than two sentences surrounding an item. By limiting quoted material in this way we sometimes forgo extensive illustration of a point, and we do not present item-by-item descriptions of test properties. Hopefully, adequate examples are presented none the less.

The following section of this report presents a description of language properties of the 12 passages studied, and of the abilities or skills which contribute to completing DRP test items. Subsequently, those findings are applied to an evaluation of whether the test actually measures reading comprehension in the intended manner.

DESCRIPTION

The DRP Test is made up of a series of untitled passages, each about 300 words in length, at specified levels of reading difficulty. Test passages consist of five to seven paragraphs of expository prose, written on nonfiction topics. From each passage, seven "content" words have been deleted: three nouns, three verbs, and one adjective or adverb. Corresponding to each item (deletion), a list of five response option words is provided. The student must choose from that list the word that "makes the best sense in the blank" (test directions).

The DRP Test is intended to measure a student's ability to read and comprehend connected prose. This is accomplished, the test-makers claim, by designing items so that comprehension of the surrounding prose context is both necessary and sufficient for selecting the correct answer. The text becomes more difficult, on a quantitative scale of readability, with each passage. The student is expected to proceed through harder and harder passages until he or she can no longer complete the items correctly. According to the design of the test, that is the point at which the student can no longer comprehend the written prose. In this way, it is claimed, the test identifies the most difficult text (in terms of the readability scale) the student can read—an "absolute" measure of reading ability (State Education Department, 1978a).

The DRP test is designed to test overall reading comprehension, "the end result of instruction," rather than the supposed reading "subskills" which traditional discrete-point reading tests claim to measure. In order to evaluate the extent to which it accomplishes this, we have first asked what it takes to complete the test items. We know that faced with a test passage, readers must select the right words for the blanks on the basis of linguistic cues provided in the text. What specific abilities, skills, or types of knowledge are necessary for them to be able to do this?

The following sections describe specific abilities which are called on by DRP test passages and items; and they show how language properties of the test shape its requirements. This is not the same as describing reading in terms of discrete subskills which can be taught and tested independently. Rather, it provides an analytic view of a complex task, by outlining a number of interrelated and sometimes overlapping abilities which together enable a reader to carry out that task.

Topics

The DRP Test passages have no titles, but recognition of what a passage is about contributes directly or indirectly to the test task. In all passages except the first two and last two, the topic is established in the first sentence. In the first two passages, where very little content is carried in a single sentence, the topic is established in the course of two or three opening sentences. In the last two passages, statement of the topic is preceded by a paragraph of background material which is relevant, but not directly related to, the passage topic. In these harder passages, then, the reader must delay a determination of what the passage is about, yet recognize the relationship of the introductory material to the rest of the passage content.

There is a striking difference between topics in earlier passages and those of later passages. Passages 1 through 6 all deal with animals or plants, the human body, and/or concrete human behavior. In contrast, the topics of passages 7 through 12 are all historical and/or abstract in nature. This contrast can be illustrated simply by comparing the opening sentences of passages 6 and 7.

passage 6:   Police doctors can learn a lot from skeletons.
passage 7:   Medieval craft guilds were associations of men practicing the same
             trade.

While some aspects of children's everyday life and experience might provide a bridge to topics in the earlier passages, it seems likely that the topics of later passages would only be encountered in an academic context.

Sentence Grammar

Readers must grasp sentence-level syntactic and semantic relations in interpreting the individual sentences of a passage. The syntactic structure of sentences shows little patterned variation across passages in the DRP Test. Test item frame sentences (i.e., those containing deletions) are uniformly short with a maximum of one embedded clause. There is no patterned distribution of simple and complex or active and passive constructions among frame sentences in the test. While 45% of item deletions are the last word in the sentence, there is otherwise no pattern to the structural location of deletions within frame sentences.

The amount of sentence embedding and conjoining in passages, in terms of the number of clauses per sentence, is indicated in Table 1. This table gives (a) the range of number of clauses per sentence in a passage (so that in passage 6, for example, sentences consist of from one to four clauses); (b) the average number of clauses per sentence in the passage, including frame sentences; and (c) the average when frame sentences are not counted. (The figures in Table 1 are based on a parsing of every sentence into relationally defined major constituents (e.g., subject, verb, object), counting independent clauses, relative clauses, complement clauses, adverbial clauses, any clause fragment containing a verb (finite, infinitive,or participial form), and certain verb-deleted constructions such as adjective comparisons and reduced relative clauses.)

The number of clauses per sentence is not in itself a sensitive measure of complexity, since sentence conjoining contributes less to complexity than most sentence embedding, and some types of embedded constructions are more complex than others. However, Table 1 accurately reflects the fact that sentences in the first three passages of the test are generally simple in structure. These passages are also characterized by repetition of sentence structure, with strings of three to seven sentences identical in grammatical form. Also, as the figures in Table 1 suggest, there is a marked increase in syntactic complexity between passages 3 and 4; the fourth passage includes infinitive and participial clauses,

Table 1. Number of Clauses per Sentence

Passage	(A) Range	(B) Average (Frame Sentences Included)	(B) Average (Frame Sentences Not Included)
1	1–2	1.09	1.07
2	1–2	1.14	1.10
3	1–3	1.49	1.53
4	1–6	2.17	2.37
5	1–5	2.0	2.23
6	1–4	1.65	1.74
7	1–4	1.77	1.86
8	1–4	1.88	2.05
9	1–6	1.85	2.11
10	1–4	2.0	2.24
11	1–5	2.0	2.35
12	1–7	2.28	2.64

that–complements, passive constructions, and embedded questions to a degree which distinguishes it from the preceding passages. Through most of the rest of the test (passages 4 through 11), syntactic complexity—in terms of the number of embeddings per sentence—does not differ markedly among passages.

Throughout the test, most of the sentence structures encountered are constructions which elementary school students can generally be expected to control in oral language (Chomsky, 1980; Gibson & Levin, 1975; Palermo & Molfese, 1972). But the perceptual complexity of sentence structure appears to increase in the second half of the test due to the occurrence of sentences in which the surface order or length of constituents might impede processing. To understand sentences in passages 7 through 12, readers must be able to process certain types of sentence structure more characteristic of written than spoken language, such as:

1. sentences with a long, wordy constituent up front, for example, a long relative clause in the subject:[1]

The likelihood that the book was plagiarized with language copied outright is absurd.

2. sentences with a dangling participial modifier, for example:

Patients with painful conditions have been sadly misled by the advertisements, *expecting to find relief from suffering with a treatment which is largely ineffective.*

3. sentences in which the object or predicate precedes the subject (other than sentences, such as questions, in which such word order would be expected), for example:

Projects that seemed most likely to succeed she considered projects of the first priority.

4. sentences with a preposed adverbial clause with inversion of subject and verb, for example:

Not before the windows, the front door, and the woodwork were painted in white could the last part of the job be finished.

These types of sentences may involve greater perceptual complexity than those more common to ordinary conversation because they present a heavy processing load; or they separate semantically related constituents; or they depart from the canonical subject–first word order of English (Davison, 1980; Green et al., 1980).

Context-dependent Items
All DRP test frame sentences are highly context dependent for interpretation. In most, this dependency derives from the use of expressions which, for purposes of this discussion, will be called "context-dependent items." These expressions

---

[1] Example sentences presented here are analogous to sentences in DRP passages in relevant aspects of grammatical structure, and length.

constitute a diverse group in terms of linguistic form and function; but in DRP test frame sentences they have an important property in common: They cannot be fully interpreted on their own, but must be understood in terms of information which the reader must retrieve from outside the frame sentence—from either linguistic or extralinguistic context. In order to interpret such an expression, the reader must make a connection between that item and another item (such as a noun phrase) in the text, or an extended portion of text, or an entity which must be identified through inference from text or application of background information. In some frame sentences, the deleted word itself is such a context-dependent item; in others, selection of the deleted word depends on correct interpretation of a context-dependent item elsewhere in the frame sentence. Expressions of this nature which occur in DRP test frame sentences include:

1. definite noun phrases (NPs) (e.g., *the effect, the number of years*), which have the same referent as some other noun phrase occurring in the preceding text, or whose referent is identifiable from extralinguistic context;
2. demonstrative definite noun phrases (NPs) (e.g., *this problem, these unusual methods*);
3. demonstratives (e.g., *this, that*);
4. pronouns (e.g., *it, he, them*);
5. identity-of-sense anaphora (e.g., *others, another,* "bare" quantifiers such as *some, most, much*), items which depend on some other nominal for interpretation although the two expressions are not coreferential;
6. verb phrase (VP) anaphora (e.g., *do so*);
7. comparative constructions (e.g., *the same, even longer hours, as nice*).

Both types of context-dependent items which occur in frame sentences, and the processes involved in their interpretation, vary from earlier to later test passages.

Table 2 shows the distribution of different types of context-dependent expressions which occur in the frame sentences of DRP test passages. As these figures indicate, pronouns are relatively common in frame sentences in the first half of the test, while frame sentences in the second half contain a relatively large number of definite noun phrases.

Most of the nominal expressions described above have an anaphoric function within the discourse, in the sense that they share the same referent with some other item: either a nonpronominal noun phrase which occurs earlier in the text, or a name which can be inferred from preceding text. Table 3 indicates where there are explicit antecedents for definite noun phrases, demonstratives and pronouns having a discourse anaphoric function in passages; and it shows the number per passage of the same types of nominals which lack an explicit linguistic antecedent. These figures show that while anaphoric items occur in all passages, there is a greater tendency in the earlier passages for such an expression to have an anaphoric relation with an explicit antecedent noun phrase in the text. At the same time, in later passages there is an increase in the occurrence

Table 2. Distribution of Context-Dependent Items in Test Frame Sentences

Passage	Definite NPs	Demonstrative Definite NPs	Demonstratives	Pronouns	Identity-of-Sense Anaphora	VP Anaphora	Comparative Constructions
1	2	1	2	2	1	0	0
2	0	0	1	4	1	0	1
3	2	1	0	1	1	0	0
4	1	0	1	5	1	0	0
5	1	2	0	3	0	0	1
6	2	1	1	0	0	0	1
7	3	1	1	0	1	1	1
8	1	2	0	5	0	0	0
9	3	1	0	1	1	0	1
10	4	1	0	0	0	0	2
11	4	0	0	1	1	1	1
12	0	4	0	1	0	0	0
1 through 6	8	5	5	15	4	0	3
7 through 12	15	9	1	8	3	2	5

Table 3. Distribution of Explicit Noun Phrase (NP) Antecedents for Anaphoric Nominal Expressions in Test Frame Sentences

Passage	Explicit NP Antecedent in Preceding Text	No Explicit NP Antecedent
1	6	1
2	3	2
3	2	2
4	6	1
5	4	2
6	1	3
7	3	1
8	1	4
9	3	6
10	3	3
11	1	3
12	4	1
1 through 6	22	11
7 through 12	15	18

of anaphoric elements whose interpretation involves some type of inference. This tendency—for the interpretation of anaphoric expressions to depend increasingly on inference as passages get harder—is clearer when we examine processes involved in picking out the referents of such expressions. The following discussion distinguishes categories of anaphoric nominal expressions occurring in frame sentences according to the location of a linguistic antecedent or, where there is none, according to how the nonexplicit antecedent is identifiable (i.e., its relationship to the text).

1. *Antecedent noun phrase in preceding sentence.* For some anaphoric expressions there is a nonpronominal noun phrase located in the immediately preceding sentence which is an obvious candidate for antecedent on formal and semantic grounds: In the case of pronouns and demonstratives it is the closest nonprominal phrase which agrees in number and gender with the anaphoric element, as in the following example:

The guide leads the visitors through the mansion and surrounding estate, showing them the major points of interest. *He* presents a brief history of the ornate 19th century mansion.

In the case of definite noun phrases, it is usually the closest preceding noun phrase, and the anaphoric noun phrase contains either a repetition of the antecedent noun (as in the foregoing example, where *mansion* is repeated), or a word closely related in meaning.

2. *Antecedent noun phrase in earlier sentence.* In some cases, an anaphoric expression is unambiguously connected to an antecedent noun phrase which occurs several sentences earlier than the frame sentence. In these cases, the anaphoric expression either explicitly repeats the earlier noun, or, most frequently, it is connected to the antecedent noun phrase through a series of sentences with nominals (usually pronouns) which all share the same referent and have the same grammatical function within the sentence. This case is illustrated in the following example, which is typical of early passages:

Cats like to hunt at night. *They* feel safe. *They* feel free. *They* roam around. *They* explore. *They* catch mice. *They* visit each other. Sometimes *they* fight. *These animals* are very independent.

3. *Demonstratives with extended reference.* In all but one use of *this* or *that* (with no following noun) in frame sentences, the demonstrative points to the descriptive content of an extended portion (one to several sentences) of the immediately preceding text, as in the following example:

She beats the clothes against the rocks. That is how she gets them clean.

The sentence with the demonstrative takes a form such as *That is how . . . , This is why . . . , This means that . . . ,* presenting a comment on the event or situation described.

4. *Pronouns with situational reference.* A few frame sentences contain deictic pronouns: *you* or *we* pointing out of the text to a referent (e.g., the reader) in the context of situation.

5. *Ambiguity in anaphoric relation.* For a few anaphoric expressions there is more than one candidate for antecedent in the text, so that contextual information must be applied to select the correct one.

6. *Inference of antecedent for definite noun phrase.* Some demonstrative definite noun phrases point to an entity whose existence is implied by the descriptive content of an extended portion of preceding text. These cases work generally like the following example:

In the presence of danger, the mother bird will flap her wings noisily as if she were injured. *This trick* is intended to divert attention away from her nest.

Here and in similar cases, the antecedent of the anaphoric noun phrase is not named explicitly in the linguistic context, but is identifiable on the basis of a description contained in the text. Other definite noun phrases in frame sentences name referents whose identity must be inferred in some other manner on the basis of what is said in preceding text. These cases do not reflect a generalizable process which can be illustrated here, since the inference in each case depends on the content and structure of the sentences. In each case, interpretation of the definite noun phrase (and of the frame sentence containing it) depends on identification of a specific referent which is not explicitly named in the linguistic context but which can be identified through inference.

The categories of anaphoric nominals described in categories 1 through 6 above differ in the processes required for their interpretation. There is no sharp distinction to be drawn (here or in general) between processes which depend upon inference and those which do not. Also, some inferences seem closely tied to the text, while others involve the application of some background information. However, among the anaphoric expressions described above, the interpretation of those in categories 1 through 3 is most clearly supported by material explicitly expressed in the text, while interpretation of those in categories 4 through 6 involves some type of inference. Table 4 shows the distribution of these expressions in frame sentences, in terms of categories corresponding to processes of interpretation. Table 4 shows that earlier passages are more likely to provide explicit support in the text for anaphoric relations; in particular, they frequently contain series of sentences with conferential nominal expressions, which are rare in later passages. It also demonstrates that the demand for inference in the interpretation of anaphoric expressions increases in the latter portion of the test.

Connections Among Sentences

In sensible and coherent prose, adjacent sentences bear some meaningful connection to each other in terms of content and discourse function. In order to comprehend a test passage a reader must be able to interpret the intended connections among its sentences. These connections may be indicated through a variety of devices, including the use of anaphoric expressions (discussed above) and ellipsis, or they may be understood through inference; they may also be "marked" through the use of explicit sentence connectors such as *but, for example, thus,* and so on. Table 5 shows the extent to which explicit indicators of sentence connections are used in DRP passages overall, and more specifically, in the seven frame sentences of each passage. As these figures indicate, there appears to be a slight increase in the use of explicit sentence connectors, in frame sentences and other sentences, as overall passage difficulty increases.

The distribution of particular sentence connectors varies more distinctly through the test. In the first six passages, 11 different connectors are used; but in 75% of marked sentence connections in these passages, the connector used is either *but, so,* or a demonstrative with extended reference. In the second half of the test (passages 7 through 12), there are 25 different connectors, of which only 6 occur in the first half of the test as well. (These are *but, so,* demonstratives, *also, and* and *then.*) In other words, relatively few types of connections are explicitly indicated in sentences in earlier passages (leaving any other type of connection implicit), while later passages are characterized by a greater number and variety of explicit connections among sentences.

The sentence-connectors used in passages 1 through 6 are all commonly used

Table 4. Distribution of Anaphoric Nominal Expressions in Test Frame Sentences According to Interpretive Processes

Passage	1. Antecedent NP in Preceding Sentence	2. Antecedent NP in Earlier Sentence	3. Demonstratives with Extended Reference	TOTAL TEXT-SUPPORTED ANAPHORIC RELATIONS	4. Pronouns with Situational Reference	5. Ambiguity in Anaphoric Relation	6. Inference of Antecedent for Definite NP	TOTAL INFERENCE-DEPENDENT ANAPHORIC RELATIONS
1	1	5	1	7	0	0	0	0
2	2	1	1	4	1	0	0	1
3	1	1	0	2	0	0	2	2
4	2	4	1	7	0	0	0	0
5	1	3	0	4	0	0	2	2
6	1	0	1	2	0	0	2	2
7	2	1	0	3	0	0	1	1
8	0	1	1	2	1	0	2	3
9	1	1	0	2	2	1	4	7
10	2	0	0	2	0	1	3	4
11	1	0	0	1	0	0	3	3
12	3	0	0	3	0	1	1	2
1 through 6	8	14	4	26	1	0	6	7
7 through 12	9	3	1	13	3	3	14	20

Table 5. Distribution of Explicit Sentence-Connectors in Passages and Frame Sentences

Passage	Percentage of All Sentences with Explicit Connector	Frame Sentences with Explicit Connector Number	Percentage
1	.14	2	.29
2	.11	5	.71
3	.20	2	.29
4	.18	4	.57
5	.27	4	.57
6	.41	4	.57
7	.29	3	.43
8	.27	5	.71
9	.27	4	.57
10	.38	4	.57
11	.46	6	.86
12	.38	4	.57
1 through 6	.22	21	.50
7 through 9	.28	12	.57
10 through 12	.41	14	.67

in ordinary conversation. In contrast, many of those which occur in later passages—such as *thus, hence, nevertheless, furthermore*—are generally not used in conversation, but are characteristic of written prose. A reader must have become familiar with the meaning and use of a variety of such connectors, in order to understand later test passages, and frame sentences in particular.

Where the intended connection between sentences is not explicitly marked, it must be understood through inference. Generally, these relationships are understood on the basis of "clues" in the structure and content of sentences, and of expectations about the author's intent (e.g., to say what is relevant and informative). Sentences may be related to each other in any number of ways, but certain types of unmarked relationships are probably characteristic of a given genre of written prose. In DRP test passages a few types of connections recur between frame sentences and sentences adjacent to them.

Sometimes a frame sentence has the effect of restating the content of all or part of the preceding sentence. In other cases, the frame sentence presents a consequence of the situation or event described in the preceding sentence. In still others, the frame sentence describes a reason for the event described in the sentence preceding it.

Sometimes the frame sentence introduces a notion (represented by a nominal marked with an indefinite) which is then given content in the sentence which follows it. For example:

Driving home, *a nagging thought* would not leave him. He had been rude and inconsiderate to his best friend.

Here, if the second sentence were absent, the notion of *a nagging thought* would be left dangling pointlessly; in the expectation of an informative discourse, the reader can take the second sentence to supply the content of the thought.

In many cases, the connection between sentences is less specific. In some pairs of adjacent sentences, each presents an independent fact, which seems to bear no special relationship to what is stated in the adjacent sentence beyond the fact that they both present information on the same topic.

Comparing earlier with later DRP test passages, we can observe a general shift in terms of the nature of connections between frame sentences and adjacent sentences, and the type and density of clues to these connections, in the text. On the one hand, earlier passages contain fewer explicit markers of sentence connections, so that understanding how sentences fit together depends to a greater extent on inference. On the other hand, in earlier passages where there is no sentence connector, frame sentences generally bear a locally constrained type of relationship to adjacent sentences—such as the more specific types of connections described above—which is largely accessible from understanding the content of the sentences in the context of general knowledge about the world. Furthermore, the frequency of anaphoric elements with explicit antecedents in early passages, and the tendency for a series of sentences to contain coreferential pronouns, provide additional indicators of how sentences are connected in these passages.

As passage difficulty increases, there is greater use of explicit sentence-connectors; there is a decrease in anaphoric relations between explicit elements in the text; and there is a tendency for unmarked sentence connections to be nonspecific, in the sense that the relevance of adjacent sentences to each other must frequently be understood in terms of the relevance of their content to the topic of the passage.

Vocabulary

All of the multiple-choice response options associated with test items are classified as very familiar words in the Thorndike-Lorge Teacher's Word List. But in the text of passages, as overall difficulty increases, more words appear which are long and/or unlikely to be familiar from everyday use.

The diversity of vocabulary in a passage also increases with overall passage difficulty. This is demonstrated in Table 6, which shows how many words (expressed as a percentage of the total number of words in a passage) occur only once in the passage (not including item deletions, which are never repeated). Earlier passages are characterized by repetition of words, while later passages include more synonyms (e.g., *motion/movement, look/appear, six/half-dozen*).

The vocabulary of passages in the second half of the test contains an increas-

Table 6.   Percent of Single-Occurrence Words in Passages

Passage	Percentage of Total Words
1	.15
3	.19
5	.23
8	.29
10	.39
12	.40

ing number of words which one would expect to encounter in written language in academic or technical contexts, but not in ordinary conversation or popular writing. In order to understand harder passages, readers must come to the test knowing these words and their meanings. This is necessary because after passage 6, there is a decreasing amount of contextual redundancy surrounding hard words. That is, it becomes harder to figure out the meaning of unfamiliar words from context because fewer clues are provided; consequently, knowing the meaning of the word itself becomes more important.

Words which indicate sentence connections (*thus, hence,* etc.) are a special category of words which must be known, since often they alone indicate how the content of sentences is related. The following examples also demonstrate the contrast which can be observed between the earlier and later portions of the test in this regard: In passage 6, the words *tell, determine,* and *establish* are all used in parallel contexts (with an object noun phrase referring to something police doctors discover from skeletons—e.g., *age, height,* and *weight*). A reader who doesn't know the word *establish,* for example, might still make sense of the passage by noticing that it is used in the same way as *determine* and *tell.* Similarly, passage 6 uses the possibly unfamiliar word *anemia,* in the clarifying phrase *sicknesses, like anemia.* In contrast, passage 7 (and those which follow it) uses words in constructions which place a greater demand for vocabulary knowledge on the reader. Words whose form might be familiar from other contexts are used in a sense which is less likely to be known—e.g., *trade* and *practice* in the sentence *Medieval craft guilds were associations of men practicing the same trade.* Here the context does not provide the kind of secondary indications of meaning illustrated above in the examples from passage 6. In this case, a reader must know what it means to *practice a trade* (as opposed to "practicing the piano," or "making a fair trade") in order to understand the definition of a *craft guild,* the passage topic.

As the diversity of vocabulary increases in passages, there is more of a tendency for synonymy to bear directly on test items, as it does in the following item from passage 9 (about Neanderthal man):

Evidence of intelligence is seen in his tools: axes, hammers, spear points, scrapers, borers, and even a saw. . . . Thus we see ancient evidence of _____ at work.

The most direct clue to the right answer, *reason,* is the parallel construction *evidence of* [*noun*] in which the slot can be filled by synonymous words. Items like this seem to depend heavily on simple word knowledge.

Background Knowledge About the World

Besides needing to know what words mean—vocabulary knowledge, in a strict sense—readers need to know facts about the things referred to by words in test passages. That is, they need to know related information about those things and their place in the world, in addition to being acquainted with the words used to name them.

Recent research in several related fields supports the view that reading is an active process whereby the reader reconstructs the author's intended meaning and integrates new information with what he or she already knows. The meaning conveyed by a text, in this view, does not reside in the language of the text, but "is the interactive product of text and context of various kinds, including linguistic, prior knowledge, situational, attitudinal, and task contexts, among others" (Spiro, 1980, p. 246).

Research on language and reading demonstrates that proficient readers predict meaning through application of knowledge of language structure, conventions of language use, and real-world factual information (Goodman & Goodman, 1977; Griffin, 1977b; Klare, 1976; Larkin, Dieterich, Freeman, & Yanofsky, 1979; Morgan, 1978). Complementary research in cognitive psychology and artificial intelligence supports a notion of simultaneous top-down and bottom-up processing in reading: As a reader integrates features of incoming data with prior knowledge at a specific level (as in word recognition), he or she simultaneously forms expectations of meaning from the activation of higher-level knowledge structures in memory (i.e., information associated with recognized concepts) (Bobrow & Norman, 1975; Charniak, 1978; Freedle & Hale, 1979; Kintsch and Van Dijk, 1978; Rumelhart, 1980; Schank, 1975).

Of particular concern here is the point that new information presented in text is assimilated to relevant prior knowledge, and that this is a necessary aspect of comprehending prose; a reader may be prevented from getting the full sense of a passage if specifically relevant facts about the world are not available to him or her (Adams, 1980; Adams and Bruce, 1980; Adams and Collins, 1979; Morgan & Green, 1980; Winograd, 1977). In other words, in order to gain new information from a text, a reader must already have enough relevant knowledge to serve as a framework for interpretation, a context within which the new information will make sense. As Bransford and McCarrell (1974, p. 204) state, "Comprehension results only when the comprehender has sufficient alinguistic information to use the cues specified in linguistic input to create some semantic content that allows him to understand."

One of the basic claims for the DRP Test is that prior knowledge about passage topics is not needed to do well on the test, and will not help a reader do better. For example (from State Education Department, 1979b, p. 14):

> All the information that is needed to select the correct response is provided in the text of the passages: there is no need to supply information concerning each passage's content from memory or past experience . . . Knowing a great deal or nothing about the content of any passage should not bias a student's ability to respond.

In fact, readers of DRP passages need factual knowledge about the world both for overall passage comprehension and specific item completion.

In earlier passages, the need for background information is not obvious because it is information of a sort which one might expect high school students to know from ordinary experience, or to have heard about—such as the fact that crop failures can result in a shortage of food; that the seasons of the year vary in terms of the number of hours of light and dark in the day; that in order to find out how wide a jawbone is, one must measure it; and so on. But in passages 7 through 12, the factual background information needed for overall passage comprehension is markedly more abstract and more removed from everyday life, than that required in the first half of the test (as examples below will illustrate). Readers need to have some factual information to which they can relate such notions as stellar magnitude, the Ice Age, ecological balance, World War II, and the abacus, to name only a few examples.

Some familiarity with the topic of a passage, and some prior acquaintance with the things, events, or concepts named in it will allow a reader to recognize what a passage is about, and to assimilate the information presented in it as integrated content. Background information allows the reader to grasp the point and the relative importance of the various facts presented, and to perceive the parts of a passage as fitting together coherently (Brown, 1980). The role of background knowledge in comprehending DRP passages is made more important by the absence of titles or pictures, either of which can promote comprehension by helping the reader see how to integrate the parts of the passage (Schallert, 1980).

For example, a reader's comprehension of passage 7, which describes functions of craft guilds in medieval society, will probably be greatly promoted if he or she already has some notion of what craft guilds are, or what it has meant, socially and historically, to practice a trade: possession of a skill as a result of long training; being socially distinguished from unskilled laborers, merchants, members of professions, and so on; having a vital economic role in common with a great many other members of medieval society; and so on. If knowledge of this sort is available to be called up by the opening sentence of the passage (*Medieval craft guilds were associations of men practicing the same trade.*), it would provide a framework within which the various facts presented in the paragraphs will fit together and make sense as a unit. Without this background information, a reader would at best face a series of disparate facts, with no means of integrating them in a way that makes sense to him or her.

Passage 9 opens with the following two sentences:

Neanderthal man, who perished during the Ice Age, is regarded nowadays as an extinct variety of man, not a separate species. In contrast to earlier viewpoints, it is presently the similarities between Neanderthal and modern man that are emphasized and considered crucial.

The first sentence, which indicates what the passage is about, contains at least five technical terms from biological science. A reader either needs to know already who Neanderthal man was, or needs to know when the Ice Age was, and what a species is, and what it means to be extinct. He or she also needs to be able to call up a relevant context of understanding about science, in order to know what is meant by *viewpoints* in the second sentence (viewpoints about what?), and to recognize that emphasizing similarities between Neanderthal and modern man is an instance of a scientific viewpoint. Recognizing this, the reader can make the necessary inferences that ''earlier viewpoints'' emphasized differences, and that the point of the passage is to list and describe similarities. A reader with enough prior knowledge about early man to know that the comparison is with a physically, mentally, and socially different creature, will approach the passage understanding that similarities are listed in a context in which the differences are most obvious. This kind of background will shape appropriate expectations about passage content, and will probably facilitate gaining new information from the passage, which presents specific facts about Neanderthal's facial features, physique, brain volume, posture, and behavior.

On a more specific level, factual background information can contribute directly to the completion of many items throughout the test. Frequently, choosing the right answer depends on making some inference from what is said in the text; prior knowledge can figure in the reader's ability to recognize and make the appropriate inference. In the following example, from passage 10,

The Welland Canal, connecting Lake Ontario to the other Great Lakes, was constructed to provide uninterrupted water passage for commercial sailing vessels from the Atlantic Ocean halfway across the continent. As expected, the benefits to ___ were large.

selection of the correct answer, *trade,* depends heavily on the reader's knowing what *commercial* means, and being able to infer that if commercial sailing vessels had an uninterrupted passage from the Atlantic to the Great Lakes, it would be good for trade. (Note that the reader also needs to recognize that the meaning of *trade* here is different from its meaning in passage 7, as cited above.) The necessary inferences would be facilitated if the reader has not only heard of the Great Lakes, but knows something about them, such as where they are, the fact that they are connected, where Lake Ontario is in relation to the others and in relation to the Atlantic Ocean, the fact that huge quantities of raw materials and manufactured products are shipped in and out of the Great Lakes, and so on. At the very least, the item would probably be much more difficult to understand and complete if the reader did not have any background knowledge on these topics.

In general, test items provide more than one path to the right answer, in the sense that a certain density of structural and content clues is associated with an item. In many cases, it appears likely that already having information about the topic will open the most direct avenue to completing the item, whereas lacking any specifically relevant knowledge will force strict reliance on linguistic clues within the text—almost certainly a more difficult procedure. In the following item from passage 7, for example, the right answer (*public*) is clued by the meaning of one word, and several relevant but unstated facts about guild membership:

By setting and maintaining standards, guilds not only protected members but also served an important communal function. The _____ was protected.

Optimally, the text may lead a reader to apply two separate pieces of knowledge, each of which enhances the relevance of the other:

1. A reader who knows that guild membership can be taken as distinct from membership in the public, and that guild members produced goods for the public, would recognize that the public would benefit from standards set by the guild (the word *standards* being understood as relating anaphorically to the noun phrase *product standards* earlier in the paragraph), and could understand the implicit contrast between *members* and *the public* as two groups who were protected.

2. A reader who knows what *communal* means may infer that the content of *communal function* is presented in the frame sentence, and connect the notion of "community" with *the public*.

On the other hand, a reader who cannot draw on any relevant information about the topic would have the difficult task of recognizing the appropriate inference solely on the basis of structural clues and the meaning of one word (*communal*). Many items thus demonstrate that relevant background knowledge makes it easier for a reader to make appropriate use of linguistic clues.

In passage 11, which deals with postwar economic recovery in Japan, the opening paragraph states that at the end of World War II Japan had a severely inflated economy, a crippled industrial capability, a starving population, and devastated cities. The paragraph concludes:

. . . Japan had suffered a loss approximately equivalent to eighteen years of economic growth. Such was the _____.

Looking back over the preceding sentences for a clue to the referent of the missing noun, a comprehending reader can recognize that the paragraph contains a description of damage and destruction. But the correct answer for the blank is *defeat*. To a reader who already knows that Japan was defeated in the Second

World War, the connection between *defeat* and the damage described might be clear. But a reader who lacks background knowledge about the war would not necessarily be led to select *defeat* by what is stated in the text; after all, the description would apply as well to many countries which were not defeated. In order to reconstruct the content of the passage in a way that makes sense to him or her, a reader will interpret the linguistic cues in light of whatever background information he or she possesses. For example, an uninformed reader, taking the paragraph as a description of the usual, predictable outcome of war, could select *custom,* another response option, for the blank. In order to understand the intended point of the paragraph, a reader needs some general background knowledge about the aftermath of war, and the specific information that Japan lost World War II.

A final example, from passage 12, further demonstrates that comprehension of a passage will be guided by the reader's background knowledge as well as by the language of the text. In this case, specific background information is needed for grammatical parsing of the first sentence, and for correct completion of the test item in the second sentence.

Babbage foresaw a computing system whose memory stored data, sequenced operations, and input information through cards. There was basically nothing wrong with these _____.

There are at least two ways to interpret the first sentence:

1. In one possible interpretation, the relative clause contains three conjoined noun phrases (two of them with premodifiers)—*data, sequenced operations,* and *input information*—as objects of *stored.* This reading might be paraphrased as follows:

Babbage foresaw a computing system whose memory stored three things through cards. Those things were: data; operations which had been ordered in a sequence; and information which had been put in.

2. In an alternative interpretation, the relative clause contains three conjoined verb phrases with *memory* as subject: *stored data, sequenced operations,* and *input information.* In other words, the sentence can be interpreted as describing three operations which the memory performed in Babbage's design for a computing system.

The extent of a reader's knowledge about modern computers or their mechanical predecessors will influence interpretation of this sentence. Readers might reject interpretation 2 if they know that some outside agent (not the computer memory itself) had to put operations in sequence and put information into the computer. Other readers might reject interpretation 1 if they know that cards are not used to store information in memory in modern computers. Other interactions are possible between interpretation of the sentence and the information a reader brings to the task, but any interpretation will be partly a function of the reader's background knowledge. A reader who is simply unfamiliar with specialized notions such as memory, operations, or input, as they are associated with the working of a computer, will probably have difficulty constructing a context in which the sentence makes any sense at all.

The test item in the second sentence of the example above presents another demand for background information. The deleted noun must refer to something which is either named, described, or otherwise indicated in the preceding text. Interpreting the sentences in the context of their background knowledge about the topic, readers might find various response options plausible in the blank. For example, a reader who knows that Babbage was right in foreseeing the use of cards in computers, might select *materials;* another reader, speculating that data, sequenced operations, and input information are not an appropriate burden for computer memory, might select *loads.* Another reader, taking the first sentence to describe different things a computer could do, might select *ideas,* the correct answer. Completion of the item, in other words, will be guided not only by the language of the text, but by how readers apply what they already know about the topic, in interpreting the text.

Background Knowledge About Written Language

Readers need to bring to the test task appropriate expectations about the structure of discourse, and some awareness of the properties of expository writing in particular. This is because the task involves not only comprehension of the passage, but also choosing the answer that makes the best sense in the blank. This latter aspect of the task involves the reader in an active role somewhat akin to that of the writer of the passage. The explicit requirement is that the reader reconstruct a sentence which is sensible in context. An implicit additional requirement is that the reconstructed sentence conform to conventions of written language use. Therefore, knowing something about how people use written language to express meaning—a kind of knowledge associated with learning how to write—can frequently enter into the choice of the best answer.

Readers need to be aware of tacit rules of discourse structure. This type of knowledge, unlike real-world background information, is generally not consciously applied, but it enters into the test task nonetheless. For example, readers need to know that a single sentence will contain no more than one element which contrasts with another element in the context. The following item is from passage 11, about Japan:

Adoption of contemporary technology was a necessary ingredient for recovery. But something else was _____.

Here a reader can correctly anticipate that a synonym for *necessary* (*needed*) is needed in the blank, by (a) recognizing that *but* and *else* signal a contrast between referents of the noun phrases *adoption of contemporary technology* and *something else;* and (b) knowing how contrasts across sentences in a discourse are structured.

The following item, from passage 7 (about craft guilds), depends in part on the conventional pressure to keep the same subject in adjacent sentences where the subject in one is not specified:

Members who cheated were quickly and openly punished. So there was good reason to be ———.

Choice of the correct answer, *honest*, requires an inference that *members* is the unspecified subject of the infinitive clause in the frame sentence, formally preserving the subject of the preceding sentence, even though the two terms are not coreferential. Another response option, *independent*, makes better sense if the reader interprets the unspecified subject as the less specific *people* (i.e., not members). The appropriate inference is guided by awareness of how discourses tend to be structured.

Some items call on a reader's knowledge about how sentences function and relate to each other in discourse. This enables him or her to have appropriate expectations about what information will be provided and how it will relate to previously presented content. The following two sentences from passage 3, for example, follow a simple explanation of how people can control the blooming season of plants indoors through artificial light.

Some people do this just for fun. But often there is another ———.

The preceding context allows a sensible and coherent discourse with either of two response options: *group* (*another group* contrasting with *some people*); or *reason* (*another reason* contrasting with what the reader must infer to be a reason, *fun*). In either case, the frame sentence introduces a new entity without specifying its identity. An informative and cooperative discourse can be expected to follow such a sentence with information which will allow a reader to infer the relevance of the new material to the old. A reader who has this expectation about discourse may be led to attend to the sentence following the frame sentence for a clue to the right answer. In this case, the following sentence explains that commercial growers can produce flowers year round; this provides the reader with relevant content for *another reason* but not *another group,* and so determines the response.

Many items call on the reader to adhere to a related rule of discourse, that a paragraph deals with a single topic. For example, this requirement constrains the choice of a word to fit in the blank in the following two sentences about tree frogs from passage 5:

They are not very fast. So they cannot ———.

These sentences come in the first paragraph of the passage, which opens by describing the tree frog's ability to change its color for protection, then describes the frog's weakness and slowness. The preceding context would allow at least two of the response options: *hunt* and *escape*. But the final sentence of the paragraph, following the frame sentence, goes back to the topic of protection. Whereas either of the two response options would produce a discourse which would be both true and sensible, only the choice of *escape* in the blank satisfies the stylistic requirement that the paragraph topic be preserved without digression.

Besides knowing about such constraints on the structure and organization of written discourse in general, readers need to be familiar with the special properties of expository prose. Experience with the genre will help prepare them to deal with structural elements, lexical items, syntactic properties, and stylistic conventions peculiar to the type of writing; to form appropriate expectations about the type of information to be presented; and to assume the external observer's point of view which expository prose (unlike personal narrative or stories) requires, particularly when the topic is abstract or historical.

Test-Taking Strategies

For many DRP test items, it is at least possible for the item to be completed on the basis of understanding the text preceding the item. That is, having understood the preceding sentences, a reader might approach the list of response options with an expectation about what type of word is needed to complete the frame sentence. For other items, however, the preceding context alone will allow the frame sentence to be completed in diverse ways. In these cases, a reader who has read only the preceding sentences will not be prepared to search among the response options for a word which fits narrowly constrained expectations about the intended meaning of the frame sentence. Some strategy is called for other than predicting and confirming meaning in the process of reading through the passage.

In some items the choice between competing response options specifically requires consideration of at least one sentence following the frame sentence. Text instructions explicitly alert the reader to this possibility: ''You may not be sure of the answer to a question until you have read the sentences that come after the blank. So be sure to read enough to answer the questions.'' One such item (discussed above), comes from passage 3:

Some people do this just for fun. But often there is another _____.

In this item and others like it, the sentence following the frame sentence provides content for the deleted noun (*reason*), information which can guide the choice of response option. A related group of items, also discussed above, includes those in which the topic of the sentences following the frame sentence constrains the choice of response by constraining the topic of the paragraph. In these cases, the preceding context would allow two or more of the response options equally well, but in the context of the following sentence, only one of the responses can be seen as not digressing from the topic of the paragraph.

In other items, the following sentence presents information which must be seen as consistent with, and relevant to, preceding content; and the choice of response option is limited by the need to meet this requirement. This is the case, for example, in an item from passage 6 (about what police doctors learn from skeletons):

As people grow, bones that once were separate join together. This means that the _____ of bones is important.

These sentences, in a paragraph about determining age from skeletons, follow a sentence which states how many bones people have at birth and at maturity. This preceding context allows the frame to be completed plausibly with the words *position, number,* or *strength;* in any case, the following sentence can be expected to explain how the position/number/strength of bones is important in determining age. As it is, the following sentence explains that age can often be determined by conting bones, thus limiting the choice of response to *number*.

Where the reader's expectations about a deleted word are not closely guided by the text surrounding the item, the multiple-choice test format invites an alternative strategy for item completion—working "backwards," in a sense, from response option list to the text. In other words, the reader can approach the task either (a) by forming a hypothesis, in the process of reading up to an item, about what word or type of word is missing from the text, and searching the response option list for a word which fits that expectation; or (b) lacking any such hypothesis, by trying out the available responses in the context of the passage, and selecting the one which produces the best "fit" in terms of a set of implicit criteria. "Wrong" response options corresponding to item deletions can fail to fit for a variety of reasons. Some, considered in the local context of the frame sentence and immediately adjacent sentences, are simply irrelevant or produce a senseless discourse—as in the following item from passage 8 (about gauging the brightness of stars):

It [the eye] cannot produce a permanent record or cumulate light from dim sources to make them visible. But _____ can.

Here the word *machines* is the only sensible possibility; none of the other response options (*distance, time, theories, movements*) will produce a semantically well-formed sentence with the elided predicate (*produce a permanent record or cumulate light . . .*). In other cases, a wrong response must be ruled out on the basis of background information—as in the following item from passage 10 (about ecological balance):

But in the absence of their natural predators and competitors, the rabbits multiplied beyond all expectations. There was no way to _____ them.

The knowledge that a population explosion of rabbits is considered undesirable would allow a reader to reject *shelter* as a response in spite of the fact that it is perfectly sensible in the preceding and following context.

Finally, there seems to be an implicit principle which can guide the evaluation of response options for many items: Where more than one response appears plausible in context, the right answer is the word which in some sense is the most direct of the possibilities, which calls for the least inferencing work to reconstruct a coherent discourse. This loosely stated principle can be illustrated by the following item from passage 6 (about skeletons):

Such sicknesses make the bones look a particular way. The bones, in effect, are _____.

Here a reader might choose *connected* or even *pulled* from among the response options, based on the possible inference that the frame sentence, thus reconstructed, specifies the "particular way" the bones look. But the intended answer, *marked,* introduces less specific new content, resulting in a frame sentence which is nearly a restatement of the content of the previous sentence. In a sense, it takes less work to make sense of the discourse with *marked* than with another response option in the blank.

Another example comes from passage 4 (about rainmaking):

He [the rainmaker] gathers some sticks and he lights them. He makes a _____.

This item comes from a paragraph which describes making smoke clouds to bring rain; subsequent sentences say that damp wood is used because it produces a lot of smoke. A reader could complete the frame sentence with *tower,* thus reconstructing a perfectly plausible scenario and avoiding the pointless repetitiveness characteristic of easy passages. But the correct answer is *fire,* producing a frame sentence which has the effect of saying the same thing as the preceding sentence. The implicit criterion for selection seems to be that the response must not only result in a sensible and coherent discourse, but that it must be the most directly and economically related to the immediate context, of the possibilities.[2]

EVALUATION

In the preceding section we have shown that a diverse array of abilities and kinds of knowledge are needed for completing DRP test items. In this section we examine the extent to which those facts support certain crucial claims about how

---

[2] Fillmore and Kay (1983), in their analysis of reading comprehension tests, propose a related "parsimony principle" to describe readers' efforts to give text coherence through the most economical interpretation whenever possible.

the test works. In doing this, we demonstrate an approach to evaluating the DRP as a test of reading comprehension.

The DRP is claimed to provide an unambiguous measure of reading ability. According to the design of the test, overall passage difficulty increases while the test task is held constant. In this way item difficulty is tied to text difficulty, and a student's performance will indicate the hardest prose he or she can read with comprehension.

In order for the test to work in the intended manner, two crucial requirements must be satisfied. It must be true, as claimed for the DRP, that

1. Comprehension of the prose surrounding an item is both necessary and sufficient for completing the item; and
2. The difficulty of prose in passages increases along a single dimension.

we will consider each of these requirements in turn to see if they are satisfied by properties of the test, which have been described in preceding sections.

Claim 1: Prose Comprehension is Both Necessary and Sufficient for Item Completion

This is a claim that in order to respond correctly to test items, a reader *must* read and understand the text of the passage, and that *only* that ability is required for item completion. The claim can be evaluated analytically by asking first, if there is any way other than by reading the passage, to answer an item correctly; and second, if any type of knowledge or ability other than reading is necessary in order to answer items.

With regard to the first question, it may be possible to complete some items in the test without understanding the passage. These are cases in which the paragraph containing the item contains a number of words whose meaning is closely associated, and the response option list contains just one word whose meaning can be similarly associated with the words in the text. The following item from passage 6 (which was discussed above) is an example:

As people grow, bones that once were separate join together. This means that the _____ of bones is important.

This item is preceded by text containing the printed numerals *400* and *206*, and is immediately followed, at the end of a line of print by the word root *count* (as part of *counting*). Response options include the easily associated word *number*, as well as semantically unrelated *surface, strength, color,* and *position.* It would probably be possible to select the right answers to items like this on the basis of word association alone, without grasping the meaning of the text. Reading comprehension is not strictly necessary wherever this strategy can be substituted. However, the distribution of test items which might allow it is scattered, and in general it appears to be true that reconstructing the meaning of at least some portion of the passage is necessary for item completion.

A more important and complex question for the test is whether understanding the surrounding prose is sufficient for item completion—or whether some independent or additional ability is needed. In earlier sections of this report we have described a number of abilities and types of knowledge demanded by the test, which are distinct from the ability to read with comprehension.

First, our examination suggests that some prior knowledge about topics and things discussed in the passages (for example, computers, the Ice Age, World War II) will, at the least, facilitate item completion, and is probably necessary in some cases. We have noted that a reader needs factual background information about the world to integrate passage content, to make necessary inferences from what the text says, and in some cases, to select the right answer or to reject wrong ones.

Second, the structure and format of the DRP demand that the reader sometimes employ certain strategies beyond ordinary reading for comprehension, in order to complete items. For example, the reader must often read at least one sentence beyond the item deletion to find enough clues to narrow the choice of an answer. If the test passage were like ordinary prose, with no deletions, information in the later sentence would serve to confirm the reader's interpretation of text up to that point—the ordinary function of redundancy in text. But the procedure required by the test format is one of reading ahead not to confirm, but to reconstruct, retroactively, the intended meaning of an earlier sentence.

Similarly, the reader as test-taker assumes the role of writer in a sense, in order to evaluate available response options in the discourse context. In one respect, this procedure—trying out words to see how they fit—might be viewed as raising a generally tacit aspect of ordinary reading to the level of a conscious, deliberate procedure: Proficient reading is generally regarded as involving a tacit procedure of hypothesis-formation and confirmation in the reconstruction of meaning; the test-taking strategy of evaluating responses is a meta-linguistic activity which partly parallels the ordinary reading process, but is distinct from reading per se (Brown, 1980). This test-taking strategy goes beyond reading comprehension in other aspects, as well. Test instructions are to "choose the word that makes the best sense in the blank," reflecting the intent that comprehension of passage meaning alone determines responses; in practice, however-er, response options must be evaluated not only in terms of the sense of the text, but according to criteria of discourse cohesion, stylistics, and what we have discussed as a principle of "least work" as well.

In short, it appears that a reader's ability to complete test items will be promoted if he or she brings to the task not only the ability to read and understand prose of a certain difficulty, but also specific types of knowledge about things in the world, some familiarity with conventions of expository prose, and ability to devise test-taking strategies specifically adapted to the format of the DRP.

But the question of what the test requires is still more complex. The DRP is claimed to measure reading directly as "the end (cumulative) result of instruction" (State Education Department, 1979a). This is vocabulary knowledge, understanding main ideas, "literal" comprehension, inference, and so on. In view of evidence that such subskills may not be independent in proficient reading, the DRP is designed to test the "composite ability" of reading which is supposed to be the "final outcome" of instruction. But while it may be true that proficient reading, in the abstract, is a holistic ability which cannot validly be measured in terms of discrete component subskills, it is not clear that the test unambiguously measures that ability. In other words, it is not clear that "*only* the ability to understand prose is required to perform well on DRP tests" (as claimed in *The College Board News,* Spring 1981).

The process of reading, in any one instance—such as reading a given DRP test passage—requires a bundle of interrelated but distinct kinds of knowledge and abilities (Dieterich, Freeman, & Griffin, 1978; Weaver, 1977). We have noted, for example, that knowledge of vocabulary is necessary for comprehension of test passages, and that this requirement grows as passage content becomes more abstract and built-in textual redundancy decreases. Some corpus of words must be shared by most English speakers, and knowing some categories of words can be claimed to be part of knowing English (Brown, 1973; Carroll & White, 1973; Sheldon, 1978). DRP test design takes advantage of this fact in providing only common words as response options throughout the test; this is intended to ensure that reader responses will not be affected by the difficulty of those words but will depend just on prose comprehension. But understanding the prose of later passages requires knowledge of vocabulary which cannot be claimed to be universally acquired as part of acquiring English. If students learn what words like *stellar, reference, rickets, inimical, sociocultural, abacus, prototype,* or *digital* mean (to name only a few random examples), it is largely a function of experience, probably school experience in most cases. While it is necessary to know what words like these mean in order to understand passages which contain them (without providing a definition or other indication of their meaning), vocabulary knowledge of this sort is independent of reading ability.

We have also noted that in order to comprehend passages, readers need relevant background knowledge about concepts and entities mentioned in the text. This is different from claiming, as we have above, that some items demand background information beyond what the reader can gain from the passage; here we are observing that real-world background knowledge is necessary at the more fundamental level of understanding the text in the first place. We have discussed how in DRP passages, as in written discourse in general, the reader's background knowledge affects his or her ability to reconstruct and integrate the information in the text so that the content of the passage can be grasped as sensible and coherent. Since some prior knowledge relevant to the content of a passage is needed even to achieve what might be called "literal" comprehension, it is impossible for DRP passages to satisfy the claim of the test makers that "all the information that is needed to answer the questions correctly is presented in the text'' (State Education Department, 1979a). On the contrary, it is inescapable that some information not explicitly encoded in the text will be needed for a reader to reconstruct the content of the passage and thereby, presumably, to answer the questions. Knowing about particular events and things in the world, like knowing particular words, allows reading comprehension to take place in some instance, but it is not part of the basic ability to read.

Finally, it is likely that reading comprehension depends to a great extent on general linguistic comprehension. While there are interpretive processes (beyond visual tracking skills) special to reading, proficient readers in processing written prose probably rely on language comprehension strategies which are mode independent (i.e., applied to comprehension of language whether written or oral).

Recent research on the reading process supports the view that the linguistic processing of written language parallels the processing of oral language (in contrast to a model of reading in which print is first decoded into sound, then processed as oral language) (Goodman & Goodman, 1977; Kleiman, 1975; Larkin et al., 1979). Research on injury-related aphasia (impairment or loss of ability to use language) also suggests that there are neurolinguistic abilities special to reading. In the typical case of brain lesion all language functions are affected, but special cases of isolated dysfunction—such as auditory agnosia or ''word deafness,'' in which reading ability is retained while ability to understand spoken language is lost—demonstrate that separate mechanisms exist for processing of written and spoken input (Whitaker & Whitaker, 1979).

But while independent mechanisms apparently exist, it is likely that general linguistic comprehension figures importantly in reading comprehension. This view is supported by research which demonstrates a high correlation between subjects' comprehension of orally presented material and of written text (e.g., Jackson & McClelland, 1979; Rubin, 1980; Sticht, 1972). These studies suggest that there are certain skills or abilities which facilitate comprehension both in listening and in reading. Recent research on American Sign Language demonstrates close parallels between the processing of signs and the processing of speech, further suggesting the existence of some general interpretive processes independent of the mode in which language is presented (Massaro, 1977). Finally, studies have demonstrated a high correlation between subject performance on traditional reading tests and listening (Oller & Perkins, 1978), suggesting that to a great extent these tests really measure mode-independent general language comprehension strategies rather than reading comprehension per se.

This discussion has presented evidence relevant to the claim that prose comprehension is both necessary and sufficient for DRP item completion so that the DRP provides a direct and unambiguous measure of overall reading comprehension as a composite ability. Having found that the ability to comprehend prose is probably necessary for completing most test items, we have raised questions about its sufficiency, which can be summarized as follows:

1. Some items may demand knowledge and abilities beyond reading comprehension—in particular, real-world background knowledge relevant to the content of the passage, and the application of test-taking strategies adapted to the DRP test format.

2. Comprehension of passages depends on the interaction of a number of distinct kinds of knowledge and abilities: knowledge of vocabulary, related information about concepts named in the text, and general language comprehension strategies are all prerequisites for reading, yet are not, strictly speaking, part of the basic ability to read.

The first of these statements points to potential counterevidence to the test-makers' claim that prose comprehension is sufficient for item completion. The second of these statements does not necessarily argue against that specific claim, but still suggests that, in order to do well on the DRP Test, a reader must bring more than just reading ability to the test. This problem derives from the fact that the test represents an attempt to measure an abstract ability by means of concrete applications of that ability; but every such concrete application also requires the application of other, distinct, kinds of knowledge and abilities.

Claim 2: Passage Difficulty Increases Along a Single Dimension

This second crucial claim for DRP test design has to do with the requirement that the difficulty of prose must increase in regular steps from passage to passage. If this requirement is satisfied and if, as claimed, item completion depends solely on prose comprehension, then the difficulty of test items will increase step by step. The passage in which the reader can no longer complete the items correctly can be taken to represent the limit of his or her reading ability.

The DRP Test is sometimes compared to jumping hurdles, as follows (from State Education Department, 1979a):

> The passages on the test may be thought of as a series of hurdles that the reader must clear. The first passages are easiest, representing the lowest hurdles. As the test progresses, the passages get harder. . . . Just as we might describe a jumper's ability in terms of the height (in feet and inches) of hurdles cleared, so can the reader's ability be defined in terms of the difficulty (readability) of text that can be understood.

Implicit in this analogy is the assumption that different passages present the same type of demands to a different degree, rather than different sets of demands. In the case of the jumper, the difficulty of clearing a hurdle is defined in terms of a single dimension, height, and that is the only way in which the hurdles vary. If, in addition, some were very wide and deep, others set on fire, and others standing in pools of water, there would be no single way to account for the jumper's performance. In order for the test to work in an analogous manner, as intended, the difficulty of reading passages must be definable in terms of some consistent set of properties, and the passages must not vary in other ways which can affect the demands they present to a reader.

DRP test design rests on the premise that differences in the difficulty, or readability, of prose can be accounted for by certain quantifiable structural features of the prose. Prose difficulty of DRP passages is scaled in terms of "DRP units," which are derived from readability scores calculated by using Bormuth's (1969) mean cloze formula. This formula predicts the readability of text from (a) the proportion of easy (i.e., common) words, (b) the average length of words, and (c) the average length of sentences, in the text. The formula, incorporating these three quantifiable features of text, yields a numerical score which can be converted to DRP units. Passages are ranked in order of difficulty on the scale of DRP units (State Education Department, 1979a).

Prose difficulty, however, unlike the difficulty of clearing a hurdle, is not tied to a single natural dimension like hurdle height. On the contrary, it derives from the combined effects of content, organization, and structural properties, of a text (Davison, Kantor, Hannah, Hermon, Lutz, & Salzillo, 1980; Freeman, 1978). The factors which are considered in calculation of DRP units (proportion of easy words, word length, and sentence length) do not themselves constitute or determine prose difficulty; they are simply taken as a reflection, or index of it. This is somewhat analogous to judging the relative wealth of people in a neighborhood by the number and make of cars each family owns. While those facts do not actually determine wealth, they may be a fair reflection of it in many cases. On the other hand, the correlation (between cars and wealth) will be imperfect; the index will sometimes yield wrong predictions. And since the notion of wealth is a composite of many contributing factors, and can vary along more dimensions than simply magnitude (e.g., permanence, liquidity, tangibility of assets), the index might sometimes fail to reflect significant qualitative differences from one case to another.

Research has shown that the quantifiable features of text which are used to predict difficulty (but which do not actually determine it) often bear a positive correlation with some properties of text which do contribute to difficulty (but which are not directly quantifiable). (For overviews of relevant readability research, see Freeman, 1978; Gilliland, 1972; Klare, 1975). But what makes a text easy or hard to read is generally a complex array of interrelated properties, and any particular text may have significant properties which escape measurement by a formula since they bear no regular relationship to word frequency, word length, or sentence length. This means that texts can vary in terms of the comprehension tasks they present to a reader, but that this variation will not necessarily be reflected in differences among the numerical readability scores assigned to them by a formula.

In the Description section of this report we described specific language properties of DRP passages which shape the comprehension tasks those passages present to a reader. Our examination showed that difficulty levels, as represented by test passages, can be differentiated in terms of the following (summarized) properties:

1. *Vocabulary.* Passage vocabulary grows more diverse as difficulty level increases and content–word vocabulary becomes more uncommon and technical.

2. *Sentence complexity.* Syntactic complexity does not show patterned variation across passages. Sentence structures of particular perceptual complexity occur only in later passages.

3. *Types of context-dependent items in frame sentences.* Pronouns are particularly common in earlier passages but relatively few in later passages. Definite noun phrases are particularly common in later passages but relatively few in earlier passages.

4. *Presence of explicit antecedent noun phrases (NPs) for anaphoric expressions.* Anaphoric elements in earlier passages are more likely to relate to explicit antecedent NPs in the text, while those in later passages are more likely to have no linguistically explicit antecedent.

5. *Demand for inference in interpretation of anaphoric relations.* Earlier passages are more likely to provide explicit textual support for anaphoric relations, particularly in the form of series of coreferential pronouns. Interpretation of anaphoric relations in later passages is more likely to depend on inferencing.

6. *Use of sentence connectors.* Use of explicit markers of sentence connections increases as difficulty level increases.

7. *Inference of unmarked sentence connections.* Where there is no explicit sentence connector, frame sentences in earlier passages tend to bear specific, locally constrained relationships to adjacent sentences. In later passages these relationships tend to be nonspecific and must be understood in terms of the relevance of each sentence to the topic of the paragraph or passage.

8. *Amount of textual redundancy.* Earlier passages tend to provide redundant indications of meaning; hard words in later passages are surrounded by less contextual redundancy, so that vocabulary knowledge is more important.

9. *Passage content.* Earlier passages deal with concrete, experience-related topics, while topics of later passages are abstract and/or historical.

10. *Demand for real-world background knowledge.* Whereas all passages demand background information about concepts, things, and events mentioned in passages, the type of background knowledge needed grows more abstract as difficulty level increases.

Variation across passages in terms of the properties listed above indicates a gross pattern of differences between the earlier (passages 1 through 6) and later (passages 7 through 12) portions of the test. This pattern—which reflects general

Table 7.   Summary of General Differences between Passages 1 through 6 and Passages 7 through 12

Earlier Passages	Later Passages
• repetition of vocabulary • common words	• diversity of vocabulary • technical, uncommon words • some perceptually complex sentence structures
• frequent pronouns in frame sentences • explicit antecedent NPs for anaphoric elements • coreferential pronoun chains linking anaphoric elements with antecedents	• frequent definite NPs in frame sentences • lack of explicit antecedent NPs • inference of anaphoric relations
• few marked sentence connections • unmarked sentence connections specific and locally constrained • concrete topics • initial "topic sentence"	• frequent uses of explicit sentence connectors • unmarked sentence connections nonspecific constrained by topic relevance • abstract topics • statement of topic delayed (in latest passages)
• demand for background knowledge related to everyday experience	• demand for background knowledge removed from everyday experience

tendencies, rather than discrete sets of characteristics—can be informally summarized as in Table 7.

Of the properties listed in Table 7, those most likely to correlate with the measurable features of word length and sentence length are vocabulary difficulty and sentence complexity. In fact, it appears that vocabulary difficulty plays a dominant role in increasing overall difficulty level in later passages. This is a predictable consequence of using the Bormuth (1969) readability formula, which is constructed so that "difficult" and long words contribute more to overall difficulty (as reflected by the readability score) than sentence length.[3] For short sentences of 4 to 6 words, an increase of one word in sentence length reduces the readability score (indicating increasing difficulty) by about .02, while for sentences of 20 to 22 words, an increase of one word in sentence length reduces the readability score by .004. (See Appendix C of this report for the Bormuth (1969) formula, with a chart detailing the contribution of sentence length to the readability score for sentences of from 1 to 22 words.) In other words, the calculated contribution of sentence length to overall difficulty shrinks steadily as sentences get longer; and at the same time, the contribution of vocabulary difficulty (as indicated by word frequency and length) grows. In ordinary-length sentences of 15 to 20 words, sentence length contributes approximately −.2 to the readability score. If the words in such sentences average 5 letters per word, word length will

---

[3] This observation and the relevant data, including those in Appendix C, were contributed by Arnold Zwicky.

contribute approximately $-.4$, or twice as much as sentence length. Word length in the last paragraph of DRP passage 12 is 6.9 letters per word, which contributes $-.58$ to the readability score, almost 3 times the contribution of sentence length. Writers trying to produce passages of increasing difficulty, using the Bormuth formula as a guide, apparently have to rely heavily on long and difficult words to achieve lower readability scores. Thus we find, for example, *flora* and *fauna* rather than *plants* and *animals, commenced* rather than *started, utilization* rather than *use,* and *delivered inadequate performance* rather than, say, *did not work well.* This tendency, motivated by technical properties of the formula, is reinforced by the fact that limitations of human memory and perceptual abilities impose an upper limit on the length and complexity of sentences which can be processed. Writers can only go so far in subordinating and lengthening sentences; beyond that point they must manipulate vocabulary to lower the readability score.

A second but less direct consequence of the formula is the fact that sentence syntactic complexity, which contributes directly to the reading ease or difficulty of passages, does not correlate well with calculated levels of readability. That is, sentences do not show a regular or patterned increase in complexity from earlier to later passages. This can be attributed in part to the diminishing contribution of sentence length to readability scores from earlier to later passages, and in part to the fact that differences in sentence length tend to reflect differences in complexity only among very short sentences. This is demonstrated by the fact that the sentences in passages 4 and 11 have virtually the same average number of subordinate and coordinate clauses (see Table 1) but the two passages are intended to represent extremes of a wide range of difficulty (separated by 28 DRP units).

It is also the case that longer sentences can vary considerably in complexity without varying much in length (Davison et al., 1980; Freeman, 1978). Thus some sentences in later DRP passages present greater obstacles to processing than others of similar length, and the distribution of these sentences does not correspond to differences in readability scores.

The DRP test passages illustrate some of the problems which can arise when a readability formula is used as a guide to writing—even by writers with good intuitions and judgments about language. (See Davison et al., 1980, for a thorough discussion of this topic.) We are not primarily concerned here with the unnaturalness which characterizes very "easy" prose written to criteria of readability formulas (see Anderson, Armbruster, & Kantor, 1980; Dawkins, 1975; Griffin, 1977b; Lutz, 1974); given the purposes of the DRP test, it seems more important to consider possible pitfalls in writing to those criteria at higher levels of difficulty. The DRP passages are written specially for the test, with the readability formula applied as a measure of the difficulty of the product (Byrne, 1980). In revising prose to achieve a specified difficulty level, there are two options available to a writer: adjusting the length of sentences, and adjusting the proportion of long and/or difficult words in the text. Either procedure can have unintended effects on the comprehensibility of the prose.

First, syntactic processes which serve to shorten sentences can, at the same time, make them more complex and more difficult to process. This is sometimes the case, for example, when nominalizations are used rather than active verbal constructions (Klare, 1976). Thus, the following sentence from passage 9 (about Neanderthal man),

Fashioning such instruments required attention to properties a tool would need for its intended job.

might be more difficult to process than a version such as the following:

In order to fashion such instruments, he had to be aware of properties a tool would need for its intended job.

But the opposite effect would be predicted by the readability formula, since the second sentence above is longer. Another structural device for shortening sentences, which frequently adds complexity, is using a prenominal modifier rather than a relative clause. For example, the following sentence from passage 2 about rain forests (where *it* refers to fruit dropped by monkeys),

It allows the ground animals to eat more.

is shorter, but probably more difficult, than a version with a relative clause:

It allows the animals who live on the ground to eat more.

Similarly, *product standards* (in passage 7) is less accessible than *standards for products,* and *stellar magnitude* (passage 8) is harder than *magnitude of stars,* since in each case the shorter form obscures structural relations (Larkin, 1977).

Other syntactic processes can make meaning more accessible, but either leave sentence length unchanged, or increase it. Thus the following sentence from passage 9, which contains a long clausal subject,

Furthermore, the opinion that [Neanderthal's] posture was bowlegged with head thrust forward is incorrect. (14 words)

may present greater processing difficulty than a version in which the long embedded sentence is shifted to the end of the sentence, as in:

Furthermore, the opinion is incorrect that Neanderthal's posture was bowlegged with head thrust forward. (14 words)

or even:

Furthermore, it is incorrect to believe that Neanderthal's posture was bowlegged with head thrust forward. (15 words)

But the greater comprehensibility resulting from such revisions would not be reflected by a readability score.

An obvious way to adjust either sentence length or the proportion of difficult words in a passage is to change or eliminate words in sentences. But it is clear that seemingly small variations in the prose of a passage, which will lower the measured level of difficulty, will increase the real difficulty of test items within the passage, by altering the density of clues provided in the context. For example, the prose in passage 7 could be made easier by substituting the easier word *another* for the difficult word *communal* in the following sentences:

By setting and maintaining standards, guilds not only protected members but also served an important communal function. The _____ was protected.

And the following would result:

By setting and maintaining standards, guilds not only protected members but also served another important function. The _____ was protected.

But this ostensible simplification in prose (according to the formula) would throw the burden, for comprehension, on the reader's background knowledge and ability to make an appropriate inference about the connection between the sentences, increasing the difficulty presented by the item. On the other hand, this item could probably be made much simpler by one or both of the following small alterations: First, the period separating the two sentences could be changed to a colon, indicating their intended relationship; and second, the complex noun phrase *communal function* could be "unpacked," as in the following:

By setting and maintaining standards, guilds not only protected members but also served an important function for the whole community: the _____ was protected.

But this clearly more accessible version involves a great increase in sentence length, so that the readability score would, falsely, predict greater difficulty.

A writer, in constructing the sentences of a passage, makes choices among the structural options available, consciously or not. As the few examples above show, small variations in prose can have unintended effects on actual reading ease or difficulty, or on the difficulty of items, contrary to predictions of the readability formula. Use of the formula, then, does not adequately control for real effects on passage difficulty; it seems likely that the subjective judgment and intuition of a writer plays the major role in determining the difficulty of prose. But there are at least two possible adverse consequences of this for the test: First, the real processing demands of a passage may not be correctly reflected by its readability score (and its place in the sequence of difficulty); and second, passages ranked along the readability scale may actually present qualitatively different sets of demands to readers, since their difficulty may derive from properties which escape measurement by formula.

Either of the abovementioned possibilities may be true for DRP passages; our examination points in particular to the second. Passages sequenced from the beginning to the end of the test are differentiated most obviously in terms of vocabulary and content, which together change in the direction of harder, more technical words, dealing with more abstract and academic topics. But the overall array of processing demands presented by each passage does not appear to be controlled or consistent with those of other passages. Some properties contributing to linguistic complexity do not necessarily change in the direction of greater difficulty. For example, passage 7 is considerably more difficult than earlier passages, both intuitively and in terms of DRP units; yet its sentence syntax is generally less complex than that of earlier passages, because it has more coordinate constructions and fewer difficult types of embeddings. Passage 4, in contrast, presents greater syntactic complexity, but is easier to read in other respects.

The linguistic complexity of every passage derives from the cumulative contributions of multiple interacting factors. Looking at any one contributing factor (e.g., the structuring of anaphoric relations, or indicators of sentence connections), there is no regular pattern of change from one passage to the next which corresponds to the sequencing of passages along the difficulty scale (even though we can see general patterns differentiating later passages as a group from earlier ones, as summarized above). Simply put, passages can be hard (or easy) for different reasons. They can be ordered on the basis of intuitive judgments of their overall difficulty, supported by the fact that the dominant contribution to that effect is from vocabulary. But even though the measurable indices of difficulty allow ranking of passages along a single scale of difficulty, passages at different points on the scale can and do present different sets of demands to readers.

Accounting for Test Results

Effects from Test Properties. In the preceding discussion we have evaluated two claims which are crucial to DRP test design:

Claim 1: Prose comprehension is both necessary and sufficient for item completion.

Claim 2: Passage difficulty increases along a single dimension.

With regard to the first claim, we have found that the DRP appears to be a test of general knowledge and vocabulary as well as of reading ability. With regard to the second claim, we have noted that test passages can be differentiated not only in terms of their overall levels of difficulty, but qualitatively as well, in terms of the types of comprehension tasks they present to a reader. After the midpoint of the test, the demand for vocabulary and background knowledge escalates. Also, the language processing tasks involved in prose comprehension change qualitatively from earlier to later passages, particularly in the degree and type of inferencing required. These findings raise questions both about the validity of the DRP as a reading test, and about policy and instruction—i.e., what the consequences of the test ought to be.

It is probably safe to say that a satisfactory score on the DRP test would reflect satisfactory reading ability. The problem lies in interpreting low scores. An inadequate performance may be due to inadequate reading ability. However, it is at least possible that the lack of some other type of knowledge or skill may contribute to a poor performance.

General knowledge and vocabulary. It is, in principle, possible that a reader may possess the skills and interpretive strategies which constitute some level of reading ability in the abstract—which ability could presumably be tapped by any appropriate task—but may lack the particular vocabulary or background information necessary for making sense of a given passage. A poor performance in this case would not, strictly speaking, indicate a lack of reading ability; but the test cannot distinguish between the contributions of these distinct types of knowledge.

Background knowledge might bias test results in at least two possible ways: First, possessing information relevant to passage content might promote comprehension and facilitate item completion; and second, lacking relevant background knowledge might impede comprehension to the point that items cannot be completed correctly. Lacking familiarity with passage topics might also interfere with comprehension indirectly, by lowering the reader's expectations about the comprehensibility of the passage (rightly or wrongly), slowing the reading process, and even leading the reader to quit—in which case a score would not necessarily reflect the point where the prose became too hard to understand, but only the point where the topic became too abstruse, intimidating, or boring.

Prior background knowledge could be claimed not to bias test scores only if it were (a) demonstrably irrelevant to comprehension of passage prose and (b) shared by all members of the speech community. The first condition should be testable; the second is, on the face of it, not satisfied by DRP test passages.

Type of prose. Research has shown that the ability to produce a coherent, well-structured discourse varies with the type of discourse, and the purpose and context of performance. For example, some speakers who have difficulty producing narratives on impersonal topics are able to produce highly structured, coherent narratives of personal experience (Labov, 1972). Pratt (1977) observed that the discourse structure of those oral narratives is not significantly different from structure in literary narrative. This suggests that for spoken production, at least, it may be that mastery of a genre will be exhibited in certain contexts but not in others. These findings also suggest that it might be easier to comprehend narratives with which they can identify as principal actors than narratives in which their point of view must be external. Fillmore (1981), discussing the importance of point of view in text comprehension, observed that in histories and descriptive texts the reader must relate to the text world as an outside observer, and from an implicit temporal reference point; sometimes sequences of sentences can be seen to cohere only in terms of that constant external viewpoint. These observations would support an expectation that expository prose, such as that of DRP passages, will be less easily read, in general, than narratives.

Fillmore (1981) also observes that readers interpret the organization of non-narrative texts in terms of their perception of the author's goals. This view is supported by Morgan (1978, p. 113): "Coherence is not a formal property of texts, nor of logical structures of texts, but a function of [the reader's] ability to relate parts of the text to [the author's] plan for achieving some goal." Comprehension and memory for text apparently suffer when text structure and organization do not correspond to the reader's expectations (Kintsch & Greene, 1978).

The DRP might not test a student's ability to read under favorable circumstances, but rather his or her ability to read a certain type of prose: exposition of the sort that might appear in a school textbook, or topics distant from ordinary life. There is a possibility that this property of the test will place at a disadvantage those readers whose experience and familiarity with this sort of expository prose is inadequate. In other words, some readers might do poorly on the tests not just because their abilities to comprehend are deficient, but because their abilities do not function well in the context of expository prose.

General language comprehension. We have noted general patterns of change from earlier to later passages, in the language processing strategies required for prose comprehension, including processing of sentence grammar, interpretation of context-dependent items, interpretation of connections among sentences and other aspects of the type of discourse structure encountered in DRP passages. While proficient reading surely depends in part on the ability to apply comprehension strategies such as these, they are probably in part a matter of general linguistic comprehension (associated with certain types of discourse) rather than strategies specific to the reading situation. The possibility exists, then, that some readers' poor test performance is related to differential requirements for mode-independent linguistic comprehension strategies in passages, rather than to increased demands for abilities associated strictly with reading. In other words, some readers who have trouble reconstructing the meaning of a passage might experience equal difficulty in gaining information from the passage if they could listen to it, suggesting that the difficulty may not be strictly a matter of reading. Here again, the issue is whether a test score reflects just reading ability, or is tied to "hidden" requirements for some separate abilities or kinds of knowledge. The question is important not just for evaluating the test as a measure of reading ability, but also for determining what the consequences of the test ought to be.

Test-taking strategies. The fact that items can demand alternative strategies independent of prose comprehension per se introduces possible inconsistency in the test task and could conceivably affect test performance. For example, items which require reading beyond the frame sentence for clues to the deletion may be harder, for some or all readers, than items where sufficient information precedes the deletion. But the effect of such items, which do not appear to be evenly distributed in the test, will be hidden.

Test format. The sequencing of passages from easiest to hardest builds into the test an assumption of the design (reflected in the hurdles analogy) that readers will continue until they are no longer able to do the task, and then quit. Another possibility is that given this sequential format, the combined effects of the test instructions (which suggest that a student should not expect to finish all the passages), time, and fatigue encourage giving up, and create a bias against later passages independent of their difficulty. This leaves open the possibility of different performance if more difficult passages were encountered early, in a format which did not indicate to the reader a priori the relative difficulty of each passage.

Readers' Background and Test Performance. Trial administrations of the DRP test during the course of its development showed that in general, black students scored significantly lower than white students, and students of low socioeconomic status (SES) did more poorly than high-SES students.[4] As evidence that the DRP is culture fair, the test-makers point to the fact that students' DRP scores correlate highly with their scores on a hard-cloze test: Black students' and low-SES students' scores were lower than white/high-SES students' scores on both tests. The prediction of hard-cloze scores from DRP test scores, in other words, was not biased by race or SES (Koslin, Koslin, Zeno, & Wainer, 1978). This experimental evidence is coupled with the test-makers' claim that prior knowledge and past experience do not affect test performance, to support the conclusion that the DRP is culture fair.

Strictly speaking, what is shown by the experimental findings mentioned above is that the DRP is no more biased than the hard-cloze task used in the study. The question still remains of why black/low-SES students, as a group, achieve lower DRP scores in the first place. Some possible explanations are suggested by our analysis, which shows that despite the test-makers' claim, the basic ability to read (under favorable circumstances, at least) may in itself not be enough for doing well on the test.

A number of researchers have explored ways in which differences between standard and nonstandard varieties of English might interfere with reading, and thus confound the results of reading tests (see Hall & Guthrie, 1980; and Wolfram, Potter, Yanofsky, & Shuy, 1979 for overviews). Dialectal variation in grammar and pronunciation is more likely to interfere with the early acquisition of reading skills than with comprehension of a particular text (Simons, 1979). Such effects would probably be overcome in any students who progress beyond the level of decoding relatively easy text. Therefore, it seems safe to predict that

---

[4] At the time of this report, patterns of scores for non-native English speaking groups were not made available by DRP Test developers.

direct interference from oral dialect differences will not have any major effect on DRP test performance.

A more likely possibility seems to be that differences in social experience, including school experience, and culture-related patterns of language use, equip some groups better than others with the knowledge and skills needed to do well on the test. We have observed that besides basic reading ability, the test demands vocabulary and general knowledge on topics distant from ordinary life (school-type subjects); familiarity with conventions of expository prose; general language comprehension skills applicable to the type of discourse and level of linguistic complexity encountered in test passages; and ability to devise and adapt test-taking strategies to meet requirements of the DRP format. These types of knowledge and abilities must typically be gained through successful school experience, a background which minorities and students of lower socioeconomic status may lack—whether because of unequal access to good facilities, instruction, and the relevant types of school experience; because of conflict between their cultural values and expectations, and those of the dominant culture; or because culture-related patterns of language use and nonverbal communication conflict with the typical instructional situation and interfere with learning (Hall & Guthrie, 1980; Hilliard, 1979; Johnson, 1979; Lewis, 1979; McDermott, 1977; Simons, 1979). Implicit demands of the test may in fact place some minority students at a disadvantage.

CONCLUSION

On the basis of our analysis of 12 DRP passages we can state, first, that the test demands knowledge and skills which can be considered separate from basic reading ability on theoretical and empirical grounds, and which may be acquired (or lacked) by a person independent from acquisition of strategies for comprehending written prose; and second, that the distribution of these implicit demands across test passages does not appear to be controlled by the measure of prose difficulty applied to passages. From this we can predict that when students get low DRP test scores it does not necessarily, or only, mean that they lack a specified level of reading ability; a student's score may be attributable at least in part to lack of some other type of knowledge or ability demanded by the test. Furthermore, it appears possible that properties of the test impose an unequal burden on any racial, ethnic, or socioeconomic groups whose background gives them unequal preparation to meet the implicit demands of the test. From these facts, several possible consequences might follow.

The Validity of the Test may be Challenged
Traditional studies undertaken to determine the validity of the DRP test show fairly high correlations between students' scores on the DRP and on a widely

used test of mental ability[5] ($r = .82$), and between DRP scores and scores on the comprehension subtest of a conventional norm-referenced reading achievement test[6] ($r = .84$) (Koslin et al., 1978). But independent research indicates that general aptitude tests such as the test used in the DRP study are largely measures of language proficiency (Oller & Perkins, 1978), and that traditional reading comprehension tests, similarly, probably test general verbal and reasoning abilities (Greene, 1977; North Dakota Study Group on Evaluation, 1978). One possible interpretation of demonstrated correlations with the DRP, then, is that the DRP also, to some extent, taps general language comprehension strategies, as our analysis suggests.

Other studies of DRP test validity depend upon the fit of DRP data to the Rasch model (Lord & Novick, 1968; Wright, 1977; Wright & Stone, 1979), a theoretical representation of factors influencing test scores. This model states that the probability of a correct response to a test item is a function of the difference between the test-taker's ability and the difficulty of the item. The Rasch model is consistent with the hurdles analogy which is used to explain the design of the DRP test: According to the logic of the model, for a person of given ability, the probability of success decreases as test items (hurdles) get harder. But for the model to be appropriately used, certain assumptions (just two of which will be mentioned here) must be satisfied.

First, the Rasch model assumes that the relative difficulty of test items is the same for all individuals. Available data on the DRP reflects only comparisons among groups (each defined by a range of test scores), in which individual differences, if they exist, would be obscured. Selection of the sample in the relevant studies did not incorporate an adequate index of socioeconomic status, and the sample did not allow separate analysis for Spanish, Asian, or other non-native English-speaking students (Koslin et al., 1978). Consequently, the fit of the data to the model in this regard has not yet been adequately demonstrated.

Second, and most importantly, the Rasch model (as applied to the DRP) assumes that reading ability and prose difficulty are unidimensional (like strength and hurdle height). As we have demonstrated in the previous section, on both points this assumption is not justified.

When a set of test items do not perfectly fit the Rasch model, it is possible to achieve a fit by removing or revising items which do not conform, a practice which has been followed, to some limited extent, in development of DRP passages (Koslin, personal communication, October, 1979). However, as Goldstein (1979, p. 216) observes, "Such a procedure holds no guarantee that the result will have a real life interpretation." What the test measures, in other words, is

---

[5] The IQ test used was the Short Form Test of Academic Aptitude, derived from the CTB McGraw Hill California Test of Mental Maturity.

[6] The California Achievement Test in Reading was used. The multiple-choice comprehension subtest is designed to test "relationships, inferences, recall of facts, and identification of main ideas" (Koslin et al., 1978, p. 73).

whatever is defined by the set of items which happen to conform to the model. Since scaling to the model assumes, rather than demonstrates, that items are consistent in what they test, it is necessary to determine what the demands of the test are independently, as we have begun to do in the present study.

Present Claims About What the Test Tests May be Revised

Since the DRP is part of the Regents Competency Testing Program, this would mean revising the standard performance for high school graduation as well, recognizing that the DRP tests educational outcomes in more areas than just reading.

Correspondences Between Test Requirements and Instruction Can be Reevaluated

The DRP Test draws on areas of knowledge and experience which may be gained outside of conventional reading instruction. Recognizing the diverse demands of the test can lead to identifying the types of language activities and social experiences which will help prepare students to meet the demands. (See Griffin, 1977a, and Smith, 1977, for discussions of the relevance of a broad range of experiences to learning reading.)

Steps Can be Taken to Diagnose Difficulties and Provide Appropriate Instructional Consequences

A mandate to provide remedial instruction to students who need it, and a test to identify those students, are only useful in the context of a program of instruction that is directly related to the abilities students need to develop. Teachers are advised to use students' DRP scores as a guide to selecting instructional materials, by matching the readability level of texts to students' ability as measured by the test (The College Board, 1980b). But a readability score is such an inadequate index of the real demands of a text for any specific reader, that this procedure can hardly increase the likelihood of instruction being directed to students' actual needs.

Since students who fail to perform adequately on the DRP test may do so for a variety of reasons, their needs will certainly be varied as well. And it may be that those needs would not be met by traditional approaches to remedial reading instruction. For example, instruction focused on specific reading skills might not strengthen the preparation of students who primarily lack general knowledge and vocabulary related to the types of topics encountered in DRP passages. Or if students lack general mode-independent strategies for comprehending connected discourse—such as making certain types of inferences about the relatedness of information in different parts of a text—their needs will not necessarily be met by ''remedial'' work on decoding skills, or even sentence-level processing or global comprehension exercises such as summarizing.

Further Work

Implicit in our discussion have been a number of hypotheses about the DRP Test, its design and its demands. We have provided one type of empirical evidence regarding the issues raised. What is needed at this point is a dialogue with other researchers about the claims presented here; one outcome of that dialogue could be the specification of methods for further qualitative and quantitative evaluation of claims we have made about the test.

REFERENCES

Adams, M.J. (1980). Failures to comprehend and levels of processing in reading. In R. Spiro, B. Bruce, & W. Brewer (Eds.), *Theoretical issues in reading comprehension*. Hillsdale, NJ: Lawrence Erlbaum Assoc.

Adams, M.J., & Bruce, B. (1980). *Background knowledge and reading comprehension* (Reading Education Rep. No. 13). Urbana-Champaign: University of Illinois, Center for the Study of Reading.

Adams, M.J., & Collins, A.M. (1979). A schema-theoretic view of reading. In R. Freedle (Ed.), *New directions in discourse processing: Vol. 2. Advances in discourse processes*. Norwood, NJ: Ablex.

Anderson, T., Armbruster, B., & Kantor, R. (1980). *How clearly written are children's textbooks? Or, of bladderworts and alfa* (Reading Education Rep. No. 16). Urbana-Champaign: University of Illinois, Center for the Study of Reading.

Bobrow, D.G., & Norman, D.A. (1975). Some principles of memory schemata. In D.G. Bobrow & A. Collins (Eds.), *Representation and understanding*. New York: Academic Press.

Bormuth, J.R. (1969). *Development of readability analyses*. Final Report, Project No. 9-0052, Office of Education, U.S. Department of Health, Education and Welfare.

Bransford, J.D., & McCarrell, N.S. (1974). A sketch of a cognitive approach to comprehension. In Weimer & D. Palermo (Eds.), *Cognition and the symbolic process*. Hillsdale, NJ: Lawrence Erlbaum Assoc.

Brown, A.L. (1980). Metacognitive development and reading. In R. Spiro, B. Bruce, & W. Brewer (Eds.), *Theoretical issues in reading comprehension*. Hillsdale, NJ: Lawrence Erlbaum Assoc.

Brown, R.W. (1973). *A first language*. Cambridge, MA: Harvard University Press.

Byrne, C. (1980). *Setting the state reference point for the reading test for New York State elementary schools*. Albany, NY: University of the State of New York, Albany State Education Department.

Carroll, J.B., & White, M.N. (1973). Word frequency and age of acquisition as determiners of picture-naming latency. *Quarterly Journal of Experimental Psychology, 25*, 85–95.

Charniak, E. (1978). "With spoon in hand this must be the eating frame. *Theoretical Issues in Natural Language Processing—2*. Urbana-Champaign: University of Illinois.

Chomsky, C. (1980). Stages in Language Development and Reading Exposure. In M. Wolf, M. McQuillan, & E. Radwin (Eds.), *Thought and language/language and reading*. Cambridge, MA: Harvard Educational Review.

The College Board. (1983a). *Degrees of Reading Power Readability Report*. New York: College Entrance Examination Board.

The College Board. (1983b). *Degrees of Reading Power: Understanding the DRP*. New York: College Entrance Examination Board.

The College Board. (1983c). *Degrees of Reading Power: User's Guide: PA Series*. New York: College Entrance Examination Board.

The College Board. (1980). *Degrees of Reading Power Users Manual*. New York: College Entrance Examination Board.

The College Board News, (1981, spring). "Degrees of reading power: New program measures reading ability, effectiveness of instruction."

Davison, A. (1980). *Linguistics and the measurement of syntactic complexity: The case of raising* (Tech. Report No. 173). Urbana-Champaign: University of Illinois, Center for the Study of Reading.

Davison, A., Kantor, R., Hannah, J., Hermon, G., Lutz, R., & Salzillo, R. (1980). *Limitations of readability formulas in guiding adaptations of texts* (Tech. Rep. No. 162). Urbana-Champaign: University of Illinois, Center for the Study of Reading.

Dawkins, J. (1975). *Syntax and readability.* Newark, DE: International Reading Assoc.

Dieterich, T., Freeman, C., & Griffin, P. (1978). *Assessing comprehension in a school setting.* Arlington, VA: Center for Applied Linguistics.

Fillmore, C. (1981, March). Ideal readers and real readers. Paper presented at Georgetown University Round Table, Washington, DC.

Fillmore, C.J., & Kay, P. (1983). *Text semantic analysis of reading comprehension tests.* Final Report, Grant No. G-790121, National Institute of Education.

Freedle, R., & Hale, G. (1979). Acquisition of new comprehension schemata for expository prose by transfer of a narrative schema. In R. Freedle (Ed.), *New directions in discourse processing: Vol. 2. Advances in discourse processes.* Norwood, NJ: Ablex.

Freeman, C. (1978). Readability and text structure: A view from linguistics. In P. Griffin & R. Shuy (Eds.), *Children's functional language and education in the early years.* Arlington, VA: Center for Applied Linguistics.

Gibson, E., & Levin, H. (1975). *The psychology of reading.* Cambridge, MA: The MIT Press.

Gilliland, J. (1972). *Readability.* London: Hodder & Stoughton.

Goldstein, H. (1979). Consequences of using the Rasch model for educational assessment. *British Educational Research Journal, 5* (2).

Goodman, K. & Goodman, Y. (1977). Learning about psycholinguistic processes by analyzing oral reading. *Harvard Education Review, 47* (3). pp. 317–333.

Green, G.M., Kantor, R.N., Morgan, J.L., Stein, N. L., Hermon, G., Salzillo, R., Sellner, M. B., Bruce, B. C., Gentner, D., & Webber, B.L. (1980). *Problems and techniques of text analysis* (Tech. Rep. No. 168). Urbana-Champaign: University of Illinois, Center for the Study of Reading.

Greene, J. (1977). *Doing linguistics on a standardized reading comprehension test: Toward an analysis of Form 5 of the reading comprehension component of the Iowa Tests of Basic Skills.* Unpublished manuscript.

Griffin, P. (1977a). How and when does reading occur in the classroom? *Theory Into Practice, 16* (5).

Griffin, P. (1977b). Reading and pragmatics: Symbiosis. In R. Shuy (Ed.), *Linguistic theory: What can it say about reading?* Newark, DE: International Reading Assoc.

Hall, W., & Guthrie, L. F. (1980). On the dialect question and reading. In R. Spiro, B. Bruce, & W. Brewer (Eds.), *Theoretical issues in reading comprehension.* Hillsdale, NJ: Lawrence Erlbaum Assoc.

Hilliard, A. (1979). Standardized testing and Afro-Americans: Building assessor competence in systematic assessment. In *Testing, teaching and learning: Report of a conference on research on testing.* Washington, DC: National Institute of Education.

Jackson, M.D. & McClelland, J.L. (1979). Processing determinants of reading speed. *Journal of Experimental Psychology: General, 108.*

Johnson, S. (1979). *The measurement mystique.* Washington, DC: Institute for the Study of Educational Policy.

Kintsch, W., & Greene, E. (1978). The role of culture specific schemata in the comprehension and recall of stories. *Discourse Processes, 1.*

Kintsch, W., & Van Dijk, T. (1978). Toward a model of text comprehension and production. *Psychological Review, 85* (5).

Klare, G. (1975). Assessing readability. *Reading Research Quarterly, 1,* 62–102.

Klare, G. (1976). A second look at the validity of readability formulas. *Journal of Reading Behavior*, *8*, (2).

Kleiman, G.M. (1975). Speech recoding in reading. *Journal of Verbal Learning and Verbal Behavior*, *14*.

Koslin, B., Koslin, S., & Zeno, S. (1979). Towards an effectiveness measure in reading. *Testing, teaching, and learning: Report of a conference on research on testing*. Washington, DC: National Institute of Education.

Koslin, B., Koslin, S., Zeno, S., & Wainer, H. (1978). *The validity and reliability of the Degrees of Reading Power Test*. Elmsford, NY: Touchstone Applied Science Assoc.

Labov, W. (1972). *Language in the inner city*. Philadelphia: University of Pennsylvania.

Larkin, D. (1977). Grammar: An important component of reading. In R. Shuy (Ed.), *Linguistic theory: What can it say about reading?* Newark, DE: International Reading Assoc.

Larkin, D., Dieterich, T., Freeman, C., & Yanofsky, N. (1979). *Theoretical considerations in the revision and extension of miscue analysis*. Rockville, MD: Montgomery County Public Schools.

Lewis, D.M. (1979). Certifying functional literacy: Competency testing and implications for due process and equal educational opportunity. *Journal of Law and Education*, *8* (2).

Lord, F.M., & Novick, M.R. (1968). *Statistical theories of mental test scores*. Reading, MA: Addison-Wesley.

Lott, W.A. (1980). *Competency testing in New York State*. Paper presented at Annual Meeting of American Educational Research Association, Boston.

Lutz, J. (1974). Some comments on psycholinguistic research and education, *The Reading Teacher*, *28* (1).

Massaro, D. (1977). Reading and listening. In Kolers, Wrolstad, & Bouma (Eds.), *Processing of visible language*. New York: Plenum.

Morgan, J. (1978). Toward a rational model of discourse comprehension. In *Theoretical issues in natural language processing—2*. Urbana-Champaign: University of Illinois.

Morgan, J., & Green, G. (1980). Pragmatics and reading comprehension. In R. Spiro, B. Bruce, & W. Brewer (Eds.), *Theoretical issues in reading comprehension*. Hillsdale, NJ: Lawrence Erlbaum Assoc.

McDermott, R. (1977). The ethnography of speaking and reading. In R. Shuy (Ed.), *Linguistic theory: What can it say about reading?* Newark, DE: International Reading Assoc.

North Dakota Study Group on Evaluation. (1978). *Standardized reading tests: Do they help or hurt your child*. Grand Forks: University of North Dakota.

Oller, J., & Perkins, K. (1978). *Language in education: Testing the tests*. Rowley, MA: Newbury House.

Palermo, D., & D.L. Molfese, (1972). Language acquisition from age 5 onward. *Psychological Bulletin*, *78*.

Pratt, M.L. (1977). *Toward a speech act theory of literary discourse*. Bloomington: Indiana University Press.

Rubin, A. (1980). A theoretical taxonomy of the differences between oral and written language. In R. Spiro, B. Bruce & W. Brewer (Eds.), *Theoretical issues in reading comprehension*. Hillsdale, NJ: Lawrence Erlbaum Assoc.

Rumelhart, D. (1980). Schemata: The building blocks of cognition. In R. Spiro, B. Bruce, & W. Brewer (Eds.), *Theoretical issues in reading comprehension*. Hillsdale, NJ: Lawrence Erlbaum Assoc.

Schallert, D. (1980). The role of illustrations in reading comprehension. In R. Spiro, B. Bruce, & W. Brewer (Eds.), *Theoretical issues in reading comprehension*. Hillsdale, NJ: Lawrence Erlbaum Assoc.

Schank, R.C. (1975). The structure of episodes in memory. In D. Bobrow & A. Collins (Eds.), *Representation and understanding*. New York: Academic Press.

Sheldon, A. (1978). *Assumptions, methods, and goals in language acquisition research*. Bloomington: Indiana University Linguistics Club.

Simons, H.D. (1979). Black dialect, reading interference, and classroom interaction. In L. Resnick & P. Weaver (Eds.), *Theory and practice of early reading* (Vol. 3). Hillsdale, NJ: Lawrence Erlbaum Assoc.

Smith, F. (1977). Making sense of reading—and of reading instruction. *Harvard Educational Review, 47*(3).

Spiro, R. (1980). Constructive processes in prose comprehension and recall. In R. Spiro, B. Bruce, & W. Brewer (Eds.), *Theoretical issues in reading comprehension*. Hillsdale, NJ: Lawrence Erlbaum Assoc.

State of New York Education Department. (1978a). *Degrees of Reading Power: Description of a new kind of reading test and its related technology.* Albany: University of the State of New York.

State of New York Education Department. (1978b). *The Regents Competency Testing Program: Information brochure.* Albany: University of the State of New York.

State of New York Education Department. (1979a). *Degrees of Reading Power: A brief technical description.* Albany: University of the State of New York.

State of New York Education Department. (1979b). *Reading test for New York State elementary schools, Forms A and B: Manual for administrators and teachers.* Albany: University of the State of New York.

Sticht, T. (1972). Learning by listening. In J. Carroll & R. Freedle (Eds.), *Language comprehension and the acquisition of knowledge*. Washington, DC: Winston and Sons.

Weaver, P. (1977). *Improving reading comprehension: Effects of sentence organization instruction.* Cambridge, MA: Harvard Graduate School of Education. Unpublished manuscript.

Whitaker, H., & Whitaker, H. (1979). *Studies in neurolinguistics* (Vol. 4). New York: Academic Press.

Winograd, T. (1977). A framework for understanding discourse. In M. Just & P. Carpenter (Eds.), *Cognitive processes in comprehension*. Hillsdale, NJ: Lawrence Erlbaum Assoc.

Wolfram, W., Potter, L., Yanofsky, N., & Shuy, R. (1979). *Reading and dialect differences.* Arlington, VA: Center for Applied Linguistics.

Wright, B.D. (1977). "Solving measurement problems with the Rasch model." *Journal of Educational Measurement*, 14(2), 97–117.

Wright, B.D., & Stone, M.H. (1979). *Best test design: Rasch measurement.* Chicago: Mesa Press.

APPENDIX A: (FROM THE COLLEGE BOARD, 1983C, PP. 4–5)

DESCRIPTION OF THE DRP

The DEGREES OF READING POWER program is a system designed to assist in the management of instruction, monitor a student's progress toward educational goals in reading, and provide an outcome measure for school accountability. The program consists of two components: tests to measure students' ability to comprehend prose and readability analyses of instructional materials.

Purposes of the Tests

DEGREES OF READING POWER (DRP) tests measure a student's ability to process and understand nonfiction English prose passages written at different levels of difficulty or readability. DRP test results can be used for several purposes: (1) to evaluate the current level of student achievement in reading, (2) to determine the most difficult prose text a student can use with instructional assistance and in independent reading, (3) to measure growth in the ability to read with comprehension, and (4) to indicate the extent of compensatory or remedial help, if any, that a student may need in order to achieve various personal as well as school-determined expectations or goals.

General Features of the Tests

DRP tests measure a student's ability to process and understand prose written at different levels of difficulty or readability. The tests identify the hardest prose that students can read at different levels of comprehension or with various probabilities of success.

Each DRP test consists of a number of prose passages on a variety of nonfiction topics. These topics are selected at random. Each passage, written specifically for the DRP tests, contains about 325 words. In each test booklet the passages are arranged in order of difficulty, beginning with easy material and progressing to difficult material. Seven of the sentences in each passage contain a blank space, indicating that a word is missing. For each blank, five single-word response options are provided. Students must select the response that most appropriately fits the blank.

DRP tests have the following properties which distinguish them from all other reading tests.

1. Test items are designed so that the *text of the passage must be read and understood* in order for the student to respond correctly. If the sentences with the blanks are considered in isolation, each response option makes a grammatically correct and semantically plausible sentence. However, when the surrounding text in which the test items are embedded is taken into account, only one response is plausible. In order for the student to choose the correct response, the student *must* understand the prose in the surrounding text.

2. All of the content information that is needed to select the correct response is provided in the text of the DRP passages. There is no need to supply information concerning passage content from memory or past experience. This feature in test design means that *only* the ability to understand prose is required for success on the DRP.

3. Regardless of the difficulty of the prose passage, all response options are common words—that is, they occur with extremely high frequency in written materials. Since students should therefore recognize and understand the response options, failure to respond correctly to test items can be unambiguously attributed to a failure to process and comprehend the prose passage.

4. Item difficulty is linked to text difficulty. The student should be able to respond correctly to most of the items in the test up to the point at which the student cannot understand the text of a passage sufficiently well to decide which word is the correct choice.

These unique properties of the DRP mean that, as much as possible, only the ability to read prose at different levels of difficulty is being measured. These properties of the DRP can be confirmed through examination of the passages in any DRP test form. Such review should make it clear that a student who comprehends the prose in a passage ought to be able to answer the items correctly;

that in order to select the correct response the student must understand the prose; and that choosing wrong answers signals a failure to comprehend. Taken together, these properties mean that the DRP is unambiguously a measure of the ability to read with comprehension. By definition, this is the central validity issue of a reading test.

The interpretation of an individual score does not depend on comparisons with the performance of students in a norming sample. The test measures student reading ability on a different type of scale. Just as height and weight can be measured accurately without reference to how tall or heavy other people are, so can reading ability be measured by determining, on the prose difficulty scale, the hardest text that can be read with comprehension. The DRP is a genuine criterion-referenced measure.

Reprinted with permission from *Degrees of Reading Power: User's Guide: PA Series,* copyright © 1983 by the College Entrance Examination Board, New York.

APPENDIX B: (FROM THE COLLEGE BOARD, 1983B)

SAMPLE DRP PASSAGE

Bridges are built to allow a continuous flow of highway and railway traffic across water lying in their paths. But engineers cannot forget that river traffic, too, is essential to our economy. The role of __1__ is important. To keep these vessels moving freely, bridges are built high enough, when possible, to let them pass underneath. Sometimes, however, channels must accommodate very tall ships. It may be uneconomical to build a tall enough bridge. The __2__ would be too high. To save money, engineers build movable bridges.

1 a) wind   b) boats
  c)weight   d) wires
       e) experience

In the swing bridge, the middle part pivots or swings open. When the bridge is closed, this section joins the two ends of the bridge, blocking tall vessels. But this section __3__. When swung open, it is perpendicular to the ends of the bridge, creating two free channels for river traffic. With swing bridges, channel width is limited by the bridge's piers. The largest swing bridge provides only a 75-meter channel. Such channels are sometimes too __4__. In such cases, a bascule bridge may be built.

2 a) levels   b) cost
  c) standards   d) waves
       e) deck

3 a) stands   b) floods
  c) wears   d) turns
       e) supports

4 a) narrow   b) rough
  c) long   d) deep
       e) straight

Bascule bridges are drawbridges with two arms that swing upward. They provide an opening as wide as the span. They are also versatile. These bridges are not limited to being fully opened or fully closed. They can be __5__ in many ways. They can be fixed at different angles to accommodate different vessels.

5 a) crossed   b) approached
  c) lighted   d) planned
       e) positioned

In vertical lift bridges, the center remains horizontal. Towers at both ends allow the center to be lifted like an elevator. One interesting variation of this kind of bridge was built during World War II. A lift bridge was desired, but there were wartime shortages of the steel and machinery needed for the towers. It was hard to find enough ___6___. An ingenious engineer designed the bridge so that it did not have to be raised above traffic. Instead it was ___7___. It could be submerged seven meters below the surface of the river. Ships sailed over it.

6 a) work   b) material
    c) time   d) power
     e) space

7 a) burned   b) emptied
    c) secured   d) shared
     e) lowered

APPENDIX C

The following explanation of Bormuth's (1969) formula is from the College Board (1983a, pp. 9–10):[*]

DRP units index the readability of prose. They are derived from the following mean cloze formula developed by Bormuth (1969):

For passage X, let the number of:
(a) letters in passage = LET,
(b) words in passage = W,
(c) Dale Long List words in passage = DLL, and
(d) sentences in passage = SEN, then

Readability (R) = .886593 − .083640 (LET/W) + .161911 (DLL/W)^3 − .021401 (W/SEN) + .000577 (W/SEN)^2 − .000005 (W/SEN)^3

Readability (R) in this formula is a cloze score, or the proportion of correct restorations that would be expected if a large sample of students, with widely varying abilities, were to be given cloze tests on passage X. Cloze tests are made by deleting words from text according to a mechanical plan and asking students to restore the missing words. The greater the proportion of correct restorations, averaging over all reading abilities, the easier the text.

Bormuth's method for developing the formula was to select at random 330, 110-word prose passages, develop cloze tests by deleting every fifth word, and then administer the tests (using all 5 forms of all passages) to matched samples of students in grades 4–12. The average portion of exact restorations, ignoring misspellings, was calculated for each passage over all students (about 2,600). These average cloze scores became the criterion scores of passage difficulty for the readability formula.

Bormuth then found a more-or-less efficient set of linguistic variables which predicted the criterion scores via multiple regression techniques. As in other research *not* using cloze scores as the criterion, he found that the proportion of easy words (words on the Dale Long List), average word length, and average sentence length predicted the difficulty of the passages as known from the average cloze scores.

The following table compiled by Arnold Zwicky shows (a) the contribution (T) of sentence length to readability score for lengths of from 1 to 22 words, and (b) the change in *t* (ΔT) for each length over the preceding length.

Table C.   Calculation of *T* for 1 ≤ w/s ≤ 22.
$T = -.021401\ w/s + .000577\ (w/s)^2 - .000005\ (w/s)^3$

w/s	T	ΔT
1	−.020829	—
2	−.040533	−.019704

(continued)

Table C. (*Continued*)

w/s	T	ΔT
3	−.059145	−.018612
4	−.076692	−.017547
5	−.093205	−.016513
6	−.108714	−.015509
7	−.123249	−.014535
8	−.136840	−.013910
9	−.149517	−.012677
10	−.161310	−.011793
11	−.172249	−.010939
12	−.182124	−.009875
13	−.191685	−.009561
14	−.200242	−.008557
15	−.208065	−.007823
16	−.215184	−.007119
17	−.221629	−.006445
18	−.227430	−.005801
19	−.232617	−.005187
20	−.237220	−.004603
21	−.241269	−.004049
22	−.244298	−.003029

CHAPTER 8

Talking With Children About Tests: An Exploratory Study of Test Item Ambiguity*

Walt Haney
Boston College
Chestnut Hill, MA 02167

Laurie Scott
The Huron Institute
Cambridge, MA 02138

INTRODUCTION

No sense, no logic, no reality. That is the impression you get from reading through test after standardized test. At first you think there must be some mistake, some one or two test-makers who do a particularly poor job. And some tests *are* truly terrible. But *all* of them I have read are at least bad. (Taylor, 1979a, p. 11)

Articles in popular and even some semiprofessional media similarly criticize individual items on familiar grounds: no right answer, more than one right answer,

---

*This paper was originally published as the seventh of a series of staff circulars distributed as part of The Huron Institute's staff work for the National Consortium on Testing (NCT). This circular was intended to spur discussion on the topic of children's perceptions and reasoning about tests, and to raise important issues worthy of additional attention, not to resolve them. Although the circular was prepared as part of staff work for the Consortium, it does not necessarily reflect the views of the Consortium nor of individual Consortium members.

Though the study reported in this paper was fairly small, the help of numerous people was essential in carrying it out. Thanks go first to Banesh Hoffmann whose gentle but insistent prodding led us to undertake the study. The helpfulness of Susan Kluver and Ken Schmidt was essential to our carrying out the study and is much appreciated. Thanks go, too, to Emily Cahan, Mark McQuillan, Elice Formann, and Mieko Kamii for their help in conducting the study. For their useful comments and criticisms, we express thanks to Anne Anastasi, Mike Garet, David Cohen, George Madaus, Vito Perrone, Michael Beck, Elinor Woods, and Anne Smith. Special appreciation is owed to Norma Robbins who cheerfully and efficiently worked through at least a half-dozen versions of this manuscript. Most of all, however, we wish to express thanks to eleven children, whom we can only call A–K for present purposes.

None of these people are, of course, responsible for any errors or ambiguities which remain in the paper.

unfairness to unconventional types of thinkers, ambiguity, dependence on factors other than those supposedly being measured, etc. Test makers respond as you would expect; instruments, like any human products, are not perfect; given the enormous number of test items in all the published tests, some poor items find their way into such tests despite maintenance of a generally high level of item quality through sophisticated editorial review and item analysis activities. Unless it is demonstrated that such items make up a significant part of a test, their existence does not vitiate its usefulness. (Lennon, 1978, p. 6)

Recent debate about standardized testing covers a wide range of educational, political, scientific, and economic issues. But one recurring theme in the debate concerns the quality of tests and test items. Critics, such as Edwin Taylor, charge that standardized test items often are ambiguous, misleading, and nonsensical. Test publishers, such as Roger Lennon, respond by saying that perhaps a few poor items do find their way into tests, but their number appears to be few and so it is unfair and inaccurate to characterize all standardized tests as ambiguous and misleading by pinpointing attention on just a few such items.

Empirical evidence can be brought to bear on this dispute. This proposition was the idea behind the pilot study reported in this paper. Specifically, the purpose of the study was to gather empirical evidence on the prevalence of ambiguity in commonly used standardized test items. The idea was simple. First, we drew a random sample of test items from several of the most commonly used standardized tests. Second, we administered the test items to a small group of children. Third, we talked with each child about how he or she answered each item. Fourth, we analyzed children's accounts of how they answered items in an attempt to estimate the frequency with which they answered items for reasons which were irrelevant to the skill or the attribute ostensibly being measured by the item.

Though the idea for the pilot study was quite simple, carrying it out was not, as we explain below. First, however, we should make clear that the idea of talking with children about how they make sense of standardized test items is not new. In fact it goes back at least half a century. In the following section, we review previous research along these lines and point out exactly what it is that the pilot study was intended to contribute to past research. In the third section, we describe how the pilot study was designed and carried out. The Analysis and Results section describes two different approaches to analyzing children's accounts of how they answered test items, and presents the results of the study. The fifth section provides a discussion of the pilot study findings, including a review of the problems and difficulties encountered in the study. Some of these will also be discussed briefly in our discussion of the pilot study since they are relevant to interpretation of results presented in the Analysis and Results section. The last section provides a summary and our conclusions from the pilot study.

Before setting out the substance of these sections, we should make clear that the work reported here represents only a *pilot* study. It was designed simply to bring some initial evidence to bear on the question of the prevalence of test item ambiguity. Nevertheless, even as a tentative inquiry the study has yielded some provocative findings. These findings will, we hope, both shed some light on the interpretation of test results and serve to spur additional research along similar lines.

TEST ITEM AMBIGUITY: A LONG-STANDING DEBATE

Concern over the quality of standardized test items and how they are interpreted goes back at least 50 years. Test-item quality was one of the points of contention in the famous series of exchanges on IQ testing between Walter Lippmann and Lewis Terman in the 1920s (see Block & Dworkin, 1976). Also around 1920, Jean Piaget began his long career in psychology by talking with Parisian school children about how they made sense of test questions. As Gruber and Voneche (1977) reported:

> Instead of administering the tests in a standardized way, he interviewed the children at length. The children did not complain. They found this "M'sier" amusing. With him, one was not bored, at all. Instead of simply noting the responses given by the children to the test items, the young Swiss biologist was interested in the how and the why of the answers. What had been at the outset nothing but a boring and annoying test situation became a real dialogue with suggestions and countersuggestions, an argument developed, a deepening of the child's thought, a new method of interrogating children was born. It leads the child to show how he formulates and solves a problem, how he thinks. (p. 53)

"M'sier" Piaget, of course, used this approach not to study the nature of tests, but instead to investigate the nature of children's thinking.

Talking with children about why they answer test questions in particular ways has been advocated by several observers as a way of evaluating test quality. In *The Tyranny of Testing* (1962), Hoffmann suggested an experiment in which students would be engaged in analyzing test quality to seek out ambiguities and errors in test items (see pp. 181–182). Anastasi has noted that test validation may include "analyses of types of errors commonly made on a test and observation of the work methods employed by examinees. The latter could be done by testing students individually with instructions to 'think aloud' while solving each problem" (1976, p. 138).

Taylor has recommended that "test developers must sit down with children individually, watch them take the test, and talk with them afterward about which questions were clear and important and which were confusing or demeaning" (1977a, p. 14).

Systematic studies along these lines appear to be quite rare. Far more common is for adult observers themselves to review tests in order to seek out items that are ambiguous, misleading, or otherwise inadequate. Indeed this practice is common among critics of standardized testing (see Hoffmann, 1962; Houts, 1977: Patton, 1975; Schwartz, 1977: Taylor, 1977a). Taylor, for example, cites the following items from published science tests as examples of ambiguous and misleading questions (1977b, pp. 303–305):

Ocean waves are caused by the
(A)   earth's gravity
(B)   moon's gravity
(C)   earth's motion
(D)   wind's patterns

Many kinds of plants are not able to live on the desert because of the
(A)   high temperature
(B)   low rainfall
(C)   bright sunshine
(D)   poor soil

The practice of having adults review tests intended for children is by no means exclusive to standardized testing critics, however. Publishers of standardized tests typically employ a variety of adults to review items in the process of test development. Commonly this includes reviews by subject matter specialists, measurement experts and, especially in recent years, minority group representatives.

After candidate items are reviewed by a variety of experts, developers typically pretest items by having a sample of children take a tryout test. Candidate items are then chosen for inclusion in the final version of the test on the basis of item tryout statistics such as item difficulties (often called the p-value or percentage of test-takers answering the item correctly) or item discrimination indices (measures of the extent to which item results differentiate between test-takers who score high and low on the total test; see Anastasi, 1976, pp. 206–215, or Henrysson, 1971, for details on how such indices are calculated). Defenders of standardized tests often claim that test critics ignore such procedures. In his critique of Hoffmann's book *The Tyranny of Testing,* Dunnelle (1964), for example, charged that

> . . . Hoffmann completely ignores the fact that statistical validation of test items is most often an effective means of discovering poor and ambiguous items. Nowhere in his book does Hoffmann mention that item analysis is primarily a means of identifying poorly keyed and ambiguous items. (p. 66)

Despite this disclaimer, these procedures do not necessarily get at the issue of test or item quality from the perspective of individual test-takers which was the point of Hoffmann's critique. This distinction is important because what it is that a test or item measures—that is, its content validity—depends not on what adult experts or critics *think* it measures nor on what item statistics suggest about the item but rather on how individual test-takers perceive and react to the test or item. As Anastasi points out, "Content validity depends on the relevance of the individual's test responses to the behavior area under consideration, rather than on the apparent relevance of item content. Mere inspection of the test may fail to reveal the processes actually used by examinees in taking the test" (1976, p. 135).

To delve into what it is that a test or test item measures for particular test-takers requires some kind of observation or communication with them on an individual basis. This is precisely the sort of interchange which takes place between test administrator and test-taker in many sorts of individualized testing, and textbooks on individually administered tests suggest a variety of approaches to dealing with unusual and ambiguous answers to individually administered test questions. Matarazzo (1972), for example, offers the following advice in a discussion of the scoring of the Picture Arrangement Test of the Wechsler Adult Intelligence scales:

> The arrangements given in the manuals cover pretty well most of the rational orders which the individual series permits. Occasionally, however, a subject does produce a different one for which he is able to give a convincing explanation, but for which no credit is allowed in the manual. In most instances, it will be found that disallowing the subject's response does not materially influence his total score on the test, but provision is made for the examiner to credit the subject with a reasonable additional score in special cases. More interesting than the question of credits allowed, in such cases, is the explanation which the subject may give for his unusual arrangement. Consistently bizarre explanations are suggestive of some peculiar mental orientation or even psychotic process. (p. 210)

Later in a discussion of extraneous factors which can influence performance on intelligence tests, he argues:

> Emotionality, anxiety, motivation, introversion, extroversion, etc., can influence test scores, but only seldom do they influence performance to such a degree as to *invalidate the test findings as a whole*. More important . . . , however, is the fact that the impacts of these personality factors, far from being sources of error, must be looked upon as significant aspects of the individual's global intellectual capacity. (p. 484, emphasis in original)

Though unusual and ambiguous interpretation of individually administered test items has thus been clearly recognized, there appears to have been little systematic research on this point from the perspective of individual test-takers, particularly with respect to group-administered tests. In the remainder of this section we describe briefly past work along these lines and identify what the pilot study was intended to contribute to it. In the concluding section, we will refer also to additional relevant research, some of which came to our attention only after our investigation was begun.

In its early years, the National Association of Educational Assessment (NAEP) undertook an unusually wide range of investigations in the course of item or, to use NAEP's term, exercise development. One of the studies involved talking with school children after they had taken the NAEP exercises (Finley & Berdie, 1970):

A small number of examinees, judged to be the least able in each class, were interviewed carefully after each group administration. They were asked about the exercises and any problems they encountered. The results of the study are based primarily upon interviewer, teacher and student comments.

The major conclusion was that the exercises, as they existed in the spring of 1967, were basically usable but needed revision. . . .

The major problems with the exercises were directions that were too complex or involved and use of vocabulary that was so difficult that low-achieving examinees had trouble understanding the task or the question. The post-test interviews were particularly productive in identifying specific words, phrases and directions that were incomprehensible to many students. (pp. 61–62)

A second set of investigations involving talking with children about how they made sense of test items were reported to Mehan (1973), MacKay (1973), Mehan and Wood (1975), and Cicourel et al. (1974). In related studies, these investigators (Cicourel et al., 1974) studied how children interpreted and answered a variety of standardized test questions:

After standardized reading, intelligence, and language development tests were given to the first grade children in both schools, a small group of children were asked to explain their answers and to provide the reasons why they answered as they did. The children's accounts were then compared to the official versions provided by test protocol. As in the classroom lesson situation, the children were not always attending to testing material in the way expected by the test protocol. Often this differential perception led the child to a wrong answer, which in turn led to a low test score. (p. 5)

In summary, these investigators (Cicourel et al., 1974) challenged

the conclusion usually drawn from incorrect test scores: that the child being examined lacked particular abilities. Instead they suggest that it is necessary to examine the structure of the child's accounting practices and reasoning processes in order to draw valid inferences about his competence. (p. 5)

Roth's (1974) study employed the individually administered Peabody Picture Vocabulary Test. After analyzing a sample of children's accounts of how they made sense of questions on this test, Roth observed that *"the Peabody Test is insufficiently verbal because it limits the child's verbal performance to matching picture and word.* When the child is encouraged to verbalize about the pictures and words, we find that he knows much more than the test score indicates" (p. 203, emphasis in original). Roth reported that this is true for both black and white, and low-scoring as well as high-scoring children.

In a companion study, MacKay (1974) analyzed how first-grade children arrived at answers to the Cooperative Reading Test (Form 12);

After the children had taken the test I went over it with them, asking them to read the stimulus word or sentence and to tell me why they had chosen the answer they marked. The interviews were audio tape recorded and later transcribed. (p. 220)

Though he does not report results of his study thoroughly, MacKay does provide several examples of what he calls ambiguous items:

> Item 18 is one example of what I am referring to [ambiguity of test items]. The stimulus sentence is "The bird built his own house" followed by pictures of (1) a twig; (2) a birdhouse; and (3) a nest. According to the national norms in the Manual the distribution of answers was: (1) 5%; (2) 59%; and (3) 35%. Number 3 (the nest) was the correct answer. If the relevant skill being measured is understood to be "Identifying an illustrative instance" then the choice of 2 or 3 seems warrantable. Indeed most children seem to have thought Number 2 to be *most* reasonable. The teacher commented on this in an interview after the test was administered:
>> "I saw somebody read the whole thing to himself 'The bird build his own' and they checked the bird house because you build a bird house and bird built . . . his own house—the word house throws them so 'bird built his own house,' well in fairy stories quite often a rabbit builds his own house. There's no reason why in make-believe . . . a bird couldn't [build] his own house. Monkeys do it. We just read a story where monkeys didn't want to build their house. To them house is misleading. If it said the bird built its own nest they would have checked that."
> Perhaps birds do build birdhouses in Walt Disney cartoons and that is the frame of reference the child uses. The test constructor's power is to enforce narrow normative conceptions. (p. 244, teacher's account edited from original)

In conclusion MacKay suggests that "the test fails within its own frame of reference because of lack of clear instructions, lack of standardization, lack of accurate time-keeping, and most importantly ambiguity in many of the items." (p. 245)

Mehan (1978) reports on these and other similar investigations of how children make sense of test items. Again results are not reported comprehensively. "Because of space limitations, only a few examples of the disparity between adult and child perspectives will be presented here" (p. 50). After presenting two such examples, Mehan observes:

> These answers did not result from a lack of knowledge; rather, they resulted from a substantively different interpretation of test materials. Students who answered test questions incorrectly were often performing the very cognitive operation being tested by the questions. Contrary to prevailing educational-testing theory, which suggests that incorrect answers may result from a lack of knowledge, these investigations of children's schemes of interpretation suggest that incorrect answers may result from a discrepancy between adult and student views of the world. (p. 51)

In a booklet entitled "Reading Tests: Do They Help or Hurt Your Children?" Cook and Meier (1976) report on items from the Metropolitan Achievement Test used with children aged seven to nine years. They note numerous instances in which items can be confusing or misleading to young children. Though they do not say how the examples cited were selected, they do suggest that "the test questions in this booklet are typical of those found on all standardized reading tests—not just the MATs" (see also Meier, 1972).

In sum, critics of standardized tests (Cook and Meier, n.d.; Hoffmann, 1962; MacKay, 1973, 1974; Mehan, 1973, 1978) have charged that standardized test items frequently are misleading and ambiguous and do not necessarily measure what they purport to measure—that is, that they lack content validity.

Defenders of standardized tests (e.g., Dunnelle, 1964; Ebel, 1973; Jensen, 1980; Lennon, 1978) have responded to these charges in three ways[1] by arguing that

1. Such criticisms ignore the fact that expert review, item tryout, and test validation procedures help to ensure that poor and ambiguous test items do not find their way into published tests.
2. What may appear ambiguous to an adult may not seem so to a child because adult perceptions of test items do not necessarily reflect how children perceive and experience those items.
3. Even if a few test items are ambiguous or misleading there is no systematic evidence to indicate that they constitute a significant portion of items on any one test, or on standardized tests generally.

The first response seems plausible, yet the fact that critics have identified ambiguous or otherwise poor items among those included on published and widely used standardized tests indicates that such procedures are not infalliable means of screening out such items. The second point is relevant also. Adults' perceptions of test items do not however necessarily pertain to how items are experienced by those with whom they are intended to be used. But the converse of the second point seems equally relevant—what seems ambiguous or misleading from the child's perspective may not seem so from the adult's viewpoint. Very few published studies appear to have addressed the question of ambiguity from the perspective of the test-taker. Among the best of these studies are the related work of Mehan (1973), MacKay (1973, 1974), and Roth (1974). Their studies with first graders in California have demonstrated that children may choose ''correct'' or intended response alternatives without actually applying the skill or knowledge ostensibly being measured by a test item and conversely that a wrong or unintended response alternative may be selected even though the child correctly applies the skill or knowledge ostensibly being measured by the item.

What is unclear from these studies, however, is the third point in the test defender's brief for the defense, namely, the extent to which these findings are generalizable. Though some observers, after recounting several examples of ambiguous or misleading items, have drawn rather sweeping conclusions about all items on a test or even items on standardized tests generally, the prevalence of items which are misleading or ambiguous, from the point of view of the test-

---

[1] Actually, defenders of standardized tests have responded in numerous other ways to the test critics. Other responses deal with such things as social philosophy and educational theory (e.g., see Dunnelle, 1964; Ebel, 1973). The three points listed above seem to us to represent only the direct substantive responses of the defenders to the critics' charges of ambiguity.

taker, has not been systematically investigated. The pilot study reported in this paper was designed to provide empirical evidence on precisely this point.

THE PILOT STUDY

The pilot study was conducted with second- and third-grade children, using items drawn from four of the most commonly used standardized test series. In this section we describe: (a) how children were selected for participation in the study; (b) how test items were selected and put together into composite tests; (c) how these tests were administered; (d) how children were interviewed about the tests; and (e) how children scored on the test.

Participants

Eleven children participated in the pilot study. All were in the same combined second- and third-grade class. The six girls and five boys ranged in age from seven years, eight months to ten years, five months. Four were in the second grade and seven in the third.

These children were not systematically selected from any broader group of children. Initially, we met with a group of parents from the school in which the study was to be conducted and solicited their interest in the pilot study. We discussed with them some of the common criticisms of standardized testing, as well as some of the reasons why standardized tests are widely used. We also described our plans for carrying out the pilot study. Parents who approved of the study plan were asked to allow their children to participate. Only those students whose parents provided written approval were included in the study.

The sample included both black and white children and appeared to include a moderate range in socioeconomic background. No data on race or socioeconomic status (SES) were included in our analyses, however. Since the study was designed as a pilot inquiry, our intent was simply to find a group of fairly typical school children willing and able to participate in the study. Identities of the participants must, of course, remain confidential. For purposes of analysis and reporting they are referred to simply as students A–K.

While the eleven students participating in the pilot study seemed to represent a fairly typical sample of lower- to upper-middle class schoolchildren, one respect in which they may have been somewhat unusual should be noted. All came from a relatively open classroom in which children were encouraged to speak freely and to question and explore their educational interests. This educational background may have made it easier for the children to discuss the test items candidly with us and may have affected the way they perceived and reacted to standardized tests. Nevertheless, all of the children were reported to have taken standardized tests on previous occasions.

Construction of Composite Tests

Items used in the pilot study were sampled from four widely used standardized achievement test series, namely the Metropolitan Achievement Test (MAT); the

Comprehensive Test of Basic Skills (CTBS); the California Achievement Test (CAT); and the Stanford Achievement Test (SAT). According to three independent surveys, these are four of the most widely used standardized achievement test series in the United States. These three surveys are (a) a survey of test use in the nation's 100 largest school districts (Dimengo, 1978); (b) an analysis of instruments used in federally sponsored research on children and adolescents (Heyneman and Mintz, 1976); and (c) a review of state Title I annual evaluation reports (Gamel, Tallmadge, Wood, & Brinkley, et al., 1975).

Relevant test levels were first identified from each of these test series (see Table 1). We attempted to select test levels appropriate for the pilot study sample; that is, levels which were appropriate according to the publishers' designations, for roughly middle of second grade through end of third grade. In two cases, however, no test level spanned this range, so levels for a slightly lower grade range were selected. This seemed preferable to choosing a higher level which might have proven especially difficult for some of the second graders in our sample.

Three subtest areas were treated in the pilot study: reading comprehension, science, and social studies. Each test series at the second–third grade level includes several other subtests, dealing, for example, with spelling, math computations, and reading vocabulary. The subtests of Reading Comprehension, Science, and Social Studies were chosen for inclusion in the pilot study for two reasons. First, for practical reasons we had to limit the areas to be covered. Second, it was assumed that if ambiguity in test items was to show up anywhere it would be in the more complex subject matter areas of reading comprehension, science, and social studies, rather than in the more concrete subject areas of vocabulary and math computations.

Reading comprehension is treated slightly differently in the four test series included in the study. For the sake of uniformity, we therefore defined comprehension for the purposes of this study to refer strictly to paragraph or passage comprehension, not to sentence or word comprehension. Science and social studies subtests are included at the second–third grade levels in only three of the four test series treated in the pilot study, namely the MAT, CTBS, and the SAT. The total pool of items defined by the relevant test levels was: Reading Comprehension, 141; Science, 97; Social Studies, 97.

Rather than administering all of these items, we selected a random sample of them. Using a formula for determining sample sizes (Krejcie & Morgan, 1970), we determined the number of items which would be necessary to attain a .10 accuracy of estimation with a confidence level of .80 (29 for the social studies and science item pools and 32 for the reading items). A random number table was then used to select science and social studies items from each test series so that the proportion selected from each corresponded to the proportion of each series' items in the total pool.

Reading comprehension items were selected in a slightly different fashion. Reading items are not independent of one another in the tests considered. In-

Table 1. Standardized Achievement Tests Used

Test Series	Publisher	Copyright Dates	Level	Intended Grade Range	Form	Subtests	No. of Items
Metropolitan Achievement Test (MAT)	Harcourt Brace Jovanovich, Inc.	1977–1978	Primary 2	2.5–3.4	JS	Reading Science Social Studies	55 40 40
Comprehensive Tests of Basic Skills (CTBS)	CTB/McGraw-Hill	1973	C	1.6–2.9	S	Reading Comprehension: Passages Science Social Studies	18 30 30
California Achievement Test (CAT)	CTB/McGraw-Hill	1977–1978	12	1.5–2.9	C	Reading Comprehension	20
Stanford Achievement Test (SAT)	Harcourt Brace Jovanovich, Inc.	1972–1975	Primary II	2.5–3.4	A	Reading, Part B Science Social Studies	48 27 27

stead, several items (typically four) are based on a single reading passage. If we had selected reading items on a strictly random basis, this would have required children to do more reading per item than is generally required in the actual tests. This likely would have made items more difficult than normal since in each of the test series studied, children are required to read only one passage in order to answer several items. Therefore, we employed a stratified random sampling approach in selecting reading comprehension items. Entire reading passages were randomly chosen from each of the test series. As many complete sets of items (i.e., the reading passage plus all attendant questions) were selected as necessary to provide the requisite number of items. In some cases more than the required number of reading items were included. We could have selected only the exact number of items from each series, but this would have required splitting up some item sets (e.g., taking only two of four items pertaining to a particular reading passage). Since this might have affected the difficulty of these items, we instead decided to take entire item sets, even though the total number of reading comprehension items thus selected was somewhat greater (37) than originally intended (32). We should note that the use of this stratified sampling procedure with the reading comprehension items has the effect of somewhat reducing the statistical power of the inferences which can be drawn with respect to the total pool of reading items. Nevertheless, this was deemed preferable to either making the test unreasonably long or selecting reading items individually rather than in sets as they normally occur in the tests.

Once items, together with relevant illustrations and reading passages, were selected, they were assembled into composite reading, science, and social studies tests. Clear photocopies of individual items were taped together; and photocopies of these ''galleys'' were then stapled together to form test booklets for each child. Although in constructing these composite test booklets we attempted to make reproductions as clear as possible, it should be noted that in some instances photocopied illustrations in the composite tests were not as clear as were the originals in the actual test series. These booklets also included sample questions drawn verbatim from the original test series.

Administration of Composite Tests and Interviews

The three composite subtests were administered under standard testing conditions on three separate days. Each subtest required about half an hour to administer. Following group administration, each child was interviewed individually about each question, with interviews audio tape-recorded for later transcription. The two interviewers both had several years teaching experience and advanced degrees in education, but no special training in interviewing young children. Following a brief conversation intended to put children at ease, each child was given the subtest he or she had just completed. For the social studies and science subtests, each child was asked to describe the alternative answer choices pictured and then, after the interviewer repeated the test question, to explain his or her reasons for selecting a particular response. For the reading subtest each child was asked to read the question and alternative-answer choices aloud (in only a small sample of cases were children asked to read the reading passages out loud) and then to explain reasons for answer selection. Duration of the interviews varied but generally lasted from 25 to 45 minutes for each child, for each subtest.

Absenteeism reduced the number of students participating for two subtests. Nine children took the social studies subtest: ten children took the reading comprehension subtest, and all eleven took the science subtest.

All three subtests were administered after lunch. Most of the interviews took place either in the afternoon immediately after the testing or the following morning. The science interviews were begun on a Thursday afternoon and concluded on Friday morning. The students were noticeably more alert and attentive in the morning than in the afternoon, thus raising the question of the effect that time of day might have on both test and interview responses.

It should be noted that children's reactions to the interview process varied considerably. While most children seemed interested and attentive during interviews, a few grew obviously restless about having to respond to much the same questions for each of 30 test items. Also, in one case, an interview had to be terminated without completing discussion of all items simply because the school-day came to a close and children had to depart to catch school buses.

Standard Test Results

Before describing how interviews with children were analyzed, let us simply summarize the overall performance of the pilot study sample on each of the composite tests. Results of the standard administration of the composite tests are shown in Table 2. The sample of children to whom the test was administered selected the keyed answer (i.e., the one designated by the publisher as the correct answer), for 72%, 67% and 71% of the items for the Reading Comprehension, Science, and Social Studies tests, respectively. Since the composite tests were constructed from items randomly drawn from complete tests, it is impossible to compare this sample performance directly with test norms. However, since the average item difficulty reported by publishers for the items included in the composite tests was .64, .63, and .70 for reading comprehension, science and social studies items, respectively, the performance of the pilot study sample seems to correspond at least roughly with typical performance of the national norm samples for these test series.[2]

One other point should be noted from Table 2. On each of the composite tests a fair number of items were skipped by children (ranging from 31, or 3%, items on the Reading Comprehension subtest, to 7, or 0.9%, on the Social Studies

---

[2] Average difficulties based on spring second-grade norm samples or fall third-grade where only these data were available. Note that while average number of items correct for the pilot sample is slightly higher than average item difficulties, 7 of 11 students were third graders.

Table 2.   **Standard Results on Composite Tests**

	Composite Test		
	Reading Comprehension[a]	Science	Social Studies[b]
Sample Characteristics			
No. of Students	10	11	8
No. of Items	37	29	29
Total No. of Item Responses	358	319	232
Test Performance			
Keyed Answer Chosen			
Total	258	214	164
Mean/Child	25.8	19.4	20.6
% of Items	72	67	71
Unkeyed Answer Chosen			
Total	69	85	61
Mean/Child	6.9	7.7	7.6
% of Items	19	27	26
Item Skipped			
Total	31	20	7
Mean/Child	3.1	1.8	0.9
% of Items	9	6	3

[a]Reading Comprehension test performance is reported on a total of only 358, since 12 items for one child were not included in the interview process.

[b]Excluded from this summary of results is the Social Studies test for one student whose interview on this test was used in the training of raters for the analytical rating of interviews with children.

subtest). In many cases students skipped items because, as they later explained they "couldn't get it" or "couldn't read it." In two instances, children skipped items because of clerical mistakes: one simply forgot to mark an answer and one girl inadvertently skipped a whole page of five items, all of which in the subsequent interview she was able to answer correctly.

ANALYSIS AND RESULTS

Ambiguity refers to uncertainty or doubtfulness of meaning. For the purposes of our investigation, ambiguity in children's perception and reasoning about test items was defined in terms of contrasts between the standard scoring of items reported above, and our interviews with children. Two types of contrasts served to define ambiguity; (a) when a child marked the "right" answer, but the interview indicated he or she had not applied the general skill ostensibly measured by the item, or (b) when a child marked an "incorrect" answer, but the interview indicated that he or she had in fact applied the skill ostensibly measured. We will explore shortly exactly how these conditions were identified in terms of our analyses. Nevertheless, we wish to make clear from the start that this general approach includes certain phenomena that often might not be considered signs of ambiguity and excludes others that might reasonably be considered to be signs of just that condition. Nevertheless, this seems to us a reasonable place to start. Later, in the Discussion and Summary sections, we will discuss alternative approaches to defining and identifying ambiguity in test items.

Tape recordings of interviews with individual children were transcribed and verified by checking them against the tape recordings. These transcriptions of interviews served as primary source materials for all subsequent analyses. Two types of analyses were performed on the transcriptions of interviews with children. The first was an analytical rating of each child's interview transcript, item by item in the order in which items appeared on each composite test. The second—what we call a holistic rating—was based on sets of item interviews, comprised of the test item and item statistics, together with an account of how all children interviewed described their perception and means of answering that particular item. In this section, we first describe the analytical rating and results, then the holistic rating and results. The concluding part of this section describes overall findings from both rating systems, in terms of how results from the two approaches compare.

Analytical Ratings

The analytical ratings consisted essentially of having two individuals (who had not been involved either in administration of the composite tests or in interviewing children about the tests) independently rate each account of how a child answered each item, using an analytical rating scheme. The two raters were both professional staff members of the Huron Institute, one trained in developmental psychology and the other in language and reading. In a moment we will describe the rating scheme, how it was applied, and how ambiguity was defined in terms of analytical ratings. First, however, let us simply describe the issues addressed in the analytical rating system.

The analytical rating scheme deals with aspects of children's thinking about test items which have been suggested to affect children's test performance. Specifically the six aspects of the rating scheme dealt with: (a) the answer alternative selected; (b) the child's perception of the item stimulus; (c) the child's perception of the response alternatives; (d) the process by which the child appeared to reach an answer to the question; (e) the apparent validity of the logic used in light of the attribute ostensibly measured by the item if the child appeared to be reasoning in answering the item question; and (f) whether or not the child cited information or applied knowledge extraneous to the item or what it ostensibly measured.[3] These were elaborated as follows:

---

[3] We should note that our rating scheme originally included a seventh issue, namely whether or not the child's account indicated that an item required any knowledge or behavior other than that ostensibly measured by the item or provided in the item stimulus. We included this because some test

Answer Alternative Selected. This was the most straightforward aspect of the analytical rating scheme; namely whether the child (a) marked the answer alternative which the test publisher's answer key indicated as correct (the keyed answer, (K); (b) marked a different answer choice, indicated by the publisher to be incorrect (an unkeyed answer, UK), or (c) no answer alternative was marked (skipped, S). Note that hereafter, we refer to "keyed" and "unkeyed" answer alternatives to indicate publishers' designations of correct and incorrect answers.

Perceptions of Item Stimulus. This refers to how the child perceives what is depicted, presented and/or asked in the item. Raters were instructed to judge whether the child perceived the stimulus as apparently *intended* (or if *unintended;* that is, where the perception was not one apparently intended by the item author, and was *not* directly related to the skill ostensibly measured by the item). These categories are abbreviated as IPS and UPS in this paper. What we were trying to get at here was whether or not the child perceived the item stimulus in unintended fashion which was *unrelated* to the attribute ostensibly measured by the item. This rating category was not applied with reading items since we decided that there would be no way in which children's reading aloud of reading passages would reveal unintended perceptions *unrelated* to the skill of reading comprehension.

Perception of Response Alternatives. Children's perceptions of response alternatives were rated in similar manner as intended or unintended (abbreviated as IPR or UPR). Thus on a reading test item if a child could not read one response alternative, his perception would be rated intended, because the perception of the response alternative related directly to the skill ostensibly measured. However, if a child perceived a picture in unintended fashion on a science item this would be rated UPR, since visual perception was not part of what the item ostensibly measured.

Process of Reaching Answer. Under this category, raters were asked to judge what process the child used to reach an answer to a question. Specifically raters were asked to indicate whether or not the child evidenced some direct logic or reasoning (R); derived the answer indirectly via process of elimination of alternative answers (E); guessed an answer or at least said he or she guessed (G): or when explaining his or her answer spontaneously recognized that he or she had made a mistake when taking the test under standard conditions and corrected him or herself without assistance from the adult interviewer (M).

---

critics have charged that some items implicitly require such knowledge and that such requirements can affect test-takers' performance in a manner irrelevant to the attribute ostensibly being measured. In no cases, however, did a rater indicate that a child's response revealed that an item assumed such extraneous knowledge. This is a substantive finding but since there was no variation with respect to this issue in the analytical ratings, we will not discuss it further in this section. Nevertheless, we will come back to this point in the Discussion section, since some items clearly do require extraneous knowledge, even if children's responses do not reveal this requirement.

Reasoning. If the child was judged to have applied some sort of direct logic or reasoning in reaching an answer, the raters were further asked to judge whether the reasoning was valid (V) or invalid (InV) *in light of the child's perceptions of the item stimulus and response alternatives.* Note that it was possible for a child's reasoning to be rated V or InV, regardless of whether or not he or she selected the keyed or unkeyed response alternative.

Extraneous Knowledge. If the child's reasoning was rated valid, the raters were further asked to judge whether the child's logic exhibited knowledge or behavior extraneous to the attribute ostensibly measured (E) or whether the child's logic was directly related to the attribute ostensibly measured (NE).

Ratings on several of these issues obviously depend on what it is that the test items ostensibly measure. On this point raters were instructed to rely directly upon publishers' statements of what it is that these reading comprehension, social studies, and science items measure. Publishers' general descriptions of what each of the three types of test items measure formed the basis for raters' judgments about what items ostensibly measured. These descriptions may be summarized as follows for each of the three types of items.

Reading Comprehension.   Reading Comprehension subtests (specifically paragraph or passage comprehension), according to manuals of the four test series employed, test two components of reading: literal comprehension and implicit, inferential, or critical comprehension. The SAT Comprehension subtest employs completion items in which students are asked to choose one of four words to complete a sentence. The other three series use complete reading passages followed by a set of multiple-choice items pertaining to the passage.

Science.   The MAT Science items are intended to measure knowledge, comprehension, inquiry skills, and critical analysis in physical science, earth and space science, and life science (Prescott, Balow, Hogan & Farr, 1978). The SAT is designed to test concepts of matter and energy, change in the physical environment, form and function of living things, environmental interaction, and basic skills of science (Madden, Gardner, Rudman, Karlsen, & Merwin, 1973). The items are intended to "assess the student's ability to investigate problems in science and, to a lesser degree, to recall scientific facts or concepts" (CTB/McGraw-Hill, 1976, p. 5). Science items from all three series are intended to be read aloud by the examiner, and response choices are in the form of illustrations.

Social Studies.   Test series' manuals also describe the content of the social studies subtests. The MAT Social Studies subtest is designed to test knowledge, comprehension, inquiry skills, and critical analysis of geography, history, economics, sociology, political science, anthropology, and psychology (Prescott et al., 1978). The SAT is said to measure achievement in geography, history, economics, political science, sociology and anthropology (Madden et al., 1973). The CTBS asserts that its items "measure the student's grasp of concepts, generalizations, and inquiry skills necessary for effective problem solving in social studies." These skills are tested in settings drawn from four content areas: the physical environment, the social environment, the political/economic environment, and history" (CTB/McGraw-Hill, 1976, p. 5). As with science items all social studies items are read aloud by the examiner; pupils select their answers from among three or four drawings.

Raters were familiarized with these statements of what each type of item ostensibly measured, and to help them keep this in mind when they were rating children's accounts of how they answered items, specific content and skill designations for each item were recorded on the rating forms they used. Also prior to rating of the transcripts it was indicated on rating forms whether a child had marked keyed, unkeyed alternatives or had skipped the item in taking the test. This was done because this aspect of rating was simply clerical, calling for no critical judgment.

Other ratings were of course not so straightforward. Ratings pertaining to children's perceptions of item stimuli and response alternatives, the process by which they reached answers, the relevance of their logic to the attribute ostensibly measured, and whether or not the child employed extraneous knowledge, all called for considerable judgment on the part of the raters. The last two rating categories were pertinent only if the rater judged the child to have applied logic or reasoning in the process of selecting an answer.

The entire process of analytically rating an interview transcript regarding a single item is depicted in Figure 1, in the form of a decision tree. In terms of this decision tree there are 48 different possible outcomes for a complete rating of any one child–item interview. These are numbered for easy reference. Rating outcome 4, for example, would indicate that the child's reasoning followed the following sequence: keyed answer (K), intended perception of stimulus (IPS), intended perception of response alternative (IPR), reasoning employed in deriving an answer (R), reasoning valid with respect to the attribute ostensibly measured (V), and no extraneous information used in deducing an answer (NE).

Application of this rating scheme obviously raises questions of reliability since raters are asked to draw some very subtle judgments. Prior to ratings, a set of written instructions regarding use of the rating scheme was prepared and discussed with both raters in order to clarify ambiguities concerning rating categories. An initial tryout of the rating scheme, by two independent raters on the same child's interview transcript, showed that the ratings had only moderate interrater reliability—less than 70% agreement. The rating scheme was again discussed with the raters and after rating instructions were refined the raters again were asked independently to rate the same interview transcript. This second

Figure 1.

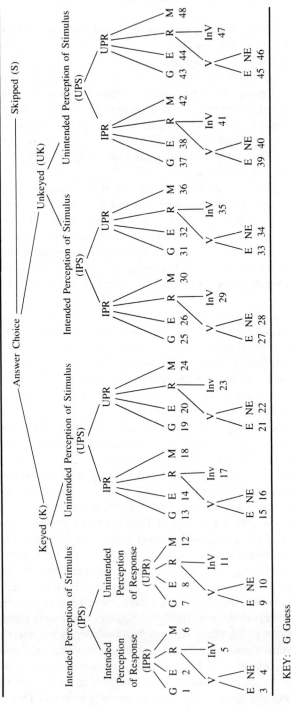

KEY: G Guess
E Elimination
R Reasoning
M Mistake
V Valid
InV Invalid
E Child Used Extraneous Knowledge
NE Child Did Not Use Extraneous Knowledge

tryout produced an interrater consistency of 78%. Inspection of items on which raters disagreed suggested that in some cases raters had simply made clerical errors or had misinterpreted particular response categories; for example, one rater had misunderstood the point that if a child showed an unintended perception of a *single* alternative answer in a way unrelated to the skill ostensibly measured, then the rating should be unintended perception of response alternatives (UPR) rather than intended (IPR). These points were brought to the attention of raters and they were asked to check over their second tryout ratings both for clerical errors and in light of a careful review of rating instructions. After these self-corrections by raters, the interrater consistency on the second tryout increased to 90%—a level of consistency which seemed reasonably acceptable.

Both raters then independently rated each transcript for each subtest for each child (excepting the social studies transcript for child B which was used in training the raters). After the ratings were corrected for clerical errors, interrater consistency for the Reading Comprehension, Science, and Social Studies subtests were 90%, 88%, and 90%, respectively.[4] For the purposes of analysis reported in the next section, items on which raters disagreed were resolved through discussion between the two raters and one of the investigators. Nevertheless, since these cases of disagreement reveal several important points about the inadequacies of the rating scheme, and also about the subtleties of drawing inferences about children's reasoning, we shall come back in the next section with a discussion of findings to recount some of the apparent causes of disagreement.

Analytical Rating Results

Findings from the analytical ratings are presented in two parts. First described are aggregate results of analytical ratings of children's accounts of how they answered particular test items, and then the detailed results of the analytical ratings.

Aggregate Results of Analytical Ratings.   Table 3 presents the results of analytical ratings of transcripts of interviews with children about how they answered items on the composite tests. Ratings pertain to the five categories under which raters were asked to make judgments concerning transcripts of interviews with children, as explained above. As depicted in the decision tree in Figure 1, the last two categories of rating were contingent on previous ones.

In only a single instance was a child rated to have perceived an item stimulus

---

[4] It should be noted that the consistency data cited here and above are based on items answered (i.e., excluding skipped items) and refer to consistency over the total set of ratings for items (i.e., consistency in where item ratings came out at the bottom of the decision tree shown in Figure 1). Thus consistency for individual ratings generally were somewhat higher than 90%. More discussion on this point is provided in the next section.

Table 3.   Aggregate Results of Analytical Ratings of Item-Interviews

	Reading Comprehension[a]		Science		Social Studies	
Total No. of Item Interviews	358		319		232	
Total No. of Interviews	327		299		224	
Perception of Item Stimulus						
Intended (IPS)	NA		299	(100%)	224	(100%)
Unintended (UPS)			0		0	
Perception of Item Response Alternatives						
Intended (IPR)	327	(100%)	285	(95%)	177	(79%)
Unintended (UPR)	0		14	(5%)	48	(21%)
Process						
Guess (G)	18	(5%)	23	(8%)	22	(10%)
Elimination (E)	4	(1%)	1	(0%)	1	(0%)
Mistake (M)	8	(2%)	11	(4%)	2	(1%)
Reasoning (R)	297	(91%)	264	(88%)	200	(89%)
Reasoning (for R items only)						
Valid (V)	237	(80%)	192	(73%)	136	(68%)
Invalid (InV)	60	(20%)	72	(27%)	64	(32%)
Information (for V items only)						
Extraneous Info. Used (E)	4	(2%)	4	(2%)	1	(1%)
No Extraneous Info. Used (NE)	233	(98%)	188	(98%)	135	(99%)

[a]Since children were not systematically asked to read reading comprehension passages, ratings concerning perception of item stimulus were not applicable to reading comprehension items.

in a way that was unrelated to the skill ostensibly measured by the item. Unintended perceptions of response alternatives were more common—in 5% of the cases for science items and 21% of the cases for social studies items. The findings of zero cases of unintended perceptions of response alternatives for reading items resulted at least in part from the point noted above—namely, that it would be hard for children's reading aloud of reading item response alternatives to reveal unintended perceptions *unrelated* to the skill of reading comprehension.

Ratings of the process of manner in which children picked response alternatives indicated that in the vast majority of cases students evidenced some direct form of reasoning or logic in selecting answers (91% for reading comprehension, 88% for science, and 89% for social studies). The second most common means of deriving answers appears to have been guessing (in 5% of the cases for reading comprehension, 8% for science, and 10% for social studies).

In a small number of cases (2% of reading items, 4% for science items, and 1% of social studies items) children had simply made a mistake in marking their answers. Instances were rated as mistakes only when children spontaneously changed their answers in the course of the interview, without prompting from the adult interviewer. In still fewer cases were children rated to have employed some form of elimination in selecting response alternatives (in 0–1% of the cases for the three subtests).

In cases where children were rated to have employed some direct form of reasoning in answering test questions, a subsequent rating pertained to validity of children's reasoning in light of their perception of item stimulus and response alternatives and in view of the attribute ostensibly measured by the item. The attribute ostensibly measured may have been validly demonstrated even though the child selected an unkeyed response alternative.

The InV rating category was intended to designate reasoning which was not a reflection of the attribute ostensibly measured, even though such reasoning might be interpreted as valid in terms of other attributes or points of view. In short a child's reasoning could be rated invalid regardless of whether the child picked the keyed or the unkeyed response alternative. In the aggregate, children's reasoned responses were rated invalid in 20% of the reading comprehension items, 27% of the science items, and 32% of the social studies items.

The last rating category, extraneous knowledge used, pertained only to those cases in which children were rated to have employed reasoning validity reflecting the attribute ostensibly measured. In such cases, raters were asked to indicate whether or not children in their reasoned accounts of how they selected response alternatives employed extraneous information not actually given in the item stimulus. Ratings indicated such use of extraneous information to be relatively rare—in only 1 to 2% of the cases rated to show reasoning validly reflecting the attribute ostensibly measured.

Detailed Results of Analytical Ratings. Detailed results of ratings, in terms of final rating categories of the decision tree depicted in Figure 1, are given in Table 4. What do these ratings mean? In particular, how might we go about defining ambiguity in test items in terms of these ratings? Let us begin by trying to define this condition (and to estimate its prevalence) by noting its absence.

Case of Clarity. To avoid a linguistic infelicity, we refer to cases of clarity in children's encounters with test items, rather than to "unambiguities." As with ambiguity there are two distinct forms of clarity in children's encounters with test items. First, children may select a correct, or in our terms keyed, answer to a question while actually applying the skill or attribute which the test item ostensibly measures. Second, they may choose an incorrect, or unkeyed, answer while failing to demonstrate, at least in some respect, the skill or attribute ostensibly measured.

In terms of our rating scheme, these two types of clarity in children's encounters with test items may be defined as follows: First, keyed answer clarity occurs when the child chooses the keyed response alternative, shows the intended perception of item stimulus and response alternatives, evidences reasoning validity related to the attribute ostensibly measured, and does not apply extraneous information in the reasoning process. In terms of notation used in ratings, this could be summarized as K–IPS–IPR–R–V–NE, leading to final categorization number 4 as shown in Figure 1. Clarity with respect to unkeyed answers can be defined to refer to cases in which the child picks an unkeyed answer, while

Table 4. Number and Percentage of Item Interviews in Each Analytical Rating Category

Rating Category # (See Fig. 1 for Explanation)		Reading Comprehension		Science		Social Studies	
		No.	%	No.	%	No.	%
	1	7	2.0	11	3.4	10	4.3
	2	2	0.8	1	0.3	1	0.4
	3	3	0.8	3	0.9	1	0.4
	4	231	64.5	182	57.0	111	47.8
Keyed	5	14	3.9	9	2.8	12	5.2
Response	6	0	0	1	0.3	0	0
Selected	7	0	0	1	0.3	4	1.7
	10	0	0	5	1.6	20	8.6
	11	0	0	1	0.3	3	1.3
	12	0	0	0	0	1	0.4
	17	0	0	0	0	1	0.4
	25	11	3.1	9	2.8	7	3.0
	26	1	0.3	0	0	0	0
	27	1	0.3	0	0	0	0
	28	1	0.3	0	0	0	0
Unkeyed	29	46	12.8	60	18.8	34	14.6
Response	30	8	2.2	9	2.8	0	0
Selected	31	0	0	2	0.6	1	0.4
	33	0	0	1	0.3	0	0
	34	1	0.3	1	0.3	4	1.7
	35	0	0	2	0.6	14	6.0
	36	0	0	1	0.3	1	0.4
Skipped		31	8.6	20	6.3	7	3.0
	Total	358	99.9	319	99.6	232	99.6

[a]No item interviews were rated as belonging in categories 8, 9, 13, 14, 15, 16, 18, 19, 20, 21, 22, 23, 24, 32, 37, 38, 39, 40, 41, 42, 43, 44, 45, 46, 47, 48.

perceiving item stimulus and response alternatives in intended fashion, but without demonstrating valid application of the skill ostensibly measured (i.e., the process being guessing or invalid reasoning). In terms of our notation this corresponds to UK–IPS–IPR–and G or R–InV, chains of rating designated by numbers 25 and 29 in Figure 1.

The proportions of item accounts so rated are given in Table 5. Given that clarity or lack of ambiguity is defined by these outcomes of our rating scheme as applied to transcribed accounts of how children reasoned about test items, it can be estimated that no ambiguity was apparent in 90%, 85%, and 68% of the cases in which children picked keyed answers on reading comprehension, science, and social studies questions, respectively. Similarly in cases in which children picked unkeyed response alternatives, no ambiguity was apparent in terms of our rating scheme in 83%, 81%, and 67% of the reading comprehension, science, and social studies item interviews, respectively. Summing across both keyed and unkeyed answers, clarity as defined above was apparent in 88%, 84%, and 68% of the three types of items, if we exclude items which children skipped (or 80%, 79%, and 66% of the cases if we *include* instances in which children skipped items while actually taking the composite tests).

Cases of Ambiguity. One might attempt to define ambiguity simply in terms of complements of the foregoing percentages, that is, by subtracting the foregoing percentages from 100%. However, all that is not clear in terms of children's perceptions of test items is not clearly unclear. In other words, the boundaries between clarity and ambiguity of children's perceptions of test items are themselves rather fuzzy. Therefore, let us here attempt to define such ambiguity more directly.

As suggested in the literature reviewed in the section Test Item Ambiguity, ambiguity is of two sorts: First, children may choose the keyed answers without applying the skill or attribute ostensibly measured; and second, children may demonstrate the skill or attribute ostensibly measured, even though they select an unkeyed or wrong answer.

Table 5. Cases of Clarity in Analytical Rating Results

		Subtest		
		Reading Comprehension	Science	Social Studies
Total No. of Item Interviews		358	319	232
Keyed		258	214	164
Unkeyed		69	85	61
Skipped		31	20	7
Clarity in Keyed Answers				
Rating Chain	*Rating Outcome*			
K–IPS–IPR–R–V–NE	*in Fig. 1*			
No.	1	231	182	111
% of Keyed Answers		89.5	85.0	67.7
Clarity in Unkeyed Answers				
Rating Chain	*Rating Outcome*			
UK–IPS–IPR–G–R–InV	*in Fig. 1*			
	25			
No.	29	57	69	41
% of Unkeyed Answers		82.6	81.2	67.2
Clarity—Total				
No.		288	251	152
% of Total (excluding skipped items)		88.1	84.0	67.6
% of Total (including skipped items)		80.4	78.7	65.5

The first instance, selection of keyed answers without clear demonstration of the attribute of interest, may be defined in terms of children's choosing a keyed answer by process of guessing (G) or mistake (M), or via direct reasoning which is not a valid reflection of the attribute of interest (InV). Numbers of cases rated as reflecting this condition are shown in Table 6.

The second instance, selection of an unkeyed response alternative, despite demonstration of the attribute of interest, occurs when children select an unkeyed response alternative even though they evidence reasoning which constitutes a valid representation of the skill ostensibly measured. Cases so rated are also shown in Table 6.

Given these definitions of ambiguity in terms of the analytical ratings of transcribed accounts of how children reasoned about test items, it can be esti-

Table 6. Cases of Ambiguity in Analytical Rating Results

		Subtest		
		Reading Comprehension	Science	Social Studies
Total No. of Item Interviews		358	319	232
Keyed		258	214	164
Unkeyed		69	85	61
Skipped		31	20	7
Ambiguity in Keyed Answers				
Rating Chain	Rating Outcome in Fig. 1			
K–IPS–IPR–G	1	7	11	10
–R–Inv	5	14	9	12
–M	6	0	1	0
K–IPS–UPR–G	7	0	1	4
–R–InV	11	0	1	3
–M	12	0	0	1
Total No.		21	23	30
% of Total Keyed Answers		8.1	10.7	18.3
Ambiguity in Unkeyed Answers				
Rating Chain	Rating Outcome in Fig. 1			
UK–IPS–IPR–R–V–E	27	1	0	0
–NE	28	1	0	0
UK–IPS–UPR–R–V–E	33	0	1	0
–NE	34	1	1	4
Total no.		3	2	4
% of Total Unkeyed Answers		4.3	2.3	6.6
Ambiguity Total		24	25	34
% of Total Item cases (excluding skipped items)		7.3	8.4	15.1
% of Total Item cases (including skipped items)		6.7	7.8	14.7

mated that ambiguity was apparent in 8%, 11%, and 18% of the cases in which children picked keyed or right answers to reading comprehension, science, and social studies items, respectively; and in 4%, 2%, and 7% of cases in which children choose unkeyed or wrong answers on these same subtests. If these two forms of ambiguity are pooled, we can estimate that overall ambiguity was apparent in 7%, 8%, and 15% of the cases for reading comprehension, science, and social studies items, respectively.

The estimates of percentages of cases of clarity and of ambiguity do not sum to 100%. The reason is simply that, as suggested above, the boundaries between clarity and ambiguity are themselves unclear. Instances in which children were rated to have employed some form of elimination, for example, have not been treated as cases of clarity or of ambiguity. Making such a distinction for cases of elimination would, we think, require examination on a case-by-case basis.

How many items were ambiguous? The foregoing estimates of cases of clarity and instances of ambiguity are based on the total number of child–item interviews. A natural next question—one which begins to address more directly the original purpose of the pilot study—is how many items were actually involved in the cases of ambiguity identified? In other words, for how many of the items included in the composite tests was ambiguity of interpretation apparent for one or more of the students interviewed?

Data bearing on this question are presented in Table 7. As these data suggest, instances of ambiguity were apparent with respect to a modest range of items. Keyed answer ambiguity (that instance in which a child picked a keyed answer for reasons unrelated to the skill ostensibly measured) was apparent for as many as 30%, 34%, and 31% of the items on the three composite tests respectively. As indicated in Table 7 most of this form of ambiguity derived from children's reasoning being invalid with respect to the attributes ostensibly measured. Unkeyed answer ambiguity (in which a child marked an unkeyed answer, even though his or her reasoning evidenced a valid application of the skill ostensibly measured) was apparent on 8%, 3%, and 7% of the items on the three composite tests respectively.

Instances of ambiguity were fairly widely distributed across children as well as across items. At least one case of keyed answer ambiguity was apparent for 54% of the children taking the reading comprehension test, 83% for the science test, and 100% for the social studies test. At least one instance of unkeyed answer ambiguity was apparent for 27%, 16%, and 37% of the children on the three composite tests, respectively.

The greater occurrence of ambiguity with respect to keyed answer choices seems largely due to two factors. First, children in the pilot study chose keyed answers (answered correctly) 72%, 67%, and 71% of the items on the three composite tests respectively, whereas they chose unkeyed answers for only 19%, 27%, and 26% of the items, respectively. Second, recall that our definition of keyed answer ambiguity (in which a child picks a keyed answer without demon-

Table 7. Items for Which One or More Instances of Ambiguity Were Apparent in Terms of Analytical Rating

	Subtest		
	Reading Comprehension	**Science**	**Social Studies**
No. of Items	37	29	29
Average No. Correct (Keyed Answer Marked)	25.8	19.4	20.6
Average No. Incorrect (Unkeyed Answer Marked)	6.9	7.7	7.6
Average No. Skipped (No Answer Marked)	3.1	1.8	0.9
Items in Which Ambiguity Is Apparent in One or More Cases in Which Child Selected Keyed Answer			
• Guess (Rating Outcomes 1, 7)			
No.	7	8	9
% of all items	19	28	31
• Reasoning Invalid (Rating Outcomes 5, 11)			
No.	11	10	8
% of all items	30	34	21
• Mistake (Rating Outcomes 6, 12)			
No.		1	1
% of all items	0	3	3
Items in Which Ambiguity Is Apparent in One or More Cases in Which Child Selected Unkeyed Answer			
(Rating Outcomes 27, 28, 33, 34)			
Total no.	3	1	2
% of all items	8	3	7

strating the skill or attribute ostensibly measured by the item) *includes* instances in which children simply guessed a keyed answer, or marked it merely by mistake. Since guessing appears to be a fairly frequent strategy by which children choose answers (see Tables 3 and 7) this accounts in part for the apparently greater frequency of ambiguity with respect to keyed answers than with respect to unkeyed answers. Before commenting further on these results, let us first recount in the next section the second approach employed in rating children's accounts of how they reasoned about test items.

Holistic Ratings

The analytical rating process described in the last few sections entailed several problems. First, our rating scheme required extracting a great deal of information from relatively brief interviews with children; specifically regarding ratings of children's perception of both item stimuli and response alternatives; of the process they used in selecting an answer; if reasoning was used, whether it was a valid reflection of the skill ostensibly measured; and also whether or not a child employed extraneous information in selecting an answer. As the individuals engaged in the analytical ratings frequently pointed out, there was simply not enough information provided in some item interviews on which to base such ratings with much confidence.

The second problem was more subtle. In our initial work with transcripts of interviews with children, some of the things children said about particular items or about why they answered particular items seemed hard to understand. Why, for example, would a child who identified a carrot as the only root among several answer alternatives refuse to identify the carrot as the root of a green plant? As we worked with transcripts, and began to compare different children's perceptions to the same item, some of the points which previously had seemed inexplicable, became easier to understand or at least to begin to understand (we will return to discuss the carrot example in detail in the next section).

For these reasons, we decided to try a second approach to rating the transcripts, an approach which we call a holistic rating. For this approach we cut apart copies of transcripts of conversations with each child and put together item sets for each item on all three composite tests. Each item set contained a description of the item stimulus including appropriate accompanying illustrations, the item question and response alternatives, the distribution of answers selected, plus portions of the interview transcripts in which each child talked about that item. Thus, each item set contained the item and accounts of how approximately ten children perceived and reasoned about that item (specifically 10 children for the reading comprehension items, 11 for the science items, and 9 children for the social studies items).

The question addressed with these item sets, using the holistic rating approach, was whether ambiguity was apparent in how one or more children perceived and reasoned about each item. Two raters were employed in making the holistic ratings. Both were advanced doctoral students in developmental psychology and were instructed as follows: First, we described the purpose and design of the pilot study. Second, we explained our definition of ambiguity, namely that it was of two types: the first, unkeyed answer ambiguity occurs when a child marks an unkeyed answer, but whose description of how he or she answered the question indicates application of the skill ostensibly measured by the item; the second, keyed answer ambiguity occurs when a child marks the keyed answer while *not* demonstrating the skill ostensibly measured by the item. It was explained that the second type, namely keyed answer ambiguity could be of three different sorts: (a) A child might simply guess a keyed answer, (b) a child could mark a keyed answer by mistake, or (c) a child might mark a keyed answer for *other* reasons *not* reflecting the skill or attribute ostensibly measured. The two individuals asked to do the holistic ratings were familiarized with publishers' statements of what Reading Comprehension, Science, and Social Studies tests ostensibly measured, and examples of each sort of ambiguity were discussed with them. Then, the holistic raters were asked to use a common form, to indicate *independently* for each item set whether one or more forms of ambiguity were relatively clearly apparent for one or more children. It should be noted that the holistic raters were not informed of the results of the analytical ratings. The raters were also encouraged to offer written comments regarding how children apparently had perceived and reasoned about each item.

After independent ratings of the item sets were performed, results were compared. Two problems with respect to the holistic rating instructions were apparent. The first pertained to whether or not children had selected keyed or unkeyed answers. Answer alternatives selected by each child had been marked on the child's item interview transcript. In a few instances, children decided during the interview on an answer different than the one they had marked during the regular test administration. In such cases, both original answer selected and the answer to which the child changed during the interview had been marked on the transcript. In 11 instances, holistic raters had judged children's accounts in terms of their changed answer rather than their original answers. The second misunderstanding in holistic ratings pertained to the instruction that raters indicate only instances in which children's accounts *clearly* indicated one of the forms of ambiguity. However, because of uncertainty, holistic raters marked twelve instances of ambiguity with question marks. In these instances, raters were asked to reconsider, and decide whether ambiguity was relatively clearly apparent, or was mainly conjectured. After these two obvious types of misunderstanding had been corrected, the interrater agreement between the two sets of holistic ratings ranged from 76 to 100%, as shown in Table 8.

Table 8.   Interrater Agreement for Holistic Ratings

	Composite Subtest		
Type of Ambiguity Identified	Reading Comprehension	Science	Social Studies
Unkeyed Answer Ambiguity (In which one or more children selected unkeyed or incorrect answer while demonstrating skill ostensibly measured)	76%	90%	100%
Keyed Answer Ambiguity (In which one or more children selected a keyed answer without demonstrating skill ostensibly measured via one of following)			
Guess	86%	90%	83%
Mistake	100%	97%	93%
Other Processs	76%	86%	76%

Table 9.   Results of Holistic Ratings

	Composite Subtest					
	Reading Comprehension		Science		Social Studies	
Type of Ambiguity	No.	% of Total	No.	% of Total	No.	% of Total
Keyed Answer Ambiguity (In which one or more children selected a keyed answer without demonstrating skill ostensibly measured via one of following)						
Guess	4	11	9	31	12	41
Mistake	0	0	0	0	2	7
Other Process	11	30	7	24	11	38
Unkeyed Answer Ambiguity (In which one or more children selected unkeyed or incorrect answer while demonstrating skill ostensibly measured)	8	22	6	21	4	14

Note: Results given here indicate items on which particular forms of ambiguity were clearly apparent to *both* of the holistic raters.

Holistic Rating Results

Results of the holistic ratings are shown in Table 9. In light of a moderate level of disagreement between the two independent holistic ratings of item sets, we have taken a conservative approach in presenting these results, namely by summarizing results in terms of the cases in which the independent raters agreed that a particular form of ambiguity was apparent in how one or more children perceived and reasoned about an item.[5] Unkeyed answer ambiguity was apparent for at least one child on 22%, 21%, and 14% of the reading comprehension, science, and social studies items, respectively. Keyed answer ambiguity, at least of two sorts, was more prevalent. At least one child was rated by both holistic raters to have merely guessed a keyed answer on 11%, 31%, and 41% of the three item types, respectively. Children were rated to have marked keyed answers by mistake for far fewer of the items—0%, 0%, and 7% with respect to the three item types. At least one child was rated to have selected keyed answers for other reasons, without demonstrating the skill ostensibly measured for 30%, 24%, and 38% of the reading comprehension, science and social studies items. Examples

[5] Note that this approach to summarizing findings was not possible with respect to the analytical ratings because of the contingent nature of the analytical ratings.

of explanations given by holistic raters with respect to this latter category (i.e., other bases on which children selected keyed answers) were as follows:

Reading Comprehension Items:

*   "uses personal experience"
*   "makes up own story"
*   "selected plausible answer"
*   "misperception carryover from previous question"
*   "without reference to story [child] personalizes"

Science:

*   "elimination"
*   "thinks fish breathe water"
*   "used preexisting knowledge"
*   "makes up story to explain choice"
*   "reason false"

Social Studies:

*   "reasons by counter example"
*   "uses other knowledge, not time line [given]"
*   "thinks South Pole gets the least heat and North Pole the most"
*   "personal knowledge about Hawaii made him choose answer"

These are simply a few examples of explanations offered by holistic raters of how children selected keyed answers without demonstrating the skill ostensibly measured by the item. Many of these explanations are impossible to understand out of context—that is, without first describing items—so let us postpone further discussion of them until the next section, when we do discuss specific items.

Overall Findings

Having presented the results of the two different approaches to analyzing transcripts of conversations with children regarding how they perceived and reasoned about test items, we may now compare the broad patterns of results from these two approaches. Second, we examine the consistency of the two rating approaches in terms of items identified as shown to lead to ambiguity of each type for one or more children. Third, we consider how inferences may be drawn from the pilot sample of items to the broader population of items from which our sample was drawn.

Patterns of Results. Results of holistic ratings presented in Table 9 may be compared with results of analytical ratings presented in Table 7. First note some of the broad similarities in the outcomes of these two different and independent approaches to rating children's accounts of how they perceived and reasoned about items. The ranges of proportions of items of each type identified as evidencing various sorts of ambiguity for one or more children were approximately equal—ranging from 0 to 34% in the analytical ratings and 0 to 41% in the holistic ratings. Frequencies with respect to types of keyed answer ambiguity are also roughly comparable in the two approaches. Selection of a keyed answer simply by mistake was rated to have been relatively rare for each of the three types of items in both rating approaches. Guessing of a keyed answer was considerably more common, occurring in 19 to 31% of items according to the analytical ratings and 11 to 41% of items according to holistic ratings. Also, under both rating approaches, keyed answer ambiguity for reasons other than guessing or mistakes was relatively common across all three subtests; for 21 to 34% according to the analytical ratings and 24 to 38% according to the holistic ratings. Second, note that there is one major difference in the pattern of results across the two rating approaches. Specifically, unkeyed answer ambiguity (in which a child picks an unkeyed answer, but whose description of how he or she answered the item, indicates actual application of the skill ostensibly measured) was more prevalent in terms of the holistic ratings (rated as apparent for at least one child in 22%, 21%, and 14% of the reading, science, and social studies items, respectively) than in the analytical ratings (occurring in only 8%, 3%, and 7% of the same types of items, respectively). The explanation for this discrepancy appears to derive from the fact that different phenomena were included under the "unkeyed answer ambiguity" rubric under the two rating approaches. Recall that under the first rating approach unkeyed answer ambiguity was defined strictly in terms of analytical rating outcomes 27, 28, 33, and 34. As depicted in Figure 1, these outcomes corresponded to instances in which children exhibited the intended perception of the item stimulus, but who chose an unkeyed response alternative even though their reasoning was rated to constitute a valid reflection of the skill ostensibly measured by the item. The holistic raters did identify this type of phenomenon as unkeyed answer ambiguity, but they also included two other types of phenomena under this rubric: (a) cases in which children made mistakes in marking answers, and (b) instances in which children had misperceived item stimuli, but still seemed to demonstrate the skill ostensibly measured by the item. These interpretations seem quite plausible, especially since the same interpretation was drawn by independent holistic raters. Thus, our judgment is that the estimates of prevalence of unkeyed answer ambiguity shown in Table 9 may represent a more accurate estimation of the prevalence of unkeyed answer ambiguity than those in Table 7, which are implicitly based on a much narrower definition of unkeyed answer ambiguity.

Consistency of Results.   Although broad patterns of results from the analytical and holistic rating approaches are somewhat similar, there was incomplete consistency in the exact items identified via the two approaches as having evidenced ambiguity for one or more children. Table 10 shows the degree of consistency between the two approaches in terms of items identified as showing

Table 10.   **Consistency in Items Identified as Ambiguous by Two Rating Approaches**

	Composite Subtest		
Categories of Ambiguity	Reading Comprehension	Science	Social Studies
Unkeyed Answer Ambiguity (Analytical Rating Outcomes 27, 28, 33, 34)	81%	76%	93%
Keyed Answer Ambiguity			
Guess (Analytical Rating Outcomes 1, 7)	92%	83%	90%
Mistake (Analytical Rating Outcomes 6, 12)	100%	97%	90%
Holistic Rating "Other"—(Analytical Rating "Reasoning Invalid" Outcomes 5, 11)	84%	83%	62%

ambiguity of four different types for one or more of the pilot-study sample of children. Two points may be noted with respect to these data. First, levels of consistency between results of different rating approaches are roughly comparable to the interrater reliability or consistency for two raters independently using each rating system (see pp. 327–328 and Table 8.) Second, the consistency between the two approaches was somewhat greater with respect to cases in which children picked keyed answers merely as a result of a guess or a mistake (the latter occurrence, recall, was relatively rare) than with respect to cases of unkeyed answer ambiguity (in which children picked unkeyed answers, but were rated to have demonstrated the skill ostensibly measured or to have reasoned validly in light of their perceptions of item stimuli and response alternatives) or keyed answer ambiguity deriving from other than guessing or making a mistake in marking answers.

Statistical Significance of Results.   Up to now, results of our analysis of ratings of transcripts of conversations with children regarding how they perceived and reasoned about test items have been presented merely in descriptive terms; that is, without calculating any tests of statistical significance. Nevertheless, a relevant question is how we can draw inferences from the particular random sample of items included in the pilot study back to the original pool of items from which the pilot study items were drawn.

The standard method for calculating confidence limits for a proportion is as follows (see Snedecor & Cochran, 1972): if m members out of a sample size n are found to possess some attribute (in our case ambiguity), the sample estimate of the proportion in the population possessing this attribute is $p = m/n$. In large samples (our sample was not very large, but this is a point to which we will return in a moment), the estimate p is approximately normally distributed about the population proportion P with standard deviation $\sqrt{PQ/n}$. Since the population proportion P is unknown, the sample estimate $\sqrt{pq/n}$ may be substituted for the true but unknown standard deviation $\sqrt{PQ/n}$. Hence the probability is approximately .80 that P lies between: $p \pm 1.28 \sqrt{pq/n}$.

Since our sample sizes were all approximately 30, we can thus estimate with .80 probability ($z = 1.28$), that when $p = .10$, the true proportion P is greater than .03 but less than .17. In other words, we can be reasonably confident that where our estimates of ambiguity are around .10 that the corresponding proportion of ambiguous items in the population of items from which our sample was drawn would be in the range of $.03 + 0.17$.

Several limitations in this estimate of confidence intervals should be noted concerning (a) the confidence level of .80; (b) our sample size; (c) redundancy of estimation on a single sample; and (d) the appropriateness of inferences, not just across items, but across children. First, regarding confidence levels, we should note that we initially choose a confidence level of .80, rather than a more typical confidence level of .90 or .95, both because our inquiry was only a pilot study and because we wanted to keep our sample size of items to a reasonable number and not subject the pilot sample children to too great a number of items (also, of course, we had no indication beforehand of the proportions p of ambiguity which we would find, so in planning a sample we used the conservative estimate of .5). However, it should be noted that if we were to increase the confidence level in our calculations of confidence intervals to .90 or .95 (with corresponding Z values of 1.64 and 1.96) that our confidence intervals would increase 28% and 53%, respectively.

Second, the method of calculating confidence intervals for proportions cited above is, strictly speaking, for large samples only, where p is not close to 0 or 1.00. Since our sample was relatively small it would be more appropriate to employ a confidence interval for proportions based on small samples. The effect of such an approach would be to move the confidence interval upward. The confidence interval for $p = .10$, $n = 30$. confidence level .95, for example is .02 to .26, whereas the large sample approximation to this is $.10 \pm .11$ (see Freund, 1973). Thus the confidence interval estimate above is somewhat biased in a downward direction (for $p < .50$).

Third, it should be noted that since we only drew three random samples of items (one each for reading comprehension, social studies, and science); it is not, strictly speaking, appropriate to calculate more than three tests of statistical significance on our findings. For all of the foregoing reasons we will not belabor the issue of formal statistical inference and calculate estimates of statistical significance separately for each of the proportions given in Tables 7 and 9.

Finally, we should note that given the design of the pilot study, statistical inference applies to generalizations across items, but does not apply formally to generalization from the pilot-study sample of children to any broader population of children. Thus statistical inference, strictly speaking, refers to the levels of ambiguity which likely would have been apparent had we administered the total population of items from which our sample was drawn to the same sample of children who participated in the original pilot study.

Generalization of our findings beyond this point depends not on tenets of formal statistical inference, but instead on plausibility and logical analysis. Before discussing such issues in our summary and conclusions we think it will be useful to discuss what seem to have been the main sources of ambiguity in test items. Hence in closing the present section, let us simply state our narrowly defined findings, based on four independent ratings (using two separate rating scheme) of transcribed accounts of how children perceived and reasoned about a random sample of items. Specifically, we estimate with 80% confidence that had our sample of children been given the total reading comprehension, science, and social studies test forms from which the sample items were drawn, ambiguity of the following forms would have been apparent for one or more children for the following percentages of items:[6]

Keyed Answer Ambiguity
  Choosing keyed answer by guessing: 17–37%
  Choosing keyed answer by mistake: 0–5%
  Choosing keyed answer for other reasons, but without demonstrating skill ostensibly measured: 19–41%
Unkeyed Answer Ambiguity: 6–20%

DISCUSSION: LIMITATIONS OF STUDY AND SOURCES OF AMBIGUITY

The calculations reported in the previous section may lend an unwarranted sense of precision and finality to the findings of the pilot study. Therefore, before we go any further in discussing our findings, let us step back a moment to discuss some of the limitations of this approach to studying the qualities of test items and children's interpretations of them. Specifically in this section we elaborate on problems of (a) the interview process, and (b the rating schemes and their application. After elaborating on these points, we discuss particular sources of ambiguity with respect to test items, and discuss the problem of defining ambiguity with respect to test items.

---

[6] A final note of clarification should be offered with regard to exactly how these estimates were derived. Since the confidence intervals for estimates of ambiguity of various sorts would overlap for the three types of items, it is reasonable to pool estimates across item types. We therefore averaged comparable estimates across the results of the two rating approaches given in Tables 7 and 9, and across the three item types, then calculated confidence intervals based on a .80 confidence level in the manner described above. Note that these estimates are conservative in that they are based on the large sample approximate method for calculating confidence intervals around proportions.

Interviews

Talking with children about how they perceive and answer test questions certainly allows us more insight into the processes by which they make sense of the questions than does mere inspection of the answers they mark. Nevertheless, such interviews are still a very imperfect means of gaining access to children's perceptions and reasoning. In this respect, we must reemphasize that our interviews with each child concerning a particular item were extremely brief, lasting on average only a minute or two, and our interviewers were not specially trained in conducting clinical interviews with children. In contrast, specially trained research psychologists sometimes devote hours, or even days, to probing the nature of a child's reasoning with respect to just a single task.[7] Also, of course, simply asking children how they make sense of test items may not be an efficient means of ascertaining certain aspects of their perceptions and reasoning. Not only are young children generally less capable than adults in articulating their perceptions and reasoning, but some psychologists have offered evidence to suggest that even with adults "there may be little or no direct introspective access to higher order cognitive processes" (Nisbett & Wilson, May 1977). Hence, our brief conversations with children about how they perceived and reasoned about test questions can be considered no more than crude inquiries into how they actually perceived and reasoned about test items. Nevertheless, this point does not, we think, detract from the significance of our findings. With relatively crude means of inquiry via brief interviews we have identified significant levels of ambiguity in children's perception and reasoning about a random sample of items. Had our means of inquiry been more refined, it seems reasonable to expect that ambiguities revealed would have been no less, and may even have been more.

Ratings

As students of nonverbal communication suggest, considerable information concerning social perception is lost when we move from face-to-face conversations to audio recordings of the same conversations. Still more information may be lost when audio recordings are transcribed onto the printed page—as has often been observed with respect to the Watergate tapes.

Nevertheless, probably a more severe diminution of information and insight into children's encounters with test items treated in the pilot study occurred in going from transcripts of our conversations to ratings of them. Though conversations concerning each item were brief, transcripts of conversations conducted in

---

[7] A sobering example of how difficult it is to discover how children perceive and reason about even as simple a task as building a bridge out of blocks is offered by Luchins & Luchins, 1977. Their account shows how several permutations on the block-building task are required simply to begin to understand how a child perceives and reasons about such a concrete task.

the pilot study run to more than 300 pages altogether. To provide more insight into these accounts of children's perceptions, we will in a moment quote directly from those transcripts. First, however, let us recount some of the problems and weaknesses of the two rating systems employed.

Analytical Ratings. The analytical rating scheme was developed in an attempt to analyze children's accounts of how they answered test questions in a systematic manner. This was necessary to provide a basis for generalizing findings from the pilot study. As recounted in subsection on Analytical Ratings (p. 319), several trials of the rating system and refinements of instructions to raters were necessary before raters could independently use it and derive reasonably consistent ratings of the same transcripts. For the sake of analyses reported in the previous section inconsistent analytical ratings were resolved through discussion between the two raters and one of the investigators.

Nevertheless, cases in which independent analytical ratings were inconsistent are worth describing for what they reveal both about our rating process and about how hard it is to tell what it is that a particular item represents for a particular child. In analytical ratings there were 93 cases altogether, across all three composite subtests, in which independent ratings disagreed in terms of the final outcome rating category shown in Figure 1. In all but two of these cases the inconsistency in final rating category derived from differing judgments concerning a single level in the rating scheme. By far the most common source of rating inconsistency (in 42 of the 93 inconsistent cases) were judgments concerning validity of reasoning, that is, whether or not a child's account of how he or she answered a question did or did not reflect a valid demonstration of the attribute ostensibly measured by the item (ratings of V or InV).

Item 21 from our composite science test, for example, was the source of analytical rating inconsistency in four cases. This item presented children with a picture of the sun and earth with top and bottom of the earth marked N and S, respectively. Children were verbally given the statement "When it's nighttime there's a full moon shining" and then were supposed to indicate "yes," "no," or "can't tell" from the picture. The answer indicated to be correct in the publisher's scoring key is "can't tell." Child A marked "can't tell" and explained his reasoning as follows:

A: Can't tell.
L: Why not?
A: Cause sometimes, sometimes it's half the moon and sometimes it's full moon and quarter moon . . . I don't know.

According to the publisher this sort of science item measures "knowledge, comprehension, inquiry skills, and critical analysis in physical science, earth and space science, and life science" (Prescott et al., 1978). One rater indicated that Child A's response indicated a valid demonstration of these attributes, while the other rater initially indicated that it did not. The apparent source of this rating inconsistency was that the second rater judged that child's response did not demonstrate the science inquiry skills apparently implicit in this item. However, upon discussion, raters agreed that the child's response did reflect a valid knowledge of earth and space science even if the child's answer was not clearly based upon the illustration accompanying this item. Thus, the inconsistency in this rating stemmed as much from ambiguity concerning what it was that the item ostensibly measured as it did from ambiguity about how the child reasoned about the item. Because of such uncertainities, ratings made in the pilot study do themselves carry some degree of ambiguity.

Also, we should explain one other aspect of the analytical rating scheme which clearly affected our findings. Recall that in our rating system, raters were asked to indicate whether children perceived item stimuli and response alternatives in intended or unintended fashion. The unintended rating categories (UPS and UPR) were used to indicate that a child perceived either stimulus or response alternatives in an unintended fashion which was not directly related to the skill ostensibly measured by the item.

Recall also that we did not systematically ask all children to read reading comprehension passages prior to talking with them about how they answered reading comprehension test items. We did not do this for two reasons, one practical and one substantive. From the practical point of view, having children read passages out loud would have greatly increased the time necessary for interviewing. From the substantive point of view we had reasoned that there would be no way in which having children read passages out loud could reveal misperceptions which were *unrelated* to the skills of reading comprehension. This assumes, of course, that specific knowledge of vocabulary used in reading passages is a component skill of reading comprehension. This assumption led us to forgo rating of children's perception of reading comprehension item stimuli, and also led directly to the relatively low frequency in ratings of unintended perception of response alternatives (UPR) with respect to reading comprehension. The assumption still seems a reasonable one to us. Nevertheless, it should be noted that we did find instances in which misunderstanding of a *single* word in either reading passages or response alternatives led to children's selecting unkeyed answers on reading comprehension items even though they seemed to comprehend most of the relevant passage. One boy, for example, did not grasp the fact that the word ''Mouser'' in a story about a cat was the cat's name, and failure to understand this single word prevented him from answering two of four items pertaining to the passage about Mouser—even though he seemed to comprehend almost all other aspects of the reading passage.

Holistic Ratings. The holistic rating system was developed in order to try to overcome some of the problems in the analytical rating approach. The second strategy for analyzing transcripts of conversations with children attempted, for example, to reduce the number of judgments which raters were called on to make. In the analytical ratings, raters were asked to make as many as 4750 discrete judgments (95 items × 10 kids × up to 5 judgments). In the holistic ratings, this judgment load was reduced nearly tenfold. Since the holistic raters were not asked to make judgments about how *each* child perceived and reasoned about each item, they were called on to make as few as 400 separate judgments (any of four types of ambiguity apparent for one or more children for 95 items). Nevertheless, despite the lower number of ratings called for in the holistic ratings there still were nearly 40 inconsistencies in judgments made by holistic raters. Although we attempted to minimize the effects of such inconsistencies in summarizing results of holistic ratings in Table 9, by counting cases as ambiguous only when *both* raters agreed in that designation, consideration of inconsistencies in holistic ratings helps to clarify why it is hard to judge precisely how children interpret test times. Question 12 on the composite science test was based on the following statement read aloud to children:

> Joan read that the surface of the Earth is about three-fourths water. Three-fourths of the Earth's surface is water. So she decided to draw a circle graph to show this. She used wavy lines for the water. What graph did she make?

Response alternatives for this question were three circles: the first was three-quarters wavy lines and one-quarter solid, the second was one-quarter wavy lines and three-quarters solid, and the third half wavy lines and half solid. Child F selected the second answer alternative while taking the test under standard conditions. The interview with child F about this question went as follows. After repeating the item stimulus the interviewer asked, "Which graph shows what Joan would have made?"

F: I don't . . . second one.
L: Why is that?
F: Because she, it's like she said, I'm three-quarters of a half . . .
L: Three-quarters of the . . . Earth . . .
F: And three-quarters is about that much. Three-quarters wouldn't be that much. Said most of the Earth.
L: Which one would say most of the Earth is covered?
F: Didn't it say most of the Earth?
L: It says about three-fourths of the Earth's surface is covered with water.
F: Say.
L: About three-fourths of the Earth is covered with water.
F: I don't get it. I did the opposite.
L: OK. You want to change your answer?
F: Yeah.

So child F went ahead and changed his answer to the first alternative, which was the keyed one.

One holistic rater judged this to be an instance of unkeyed ambiguity, on the grounds that the child had made a mistake and "corrects self." The other holistic rater did not indicate that this was a clear instance of ambiguity, but did comment that the child "may have the skill, but probing may have evoked change to keyed answer." One could plausibly make a case for either interpretation, but given our approach to summarizing the holistic ratings this was not counted as a case of ambiguity.

Sources of Ambiguity

The point of the foregoing examples is simply that there clearly was a certain degree of ambiguity in two important stages of the pilot study, namely the interview process, the two processes of rating interview transcripts. Therefore, in this section let us more directly explain and illustrate some of the common sources of ambiguity in children's interactions with test items. Specifically, we discuss examples from our interview transcripts as illustrations of the following sources of ambiguity in children's interactions with test items:

- rules of test-taking
- unusual and perceptive interpretation of questions
- personal experience and egocentric interpretations
- concrete sequential reasoning
- visual interpretation
- item format

It is impossible in most instances to say with certainty that ambiguity derived from any single one of these factors, but to illustrate what seems to have happened let us cite some specific examples.

Rules of Test-Taking. For each of the subtests, children were instructed to mark only *one* answer for each question. Since all children had taken standardized multiple-choice tests on previous occasions, according to their teacher, this was a rule of test-taking which might be assumed to be quite familiar to them. Yet, we found eight cases in which children seemed to forget this rule of test-taking and to mark more than one answer alternative.

Item number 23 on the Reading Comprehension composite test (MAT-2-1) was based on the following reading passage:

> Mother said, "Here is the cake I made. Would you like some?"
> Sue and Nick said, "Yes, thank you. We would."
> But their dog Red took Sue's cake and ran away with it. Mother got Sue some new cake. Then they all had cake to eat. Red too.

Question 23, based on this passage asked "Who made the cake?" Answer alternatives were:

(A) Sue
(B) Nick
(C) Mother
(D) Red

Nine out of ten children selected only the keyed alternative "Mother." Child J, however, marked both "Mother" and "Sue" and drew a line between the two. During our interview, child J explained his answers as follows:

> I marked "Mother" and then I didn't think that made any sense because it could be anybody's mother, so I just wrote Sue's and then I drew a line to Mother, Sue's Mother.

Clearly J comprehended the reading passage. His inferential comprehension seemed, if anything, more sophisticated than that reflected in the answer alternatives available. His solution to his dilemma was to mark two answers, transgressing the rule of marking only one, and hence to a response which would have been counted as incorrect under standard scoring procedures.

Unusual and Perceptive Interpretation. The above example was not, by any means, the only case of an unusually perceptive interpretation of a test item. Item 8 on our composite science test (SAT-20-13) consisted of the question "Which plant needs the least amount of water?" given orally with respect to the three illustrations shown in Figure 2:

Figure 2.

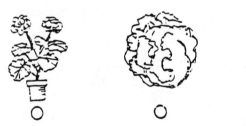

Children most commonly described these three illustrations as a "flower" or "some kind of plant"; "cabbage," "lettuce," or a "leafy vegetable"; and "catus," or "a prickle." Nine out of eleven children selected the keyed answer alternative, the cactus, as the plant needing the least amount of water.

Child A, however, selected the cabbage as the correct answer and explained his reasoning as follows:

L: Which one needs the least amount of water?
A: That does.

L: Why is that?

A: 'Cause it's a cabbage. Doesn't need as much water. Only when you clean it.

This child apparently reasoned that the cabbage needed less water than the two potted plants because it was not depicted as a potted cabbage. From this point of view, the logic of the child's reasoning is hard to deny. A head of cabbage once harvested can be kept well and long without water—water is needed only when you clean it.

Personal Experience and Egocentrism.   Another factor which clearly influenced children's perception and reasoning about test items was their own personal experience and egocentrism—that is, their tendency to view things from their own personal point of view.

Children's reactions to item number 1 from our Reading Comprehension Composite subtest (SAT-5-3) illustrate this tendency. This item was of the sentence completion type. The item stimulus was:

Eve likes to watch TV. She thinks it is _____.

Answer alternatives were:

(A)   fun
(B)   dull
(C)   hard
(D)   petty

Nine out of ten children selected the intended correct answer "fun." Interestingly, however, all ten children read the last alternative not as "petty" but as "pretty." This illustrates a type of ambiguity which was not covered under our definition of ambiguity, but this is a point to which we will return in conclusion. For the moment let us simply consider two children's accounts of how they answered this question. The interview with child J went as follows:

L: Why don't you just start at number one, OK?

J: Eve likes to watch TV. She thinks it is fun.

L: What are the other words?

J: Dull, hard, pretty.

L: Hm-hum. And why did you pick the first one?

J: Because I think it's fun.

L: Oh.

J: I like to watch TV.

Clearly child J interpreted this question in terms of her own personal experience, not necessarily in terms of an inference that because *Eve* likes to watch TV she must think it fun.

Child H also seemed to answer this question in terms of his own personal experience, but it was a different personal experience.

W: OK, you want to just read this? You don't read the sample, just start on number one, OK.
H: We are, we saw . . .
W: No, that's the sample. Why don't we just start here?
H: No, I want to start here.
W: But we already talked about that in class, though. That's why I thought it wouldn't be necessary.
H: Oh. Eve likes to watch TV. She thinks it is . . . fun, dull, hard, or pretty. Dull.
W: OK. Why did you pick that one?
H: Because your eyes could get, us, your eyes could get, um, um, your eyes could get, you know, your eyes could get, you could get blind.
W: Uh . . . if you like to watch TV, you mean?
H: Yeah, if you watch TV a lot.

From his experience, this child reasoned that someone who likes TV, who watches it a lot will think it dull in the sense that watching TV a lot can hurt one's eyes. There are, of course, other grounds for thinking TV dull, but child H's interpretation of this question apparently stems from his own personal experience. The child seemed to understand the reading passage as well as other children, but his personal frame of reference in drawing inference from it was quite different, for example, than that of the girl who answered "fun" because she thinks TV is fun.

Another interesting example of how personal experience can affect children's perceptions of test items comes from child B's answer to item 26 on our composite Science test (CTBS-30-23). The science item consisted of the instructions and response alternatives shown in see Figure 3. There's a heavy boy and a lighter boy. How should they sit to balance on the seesaw?

Five of eleven children chose the keyed answer alternative, the second pic-

Figure 3.

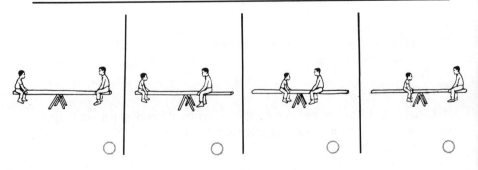

ture. Five selected the first and one gave no answer to this item. Child B explained his choice of the first picture as follows:

B: Well, usually when my little brother and I get on the seesaw we sit at the ends because if I sit closer then we might—he'll say, "get back, get back." He's afraid he'll fall.
L: And is he bigger or smaller than you are?
B: Smaller.

Concrete Sequential Reasoning. One could interpret the two examples concerning TV-watching not only as showing that children interpret test items in light of their own experience, but also that their reasoning may be concrete and sequential. A child may be able to read the sentence "Eve likes to watch TV," but the next incomplete sentence is viewed separately, not necessarily in terms of Eve, but in terms of a separate consideration of what it is reasonable to think about TV. From this perspective one could, of course, argue that child H's answer in the example cited above exhibited concrete reading comprehension. The point seems debatable with respect to the case above, but there are other examples which even more clearly demonstrate children's tendency to think concretely and sequentially about the problems posed in test questions. Item number 14 from our composite science subtest (MAT-19-21) provides a particularly interesting example. The item stimulus, read aloud to children, was

Which one is the root of a green plant?

Answer alternatives were as shown in Figure 4.

Children identified these pictures as "carrot" or "carrot without the top"; "cabbage," "lettuce," or "head of lettuce"; and "tomato," or "I don't know what that is." Despite the apparent ease with which most children identified these pictures, only 3 of 11 selected the keyed answer which was the picture of the carrot. Six had marked the cabbage or lettuce as the correct answer, and two had not marked any answer to this question. The interview with child D, who had not marked any answer went as follows:

Figure 4.

L: Number fourteen. What are those pictures?
D: Carrot without the top, lettuce and I don't know what that is.
L: The last one?
D: Yes.
L: OK. Which of those is the root of a green plant? . . . What's a root?
D: It's the bottom of a plant.
L: Are any of those the bottom of a plant?
D: Ya.
L: Which one?
D: The carrot.
L: The carrot is. Is that the root of a green plant?
D: No! It's the root of an orange one.

Most of the children who had marked the cabbage or lettuce as the correct answer to this question, seemed to experience the same trouble as child D. They knew what a root is, knew that a carrot is orange, a cabbage (or lettuce) green, and a tomato red. But since there seemed to be no really correct answer to this question, they picked the cabbage picture as the best of several bad alternatives, since the question did clearly refer to a green plant. At one level, these children appeared to engage in a sort of concrete sequential reasoning. Since none of the answer alternatives seemed to make sense, they focused on a single part of the question, the reference to a green plant, and simply marked what clearly was a green plant.

At another level, an epistemological one, it could be argued that child D's response, namely a refusal to mark any of the response alternatives was the most thoughtful. After all, the root is a part of a plant—the "bottom of a plant" as child D put it—and if a plant has an orange root it is therefore not a green plant. Even though children may have thought in such terms it seems unlikely that they could verbalize them very well. But whatever the case it seems clear that some of the ambiguity in this item derived from the fact that children may think in concrete, sequential ways about answers to such problems.

Another reading passage and a child's interpretation of a question about it also suggests children's attention to concrete details, but also reveals real ambiguity with respect to the inferential comprehension expected of children. The reading passage, on which composite reading test questions 12 to 16 (CAT-10-15-19) were based, was as follows:

Jane Addams cared about people all her life. When she lived in Chicago, she saw many children who did not have a good place to play. They played in the streets. Jane Addams thought the children were not safe. She wanted to do something for them.
Jane Addams was given a large lot. The lot had many old, unused houses on it. She had the houses torn down so that the lot would be empty.
Jane Addams worked hard to clean up the lot. Then she bought swings and

seesaws. This became the first playground in Chicago. The children had a safe place to play!

Five comprehension questions were based on this passage. One of them, and the answer alternatives posed for it, was: "What did Jane Addams do with the swings and seesaws?"

(A) cleaned them
(B) played with them
(C) had them put on the lot
(D) used them in the streets

Six out of ten children marked the third answer alternative, which was the intended correct answer. Two marked "played with them"—apparently reflecting the natural view of children about what one ought to do with swings and seesaws. One child, asked why he choose this answer alternative, explained "Because she could have lots more fun instead of sitting around in the house." One girl marked the first answer alternative. The conversation regarding her answer to the question went as follows:

L: What about number fifteen?
B: What did Jane Addams do with the swings and seesaws? "Played with them," "had them put in the lot," "used them on the streets." I just said "cleaned them."
L: Why did you choose "cleaned them"?
B: 'Cause she doesn't, she doesn't want the kids to go on dirty things.

According to the publisher's scoring key this is, of course, an incorrect answer. The reading passage does not say that Jane Addams cleaned the swings and seesaws—but neither does it say that she had them put on the lot. This is not surprising since this item is aimed at testing inferential not literal comprehension. But in terms of plausible inference it seems hard to argue that child B's answer is really less correct than the keyed one. The passage does after all clearly reveal Ms. Addam's concern for cleanliness.

Visual Interpretation.   If inferential interpretation was a source of ambiguity in children's perception and reasoning about test items, so was visual interpretation—specifically how they perceived and reasoned about pictures. Pictures are used in tests for young children far more commonly than in tests for older children. In the tests series included in the pilot study, for example, almost all answer alternatives for science and social studies items (specifically in the CTBS Level C Form S, MAT Primary II Form JS, and SAT Primary Level II Form A) consist of pictures and illustrations among which children are supposed to choose in response to an oral question.[8] The apparent rationale for such heavy reliance

---

[8] The main exception to this general pattern are six sets of items on the MAT for which answer alternatives are posed in terms of the written words "yes" and "no" and "can't tell." We discuss this item type in the sub-section Item Format, p. 351.

on pictures instead of words is to avoid confounding of science and social studies skills with those of reading.

What the pilot study revealed, however, is that visual interpretation, like reading interpretation, sometimes may be confounded with other skills ostensibly measured by test items. Specifically, different children seem to see different things in the same pictures, and what is seen sometimes influences how children answer test questions.

Some of the conversations with children already quoted show that children can perceive or at least describe pictures differently. The relationship between perception and putting names on things is, of course, often unclear. How one perceives something clearly influences the name put on it. The converse may also happen: The names one knows and puts on things may also influence perception. Often, however, the exact relationships between naming and perception are unclear. Thus, when different children identify the same picture as "cabbage," "lettuce" or "leafy vegetable," it is not clear that they are perceiving the picture in fundamentally different ways—or at least not in ways different enough to lead to ambiguity in terms of answering a test item.

But in some cases perception and naming seems more clearly to influence interpretation. Item 20 from our composite social studies test (CTBS-32-4), provides a relevant example. This item was based on the following passage, written in children's test booklets, but also read aloud to students:

> One of the most powerful rulers of Russia was Peter the Great. During his rule, Peter changed a swampy piece of land into a new capital city and seaport. He also formed the first Russian navy.

Children were then instructed as follows:

> Find the picture that shows on what kind of land Peter the Great built the capital city. Mark the circle under the picture.

Answer alternatives consisted of the four pictures shown in Figure 5. Below each picture are listed the words which children used to describe it, and in parentheses the number of children using each descriptive word or phrase.

Five of nine children chose the fourth picture which was the keyed answer. Three chose the third picture and one chose the second. It seems significant that three out of four children who got this question "wrong" described the keyed answer alternative not as a swamp, but as field, pond and ocean, and conversely that four out of five children who described the fourth picture as a swamp did choose that answer alternative.

Children's responses to this item also raise questions about what it is that this item reveals about children's understanding and reasoning about social studies. The children who picked the keyed answer may have simply been relying on verbal comprehension—as one child explained his answer, "It said the swamp, and I picked the swamp." However, the children who picked the third alternative

Figure 5.

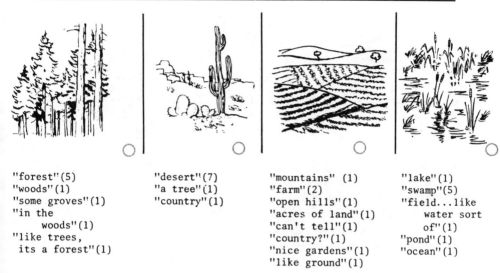

```
"forest"(5)          "desert"(7)       "mountains" (1)      "lake"(1)
"woods"(1)           "a tree"(1)       "farm"(2)            "swamp"(5)
"some groves"(1)     "country"(1)      "open hills"(1)      "field...like
"in the                                "acres of land"(1)      water sort
   woods"(1)                           "can't tell"(1)         of"(1)
"like trees,                           "country?"(1)        "pond"(1)
 its a forest"(1)                      "nice gardens"(1)    "ocean"(1)
                                       "like ground"(1)
```

seem to have applied broader social knowledge regarding where it is reasonable to build a city. The three children who chose the third answer alternative explained their reasoning as follows:

Child B: I thought it was right here because it looks like there was more room in that one than any of them.

Child E: I would say the third one because it has enough room and enough . . . and they could cut the grass and stuff, but it's not much work. 'Cause if it was like in the forest or something, they would have to do all their stuff.

Child F: I choose the third one.

L: The third one? Why?

F: Because right here, that looks more like a farm to me.

L: It looks more like a what?

F: A farm where people could go home.

Differential visual perception does not of course always interfere with children's selection of the intended or keyed answer alternative. This point is well illustrated by item number 10 on our composite social studies test (MAT-21-8). For this item children were orally instructed to "Mark the space under the picture showing someone who is probably following a rule." The three answer alternatives pictured are shown in Figure 6.

All nine children selected the third answer alternative which was the intended correct answer, even though they offered *nine different* interpretations of the second alternative:

Figure 6.

- "Two girls that are going on a picnic."
- "Girls, and they're just dropping things on the ground."
- "Two women talking in a parking lot."
- "[Two girls] walking through a parking lot."
- "Two girls walking between some cars."
- "Two ladies walking across a street."
- "I can't tell . . . They're walking in front of a car."
- "Somebody talking to somebody."
- "They are walking when cars are going back and forth . . . "

In other items, however, differential visual interpretation clearly affected children's test performance. Probably the clearest example of this occurrence was item 26 on our composite social studies test (CTBS-36-26). Instructions for this item were as follows:

> Look at the story at the bottom of the page. Read the story silently while I read it aloud.
>
> Nomads are people who move from place to place. They make their living by raising sheep and goats. They move to a new place when their herds need more grass and water.
>
> Now look at Number 26. Find the picture that shows how a nomad makes his living. Mark the circle under the picture.

The answer alternative pictures are presented in Figure 7.

Only two children selected the second picture which was the keyed answer alternative. Three chose the third. Three chose the fourth and one child marked both the second and third.

During interviews, two children commented on how hard it was to tell what these illustrations depicted. Comments along these lines were:

Child A: Um, I can't see them good.
Child G: I can't tell in this one, and this one or this one.

In this respect, it should be noted that our practice in constructing the composite tests, namely by photocopying illustrations from original test booklets, made our illustrations more difficult to interpret than those in the original book-

Figure 7.

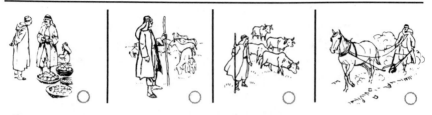

lets. Nevertheless, children's descriptions of what they saw in these illustrations clearly indicate that what they saw in answer alternatives influenced which answer they selected.

Two children who chose the third answer alternative, for example, described their choice as follows:

Child C: (who changed his answer during the interview): Now I would say number two, because I just realized those are cows [in number three].

L: Do you remember why you chose number three?

C: Because it looked like somebody watching sheep to me at the time, anyways.

Child G: I think 'cause he, there's goats, and in the story it says goats.

L: Um-hum, and are there goats in that picture?

G: Um-hum, like goats.

The three children who chose the fourth answer alternative explained their reasoning as follows:

Child A (describing the answer alternatives):
Two men and a little girl near the food . . . And a man guarding his sheep. And then a man and the cows are running off, and the horse, a man's on the horse and he's riding going away.

L: OK, which one shows how the nomads make their living?

A: That one because they keep on going place to place and place to place.

Child D: (who decided to change his answer from the fourth to the third answer alternative, during the interview)

L: OK and which one shows how the nomad makes his living?

D: The third one.

L: The third one?

D: Yeah.

L: OK, why is that?

D: Because he's raising goats, goats, goats, goats, goats.

L: Then why did you first choose the last one?

D: Umm, I didn't know that was goats.

L: What's the last picture?

Child H: Somebody going somewhere.

L: Someone going somewhere. Which one shows how nomads make their liv-
     ing? . . . The last one? Why is that?

H: Because, because, em, somebody are moving somewhere.

And finally, child I, another child whose answer to this item would have been
marked wrong under standard scoring conditions, because he marked both the
second and third alternatives, described the answer alternatives as follows:

L: What's going on in each picture?

I: Well, he's buying something from another person, and there he's watching his sheep,
     and there he's watching his goats. And now he's plowing his lawn or something like
     that.

In short, in most of these instances children selected ostensibly wrong answer
alternatives for the single reason that they saw things in the pictured alternatives
other than the test publisher apparently had intended. Some chose the third
picture because they saw goats in it and two clearly chose the fourth alternative
because they saw this picture as depicting someone "going place to place" and
"moving somewhere." These perceptions are particularly interesting because in
both cases the children did perceive sheep in the keyed answer alternative (Child
A: "a man guarding his sheep;" Child H: "somebody helping with sheep"), but
chose the fourth answer alternative apparently because they perceived moving
from place to place as being a more fundamental aspect of how nomads make
their living than "guarding" or "helping" with sheep. It is a nice question as to
whether such perceptions reveal any less understanding of nomads or social
studies than children who picked the keyed answer alternative, perhaps in reaction to the literal statement that "they [nomads] make their living by raising
sheep and goats."

There are many other examples of children's descriptions of illustrations
which suggest that visual interpretation influenced their perceptions of and answers to test items. Let us recount only one more because it seems to us to be a
particularly fascinating example. Item number 24 (see Figure 8) on our composite social studies test (CTBS-34-24) consisted of the following instructions
and answer alternatives:

Figure 8.

24. Find the picture that shows a person who is running for public office. Mark the circle under the picture.

Only one of nine children selected the fourth answer alternative, which was the keyed or ostensibly correct answer. The eight who got this item "wrong" all picked the first answer alternative. Here is how all nine children described these two answer alternatives, namely the first and fourth picture above:

	First	*Fourth*
Child A:	A man in an office.	President talking.
B:	A man sitting at a desk.	He's making a speech.
C:	Looks like somebody in an office.	Somebody giving a lecture.
D:	A man sitting by a flag at a desk.	An eye doctor.
E:	Somebody sitting down at a desk or like a principal.	It's like the president looks, like they're voting for something.
F:	A guy in his office.	Like a governor, . . . a governor talking, speaking, giving a speech.
G:	Like a president or a governor, somebody that's a leader.	
H:	Somebody looking for public office.	Somebody talking.
I:	Like a judge.	Someone at a concert or something . . . , or talking about a person.

The only child to pick the fourth, keyed, alternative was child A. All the others picked the first; some because they seemed to confuse running *for public office*, with running *an office*, but others, such as Child H, because they clearly perceived the first answer alternative as somebody looking for public office. Child D who perceived the fourth illustration as an eye doctor instead of someone giving a campaign speech seems to have been clearly led away from the ostensibly correct answer by this perception. Child I explained his selection of the first answer alternative as follows:

L: The first one? Why is that?
I, 'Cause he, em, a judge, you know, he owns things.
L: He owns things?
I: Well, not really owns things but he owns like big, . . . part . . . I don't know what it's called, but . . . I don't know what it's called . . .
L: OK.

In this case, the child's ability to verbalize and name things clearly seemed to fall short of perception. One can only wish in retrospect that the interview process had been able more clearly to elicit the tie which the child perceived between running for public office and owning things.

Item Format.   As discussed already, certain formalities of test-taking like choosing only one answer even if more than one seemed correct, and choosing one even if none seemed appropriate, were apparent sources of ambiguity for some children. In addition one particular type of item format seemed to be a particular source of ambiguity for several children. This type of item, what might be called an information sufficiency format, called for children to listen to a statement while looking at an illustration and then to mark "yes," "no." or "can't tell from the picture what the answer is." In our random sample of items this format appeared in 10 items—6 on our composite science test and 4 on our composite social studies test. All of these items came from the MAT Primary 2, Form JS. This type of item format does not appear in forms and levels of other test series included in the pilot study.

This type of item was the source of six out of eight cases in which children marked more than one answer alternative while taking the test under standard testing conditions. This item type was also one concerning which children frequently decided to change answers during our conversations about these items. To illustrate why this type of item may have been confusing to children let us recount one science item of type.

In item number 17 on our composite science test (MAT-20-28), children were instructed to look at the following illustration and then to mark "yes," "no," or "can't tell from the picture (see Figure 9) what the answer is" with respect to the following statement:

The fish had to jump out of the water to get oxygen.

Of 11 children taking the Composite Social Studies test, 1 marked "yes," 6 marked "no," 3 marked "can't tell," and 1 marked "yes," "no," *and* "can't

Figure 9.

tell,'' while taking the test under standard conditions. Five children decided to change their answers during our conversations regarding why they answered this item in the way they did. In case the reader is uncertain what the ''correct'' answer to this question is, we will indicate the publisher's designation of the keyed answer to this item after we recount how the first five children in the pilot study dealt with their own uncertainty on this point.

Child A: (who changed his original answer of ''can't tell'' to ''no'' during the conversation about this item).

    L: And number seventeen. The fish has to jump out of the water to get oxygen.

    A: I didn't really hear that 'cause someone was saying something.

    L: Oh, would you like to do it now, then?

    A: OK.

    L: I'll say it again. The fish has to jump out of the water to get oxygen.

    A: Nope.

    L: ''No''?

    A: Not all the time.

    L: OK, so you want to choose the answer ''no''?

    A: Yes.

    L: OK. And why do you think ''no''? How do fish get their oxygen?

    A: In the water. They have gills.

    L: Um-hum, good. Number . . .

    A: But flying fish go up. That's why I wanted to know if it was a flying fish.

Child B:

    L: OK, number seventeen. A fish has to jump out of the water to get oxygen.

    B: It doesn't (laughs).

    L: No, it doesn't. How do you know?

    B: If it jumped out of the water to get oxygen then it would probably die.

    L: OK.

Child C: I said ''no'' to that because fish do not live like we do, you know, they can't get out. They get oxygen under water. Think it's called their gills. I'm not too sure.

Child D: ''No.''

    L: Why not?

    D: Because fish don't need oxygen. They breathe water.

    L: OK.

    D: I don't know. Some fish can stay out of water, for at least two years.

    L: Two years—fish can?

    D: Some of them.

    L: Wow. OK.

Child E: (who changed from ''no'' to ''yes'' during the conversation).

    L: In number seventeen, a fish has to jump out of the water to get oxygen.

E: Yeah, that—ohh.

L: You can change your answer if you want to. What do you want to say on that
     one?

E: "Yes." Because . . .

L: Because you think the fish has to jump out of the water to get oxygen?

E: Well, sometimes.

L: Sometimes? Can you tell from the picture?

E: Uh—not really.

L: OK. Number seventeen.

E: Seventeen?

L: We filled in seventeen—you said "no"—tell you what, why don't you just
     put an "X" through the one you want to choose on that one. Then you don't
     have to worry about erasing.

E: "X" in the one . . .

L: In number seventeen. I'll read number seventeen again. The fish has to jump
     out of the water to get oxygen.

E: I say "yes," so I put a "X" . . .

L: Why not put an X through the "yes", 'cause that's your new answer.

E: Yes. There.

L: Why do think the fish has to jump out of the water?

E: Some fish do, not all though, 'cause sometimes fish need oxygen.

L: OK.

The ostensibly correct answer to this question, should there be any doubt in
the reader's mind, is "no."

Although other "yes," "no," "can't tell" items seemed almost as confusing
for children as the one cited above, we should hasten to point out that not all
items of this type seemed confusing to children. For example, one item asking
children to respond to statements concerning numbers on a picture of the earth
(e.g., the line marked number 3 is the equator), seemed relatively free of
ambiguity.

The Ambiguity of Ambiguity

We have quoted at some length from transcripts of conversations with children in
order to help add meaning to the relatively abstract analyses of test item ambiguity reported in the previous section. In addition, however, these examples have
also served to show that there is a real degree of ambiguity in the concept of item
ambiguity itself. Our approaches to defining test item ambiguity in terms of the
analytical and holistic ratings reported in the previous section, were clearly
limited in two respects. First, we limited our definition of ambiguity to those
instances in which children seemed to evidence the general skill ostensibly
measured by an item, but to select an unkeyed answer alternative (unkeyed
answer ambiguity) and instances in which children did not evidence the general

skill, ostensibly measured, but did still select the ostensibly correct answer (keyed answer ambiguity). In other words, our study has focused on only aspects of ambiguity which were salient enough to affect how children answered test items. There were other aspects of ambiguity revealed in the study (for example, in a reading comprehension passage when all children misperceived the answer alternative "petty" as "pretty," but this did not prevent them from selecting the keyed answer alternative), but these sorts of ambiguity were apparently not prominent enough to affect answer alternatives selected, and hence were not covered in our analyses.

Second in the ratings described in the previous section, we relied upon very general statements by publishers of what reading comprehension, science, and social studies items were intended to measure (see p. 316). Had we attempted to rely upon *specific* designations of what each item was intended to measure, it is possible that estimates of ambiguity might have been somewhat higher. Recall, for example, the flexible manner in which we interpreted that composite science test item number 21 was intended to measure either science inquiry skills, or science knowledge (discussed on pp. 336–337).

Clearly there are other ways in which one might define test item ambiguity. For example, ambiguity might be defined in terms of inconsistency in children's interpretation of illustrations, reading passages and/or oral instructions. Alternatively, one might analyze the degree to which items require or are influenced by children's prior knowledge, when they purport to be measuring something other than such knowledge. In the next and final section, we will suggest some specific ways in which research on children's perceptions of test items might be extended along these and other lines.

Here, in closing, let us simply comment briefly on what are probably the two main sources of ambiguity in the notion of ambiguity explored in the pilot study. Repeatedly we have referred to the phrase "test item ambiguity." Yet as we pointed out in the section on test ambiguity, the most famous researcher to use the technique of talking with children about test items, namely Jean Piaget, used this technique not to study test items, but to study children's reasoning. What this contrast points out is that ambiguity—that is, doubtfulness or uncertainty of meaning—resides not in test items per se nor necessarily in children's perception and reasoning per se, but rather in the *Interaction* between the two.

The second general point to be made with respect to the ambiguity of ambiguity is that ambiguity is in essence a relative concept. Apart from death and taxes, little in life is certain. Indeed, if we discount visits from the grim reaper and the IRS man, there may be no social interactions whatsoever which are altogether devoid of doubtfulness or uncertainty of meaning. Specifically, few if any interactions in educational endeavors are altogether free of ambiguity. A good way of illustrating this point is to briefly describe another line of research carried out by Cicourel, MacKay, Mehan, Roth, and their colleagues, who as we observed have conducted some of the best research to date on children's interpretations of test items. These investigators (who ironically enough variously describe what they do as sociolinguistics, constitutive ethnography, and ethnomethodology) have not only investigated uncertainty of meaning of children's performance on tests, but also have conducted similar investigations of the meaning of classroom lessons. From interviews with teachers and children, and videotape recordings and analyses of classroom interactions they (see Cicourel et al., 1974) drew the following observations:

> Comparing the teachers' accounts of the lesson before and after it was presented, and comparing the teacher's version with those of the children produced different accounts of the "same" scene. It was sometimes difficult to recognize that the children and the teacher witnessed the same event. The children's responses during the lesson provided different conceptions of correct and incorrect answers which contrasted with the teacher's expectations stated prior to and subsequent to the lesson. The children seemed to receive and organize the lesson in terms of their own orientations at the time of the event, and these conceptions do not always match the teacher's account of the lesson's purpose and conduct. (p. 4)

So the findings of our pilot study should not be interpreted to mean that ambiguity in children's perception and reasoning about test items is necessarily any greater than uncertainty of meaning in other sorts of educational endeavors. Rather the essential interpretation we would draw is that, as with other interactions in educational settings, and in social life generally, one may see another side to the meaning of test performance by adopting a perspective on it other than the standard one. When test items are viewed from the perspective of children, as we attempted to do in the study reported here, test items do not always seem to represent what is commonly assumed.

The point perhaps needs special emphasis with respect to test items and test scores. Because test items are typically marked "right" or "wrong" and seemingly precise numbers are derived from children's performance on them, it is easy to be lulled into a false sense of certainty with respect to their social meaning. But the essential point of our investigation—what might in summary fashion be termed the contextual dependency of children's perception and reasoning about test items—is not a new one. The concern is reflected in even as staid a document as the 1974 *Standards on Educational and Psychological Tests* (APA, AERA & NCME, 1974, standards J1, J1.1 and J7), which advises in three "essential" standards regarding test use that:

- A test score should be interpreted as an estimate of performance under a given set of circumstances. It should not be interpreted as some absolute characteristic of the examinee or as something permanent and generalizable to all other circumstances.
- A test-user should consider the total context of testing in interpreting an obtained score before making any decisions (including the decision to accept the score).
- A test-user should consider alternative interpretations of a given score.

On the basis of work reported in this paper, this seems to us like very sound advice. What is needed, perhaps, are better and more widely accepted means of considering the contexts of testing and alternative interpretation of the meaning of test items and scores derived from them.

SUMMARY AND CONCLUSIONS

In this concluding section, we recap what has been said in previous sections, and offer our conclusions from the pilot study as well as suggestions for research and other activities which might help to clarify some of the issues revealed in the pilot study.

Background

Critics of standardized tests have charged that test items often are ambiguous or otherwise misleading. Several have offered specific examples to illustrate their criticisms. Defenders of standardized tests have rebutted these criticisms by arguing that (a) item tryout procedures help to ensure that few such items find their way into published tests; (b) items that appear ambiguous or otherwise misleading to adults may not be so to the children for whom they are intended; and (c) even if a few ambiguous or otherwise misleading items do appear in published tests, there is no systematic evidence to show that they constitute a significant proportion of items on any one test or on standardized tests generally.

The Pilot Study

The pilot study was designed to bring empirical evidence to bear on this dispute. First, we located a group of 11 second- and third-grade children whose parents gave permission for them to participate in the pilot study. Second, we drew a random sample of items from appropriate levels of four of the most commonly used standardized tests (the MAT, CTBS, CAT, and SAT). Specifically, items were drawn from the Reading Comprehension, Science, and Social Studies subtests of these four test series (except for the CAT which did not have a Science or Social Studies subtest). These subtests were chosen on the theory that ambiguous items would be more likely to show up in these more complex subject areas than in more concrete skill areas like vocabulary and math computations.

Third, these randomly drawn items were put together to make composite Reading Comprehension, Science, and Social Studies tests, and these tests were administered to pilot study children under standard testing conditions. We then talked individually with children about how they had perceived and answered each item. These conversations were audio tape-recorded and subsequently transcribed. Under standard testing conditions, results indicated that on each of the subtests children answered about 70% of the items correctly in terms of the publisher's designated correct answers.

Analysis

Two types of analyses were performed on the transcriptions of interviews with children—what we call analytical and holistic ratings. The analytical ratings consisted of having two individuals independently rate each account of how children answered each item using an analytical rating scheme. This scheme dealt with six aspects of children's perception and reasoning about test items: (a) the answer alternative selected; (b) the child's perception of the item stimulus; (c) the child's perception of the response alternatives; (d) the process by which the child appeared to reach an answer to the question; (e) if the child appeared to be reasoning in answering the item question, the apparent validity of the logic used in light of the attribute ostensibly measured by the item; and (f) whether or not the child needed to apply information extraneous to what the item ostensibly measured.

The holistic ratings were organized and carried out somewhat differently. Instead of rating each child's responses regarding each item, under this approach we put together sets consisting of all children's responses regarding one item. We then had independent raters review these item sets, and indicate whether ambiguity was apparent in how one or more children reasoned about each item. Holistic raters were asked to judge four types of potential ambiguity: (a) unkeyed answer ambiguity (occurring when a child marks an ''incorrect'' answer, but whose description of how he or she answered the question indicates application of the skill ostensibly measured by the item), and keyed answer ambiguity due to (b) merely guessing a keyed or ''correct'' answer; (c) marking a keyed answer by mistake; or (d) marking a keyed answer for reasons other than mistake or guessing but still *not* reflecting the skill or attribute ostensibly measured by the item.

Problems of interrater consistency were apparent in the initial tryouts of both the analytical and the holistic rating schemes. Some of this inconsistency was, however, due to raters' misunderstanding of particular aspects of each rating scheme. After rating instructions were clarified and ratings corrected for obvious clerical errors, the interrater consistency for both rating approaches reached acceptable levels (i.e., interrater consistency of 88–90% for analytical ratings and 76–100% for the holistic ratings).[9]

In both rating schemes, ambiguity in children's interactions with test items was defined as being of two types: (a) keyed answer ambiguity in which the ostensibly correct answer was chosen without demonstration of the skill ostensibly measured and (b) unkeyed answer ambiguity in which an ostensibly incorrect answer alternative was selected even though the skill ostensibly measured was demonstrated in the child's description of how he or she perceived and reasoned about the item. We attempted to distinguish three types of keyed answer ambiguity in both types of ratings; namely, selection of a keyed answer simply by

---

[9] The interrater consistencies approaching 100% should not be misinterpreted. They derived strictly from ratings of phenomena which occurred rarely or not at all.

Table 11.   Proportions of Items Showing Different Kinds of Ambiguity for One or More Children According to Two Rating Approaches

		Keyed Answer Ambiguity		Unkeyed Answer Ambiguity
	Guess	Mistake	Other or Reasoning Invalid with Respect to Attribute	
Analytical Ratings				
Reading	19%	0%	30%	8%
Science	28%	3%	34%	3%
Social Studies	31%	3%	21%	7%
Holistic Ratings				
Reading	11%	0%	30%	22%
Science	31%	0%	24%	21%
Social Studies	41%	7%	38%	14%
Average of Two Rating Approaches				
Reading	15%	0%	30%	15%
Science	30%	2%	29%	12%
Social Studies	36%	5%	30%	10%

Note: Summary data drawn from Tables 7 and 9.

guessing, by mistake, or by other reasoning which did not reflect the skill ostensibly measured.

Table 11 summarizes the proportions of types of ambiguity occurring for one or more children in the pilot study as estimated via the two rating approaches. In general, levels of ambiguity identified via the two rating approaches are roughly comparable.[10] The main differences in results from the two rating approaches have to do with the prevalence of unkeyed answer ambiguity. Estimates of proportions of items showing this kind of ambiguity for one or more children were 7 to 18% higher under the holistic rating approach than under the analytic rating approach. The apparent cause of this discrepancy was that while in terms of analytical ratings unkeyed answer ambiguity was defined strictly in terms of four specific rating outcomes, holistic raters appeared to include other phenomena under this rubric, for example, cases in which children picked an unkeyed answer by mistake or in conjunction with an unintended perception of item

---

[10] It should be noted that for the purposes of presenting results, inconsistencies in ratings were handled differently in the two schemes. For analytical ratings inconsistencies were resolved through discussion between the two analytical raters and one of the principal investigators. For holistic ratings, items were considered ambiguous only if both holistic raters had indicated them to be so for one or more children in the pilot study.

stimuli, but still did seem to demonstrate a valid application of the skill ostensibly measured.

While the latter approach to judging unkeyed answer ambiguity may for these reasons be more appropriate, for the purposes of estimating the generalizability of our findings, we have simply averaged the proportions of ambiguity estimated via both approaches, as shown in Table 11. We then applied statistical tests for confidence intervals around proportions. Since we found confidence intervals for each type of ambiguity to overlap substantially across the three subtests, we pooled estimates across subtests, and estimated confidence intervals across pooled estimates. Using an 80% confidence level, we estimated that had our pilot-study sample of children been given the total reading comprehension, science, and social studies test forms from which the sample items were drawn, ambiguity of the following forms would have been apparent for one or more children for the following percentages of items:

Keyed Answer Ambiguity:

- Choosing keyed answer by guessing: 17–37%
- Choosing keyed answer by mistake: 0–5%
- Choosing keyed answer for other reasons, but without demonstrating skill ostensibly measured: 19–41

Unkeyed Answer Ambiguity: 6–20%

Discussion

Such findings must be interpreted in light of the fact that our inquiry was only a pilot study and as such was limited in several important respects. Regarding interviews with children, we must point out that simply talking with children may not be a very efficient way of gaining access into their perceptions and reasoning about test items. Also, the particular way we went about interviewing children clearly had its drawbacks. Interviews with children about each item lasted only a minute or two on the average and neither of the interviewers participating in the pilot study had received special training in interviewing children (though both did have several years teaching experience). Nevertheless, even our relatively crude means of inquiry revealed significant levels of ambiguity in children's perceptions and reasoning about test items.

A more severe limitation of the pilot study was the way in which we went about rating our transcripts of conversations with children. In order to provide a basis for generalization, we needed some systematic means of analyzing transcripts of conversations with children. Two rating approaches were developed and tried out. The analytical rating scheme, as explained above, was developed in an effort to analyze each child's account of how he or she reasoned about each item, in terms of several factors which have been suggested to interfere with children's understanding of test items (specifically, how children perceive item stimulus and response alternatives, the process by which they choose an answer, the relevance of reasoning in that process to the attribute ostensibly measured and whether extraneous information not given in the item is required to answer it). The main problem in applying the analytical rating scheme was that in many interviews there was simply not enough information regarding children's perception and reasoning about each item on which to judge each of these issues with much confidence. A second limitation of the analytical rating approach was that we relied on publishers' general statements of what each item type measured rather than specific statements of what attributes were ostensibly measured by each item. Such general statements of attributes intended to be measured clearly caused some confusion for analytical raters.

The holistic rating approach was developed in part to try to overcome some of the problems in the analytical rating approach. Nevertheless, limitations were also apparent in this approach. One limitation, also relevant to the analytical ratings, was the extent to which the interview process itself may have affected children's perceptions and reasoning about items. There were altogether 44 cases in which children decided during interviews to change answers from what they had marked (or *not* marked) while taking the composite tests under standard conditions (12 cases on the reading comprehension items, 22 on the science, and 10 on the social studies). In some cases the changes seemed to be a result of the interview process, in others they seemed spontaneous. What the holistic ratings (and particularly holistic rating inconsistencies) made clear, however, was that it was often difficult to tell when such changes were spontaneous and when they were prompted by the interviewers' questions.

One way of circumventing some of the limitations in the rating schemes employed in the pilot study (although not those in the interview process itself) is to consider directly some samples from our transcripts of interviews with children. Thus in the previous section, we presented specific examples from transcripts in terms of six apparent sources of ambiguity in children's interactions with test items.

Specifically we provided examples to show how ambiguity (other than that associated strictly with guessing or choosing a keyed answer simply by mistake) seemed to derive from the following:

- Children sometimes forgot the test-taking rule of marking one and only one answer.
- Unusual and perceptive interpretation occasionally led children to select an unkeyed answer, even though they seemed to demonstrate skills ostensibly measured.
- Personal experience and egocentric interpretation led to keyed answer ambiguity (such interpretation also, of course, often led children to select unkeyed answers, but this would not be included in our definition of ambiguity unless skill ostensibly measured by item was also demonstrated).
- Concrete and sequential reasoning caused children to focus on specific details of a problem or a reading passage, and sometimes seemed to lead to both

forms of ambiguity (and more generally to cause confounding of assessment of specific skills ostensibly measured with more general reasoning skills, though this is not a point studied directly in the pilot study).

- Children often interpreted pictures and illustrations in different ways and this occasionally (though by no means always) led to unkeyed answer ambiguity.[11]
- One particular kind of item format, namely information sufficiency questions with answer alternatives in the format "yes," "no," or "can't tell from the picture what the answer is" seemed particularly troublesome to some children, and also quite unclear in terms of how the test publisher expected children to interpret such questions.

In most cases it was impossible to say with certainty that ambiguity in children's interaction with test items derived strictly from any one such apparent source. Thus there is a real degree of ambiguity in the notion of ambiguity itself. Specifically, our definition of ambiguity was strictly conditional on whether children picked a keyed or unkeyed answer (without or with demonstration of the skill ostensibly measured, respectively). What the pilot study made clear, however, was that there were other forms and elements of ambiguity not covered under our approach.

Second, in terms of what items ostensibly measured, we relied upon publishers' general descriptions of what reading comprehension, science, and social studies items measured. Thus, a science item might be interpreted to measure science inquiry skills for one child but science knowledge for another. Had we relied upon specific descriptions of what each item ostensibly measured, estimated levels of ambiguity in children's interpretations of test items might have been somewhat higher.

The pilot study clearly shows, nevertheless, that ambiguity does not necessarily reside in particular test items per se nor in children's perception and reasoning per se, but rather in the interaction or lack of congruence between the two. And as a final point of interpretation, it should be noted that ambiguity itself is a relative concept. Doubtfulness or uncertainty of meaning arises not only in children's interactions with test items, but also in children's interactions with teachers, with parents, and certainly in interactions with interviewers, such as those employed in the pilot study.

Conclusions

The pilot study was designed to bring empirical evidence to bear on disputes concerning the prevalence of ambiguity in standardized test questions. What then

---

[11] One particular limitation of the pilot study should be noted with respect to this finding. The pilot study composite tests were put together from photo-copies of actual test booklets. Since photocopies of some small-scale pictures were less clear than the originals this clearly did make visual interpretation of some pictures more difficult and may therefore have contributed to the diversity of interpretations made of some pictures.

can we say in conclusion about this dispute? Keeping in mind that our study was only a pilot inquiry, and was based on only a small, formally unrepresentative sample of second and third graders, we conclude that

1. Ambiguity in children's interactions with test items is a phenomenon which occurs in a significant number of cases. If defined, as we have done, as selection of a keyed answer without demonstration of the skill ostensibly measured or selection of an unkeyed answer with demonstration of the skill ostensibly measured, ambiguity was apparent in from 7 to 15% of the total child–item interactions. If an item is defined to be ambiguous when ambiguity of interpretation, as defined above, is apparent for one or more children in the pilot study, then inferential statistics suggest that some 6 to 40% of the items on the test levels and forms included in the pilot study can be estimated to be ambiguous, (if we ignore keyed answer ambiguity caused by children's guessing or marking keyed answers by mistake, see p. 360).

2. While ambiguity was apparent in a significant proportion of child–item interactions and a significant proportion of items for one or more children in the pilot study, these proportions were consistently far less than 50%.

In other words, in the dispute over test item ambiguity, as in so many important public controversies, there appears to be some merit to both sides of the argument. Ambiguity appears to be a real phenomenon, but it also appears to be substantially less of a problem than some critics have suggested.

These conclusions may be compared to more traditional means of evaluating test quality, namely, reliability and validity. Test reliability traditionally is evaluated in terms of a variety of correlation coefficients or standard errors of measurement. Standard error of measurement refers to the standard deviation of a point estimate of something measured, like a child's standardized test performance. To compare such traditional means of assessing test reliability with results of the pilot study we can calculate .80 confidence intervals (i.e., ± 1.28 × standard error) for each of the test forms included in the pilot study and then as a rough base of comparison to the pilot study, calculate the .80 confidence interval as a percentage of the total number of items on each subtest. These data are shown in Table 12. These confidence intervals, calculated on the basis of publishers' reported standard errors of measurement for these subtests, amount to 14 to 22% of the total number of items on each subtest. From this perspective, the findings of the pilot study appear to be not too surprising. The analytical rating scheme resulted in estimates of ambiguity as a proportion of total child–item interactions ranging from 7 to 15% overall (see Table 6). These proportions are well within the levels reported in Table 12 of .80 confidence intervals as percentages of numbers of items on each subtest.[12]

---

[12] It should be noted that we did not apply inferential statistics to the Table 6 estimates since the pilot-study sample of children was not a random sample of any broader group.

Table 12.   Number of Items, Standard Errors and .80 Confidence Intervals for Subtests Included in Pilot Study

Test Level, Form, and Subtest	No. of Items	Standard Error (SE)	.80 Confidence Interval (Z ÷ 1.28) (±1.28SE)	.80 Conf. Interval as % of No. of Items
MAT (Primary 2 Form JS)				
Reading	55	2.9	7.4	14
Science	40	2.7	7.0	18
Social Studies	40	2.6	6.6	16
CTBS (Level C Form S)				
Reading Comprehension: Passages	18	1.5	3.8	22
Science	30	2.4	6.2	20
Social Studies	30	2.4	6.2	20
CAT (Level 12 Form C)				
Reading Comprehension	20	1.7	4.4	22
SAT (Primary II Form A)				
Reading Comprehension: Part B	48	2.7	7.0	14
Science	27	2.2	5.6	20
Social Studies	27	2.7	5.4	20

Note: Standard error estimates are drawn from publishers' norming data reports for either end of second grade or beginning of third grade, specifically Prescott, et al., *Teacher's Manual for Administration and Interpretating,* 1978, p. 105; CTB/McGraw-Hill *CTBS Technical Bulletin No. 1,* 1974, p. 31; CTB/McGraw-Hill *CAT* Technical Bulletin No. 1 (Draft) Table 66; and Madden, R., et al., *Technical Data Report,* 1975, p. 57. Although some publishers report standard errors to the second decimal place, for the sake of consistency all estimates here are rounded to the first decimal place.

Nevertheless, issues raised by the pilot study are not essentially ones of reliability or measurement error. Rather they are ones of validity, namely, what it is that test items are measuring for particular children. Specifically, the essential point raised in the pilot study is that insofar as we can tell from brief accounts of how children perceived and reasoned about test items, in a significant proportion of cases these items do not appear to be measuring what they are purported to measure. In other words even if levels of ambiguity are within .80 confidence intervals of measurement error, the point is that this is not simply random error. In the previous section, we discussed some of the extraneous factors which seem to be confounded with children's test performance; namely, their adherence to rules of test-taking, unusual and perceptive insights, egocentric thinking in terms of children's own experience, children's attention to concrete detail and sequential reasoning, their differing interpretations of pictures, and their ability to cope with a difficult item format.

Since the pilot study itself carried many ambiguities, we suggest considerable caution in drawing broader conclusions from our study. Nevertheless, we would like to suggest the following implications, with respect to test development, further research into children's perception and reasoning about tests and test items, and perhaps most important test interpretation and use. With respect to research, we refer briefly to past research relevant to points raised in the pilot study.

Test Development. As a result of our experience in conducting the pilot study and in light of conclusions drawn from it, we completely concur with the recommendations of Anastasi and Taylor concerning the need for talking individually with children as part of the process of developing and validating tests (see p. xxx for their specific recommendations). While traditional means of item tryout and selection (in terms of various item statistics) may help to eliminate some ambiguous or otherwise misleading questions, the results of the pilot study suggest that such procedures fail to screen out significant numbers of items which are ambiguous in that they do not seem to measure what they are purported to measure, for at least some children. Therefore it seems plausible to explore alternative means of test and item validation, including, as Anastasi and Taylor have suggested, talking with children about how they perceive and reason about test questions.

Research. [13]   In addition the pilot study has suggested to us several lines of research which might usefully be pursued. At a minimum, of course, it would be useful to repeat such a systematic analysis of children's accounts of how they perceive and reason about test items in order to test the generalizability of our results. Nevertheless, were we ourselves to undertake another such inquiry, we would alter the study in the following ways. First, we think it would be useful to have children read reading passages aloud. This likely would not help settle questions regarding the component skills of reading comprehension, but it would help clarify, more than we have been able to do in the pilot study, which aspects of reading skills influence children's selection of keyed or unkeyed answer alternatives. Second, as a basis for evaluating the relevance (or validity) of children's accounts with respect to the attribute ostensibly measured, we think in retrospect that it would be better to rely insofar as possible on specific descriptions of what each item is designed to measure rather than on general statements of what particular subtests are designed to measure. In this respect it might be useful to attempt an analysis of what particular items represent for individual children, altogether independent of what items are intended to measure. Results of such an analysis might then be compared on a post-hoc basis with what particular items are intended to measure.

More generally we would like to suggest that these general lines of research

---

[13] Since we do not attempt to describe research mentioned in any detail, we should point out that almost all of the work cited in this sub-section is based on types of tests different than the ones treated in the pilot study.

might usefully be extended to compare the perceptions and reasonings of children of different age or grade levels. The apparent contrast between our own findings and those of the related investigations of Cicourel, MacKay, Mehan, Wood, and Roth, and (discussed on pp. 305) may, for example, be explained by the fact that their studies involved first graders while our own were based on interviews with second and third graders. Since understanding of and adherence to rules of test-taking seems to be one source of ambiguity in children's perceptions and reasoning about test items, it might be useful to investigate how children, as they progress through school and typically gain experience in taking standardized tests, become socialized into the norms of test-taking. The relevance of such inquiry is clearly supported by the work of Powell which, though highly unusual, indicates that systematic patterns are apparent in wrong answers to standardized test questions by children of different ages and that these patterns exhibit developmental trends (the most recent summary of this work is Powell, 1979. See also Powell, 1968, 1977; and Powell & Isbister, 1974.).

Additionally, it might prove worthwhile to investigate some of the issues raised in the pilot study in different ways. One could, for example, engage children directly in conversations about what they perceive tests to measure or about what they think of proper ways of taking tests. From their application of this approach with antonym and verbal analogies items from the Scholastic Aptitude Test, Connolly and Wantman (June 1964) suggested, among other things, that having students talk aloud about their perceptions and reasoning would be a useful means of pretesting such items, and of exploring stylistic differences in students' methods of attacking and analyzing such items.

Also, one could assess the influence of factors such as visual interpretation, personal experience, and egocentrism either by employing some independent background information on children interviewed or by manipulation of different aspects of test items. For example, if children's performance on our reading comprehension item number 1 ("Eve likes to watch TV. She thinks it is (_____)." Answers: *fun, dull, hard, petty*), is influenced by the fact that most children think watching TV is fun, it would be interesting to compare performance on the item as given with an item which read "Eve hates to watch TV. She thinks it is (_____)." A variety of past investigations suggest the value of such manipulation as a means of investigating children's perceptions and reasoning about tests. Bally's (1976) study with second-grade children, for example, showed that a standardized test of auditory discrimination confounds measurements of the skill ostensibly measured with the familiarity of words used to test that skill. Similarly, Franklin's (1974) study with first- and second-grade children suggests that picture preference may be a significantly influencing factor on word–picture vocabulary tests typical of achievement and aptitude tests used in the early grades. Also, a variety of passage dependency studies, in which children were asked to answer reading comprehension test items without reading the passages on which they were based, have raised questions about the extent to which such items measure attributes other than reading comprehension. (Of more than a dozen references on this topic, Hanna & Oaster, 1978, 1978–79; Scherich & Hanna, 1977, are three of the more recent.)

Test Interpretation and Use. While new methods of research and test development, including talking with children about test items, may hold some potential for improving the quality of test items, it seems to us that this potential may be limited by two factors, the first having to do with how test quality is judged, and the second with the sometimes idiosyncratic nature of children's perception and reasoning about tests.

Regarding standards for judging test and test item quality, let us refer to Thorndike's *Educational Measurement* (1971) which is probably one of the most authoritative sources of advice on a variety of testing issues. In a chapter giving advice on writing test items, Wesman (1971) suggests "a portion of the art of item writing is the ability to conceive of distractors which are incorrect by any standard, and yet are attractive to those not knowing the answer" (p. 82). In a later chapter discussing pre-tryouts of test items, Henrysson (1971) suggests that if an item distractor—that is, an unintended response alternative—"is obviously a wrong answer to almost everyone, and thus very implausible," then "this distractor probably should be replaced by a more plausible answer" (pp. 136–137). Obviously there is a real tension implicit in such advice. How is it that an unintended answer alternative or distractor can be "wrong by any standard" but still be attractive or plausible to those not knowing the intended answer? The point of this contrast is that it represents a real ambiguity in the norms of standardized test construction. Typically, in the process of test development less priority is given to direct evaluation of what items reveal about what test-takers do or do not know, than to indirect evaluations in terms of item discrimination indices regarding either whole test scores or external criteria. The test-score indices corresponding to these item statistics are coefficients of internal consistency and criterion-related validity. It is just such indices in terms of which the technical quality of tests typically is judged. Thus, it seems to us that if talking with children about how they perceive and reason about test items does have potential for improving test quality, it will not likely be so much in terms of improving such traditional indices of test quality, as in clarifying the meaning of test items, both for children who take then and adults who try to view and understand children through them.

The second limitation regarding the potential value of interviewing children as a means of test improvement is simply the diversity of how items are perceived and attacked. The pilot study has, we think, raised some important general issues about children's concrete reasoning and egocentrism in dealing with test items, but some of the interpretations drawn by children in the pilot study, particularly those reflecting unusual personal experience, probably would be quite rare. In response to the science question about where a heavy boy and a lighter boy should sit to balance a seesaw, for example, how often might it happen that children would explain the choice of the unkeyed answer alternative showing boys sitting at far ends of the seesaw (see p. xxx) in quite the same way as Child B:

> Well, usually when my little brother and I get on the seesaw we sit at the ends because if I sit closer then we might—he'll say, "Get back, get back." He's afraid he'll fall.

But if unique and idiosyncratic interpretations of test questions by individual children would make the task of test-developer in trying to eliminate ambiguity seem neverending, they would seem to hold considerable potential, simply by way of illustration, for helping to prevent mis- or overinterpretation of test scores. As Judge Skelly Wright remarked in the *Hobson v. Hanson* case in Washington, DC, in 1967, "Although test publishers and school administrators may exhort against taking test scores at face value, the magic of number is strong" (*Hobson v. Hanson* 269, F. Supp. at 489). Testing experts often attempt to prevent misplaced faith in the precision of test scores by explaining statistical concepts such as standard error of measurement and test-score reliability. It seems to us that concrete illustrations of the unique ways in which children may interpret test questions may be a more effective means of communicating such concerns to those unfamiliar or uncomfortable with statistics.

In this respect, we would like to suggest, too, that it might be quite constructive, not only for test publishers, but also for those who regularly engage in administering or using test scores, to try talking with individual test-takers about how they perceive and interpret test scores. Teachers who have used this approach, such as Cook (Cook & Meier, n.d.) attest to the value of this approach, and there is at least some research evidence (Shemer, 1975) to suggest that teachers rate information on how and when children understand test questions to be more useful than traditional test scores. In short, talking with children about the meaning of tests not only might help people to avoid succumbing overmuch to the magic of numbers and test scores, but also would, we suspect, help more generally to remind them, as the pilot study has reminded us, of how different the worlds of children and adults can be.

REFERENCES

American Psychological Association, American Educational Research Association, and National Council on Measurement in Education. (1974). *Standards for educational and psychological tests.* Washington, DC: American Psychological Association.

Anastasi, A. (1976). *Principles of psychological testing.* New York: Collier Macmillan.

Bally, E.B. (1976). *The effects of levels of word familiarity on tests of auditory discrimination and its relationship with socioeconomic level and race.* Unpublished doctoral dissertation, Catholic University of America, Washington, DC. (University Microfilms No. 76–19, 362)

Block, N., & Dworkin, G. (Eds.). (1976). *The IQ controversy.* New York: Pantheon.

Cicourel, A., et al. (1974). *Language use and school performance.* New York: Academic Press.

Connolly, J., & Wantman, M. (1964). An exploration of oral reasoning processes in responding to objective test items. *Journal of Educational Measurement, 1,* (1), 59–64.

Cook, A., & Meier, D. (1976). *Reading tests: Do they help or hurt your child?* New York: Community Resources Institute.

CTB/McGraw Hill. (1973, 1974, 1976, 1977). *Comprehensive tests of basic skills (exp. ed.).* Monterey, CA: Author.

CTB/McGraw Hill. (1977). *California achievement tests.* Monterey, CA: Author.

Dimengo, C. (1978). *Basic testing programs used in major school systems throughout the United States in the school year 1977–78.* Akron, OH: Akron Public Schools Division of Personnel and Administration.

Dunnelle, M.D. (1964). Critics of psychological tests: Basic assumptions: How good? *Psychology in the Schools, 1,* 63–69.

Ebel, R.L. (1973). What do educational tests test? *Educational Psychologist, 10,* 76–79.

Finley, C, & Berdie, F. (1970). *The national assessment approach to exercise development.* Ann Arbor, MI: National Assessment Educational Programs. (ERIC No. ED 067 402)

Franklin, E.R. (1974). *The effect of a picture on a child's error on a test.* Unpublished doctoral dissertation, Columbia University, New York. (University Microfilms No. 74–28, 493)

Freund, J. (1973). *Modern elementary statistics* (4th ed.). Englewood Cliffs, NJ: Prentice-Hall.

Gamel, N.N., Tallmadge, G.K., Wood, C.T., & Binkley, J.L. (1975). *State ESEA Title I reports: Review and analysis of past reports and development of a model reporting system and format.* Mountain View, CA: RMC Corp.

Gruber, H., & Voneche, J. (1977). *The essential Piaget.* New York: Basic Books.

Hanna, G.S., & Oaster, T. R. (1978). How important is passage-dependence in reading comprehension? *Journal of Educational Research, 71,* 345–348.

Hanna, G.S., & Oaster, T.R. (1978–1979). Toward a unified theory of context dependence. *Reading Research Quarterly, XIV*(2), 226–243.

Henrysson, S. (1971). Gathering, analyzing and using data on test items. In R. Thorndike (Ed.), *Educational Measurement (2nd ed).* Washington, DC: American Council on Education.

Heyneman, S., & Mintz, F. (1976). *The frequency and quality of measures utilized in federally sponsored research on children an adolescents.* Washington, DC: George Washington University, Social Research Group.

Hobson v. Hansen, 269 F. Supp. 401 (D.D.C. 1967).

Hoffman, B. (1962). *The tyranny of testing.* New York: Crowell-Collier.

Houts, P.L. (Ed.). (1977). *The myth of measurability.* New York: Hart.

Jensen, A. (1980). *Bias in mental testing.* New York: Free Press.

Krejcie, R., & Morgan, D. (1970). Determining sample sizes for research activities. *Educational and Psychological Measurement, 30,* 607–610.

Lennon, R. (1978). Perspective on intelligence testing. *Measurement in Education, 9*(2), 1–8.

Lunchins, A.S., & Luchins, E.H. (1977). Wertheimer's seminars revisited: Diagnostic testing for understanding of structure. In P.W. Jonson-Laird & P.C. Wason (Eds.), *Thinking readings in cognitive science.* New York: Cambridge University Press.

MacKay, R. (1973). Conceptions of children and models of socialization. In H.P. Dreitzel (Ed.), *Childhood and socialization.* New York: Macmillan.

Mackay, R. (1974). Standardized tests: Objective/objectified measures of competence. In A. Cicourel et al. (Eds.), *Language use and school performance.* New York: Academic Press.

Madden, R., Gardner, E.F., Rudman, H.C., Karlsen, B., & Merwin, J. (1972, 1973, 1975). *Stanford achievement test.* New York: Harcourt Brace Jovanovich.

Matarazzo, J. (1972). *Wechsler's measurement and appraisal of adult intelligence.* Baltimore, MD: Williams & Wilkins.

Mehan, H. (1973). Assessing children's language using abilities. In J. Armer & A. Grinshaw (Eds.), *Methodological issues in comparative sociological research.* New York: Wiley.

Mehan, H. (1978). Structuring school structure. *Harvard Educational Review, 48*(1), 32–64.

Mehan, H., & Wood, H. (1975). *The reality of ethnomethodology.* New York: Wiley-Interscience.

Meier, D. (1972). *What's wrong with reading tests?* New York: City University of New York, Workshop Center for Open Education.

Nisbett, R.F., & Wilson, T.D. (1977). Telling more than we can know: Verbal reports on mental processes. *Psychological Review, 84*(3), 231–259.

Patton, M. (1975). Understanding the gobble-dy-gook: A people's guide to standardized testing. In V. Perrone & M. Cohen (Eds.), *Testing and evaluation: New views.* Washington, DC: Association for Childhood Education International.

Powell, J.C. (1968). The interpretation of wrong answers for a multiple choice test. *Educational and Psychological Measurement, 28*(2), 403–412.

Powell, J.C. (1977). The developmental sequence of cognitions as revealed by wrong answers. *Alberta Journal of Educational Research, 23*(1), 43–51.

Powell, J.C. (1979). *Can developmental status information be obtained from wrong answers?* Paper presented to the Annual Conference of the National Council on Measurement in Education, San Francisco, CA.

Powell, J.C. & Isbister, A.G. (1974). A comparison between right and wrong answers on a multiple choice test. *Educational and Psychological Measurement, 34*(3), 499–509.

Prescott, G.A., Balow, I.H., Hogan, T.P., & Farr, R.C. (1977, 1978). *Metropolitan achievement tests.* New York: Harcourt Brace Jovanovich.

Roth, D. (1974). Intelligence testing as a social activity. In A. Cicourel et al. (Eds.), *Language use and school performance.* New York: Academic Press.

Scherich, H.H., & Hanna, G.S. (1977). Passage-dependence data in the selection of reading comprehension test items. *Educational and Psychological Measurement, 37,* 991–997.

Schwartz, J. (1977). A is to B as C is to anything at all: The illogic of IQ tests. In P. Houts (Ed.), *The myth of measurability.* New York: Hart.

Shemer, R. (1975). *Testing the limits with the Stanford-Binet intelligence scale for children.* Unpublished doctoral dissertation, University of Illinois at Urbana-Champaign. (University Microfilms No. 76–6956)

Snedecor, G., & Cochran, W. (1972). *Statistical methods.* Ames, IA: University of Iowa Press.

Taylor, E.F. (1977a). The looking glass world of testing. In *Standardized testing issues: Teachers' perspectives.* Washington, DC: National Education Association.

Taylor, E.F. (1977b). Science Tests. In P. Houts (Ed.), *The myth of measurability.* New York: Hart.

Thorndike, R. (Ed.). (1971). *Educational measurement* (2nd ed.). Washington, DC: American Council on Education.

Wesman, A. (1971). Writing the test item. In R. Thorndike (Ed.), *Educational measurement* (2nd ed.). Washington, DC: American Council on Education.

CHAPTER 9

Styles, Reading Strategies and Test Performance: A Follow-Up Study of Beginning Readers*

Edward A. Chittenden
Educational Testing Service
Princeton, NJ

BACKGROUND

During a six-year period members of the Educational Testing Service (ETS) research staff collaborated with teachers in two large-city school systems in a study of young children learning to read. The goal of this research was twofold: to produce carefully documented case histories of children learning to read in the classroom (histories that are almost nonexistent in the professional literature); and to undertake a theoretical analysis of early reading, grounded on substantial observational accounts of individual learning patterns (Bussis, Chittenden, Amarel, & Klausner, 1985).

The research proceeded in two three-year cycles of data collection and analysis. The first, a 'pilot' cycle, included children from upper elementary grades as well as children from the primary grades. During the second, ''operational'' cycle we restricted the focus to children in the primary grades. In combination the two cycles yielded records for 40 beginning readers (14 from the pilot cycle, 26 from the operational phase). Data collection in both cycles were carried out by a collaborative team that followed two children within each classroom. The teams consisted of the classroom teacher, an ETS researcher, and a field-based observer (usually someone on the staff of a teacher center). The majority of the 40 children were studied during their first and second grade years, although four were followed during the kindergarten–first period and two during the second–third period.

Insofar as possible we sought to document the learning progress of ''normal'' beginning readers. Pupils with significant intellectual or emotional handicaps were therefore excluded from the study as were children who appeared to be precocious readers. In each classroom, one of the two children to be followed was selected by the teacher, the other selected at random. Two-thirds of the

---

* This research was supported by the Ford Foundation, Grant No. 815-1037, and by Educational Testing Service.

children were black, and one-third white. The group, all native English speakers, was evenly split between boys and girls.

The documentation on each child in the research consisted of four kinds of data: (a) teacher observations, directed by observation guidelines and obtained by means of periodic "debriefing" interviews; (b) narrative accounts by an outside observer of the child's functioning in different classroom activities and contexts; (c) samples of a child's work, for example, writing, drawing, painting, three-dimensional constructions; and (d) taped oral reading samples. The complete documentary record for each child consisted of all teacher observations and observer accounts, together with descriptions and analyses of the work products and oral reading samples. This complete record was then analyzed by a team of six collaborators to identify recurrent patterns, or themes, in the child's actions that cohered the record over time and across settings and data sources.

Although the overall configuration of patterns in each record was unique, comparisons across children revealed interesting commonalities and contrasts in stylistic kinds of behavior. A major outcome of the research was the identification of three stylistic dimensions of children's learning–dimensions that highlight how individual children approached the activities and materials in their classroom, how they related to their classmates and teacher, how they went about their classroom work, and how they seemed to perceive classroom life in general. The significance of stylistic variation for the children's early reading strategies is discussed more fully in a subsequent section of this report. What follows here is a summary description of each style as it was manifest across a variety of classroom activities.

Preferred Expressions of Meaning (Imaginative vs. Realistic). The contrasting poles of this dimension characterize children who gave freest rein to their imaginative resources versus those who drew most heavily on ideas and images about the real world. Evidence of stylistic preferences was most apparent in situations where the children could act on either inclination without adverse consequences. Some children, for example, typically stressed fantasy elements in dramatic play, and they tended to create their own fanciful expressions of meaning in painting and drawing. Other children clearly preferred more realistic enactments in dramatic play, and they typically created recognizable and/or usable products in art and craft mediums.

Attentional Scope and Emphasis (Broad and Integrative vs. Narrowed and Analytic). This style refers to basic differences in how children perceived and represented their environment as well as in how they accomplished tasks. A broad preference was seen in those children who not only deployed visual attention broadly ("taking in" a lot), but who tended to accentuate similarities and connections between objects and events. A narrowed preference was seen in those who focused attention more narrowly, and who tended to accentuate the details and distinctions that set one object or event apart from another. Whereas the former tended to be children whose manner of work was marked by fluid and flexible qualities, the latter worked in a more methodical manner, and they typically created a distinct working area for themselves and their materials.

Sequencing of Thought Processes (Parallel versus Linear). The contrasting poles of this style imply two distinct ways of processing information and creating meaningful structures. One preference entails juggling diverse information, entertaining a wide range of associations, and making apparent leaps in connections to new meanings. The other preference is for a more systematic, step-by-step process in which the structure or line of thought builds cumulatively. This style dimension was particularly evident in the way children told or retold stories, in the way they willingly followed or worked around the linear structure implicit in many classroom materials and activities.

A few children in the study were notable for the balance they exhibited in the styles described above, but detectable preferences characterized the majority of children. Where preferences were clear, the styles clustered in a pattern. That is, evidence of parallel sequencing of thought processes was associated with imaginative preferences and the tendency to deploy attention broadly—an *imaginative/broad/parallel processing* cluster. Evidence of linear sequencing was associated with realistic preferences and the tendency to focus attention more narrowly—a *realistic/narrowed/linear processing* cluster. These two clusters provided the basis for categorizing children's learning style in the present follow-up study.

The difference between the two style clusters was manifest in the children's distinctive approaches to the complex task of reading. This became especially evident in their strategies for handling a pivotal problem of initial reading, that of balancing an effort toward meaning with attention to print. Described another way, this problem or tension is one of maintaining an appropriate balance between being *accountable* to the text (being accurate, figuring out words, etc.) while at the same time maintaining a *momentum,* driven by anticipation of meaning, which keeps the whole process moving ahead. Since beginning readers are working at the limits of their cognitive processing capacities, there is often the need to favor one of these obligations over the other. Thus accountability may be sacrificed in the interests of forward motion, as the reader plunges or leaps ahead; conversely, a focus upon word identification and literal translation of the passage may replace the larger effort toward personal meaning. In their early reading efforts, children in the first style cluster, described above, tended to opt for the momentum of anticipated meaning, while those in the second cluster opted for text accountability. These differences among children in "styles of comprehending," to borrow a phrase from Spiro (1980), have clear implications for teaching and for the assessment of beginning reading.

FOLLOW-UP STUDY

A major purpose of the follow-up study is to consider how stylistic differences may be manifest in the test performance of young readers. Is there evidence that styles are differentially associated with general ability in beginning reading, when comparative estimates of ability, such as test scores and ratings, are considered? How might styles influence children's abilities to handle the distinctive conditions of testing and the demands of particular item characteristics? Such analyses should enhance the interpretation of individual children's performance on tests. More important perhaps, a consideration of stylistic aspects of early reading should shed light on the validity of test content and upon the meaning of test scores. The latter issues become particularly important as large-scale testing has become increasingly linked to instructional action.

Data collection in the present study consisted of obtaining new data on children who had been followed in the previous research as well as extracting additional information from their case history files.

1. *Standardized test scores.* The California Achievement Tests have been administered annually for a number of years in both school systems participating in the study. In one system, the tests (CAT–1970 edition) are administered from the first through the sixth grades; in the other (CAT–1977 version), they encompass second through sixth grades. With the assistance of school staff, scores from the Reading section of the CAT were obtained for children who had participated in the previous research. The scores of particular interest were those spanning the period from first or second grade through fourth grade. In addition, in the case of some pilot-study children, we were able to obtain results from testing at higher grade levels. The CAT yields a single total score for reading as well as scores on various subtests. Although we were able to obtain total scores for most children, subtest scores were not as consistently available.

2. *Teacher ratings.* Teachers who had instructed the children while they were in the second or third grades were asked to comment on the children's styles, particularly as styles pertained to performance on tests or testlike tasks. Teachers were also asked to rate the child's overall proficiency in reading with respect to his/her age level (A five-point scale was used: extremely competent; above average; average; below average; barely functioning). To supplement the teacher ratings we also obtained ratings from observers and/or researchers who had been part of the original documentation team for the child in question.

3. *Performance on an oral reading inventory.* A standardized individual measure of reading ability, a subtest of the CIRCUS battery, (1979) had been administered in second grade to children in the operational study. Because of our earlier integration of case study material drew only on observations and work samples, the results from this measure had not previously been

examined. In the present investigation, children's oral reading behavior on this measure and their answers to questions about the passage's content serve as supplementary sources of evidence regarding test performance.

The data for 26 children met the prerequisites for the follow-up study: (a) availability of test score information and (b) a sufficiently completed analysis of the case history material.[1] The first step in data analysis was to review the learning patterns that had been identified in the observational records for these children in order to establish two groups with clearly contrasting styles. The first group, Cluster A, represents children whose stylistic preferences, along the dimensions described above, are in the direction of imaginative/broad/parallel processing. The second group, Cluster B, represents preferences in the alternate directions of realistic/narrowed/linear processing. Three members of the ETS research staff participated in this review of the case history files. For each cluster we identified the ten children whose style configurations best matched the cluster description. It is the performance of these 20 children on tests, and testlike tasks that constitutes the data of central interest in the remainder of this report.

The California Achievement Tests—Reading

The California Achievement Tests (CAT) is one of the three most widely used standardized testing systems in the country. It offers measures of achievement of six "content areas": Prereading, Reading, Spelling, Language, Mathematics, and Reference Skills. In aggregate, the tests constitute a series of batteries that are designed to measure pupil achievement from kindergarten through the twelfth grade.

The latest form of the CAT, Forms C and D (1977), represents an important departure from the earlier CAT (1970 edition) in its attempt to establish a more direct link between test scores and instruction. To accomplish this, the CAT has incorporated features of criterion-referenced testing within the norm-referenced paradigm. In addition to the customary estimates of pupil status (percentile ranks, grade equivalent scores, etc.) the CAT now provides a detailed profile for evaluating a pupil's performance on the various subtests, or skill areas, within the battery. This profile, described as a "learning objectives" profile, indicates those areas or skills for which a pupil may need more instruction. For each learning objective that is tested, the CAT provides a Guide with specific suggestions for appropriate instructional activities.

It should be noted parenthetically, that this new direction of the CAT is symptomatic of a general trend in large-scale achievement testing. Designing standardized measures for the purpose of shaping instruction is a relatively recent

---

[1] Of the original 40 beginning readers, 6 had moved from the district of participating schools and test scores were therefore not accessible. In addition, there were 8 children, mainly from the pilot phase, whose case history material had not been analyzed to the point of identifying stylistic preferences.

event in the history of educational testing. As Popham notes, until the sixties "it was the mission of standardized achievement tests to reflect the effects of the educational system—not to shape it" (1982, p. 3). Given this new development in testing, it has become especially important to examine the nature of test content and to appraise the meaning of test outcomes.

At the primary levels the content of the 1977 CAT is organized around four sections: Phonic Analysis, Structural Analysis, Reading Vocabulary, and Reading Comprehension. The first two sections are measures of word analysis abilities which, according to the test manual, are commonly stressed in early reading instruction. These sections did not appear in the 1970 CAT. At the upper grades, the tests (both 1970 and 1977) consist of Vocabulary and Comprehension sections only.

Test results for a pupil are reported to teachers and parents via computer-generated report forms. Norm-referenced scores, that is, grade equivalents and/or national percentile ranks, are reported for each section of the test along with a Total Reading score for the sections combined. Criterion-referenced scores are reported for each learning objective within a section of the test. (For example, at third-grade level there are four learning objectives within the Phonic Analysis section: consonant clusters, short/long vowels, diphthongs, and variant vowels.) In most instances, five items are associated with each objective and the child's performance is categorized as "satisfactory" on an objective, if four of those items are answered correctly. If three or less items are passed, the report indicates that "more instruction" is needed in the particular objective.

Although the criterion-referenced component of the CAT is described by its developers as a major advance in testing, it was not so highly regarded by school staff who collaborated in our research. The follow-up interviews with teachers, in these schools at least, indicated that the criterion-referenced information was disregarded by most staff. Aside from questioning the meaning of scores based on five items, the teachers found the distinctions among the learning objectives to be quite artificial. By contrast, norm-referenced information was regarded more seriously, whether or not with misgivings. It is significant that it is the latter information that is abstracted for school records and entered into pupil folders. In city systems, this information may have significant impact upon curriculum and the educational careers of the pupils. Percentile rank can be the critical factor determining whether or not a child will be promoted. Our subsequent analysis of test scores will focus primarily upon the norm-referenced information provided by the CAT.

Test Results: Total Reading Scores
In this section the children's Total Reading scores for the CAT are discussed. Two principal questions are considered. Do the scores, as comparative estimates of overall reading ability, indicate a difference in general ability between the two style clusters? And, what do the scores contribute to an understanding of the reading attainment of this sample in comparison to the larger school population?

Table 1 depicts distributions of the children's Total Reading scores on the CAT that was administered in the spring of their third-grade year. A comparison of the test performance of the two clusters supports a conclusion from our original analyses across all case studies, namely, that the style dimensions under consideration in themselves are not predictive of reading attainment by the end of the primary grade period. Our observational records had shown that there were children in both clusters who moved rapidly and easily into initial reading skill, just as there were children in both groups whose progress was slow and more arduous. This observed variation among children is reflected in the score ranges for the two groups.

The "Combined" column in Table 1, showing the distribution for the sample as a whole, sheds some light on the representativeness of children in our original sample and permits a comparison of the children's performance to that of the school population in their districts. As can be seen, the sample does not include children who obtained very low test scores and is to that extent not representative of the national norms provided by the CAT. The lack of scores at the lower deciles is not unexpected, however, given the criteria for selecting children for the original research. Teachers were asked not to choose children exhibiting evidence of severe learning problems, just as they were asked not to choose precocious readers. Although teachers reported that the number of children excluded on grounds of problems was small (rarely more than four), the criteria undoubtedly screened out those who perform very poorly on tests. With this qualification the performance of the sample on the CAT aopears to be in line with test results as reported by their districts.

Ratings. As a supplementary investigation of the question of styles and general progress in reading, we asked teachers to rate the children's overall

Table 1. Frequency Distributions of Total Reading Score (CAT) for Two Style Groups

Percentile Rank	Style Group		
	Cluster A	Cluster B	Combined
90		| |	| |
80	| |	|	| | |
70	|	| |	| | |
60	|	|	| |
50	| | |	|	| | | |
40	| | |	| |	⊬⊤
30		|	|
20			
10			

Note: CAT for the third-grade level

Table 2. Frequency Distributions of Teacher/
Observer Ratings of Reading Ability for Two
Style Groups

		Style Group	
Rating		Cluster A	Cluster B
Extremely competent	(5)	| |	| | |
Above average	(4)	| | | |	|
Average	(3)	| |	| | |
Below average	(2)	| |	| |
Barely functioning	(1)		|

reading ability, attained by the end of second grade or beginning of third grade. (A five-point scale was used: extremely cojpetent; above average; average; below average; barely functioning.) We also obtained ratings from observers and researchers who had first-hand familiarity with the child's second-grade attainment. In instances of discrepancy among raters, the median estimate was used. The results, shown in Table 2, are congruent with the conclusion that style dimensions are not directly predictive of overall reading progress. It is, of course, not surprising to obtain this additional confirmation since the present ratings and our earlier review of observational data are based on overlapping sources of evidence and involve some of the same judges. Nevertheless, the ratings provide a useful quantitative summary, reflecting practitioners' estimates of pupil status toward the end of the primary grades.

Discussion of Total Reading Scores. An important question to raise is, To what extent might the finding of "no difference" between clusters be attributable to the nature of the children's early reading instruction? The teachers of these children, by professional choice and with the school's endorsement, sought to adapt materials and methods to the individual pupil's reactions and preferences. While each teacher necessarily relied upon certain core procedures and materials for the class as a whole, s/he gave equal (if not greater) weight to reading activities that were responsive to individual differences in styles. For example, the free-reading period in these classrooms was central to the reading program, and not a peripheral extra. Children not only had options of what to read, but within the limits of quiet reading activity, could also choose how to go about reading; they could skim the entire book and then read selectively, they could reread or jump ahead, or they could proceed in a more linear fashion. The teachers were also tolerant of variation in strategies when children read aloud to them.

The children's distinctive beginning reading strategies, associated with stylistic differences, were allowed expression and were, in fact, regarded by teachers as initial strengths in reading. The question raised here is, Would children with such stylistic differences fare equally well in programs that tolerate little variation in early reading strategies? Would there, for example, be a mismatch between certain stylistic preferences and those programs that place major constraints on what to read and how to read it? How do children in Cluster A whose approaches to reading are less text oriented than those in B, handle a strict decoding program? Under such conditions there may well be predictable associations between styles and success in learning to read in school.

Test Results: Subtest Scores

The CAT (1977 edition) yields scores for each of four subjections: Phonic Analysis, Structural Analysis, Reading Vocabulary, and Reading Comprehension. We will treat the two "word analysis" sections of the test separately from the Vocabulary and Comprehension sections.

Subtests: Phonic Analysis and Structural Analysis.   A distinction needs to be drawn between the types of items that ask children to demonstrate explicit knowledge about the writing system (Phonic and Structural Analysis) and items that may be regarded as closer approximations to the conditions of reading (Vocabulary and Comprehension). While knowledge of the writing system, including conscious awareness of information that may be embedded in print, is obviously relevant to reading, such knowledge is not equivalent to the skill itself. When children are asked, as in the example below, to locate beginning or ending sounds, they are being asked to give proof of explicit knowledge about letter–sound regularities, but they are not being asked to *read* in the sense of deriving meaning from text; indeed, they are not even responding to meaning at the level of individual words, as is the case in Vocabulary items.

Phonic Analysis Item [Third Grade Level][2]

Teacher: (reading aloud from the examiner's manual) Find the word that has the same beginning sound as the word "*scribble . . . scribble.*"

Item: O   skip
     O   struck
     O   scratch

Items in the Structural Analysis section of the CAT are similarly distant from the criterion skill of reading; moreover, they are often overlaid with extra procedural requirements. For example, the items below require the child to undertake a sequence of steps in problem-solving, which include paying careful atten-

---

[2] From California Achievement Tests, Form C. Reprinted by permission of the publisher, CTB/McGraw-Hill, Monterey, CA 93940. Copyright ©1977 by McGraw-Hill, Inc. All rights reserved.

tion to the instructions and discriminating the underlined letters. These steps, in themselves, have little to do with the process of reading. In fact, a number of adults experienced difficulty with such an item.

Structural Analysis Item [Third Grade Level][2]

Teacher: (reading aloud from the examiner's manual) A suffix is the letter or letters added to the end of a word to make a new word. For Items 10 and 11, read the words. For each item find the word that has the *suffix,* and only the *suffix,* underlined. Fill in the space that goes with the answer you choose. Stop after Item 11.

Item #10: ○ brave<u>ly</u>   Item #11: ○ old<u>est</u>
           ○ gre<u>ener</u>   ○ slee<u>py</u>
           ○ ligh<u>ten</u>   ○ hous<u>eful</u>
           ○ read<u>able</u>   ○ power<u>less</u>

Scores on the word analysis sections of the test were available only for children in the schools using the 1977 CAT (one district was still used the 1970 edition). Within this sample there is some evidence suggesting that the word analysis sections were the principal source for disagreement between a teachers' rating of reading ability and the Total Reading score. The profile scores of Carrie and Tommy in Table 3 reflect this disagreement. For example, Carrie was a particularly strong reader who could handle complex material by the end of second grade. In the follow-up interviews, her second- and third-grade teachers both rated her "extremely competent," yet the CAT total placed her at the 68th percentile nationally. Carrie's profile of subscores reveals that her difficulties with the word analysis sections (56th and 40th percentiles) offset her competence on the Vocabulary and Comprehension sections (91st and 86th percentiles), a competence that in fact correlated with the teacher's views. The result was a total score that did not correspond to observed proficiency. Tommy's profile, on the other hand, illustrates discrepancy in the other direction. He attained an above average total, although rated by teachers as "below average." His profile bears out the teacher's interpretation that his total score had been unduly inflated by the

Table 3.   Score Profiles for Two Children on the 1977 CAT

	Carrie	Tommy
	(National Percentiles)	
Phonic Analysis	56	52
Structural Analysis	40	94
Reading Vocabulary	91	57
Reading Comprehension	86	44
Total Reading	68	55

effects of coaching. Just prior to the city-wide testing, Tommy had been one of the children receiving help from a reading specialist, and consequently he had ample opportunity to practice the types of items found in the word analysis sections. While Tommy's proficiency in reading did not noticeably improve, his test performance did.

The fact that a proficient reader can perform poorly on word analysis and that a struggling reader can do relatively well supports our characterization of this section of the CAT as a test of explicit word knowledge—a test of information that does not necessarily tap the child's abilities to draw upon such classes of information while actually reading.

Subtests: Vocabulary and Comprehension. The Vocabulary section of the CAT requires attention to the meanings of words that are presented with little or no context. The item format requires the reader to select the particular word, among four options, which has the "same" (or "opposite") meaning as the stimulus word in the stem of the item. The Comprehension section requires the reading of passages, which range in length from one sentence to several paragraphs. A passage is followed by a series of question stems, each with three or four options, one of which is the correct answer to the problem posed in the stem. Both types of items are common to many reading tests. They represent the more significant components of the CAT since they appear at all grade levels, constituting the only sections in the upper grades. Moreover, in contrast to the word analysis items, the tests of Vocabulary and Comprehension entail reading for meaning, and hence come closer to the experience of reading.

A case-by-case review of the subtest scores from successive years of testing revealed that a number of the children scored consistently higher, sometimes strikingly so, on one subtest over the other. Moreover, the nature of this subtest "preference" was associated with style clusters; children in Cluster A tended to obtain the higher score on Vocabulary, while those in Cluster B obtained the higher score on Comprehension.

Subtest scores for Cluster A. The scores (percentile ranks) shown in Table 4 are from the test records of Shirley, a child in the pilot study. As can be seen, Shirley's scores on the Comprehension (C) section are consistently lower than

Table 4. Longitudinal Test Score Record: Shirley

Grade	V	C	Total
2	85	72	(80)
3	82	59	(58)
4	(not available)		(82)
5	69	64	(65)
6	92	85	(89)

Table 5. Longitudinal Test Score Record:
Child J

Grade	V	C	Total
(primary grades)	(subscores not available)		
4	60	35	(48)
5	66	39	(52)
6	44	32	(39)

her scores on the Vocabulary (V) section. This relationship is maintained despite considerable fluctuation from year to year in Total Reading. Not only is the direction of the difference between V and C consistent across grade levels, but in three of the four score comparisons, the magnitude is one stanine or more.

The observational record for Shirley revealed the kind of stylistic preferences that clearly place her in the A cluster. Her scope of attention was broad, as she characteristically monitored her classroom environment. The observer noted that "she attends to what she's doing, but at the same time takes in what's going on around her." Her imaginative approach to play and her dramatic approach to reading became forceful ways of introjecting meaning into her classroom work and activities. The teacher observed, early in first grade, that Shirley liked to "read" to other children, making up stories at those junctures in the book where she could not handle or remember the actual text: "She 'reads' dramatically, with detail and changes in voice quality for the different characters . . . very expressive. The other children like to hear her."

The subscore pattern in Shirley's record was apparent in the test records of a number of other children who had also been classified in the A group. For some the evidence was equally consistent, for others more tenuous. Child J, for example, also a child from the pilot study, did not perform as well on tests as did Shirley but nevertheless displayed the same imbalance between Vocabulary and Comprehension (see Table 5).

A third child, S, performed well on tests overall but again exhibited the same relative difficulty with the Comprehension section (see Table 6). In this particular record the discrepancy between the two subscores on the first-grade testing is the most extreme found in any of the records.

Table 6. Longitudinal Test Score Record:
Child S.

Grade	V	C	Total
1	92	23	(86)
2	95	77	(91)
3	96	79	(88)

Table 7. Longitudinal Test Score Record: Child T.

Grade	V	C	Total
1	53	40	
2	64	64	
3	81	86	

For these three records (see Tables 4, 5, 6) the differences between subscores is striking; the magnitude is appreciable and the direction of the difference is maintained across successive test administrations. For three additional children in this cluster, the evidence points in a similar direction but in less pronounced fashion. Child T, for example, manifests the pattern on the first-grade testing but not thereafter (see Table 7). Of the remaining four children in the group, three exhibited no preference as the differences between subscores was minimal. For another the subscore report was not available.

Subtest Scores for Cluster B. The records of several children in Cluster B showed strong performance on the Comprehension section, relative to scores on Vocabulary. Louis, for example, is comparable to Shirley in general reading ability, but the pattern of his subscores is in the alternate direction being especially marked in the first and third grades (see Table 8). And, just as Shirley's learning styles were examplary of the A cluster, so Louis's approaches in classroom activities were unmistakably those of Cluster B, almost in the extreme. Louis tended to work in a singularly focused manner, not scanning broadly. It was characteristic of him to approach any task in incremental, linear fashion, whether building with Lego toys or working in workbooks. Unlike Shirley he did not impose stories upon the material but proceeded in a more literal manner. His preference for accurate, realistic representation was manifest in a typical reluctance to guess, whether in reading or in spelling. As the teacher observed, "He will not write a word unless he is entirely sure of the spelling, or can find it around the room and copy it. When I tried to get him to try to spell a word the other day, it was like pulling teeth."

Four other children in Cluster B had score patterns that indicated relative strength on the comprehension subtest. The difference was not always pro-

Table 8. Longitudinal Test Score Record: Louis

Grade	V	C	Total
1	50	92	(65)
2	81	97	(91)
3	39	97	(77)

Table 9. Longitudinal Test Score Record:
Reggie

Grade	V	C	Total
2	47	64	(55)
3	75	79	(78)
4	65	68	(66)
5	47	54	(51)

nounced, however, as can be seen in the case of Reggie (see Table 9). Or, as shown in Table 10, the score difference was a large one on only one occasion.

One child in the B cluster had become a very capable reader even by the conclusion of first grade, and consequently topped out on the tests in the early grades. In this case, evidence of a significant difference between subtests appeared later, at the fourth-grade level when the subtest sections are more extensive (see Table 11).

Of the remaining children in the cluster, one exhibited score preference that was characteristic of the A group. For three the differences were minimal and inconsistent while a fourth showed relatively strong performance on Comprehension in the third grade but clearly reversed the pattern in the fourth grade.

In sum, subscore patterns associated with the two style clusters are clearly manifest in the records of half of the children. The remaining children either exhibited no consistent preference or, in one case, a preference in the opposing direction. It is worth noting that subscore patterns were discernible for children, such as Louis or Shirley, whose styles most strongly exemplified the characteristics of their cluster. The limitations of sample size and the reliability of subtest scores means that this relationship between styles and score patterns is tentatively identified. Nonetheless the magnitude of the score difference and its persistence in some of the records, when combined with the behavioral evidence discussed in the subsequent sections, make this finding a plausible one.

Table 10. Longitudinal Test Score Record:
Children K and Sn

Grade	V	C	Total
Child K			
2	(not available)		(48)
3	41	44	(40)
4	53	94	(74)
Child Sn			
2	58	73	(64)
3	82	89	(78)

Table 11. Longitudinal Test Score Record: Child C

Grade	V	C	Total
2	95	92	(98)
3	96	94	(96)
4	71	95	(92)

ANALYSIS: STYLES, STRATEGIES, AND TEST PERFORMANCE

In this section we will examine the reading strategies of children in Clusters A and B for their possible contribution to performance on subtests. We will draw particularly upon samples of children's responses to testlike materials and tasks, since the demands of these situations are comparable to the requirements of comprehension items in the CAT.

Momentum versus Accountability

When faced with the problem of gaining access to relatively unfamiliar material, the reader, whether child or adult, has certain strategic options. One option, manifest in the reading of children in Cluster A, is to build momentum by moving ahead into the material with the expectation that meaningful connections can be established. Such a strategy calls for maximum reliance upon extra-print knowledge and a willingness to entertain multiple possibilities regarding the substance of the passage or book. As a strategy it also requires suspending concern for total word accuracy and for literal translation of a sentence, at least until the reader has gained some sense of what the material is about. This strategy for reading is highly congruent with the broader style dimensions for children in Cluster A. It is characteristic of the children's entry into particular texts and descriptive of their approach to reading more generally.

An alternate strategy is to throw primary allegiance to constructing an accurate rendition of the text, with the expectation that cumulatively, word for word and sentence for sentence, its meaning is revealed. This strategy, highly congruent with the stylistic preferences of Cluster B, requires careful monitoring of performance by the reader to ensure a veridical account. While the strategy necessarily draws heavily upon the use of information embedded in print, such as knowledge of letter–sound correspondence and orthographic patterns, it should be emphasized that it does not constitute "barking at print." Rather, the reader continually strives for sense while accommodating to the visual information in the writing.

Ultimately, proficient reading entails a blend of these concerns for momentum and accountability to text. Indeed, even in the early stages of reading the children in either cluster acknowledge the dual requirements of reading. Thus children in Cluster A were well aware that their projection of meaning must be grounded on the actual text, and therefore they sometimes self-corrected and engaged in deliberate word-focused behaviors. Similarly, children in Cluster B know that there is a difference between word calling and reading; moreover, they too would guess and read "casually" on occasion. The children's differential preference for strategy was most clearly evident under conditions of challenge, when they were near the limits of their processing capacity and had to allocate their resources to optimal advantage. Such conditions are, of course, a common experience for the beginning reader, especially when dealing with opening sections of a new book or story, or when approaching the passages in tests.

In behavioral terms, the difference between the two strategies is clearly discernible in oral reading performance. The clearest signals of preference for momentum, associated with Cluster A, are found in the reader's errors that support the cadence of the performance, albeit with some loss of precision. For example, the child may skip a word or substitute a word that does not appear in the passage but nonetheless aptly fits the flow. Whether or not aware of the discrepancy, the reader continues to maintain the forward motion of the performance. Such errors may be considered "unmodified deviations" since the reader makes no overt effort to correct the error or to otherwise modify the rendition. By contrast, the clearest signals for concern for accountability to text associated with Cluster B are found in the breaks in the reader's pace. For example, the child pauses, sometimes for prolonged periods, in an effort to figure out a word; there is a definite reluctance to move ahead unless a satisfactory resolution has been reached. The child may insist upon adult help or confirmation. Other examples are found in self-corrections, even of errors that do not appear to have major consequences on meaning. All such interruptions of pace may be considered "modified deviations" since the reader takes action which modifies performance in the direction of closer alignment to the text.

The results in Table 12 depict behavioral indications of the differences between opting for momentum and opting for accountability. The data are from the standard oral reading sample that was administered to children in the operational research. The text for this sample was a children's book; hence the content of the material approximated natural conditions of reading. However, the sample is pertinent to consideration of test performance since, similar to testing, children were presented with unfamiliar material and asked to "read upon demand"; moreover, adult help was kept to a minimum. As can be seen in the table, the error patterns of Cluster A indicate preference for momentum (46% unmodified vs. 36% modified) while those for Cluster B reveal concerns for accountability (26% vs. 52%).

Since our research indicates no appreciable difference between Clusters A and B in general progress in reading, or indeed, in how well they understood a book such as the standard sample, the children's preferred strategies for gaining access

Table 12.   Distribution of Errors by Category
for Two Style Groups: Standard Oral Reading
Sample

	Style Cluster	
Error Category	A[a] (n = 8)	B[b] (n = 9)
Unmodified (pace maintained)	.46	.26
Modified (pace interrupted)	.36	.52
Repeated words[c]	.18	.22

[a]Cluster A: Total errors + repetitions = 179.
[b]Cluster B: Total errors + repetitions = 174.
[c]Repetitions of correctly read words are not considered as errors, but they do represent deviation from fluent reading and are included in percentage distribution.

to meaning generally seemed to have initially served them in good stead. The strategy of plunging ahead for children in Cluster A offered them an uninterrupted flow of information, and information is what they seemed to seek, no matter what the setting. Their styles of classroom learning were geared to searching out multiple information cues and to weaving these into meaningful patterns. Conversely, the stylistic strengths of children in Cluster B were ones of constructing meaning in a cumulative, inferential manner. Had these children plunged ahead in their reading by skipping words or playing loose with word identification, their careful step-by-step approach to deriving meaning would have been undermined.

Reading Strategies and Performance on Test Items

The stimulus passages in comprehension tests for the primary grades tend to be relatively brief and thin in substance. In the interests of measurement, the passages are tightly written and the lexicon controlled. Pictorial support and other extraneous cues (ordinarily found in books for children), such as layout, or a title and a cover are missing. Text that is sparse in information and meager in its possibilities for anticipated meaning poses a challenge to all children, but a major one for children in Cluster A.

Children's problems in responding to material that resembles comprehension items are well documented in our research records. The following illustrations involve passages from specialized instructional material and from a reading inventory.

Perhaps the most obvious drawback in the momentum strategies of Cluster A for reading abbreviated material is that a reader who plunges into text in search of connections may run out of ground before gaining sufficient grasp of the content. Here is a passage from the CIRCUS Oral Reading Inventory.

A goat in a pen had no food. At noon it began to rain. The goat was gloomy. When the sky was clear, Farmer Ben gave the goat her oats. Soon the goat was happy. She began to dance and cheer.

This is what happens to Margo on her first encounter with the passage.

Margo: A *great* . . . A *giant* in a pen had no food.

As is her style, she launches confidently into the paragraph but trips over the second word, *goat,* misreading it as *great.* She senses this mistake, however, most likely because of its grammatical inappropriateness. She then shifts to *giant,* a substitution that is more fitting because it responds to syntactic as well as graphic requirements. (*Giant* also makes sense in this sentence, provided that a rather large pen is envisioned.) Margo has difficulty with other words in this passage but she continues to move ahead and to stay with *giant* throughout. Although the substitution's semantic appropriateness to this story is questionable, she persists with it, perhaps viewing the passage as a truncated fairy tale. At the conclusion of the oral reading the interviewer poses the first test question for this passage:

Interviewer: Where was the goat?
Margo: Goat! I thought it was a giant!

Parenthetically, it is interesting to note that despite her substitution error, Margo provides the correct answer to the interviewer's question by replying that the goat/giant "was in the pen."

Margo's classmate, a child in the B cluster, also encounters opening problems with *goat.* Like Margo, he comes up with a substitution, that is, *ghost,* that responds to both the graphic information and to the grammar. Unlike Margo, however, upon completing the first sentence he does not proceed to the next one but cycles back to correct the deviation, apparently suspicious of the accuracy of his initial rendition.

Reggie: A *ghost* in a pen had no food. (pause) A *goat* in a pen . . .

This difference exhibited in their reading of contrived material is consistent with behavioral evidence from other samples in their files. Presumably, too, they approached CAT items in characteristic fashion, Margo opting for momentum and Reggie monitoring his translation for closer adherence to text.

Since readers in Cluster A converge upon meaning from differing directions and seek multiple possibilities, the broader the array of information in the material the better. Consequently, restricted material as found in some commercial reading series, workbooks, reading inventories, or test items, is not as easily accessed by Cluster A children nor is its content as readily recalled. By contrast, the linear, incremental step-by-step construction of meaning, manifest by Cluster B is better suited to the challenge. The following sample of prose does not come from a test but is taken from a commercial reading program that had been adopted by one of the participating school systems. It is an extreme example of material that demands a text-based orientation:

The Nap[3]

Nan ran to a mat.	Dan had a bat.	Nan sat.
Nan had a nap.	Tap! Tap! Tap!	Nan ran at Dan.
Dan ran to Nan.	Dan can tap the bat.	Dan ran.

One of the children in Cluster B read this story, word-by-word, stopping for long intervals on occasion to get help from the teacher. Despite the somewhat laborious nature of the child's reading performance, when the teacher asked a "comprehension" question (taken from the manual for the program), the child answered quickly and correctly. (This question, incidentally, is one that a number of adults cannot answer without rereading the passage.)

Teacher: *Why do you think Nan ran at Dan?*
Child: 'Cause he woke her up.

The incremental approach of Cluster B, linking one statement to the next, apparently allows the reader to rehearse what is happening in the "story" at each step along the way. Thus prolonged pauses to identify a word or to get help from the teacher do not jeopardize performance, as they may for Cluster A, since the reader can adhere to the chain of statements or events, cycling back if necessary. Such careful construction presumably prepares the reader for questions of fact and literal interpretation, making it possible, as in the example above, to answer specific questions with assuredness and little hesitation.

The response of a child in Cluster A to the same instructional material illustrates the differences in styles of comprehending.

Tanya: (reading accurately) *Nan had a fan. Nan can fan the sad man.*
Teacher: (following questions in manual) *What can Nan do?*
Tanya: She can fix everything up and make the man happy.

Tanya, having no idea of what *fan* means in this context, responds to the teacher's question by dwelling on the presumed effects of Nan's actions, but she does not define *fan*, the intended focus of the question. In response to further probing by the teacher, Tanya continues to elaborate upon Nan's activities, citing information that is nowhere apparent in this text. The teacher becomes curious about the source of Tanya's remarks.

Teacher: Where (in the story) does Nan do that?
Tanya: In our workbook on that page you didn't want me to do because it had some new things.

---

[3] From the Basic Reading Series: Level A, *A Pig Can Jig* by Donald E. Rasmussen and Lenina Goldberg. ©1976, 1970, 1964 by Donald E. Rasmussen and Lenina Goldberg. Reprinted by permission of the publisher, Science Research Associates, Inc.

Tanya's recourse to a larger realm of information for interpreting this text, and her difficulty in handling text-bound questions, stand in sharp contrast to the approach of the child in Cluster B to this same material. (It should be noted that Tanya made steady progress when reading conventional basal stories, whereas she floundered on her few attempts with the above mentioned material).

The introjection of meaning, characteristic of Cluster A, is evident even when children can read the material with ease. Tim and Debbie, for example, both in Cluster A, were fairly proficient readers when asked to read the CIRCUS passage below. Their oral reading renditions were almost flawless, yet they failed one of the comprehension questions for reasons that are more typical of the A group than of the B group.

Bud ran to a hut. He saw a pup on the rug.
Bud had fund. He fed the pup. The pup ate a bun.
Bud and the pup ran in the sun.
What did the pup eat?

In reply to this question Debbie erroneously answers, "a bone." This response reflects the fact that the only error in her fluent performance was a substitute *bone* for *bun*. Such a deviation is a good example of a momentum-generated error, stemming as it does from Debbie's knowledge about the kind of food that is ordinarily fed to puppies. The error, in effect, helps to connect this meager passage to the larger realm of puppies and what they eat. Technically, the passage was no challenge for Debbie, but her one error is typical of readers who are not highly attuned to the surface features of the material. (It is symptomatic in this respect that those children in the B group who did not recognize *bun* were more responsive than Debbie to the short vowel redundancy of the passage. They produced such phonetically mediated efforts as *bin* or *ben,* and when this didn't make sense they requested assistance from the adult. One of them remarked, "There are a lot of *u* words here!")

Tim also fails this comprehension question. He reads the passage accurately, including the word *bun,* but when asked, "What did the pup eat?," he replies, "Some food." Because his answer falls outside of the category of acceptable responses (*bun, roll*) he receives no credit toward the comprehension score. Yet, like Debbie, he has actually enlarged upon meaning. For a second-grader, the word *bun* may carry little loading; not being content with literal translation, Tim has placed it within a larger semantic space.

By themselves, these errors in the children's responses to the CIRCUS items are of little consequence. Cumulatively, however, the effects upon test scores of such strategies of reading can be appreciable. The illustrations above involve materials that were not central to the instructional program in the classrooms of these children, since their teachers relied primarily upon trade books and upon basals that are written in more conventional style. The samples are instructive, however, because they represent situations in which options for strategies of reading are clearly restricted; they thus throw into relief the differences among readers. Although test content is not as bizarre as some of the passages above, it nonetheless poses analogous restrictions.

In light of the characteristics described above, there are a number of ways in which the strategies of Cluster B are better suited to meeting the questions posed in the CAT Comprehension section. First, many of the CAT items require the reader to recall specific details of the stimulus passage. For example:

Item: Who is Mike's friend in the story?
Item: Where did the children eat lunch?

Items also require attention to the *sequence of events* in the narrative, as in:

Item: Which one of the following did Jane Addams do *last?*
Item: When does this story begin?

For both sorts of requests the more incremental reader of Cluster B would be better prepared.

A some what more complicated hurdle for all children, but especially for those in Cluster A, is the need to set aside multiple personal meanings in favor of an orientation to the intended meaning of the passage. Children need to learn, for example, that the question ''What *is* this story mainly about?'' is not the same type of question as, ''What *do you think* this story is mainly about?'' A test does not solicit the reader's opinions even though its question may resemble the teacher's queries when she is actually seeking to stimulate children's ideas and imagination. Through experience with workbooks and teacher-made and commercial tests, most children eventually learn that personal interpretation and expansion upon meaning are not appropriate ways of responding to certain instructional and testing conditions. They learn that ''best'' answer means ''correct'' answer; they begin to understand that the following types of questions are not open to debate (italics mine):

Item: How did Larry *probably* feel when he won a prize?
Item: Which of the following *best* tells what this story is about?
Item: Which word *best* tells about Kip during the walk in the forest?

Learning to handle the request for best answer appears fundamental to scholastic success, and while most children in the early grades begin to make appropriate differentiations, it remains an elusive matter, especially for those who juggle multiple levels of meaning, whether reading by themselves or listening to someone else. Our observations indicate that children of this age do understand a straightforward request for recall of fact, however well they may be prepared to comply with it. But the problem of selecting best titles, best designations of feeling, and so on presents a task for which they are only beginning to understand the ground rules.

CONCLUDING COMMENT: IMPLICATIONS FOR TESTING

Much of our analysis has focused upon item characteristics and their differential compatibility with children's strategies for reading. Such analysis should contribute to a better understanding of test score information. However, when our studies of styles in early reading are considered within the larger field of reading research, the implications for testing go beyond analysis of item characteristics and extend to questions about test content and test construction.

Tests such as the revised CAT reinforce the view that learning to read is essentially a sequential matter, proceeding from the acquisition of the rudimentary "decoding skills" to higher levels of processing. At primary levels the Word Analysis sections are given equal weight to Vocabulary and Comprehension. Yet research of the past several decades has failed to substantiate this long-held essential skills position. Acquiring knowledge of print is only half the story, and not necessarily the first half, at least for a great many children. Much of the contemporary literature shows reading to be a reciprocal and multilayered exchange between the reader and the text involving interacting levels of processing, perceptual, linguistic, and cognitive (Resnick & Weaver, 1979; Spiro, Bruce, & Brewer, 1980). Although young children are less skilled in the reading process, they are nevertheless equally engaged by its complexities. Tests which fractionate this skill therefore create a considerable distance between the real criterion performance, that is, reading, and what is actually tapped by the various sections of the instrument.

In general, the gap between our research knowledge of children's learning and our tests for assessing that learning continues to widen. The proceedings of the National Conference on Research on Testing (Tyler & White, 1979) point up this discrepancy. While the cognitive sciences have added substantially to our understanding of reading, of mathematics learning, and so on, the paradigm for achievement testing, constructed in the 1920s, has remained essentially unaltered (Buros, 1977). The paradigm is well suited to sequential models of learning, but poorly responsive to multifaceted accounts and to the fact that individual children may follow different routes to comparable levels of attainment. For both theoretical and practical reasons, the field of reading assessment appears especially overdue for development of new measures. The present analysis of implications of stylistic differences in children's learning draws attention to a dimension that is neglected in much of the current reappraisal of testing.

REFERENCES

Buros, O.K. (1973). Fifty years in testing: Some reminiscences, criticisms, and suggestions. *Educational Researcher, 6*, 9–15.
Bussis, A.B., Chittenden, E.A., Amarel, M., & Klausner, E. (1985). *Inquiry into meaning: An investigation of learning to read.* Hillsdale, NJ: Lawrence Erlbaum Assoc.
CTB/McGraw-Hill. (1970). *California Achievement Tests* (Reading, Levels 1–3, Form A) Monterey, CA: Author.

CTB/McGraw-Hill (1977). *California Achievement Tests* (Reading, Levels 1–6, Forms C and D), Monterey, CA: Author.

Educational Testing Service. (1979). *CIRCUS: (Oral Reading)*. Princeton, NJ: Author.

Popham, W.J. (1982, October). *Measurement as an instructional catalyst.* Paper presented at the 43rd Invitational Conference sponsored by Educational Testing Service, New York City.

Resnick, L., & Weaver, P. (Eds.). (1979). *Theory and practice of early reading* (Vols. 1–3). Hillsdale, NJ: Lawrence Erlbaum Assoc.

Spiro, R. (1980). Constructive processes in prose comprehension and recall. In R. Spiro, B. Bruce, & W. Brewer (Eds.), *Theoretical issues in reading comprehension.* Hillsdale, NJ: Lawrence Erlbaum Assoc.

Spiro, R., Bruce, B., & Brewer, W. (Eds.). (1980). *Theoretical issues in reading comprehension.* Hillsdale, NJ: Lawrence Erlbaum Assoc.

Tyler, R.W., & White, S.H. (Chairmen). (1979). *Testing, teaching and learning: Report of a Conference on Research on Testing.* Washington, DC: National Institute of Education.

Author Index

Subject Index